ECE/TRANS/182 (Vol. I)

ECONOMIC COMMISSION FOR EUROPE

Inland Transport Committee

European Agreement concerning the International Carriage of Dangerous Goods by Inland Waterways (ADN)

- **Final Act final of the Conference**

- **Resolution on the Follow-up to the Conference**

- **Agreement as adopted on 25 May 2000**

- **Annexed Regulations, as revised as of 1 January 2005**

UNITED NATIONS
New York and Geneva, 2004

NOTE

The designations employed and the presentation of the material in this publication do not imply the expression of any opinion whatsoever on the part of the Secretariat of the United Nations concerning the legal status of any country, territory city or area, or of its authorities, or concerning the delimitation of its frontiers or boundaries.

ECE/TRANS/182 (Vol. I)

Copyright © United Nations, 2004

UNITED NATIONS PUBLICATIONS
Sales No.: E.04.VIII.2
ISBN 92-1-139102-4 *(Complete set of 2 volumes)*
ISBN 92-1-139100-8 (Vol. I)

Volumes I end II not to be sold separately.

FOREWORD

The European Agreement concerning the International Carriage of Dangerous Goods by Inland Waterways (ADN) was adopted on 25 May 2000 by a Diplomatic Conference held in Geneva from 22 to 26 May 2000 under the auspices of the United Nations Economic Commission for Europe (UNECE) and the Central Commission for the Navigation on the Rhine (CCNR). The ADN was elaborated jointly by the UNECE and the CCNR.

The Agreement itself and the annexed Regulations in their original version, which form an integral part of it, as well as the Final Act of the Conference and the Resolution adopted by the Conference, were published in 2001, under the symbol ECE/TRANS/150.

The Final Act was signed on 26 May 2000 by the accredited representatives of the following fifteen countries: Austria, Belgium, Bulgaria, Croatia, Czech Republic, France, Germany, Hungary, Italy, Netherlands, Poland, Romania, Russian Federation, Slovakia and Switzerland.

The Agreement was opened for signature from 26 May 2000 until 31 May 2001. It has been signed (subject to acceptance, approval or ratification) by the following States: Bulgaria, Croatia, Czech Republic, France, Germany, Italy, Luxembourg, Netherlands, Republic of Moldova and Slovakia.

States which have not signed the Agreement may accede to it. The Agreement will enter into force one month after the date on which the number of States having signed it definitively, or having deposited their instruments of ratification, acceptance, approval or accession, has reached a total of seven.

The Netherlands deposited an instrument of acceptance on 30 April 2003. The Russian Federation and Hungary acceded to the ADN on 10 October 2002 and 4 May 2004 respectively.

The annexed Regulations contain provisions concerning dangerous substances and articles, provisions concerning their carriage in packages and in bulk on board inland navigation vessels or tank vessels, as well as provisions concerning the construction and operation of such vessels. They also address requirements and procedures for inspections, issue of certificates of approval, recognition of classification societies, monitoring, and training and examination of experts.

The annexed Regulations, in their original version, should apply twelve months after the entry into force of the Agreement (Article 11). However, in view of the delays for entry into force inherent to the processes of ratification and accession, the Resolution adopted by the Conference holds that the annexed Regulation will be updated on a regular basis by a Joint Meeting of Experts before the entry into force of the Agreement. It recommends that States interested in becoming Parties to the Agreement regularly implement these updates, at the national level, without waiting for the entry into force of the Agreement.

On the entry into force of the Agreement, the most recent version of the annexed Regulations will be submitted for adoption to the ADN Administrative Committee (see Article 17) in order to ensure that the annexed Regulations, which will apply twelve months after the entry into force of the Agreement, are the updated version.

Since the adoption of the Agreement in May 2000, a Joint Meeting of experts has been organized five times jointly by the UNECE and the CCNR, and has adopted amendments to the original annexed Regulations (reports TRANS/WP.15/AC.2/9, -/11, -/13, -/15, -/15/Add.1, -/17, -/17/Add.1 and -17/Add.1/Corr.1).

As a consequence, a new publication, including the text of the Final Act of the Conference held in May 2000, the Resolution adopted by the Conference, the Agreement itself and the updated version of the annexed Regulations as revised by the Joint Meeting for implementation as from 1 January 2003 was issued under the symbol ECE/TRANS/170.

This publication contains a new updated version of the annexed Regulations, as adopted by the Joint Meeting for implementation as from 1 January 2005.

Additional information on the status of the Agreement and the work of the Joint Meeting of Experts is available on the website of the UNECE Transport Division (http://www.unece.org/trans/danger/danger.htm).

TABLE OF CONTENTS

VOLUME I

Table of contents (cont'd)

Table of contents (cont'd)

Table of contents (cont'd)

Table of contents (cont'd)

- xi -

Table of contents (cont'd)

Table of contents (cont'd)

PART 8   **PROVISIONS FOR VESSEL CREWS, EQUIPMENT, OPERATION AND DOCUMENTATION**

Chapter 8.1   **General requirements applicable to vessels and equipment**

Chapter 8.2   **Requirements concerning training**

Chapter 8.3   **Miscellaneous requirements to be complied with by the crew of the vessel**

Chapter 8.4

Table of contents (cont'd)

Table of contents (cont'd)

Table of contents (cont'd)

FINAL ACT OF THE DIPLOMATIC CONFERENCE FOR THE ADOPTION OF A EUROPEAN AGREEMENT CONCERNING THE INTERNATIONAL CARRIAGE OF DANGEROUS GOODS BY INLAND WATERWAYS (ADN)

1.   The Diplomatic Conference for the Adoption of a European Agreement concerning the International Carriage of Dangerous Goods by Inland Waterways (ADN) was convened jointly by the Executive Secretary of the United Nations Economic Commission for Europe (UN/ECE) and the Secretary-General of the Central Commission for the Navigation of the Rhine (CCNR) pursuant to a decision of the UN/ECE Inland Transport Committee at its fifty-eighth session (12-16 January 1998) and CCNR Resolution 1994-II-6.

2.   The Conference was held at the Palais des Nations, Geneva, from 22 to 26 May 2000.

3.   Representatives of the following States took part in the work of the Conference: Austria; Belgium; Bulgaria; Croatia; Czech Republic; France; Germany; Hungary; Italy; Netherlands; Poland; Republic of Moldova; Romania; Russian Federation; Slovakia; Switzerland; Ukraine.

4.   Representatives of Turkey took part as observers.

5.   The European Commission also took part in the Conference.

6.   The following intergovernmental organization sent observers to the Conference: Danube Commission.

7.   The following non-governmental organizations also sent observers to the Conference: European Petroleum Industry Association (EUROPIA); International Association of Classification Societies (IACS); International Consortium of Rhine Inland Navigation (IAR); International Union for Inland Navigation (UINF).

8.   Mr. R.J. van Dijk of the delegation of the Netherlands was elected President of the Conference.

9.   The secretariat of UN/ECE and the secretariat of CCNR acted jointly as the secretariat of the Conference.

10.   The Conference adopted its draft agenda (ECE/TRANS/ADN/CONF/1-CCNR/MD/ADN/CONF/1 and ECE/TRANS/ADN/CONF/1/Add.1-CCNR/MD/ADN/CONF/1/Add.1).

11.   The Conference adopted document ECE/TRANS/ADN/CONF/2- CCNR/MD/ADN/CONF/2 proposed by the secretariat as its rules of procedure, with an amendment to rule 7 where the words "or alternate representatives" were inserted after "representatives".

12.   The Conference elected the following two Vice-Presidents:

Mr. M. Rak (Czech Republic);
Mr. G. Kafka (Austria).

13.   In accordance with rule 5 of the rules of procedure of the Conference, the secretariat of the Conference examined the credentials and reported to the Conference. On the basis of this report, the Conference accepted the credentials of the States named in paragraph 3.

14.   The Conference based its proceedings on the following documents:

-     Draft European Agreement concerning the International Carriage of Dangerous Goods by Inland Waterways (ECE/TRANS/ADN/CONF/3-CCNR/MD/ADN/CONF/3);

-     Annexes A, B.1 and B.2 of the annexed Regulations (TRANS/WP.15/AC.2/5 and TRANS/WP.15/AC.2/5/Corr.1-CCNR/MD/ADN/CONF/A, B.1, B.2);

- Annex C of the annexed Regulations (ECE/TRANS/ADN/CONF/4-CCNR/MD/ADN/CONF/4);

- Annexes D.1 and D.2 of the annexed Regulations (ECE/TRANS/ADN/CONF/5-CCNR/MD/ADN/CONF/5);

- Draft Conference resolution (ECE/TRANS/ADN/CONF/6-CCNR/MD/ADN/CONF/6).

15. The Conference also had before it a number of documents containing proposals and observations by Governments or the secretariat concerning the above-mentioned draft texts:

- ECE/TRANS/ADN/CONF/7-CCNR/MD/ADN/CONF/7 (France);
- ECE/TRANS/ADN/CONF/8-CCNR/MD/ADN/CONF/8 (Russian Federation);
- ECE/TRANS/ADN/CONF/2000/CRP.1-CCNR/MD/ADN/CONF/9 (Belgium);
- ECE/TRANS/ADN/CONF/2000/CRP.2-CCNR/MD/ADN/CONF/10 (France);
- ECE/TRANS/ADN/CONF/2000/CRP.3-CCNR/MD/ADN/CONF/11 (Germany and France);
- ECE/TRANS/ADN/CONF/2000/CRP.6-CCNR/MD/ADN/CONF/12 (Netherlands);
- ECE/TRANS/ADN/CONF/2000/CRP.7-CCNR/MD/ADN/CONF/13 (Netherlands);
- ECE/TRANS/ADN/CONF/2000/CRP.8-CCNR/MD/ADN/CONF/14 (Secretariat).

16. Following the debate, the Conference adopted the European Agreement concerning the International Carriage of Dangerous Goods by Inland Waterways (ADN) in English, French, German and Russian for the Agreement proper (document ECE/TRANS/ADN/CONF/2000/ CRP.10) and in French only for the annexed Regulations (document TRANS/WP.15/AC.2/5 and -/Corr.1 for annexes A, B.1 and B.2 and document ECE/TRANS/ADN/CONF/2000/CRP.11 for annexes C, D.1 and D.2).

17. The Agreement will be deposited with the Secretary-General of the United Nations. It will be open for signature in the Office of the Executive Secretary of UN/ECE in Geneva until 31 May 2001. Thereafter it will be open for accession.

18. The Conference also adopted a resolution contained in the document annexed to this Final Act.

19. Belgium made a declaration the text of which will be annexed to the Final Act.

IN WITNESS WHEREOF, the undersigned have signed this Final Act.

DONE at Geneva, this twenty-sixth day of May two thousand, in a single original copy, in the English, French, German and Russian languages, which will be deposited with the Secretary-General of the United Nations.

Resolution

Follow up to the Conference

<u>The Conference,</u>

<u>Recognizing</u> that the Regulations annexed to the European Agreement concerning the International Carriage of Dangerous Goods by Inland Waterways (ADN) meet the level of safety required for navigation on European waterways covered by the European Agreement on Main Inland Waterways of International Importance (AGN), particularly on the Rhine, at the time of adoption of this Agreement;

<u>Considering</u>, however, that this level of safety might no longer be deemed suitable at the time of entry into force of the Agreement, depending on the evolution of safety and transport techniques;

<u>Recognizing also</u> the need for harmonization of the provisions of the Regulations annexed to this Agreement with those of other agreements governing other modes of transport for the purpose of facilitating multimodal transport;

<u>Aware of</u> the request by the Central Commission for the Navigation of the Rhine that the level of safety at the time of entry into force of the Agreement should correspond to that applicable at that time on the Rhine;

<u>Aware also</u> of the desire of the Central Commission for the Navigation of the Rhine and of the Danube Commission to remain closely associated in the regulating process;

<u>Noting</u> that the United Nations Economic Commission for Europe, the Central Commission for the Navigation of the Rhine and the Danube Commission have bodies dealing with the transport of dangerous goods by inland waterways;

<u>Considering</u> that, once the Agreement has entered into force, any proposal relating to the annexed Regulations should in principle, before submission to the Administrative Committee, be discussed at meetings of experts of the Contracting Parties and, if necessary, of the other States and international organizations mentioned in article 17, paragraph (2);

1.   <u>Invites</u> the United Nations Economic Commission for Europe, the Central Commission for the Navigation of the Rhine and the Danube Commission to establish a joint meeting of experts with the following mandate:

(a)   before entry into force of the Agreement:

(i)   to prepare the updates of the annexed Regulations in order to enable the Administrative Committee, once the Agreement has entered into force, to adapt them to the evolution of transport techniques and to the ongoing restructuring of the other European regulations governing the carriage of dangerous goods and to bring them into line with the level of safety required for navigation on European waterways covered by AGN, particularly on the Rhine;

(ii)   to recommend regular implementation, at national level, of the updated provisions of the relevant annexes by all countries interested in becoming parties to the Agreement;

(iii)   to appoint, amongst Contracting States and Signatory States, provisional committees of experts in accordance with Annex C, Chapter 2, paragraph 2.2.2 of the annexed Regulations to consider on a preliminary basis requests from classification societies which wish to be recommended for recognition;

(b)   after entry into force of the Agreement:

to take the place of the Safety Committee referred to in article 18.

2.   <u>Requests</u> the Executive Secretary of the United Nations Economic Commission for Europe to convene a meeting of the Administrative Committee as soon as possible after the entry into force of the Agreement with a view to:

(a)   adopting proposals for the revision of the annexed Regulations as prepared in accordance with paragraphs 1 (a) (i) and 1 (b) above so that the Regulations will be applicable on the date scheduled in Article 11, paragraph 1;

(b)   adopting a list of recommended classification societies on the basis of the preliminary work carried out in accordance with paragraph 1 (a) (iii) above, or appointing new committees of experts in accordance with Annex C, Chapter 2, paragraph 2.2.2 to consider requests from classification societies which wish to be recommended for recognition.

Adopted on 25 May 2000

———————

EUROPEAN AGREEMENT CONCERNING THE INTERNATIONAL CARRIAGE OF DANGEROUS GOODS BY INLAND WATERWAYS (ADN)

THE CONTRACTING PARTIES,

DESIRING to establish by joint agreement uniform principles and rules, for the purposes of:

(a)   increasing the safety of international carriage of dangerous goods by inland waterways;

(b)   contributing effectively to the protection of the environment, by preventing any pollution resulting from accidents or incidents during such carriage; and

(c)   facilitating transport operations and promoting international trade,

CONSIDERING that the best means of achieving this goal is to conclude an agreement to replace the "European Provisions concerning the International Carriage of Dangerous Goods by Inland Waterways" annexed to resolution No. 223 of the Inland Transport Committee of the Economic Commission for Europe, as amended,

HAVE AGREED as follows:

CHAPTER I

GENERAL PROVISIONS

Article 1

Scope

1.   This Agreement shall apply to the international carriage of dangerous goods by vessels on inland waterways.

2.   This Agreement shall not apply to the carriage of dangerous goods by seagoing vessels on maritime waterways forming part of inland waterways.

3.   This Agreement shall not apply to the carriage of dangerous goods by warships or auxiliary warships or to other vessels belonging to or operated by a State, provided such vessels are used by the State exclusively for governmental and non-commercial purposes. However, each Contracting Party shall, by taking appropriate measures which do not impair the operations or operational capacity of such vessels belonging to or operated by it, ensure that such vessels are operated in a manner compatible with this Agreement, where it is reasonable in practice to do so.

Article 2

Regulations annexed to the Agreement

1.   The Regulations annexed to this Agreement shall form an integral part thereof. Any reference to this Agreement implies at the same time a reference to the Regulations annexed thereto.

2.   The annexed Regulations include:

(a)   Provisions concerning the international carriage of dangerous goods by inland waterways;

(b)   Requirements and procedures concerning inspections, the issue of certificates of approval, recognition of classification societies, derogations, special authorizations, monitoring, training and examination of experts;

(c)   General transitional provisions;

(d)   Supplementary transitional provisions applicable to specific inland waterways.

Article 3

Definitions

For the purposes of this Agreement:

(a)   "*vessel*" means an inland waterway or seagoing vessel;

(b)   "*dangerous goods*" means substances and articles the international carriage of which is prohibited by, or authorized only on certain conditions by, the annexed Regulations;

(c)   "*international carriage of dangerous goods*" means any carriage of dangerous goods performed by a vessel on inland waterways on the territory of at least two Contracting Parties;

(d)   "*inland waterways*" means the navigable inland waterways including maritime waterways on the territory of a Contracting Party open to the navigation of vessels under national law;

(e)   "*maritime waterways*" means inland waterways linked to the sea, basically used for the traffic of seagoing vessels and designated as such under national law;

(f)   "*recognized classification society*" means a classification society which is in conformity with the annexed Regulations and recognized, in accordance with the procedures laid down in these Regulations, by the competent authority of the Contracting Party where the certificate is issued;

(g)   "*competent authority*" means the authority or the body designated or recognized as such in each Contracting Party and in each specific case in connection with these provisions;

(h)   "*inspection body*" means a body nominated or recognized by the Contracting Party for the purpose of inspecting vessels according to the procedures laid down in the annexed Regulations.

CHAPTER II

TECHNICAL PROVISIONS

Article 4

Prohibitions on carriage, conditions of carriage, monitoring

1. Subject to the provisions of Articles 7 and 8, dangerous goods barred from carriage by the annexed Regulations shall not be accepted for international carriage.

2. Without prejudice to the provisions of Article 6, the international carriage of other dangerous goods shall be authorized, subject to compliance with the conditions laid down in the annexed Regulations.

3. Observance of the prohibitions and the conditions referred to in paragraphs 1 and 2 shall be monitored by the Contracting Parties in accordance with the provisions laid down in the annexed Regulations.

Article 5

Exemptions

This Agreement shall not apply to the carriage of dangerous goods to the extent to which such carriage is exempted in accordance with the annexed Regulations. Exemptions may only be granted when the quantity of the goods exempted, or the nature of the transport operation exempted, or the packagings, ensure that transport is carried out safely.

Article 6

Sovereign right of States

Each Contracting Party shall retain the right to regulate or prohibit the entry of dangerous goods into its territory for reasons other than safety during carriage.

Article 7

Special regulations, derogations

1. The Contracting Parties shall retain the right to arrange, for a limited period established in the annexed Regulations, by special bilateral or multilateral agreements, and provided safety is not impaired:

    (a) that the dangerous goods which under this Agreement are barred from international carriage may, subject to certain conditions, be accepted for international carriage on their inland waterways; or

    (b) that dangerous goods which under this Agreement are accepted for international carriage only on specified conditions may alternatively be accepted for international carriage on their inland waterways under conditions different from those laid down in the annexed Regulations.

    The special bilateral or multilateral agreements referred to in this paragraph shall be communicated immediately to the Executive Secretary of the Economic Commission for Europe, who shall communicate them to the Contracting Parties which are not signatories to the said agreements.

2.   Each Contracting Party shall retain the right to issue special authorizations for the international carriage in tank vessels of dangerous substances the carriage of which in tank vessels is not permitted under the provisions concerning carriage in the annexed Regulations, subject to compliance with the procedures relating to special authorizations in the annexed Regulations.

3.   The Contracting Parties shall retain the right to authorize, in the following cases, the international carriage of dangerous goods on board vessels which do not comply with conditions established in the annexed Regulations, provided that the procedure established in the annexed Regulations is complied with:

(a)   The use on a vessel of materials, installations or equipment or the application on a vessel of certain measures concerning construction or certain provisions other than those prescribed in the annexed Regulations;

(b)   Vessel with technical innovations derogating from the provisions of the annexed Regulations.

Article 8

Transitional provisions

1.   Certificates of approval and other documents prepared in accordance with the requirements of the Regulations for the Carriage of Dangerous Goods in the Rhine (ADNR), the Regulations for the Carriage of Dangerous Goods on the Danube (ADN-D) or national regulations based on the European Provisions concerning the International Carriage of Dangerous Goods by Inland Waterways as annexed to resolution No. 223 of the Inland Transport Committee of the Economic Commission for Europe or as amended, applicable at the date of application of the annexed Regulations foreseen in Article 11, paragraph 1, shall remain valid until their expiry date, under the same conditions as those prevailing up to the date of such application, including their recognition by other States. In addition, these certificates shall remain valid for a period of one year from the date of application of the annexed Regulations in the event that they would expire during that period. However, the period of validity shall in no case exceed five years beyond the date of application of the annexed Regulations.

2.   Vessels which, at the date of application of the annexed Regulations foreseen in Article 11, paragraph 1, are approved for the carriage of dangerous goods on the territory of a Contracting Party and which conform to the requirements of the annexed Regulations, taking into account where necessary, their general transitional provisions, may obtain an ADN certificate of approval under the procedure laid down in the annexed Regulations.

3.   In the case of vessels referred to in paragraph 2 to be used exclusively for carriage on inland waterways where ADNR was not applicable under domestic law prior to the date of application of the annexed Regulations foreseen in Article 11, paragraph 1, the supplementary transitional provisions applicable to specific inland waterways may be applied in addition to the general transitional provisions. Such vessels shall obtain an ADN certificate of approval limited to the inland waterways referred to above, or to a portion thereof.

4.   If new provisions are added to the annexed Regulations, the Contracting Parties may include new general transitional provisions. These transitional provisions shall indicate the vessels in question and the period for which they are valid.

Article 9

Applicability of other regulations

The transport operations to which this Agreement applies shall remain subject to local, regional or international regulations applicable in general to the carriage of goods by inland waterways.

CHAPTER III

FINAL PROVISIONS

Article 10

Contracting Parties

1. Member States of the Economic Commission for Europe whose territory contains inland waterways, other than those forming a coastal route, which form part of the network of inland waterways of international importance as defined in the European Agreement on Main Inland Waterways of International Importance (AGN) may become Contracting Parties to this Agreement:

   (a)   by signing it definitively;

   (b)   by depositing an instrument of ratification, acceptance or approval after signing it subject to ratification, acceptance or approval;

   (c)   by depositing an instrument of accession.

2. The Agreement shall be open for signature until 31 May 2001 at the Office of the Executive Secretary of the Economic Commission for Europe, Geneva. Thereafter, it shall be open for accession.

3. The instruments of ratification, acceptance, approval or accession shall be deposited with the Secretary-General of the United Nations.

Article 11

Entry into force

1. This Agreement shall enter into force one month after the date on which the number of States mentioned in Article 10, paragraph 1, which have signed it definitively, or have deposited their instruments of ratification, acceptance, approval or accession has reached a total of seven.

   However, the annexed Regulations, except provisions concerning recognition of classification societies, shall not apply until twelve months after the entry into force of the Agreement.

2. For any State signing this Agreement definitively or ratifying, accepting, approving or acceding to it after seven of the States referred to in Article 10, paragraph 1, have signed it definitively or have deposited their instruments of ratification, acceptance, approval or accession, this Agreement shall enter into force one month after the said State has signed it definitively or has deposited its instrument of ratification, acceptance, approval or accession.

   The annexed Regulations shall become applicable on the same date. In the event that the term referred to in paragraph 1 relating to the application of the annexed Regulations has not expired, the annexed Regulations shall become applicable after expiry of the said term.

Article 12

Denunciation

1.   Any Contracting Party may denounce this Agreement by so notifying in writing the Secretary-General of the United Nations.

2.   Denunciation shall take effect twelve months after the date of receipt by the Secretary-General of the written notification of denunciation.

Article 13

Termination

1.   If, after the entry into force of this Agreement, the number of Contracting Parties is less than five during twelve consecutive months, this Agreement shall cease to have effect at the end of the said period of twelve months.

2.   In the event of the conclusion of a world-wide agreement for the regulation of the multimodal transport of dangerous goods, any provision of this Agreement, with the exception of those pertaining exclusively to inland waterways, the construction and equipment of vessels, carriage in bulk or tankers which is contrary to any provision of the said world-wide agreement shall, from the date on which the latter enters into force, automatically cease to apply to relations between the Parties to this Agreement which become parties to the world-wide agreement, and shall automatically be replaced by the relevant provision of the said world-wide agreement.

Article 14

Declarations

1.   Any State may, at the time of signing this Agreement definitively or of depositing its instrument of ratification, acceptance, approval or accession or at any time thereafter, declare by written notification addressed to the Secretary-General of the United Nations that this Agreement shall extend to all or any of the territories for the international relations of which it is responsible. The Agreement shall extend to the territory or territories named in the notification one month after it is received by the Secretary-General.

2.   Any State which has made a declaration under paragraph 1 of this article extending this Agreement to any territory for whose international relations it is responsible may denounce the Agreement in respect of the said territory in accordance with the provisions of Article 12.

3.   (a)   In addition, any State may, at the time of signing this Agreement definitively or of depositing its instrument of ratification, acceptance, approval or accession or at any time thereafter, declare by written notification addressed to the Secretary-General of the United Nations that this Agreement shall not extend to certain inland waterways on its territory, provided that the waterways in question are not part of the network of inland waterways of international importance as defined in the AGN. If this declaration is made subsequent to the time when the State signs this Agreement definitively or when it deposits its instrument of ratification, acceptance, approval or accession, the Agreement shall cease to have effect on the inland waterways in question one month after this notification is received by the Secretary-General.

    (b)   However, any State on whose territory there are inland waterways covered by AGN, and which are, at the date of adoption of this Agreement, subject to a mandatory regime under international law concerning the carriage of dangerous goods, may declare that the implementation of this

Agreement on these waterways shall be subject to compliance with the procedures set out in the statutes of the said regime. Any declaration of this nature shall be made at the time of signing this Agreement definitively or of depositing its instrument of ratification, acceptance, approval or accession.

4. Any State which has made a declaration under paragraphs 3 (a) or 3 (b) of this article may subsequently declare by means of a written notification to the Secretary-General of the United Nations that this Agreement shall apply to all or part of its inland waterways covered by the declaration made under paragraphs 3 (a) or 3 (b). The Agreement shall apply to the inland waterways mentioned in the notification one month after it is received by the Secretary-General.

Article 15

Disputes

1. Any dispute between two or more Contracting Parties concerning the interpretation or application of this Agreement shall so far as possible be settled by negotiation between the Parties in dispute.

2. Any dispute which is not settled by direct negotiation may be referred by the Contracting Parties in dispute to the Administrative Committee which shall consider it and make recommendations for its settlement.

3. Any dispute which is not settled in accordance with paragraphs 1 or 2 shall be submitted to arbitration if any one of the Contracting Parties in dispute so requests and shall be referred accordingly to one or more arbitrators selected by agreement between the Parties in dispute. If within three months from the date of the request for arbitration the Parties in dispute are unable to agree on the selection of an arbitrator or arbitrators, any of those Parties may request the Secretary-General of the United Nations to nominate a single arbitrator to whom the dispute shall be referred for decision.

4. The decision of the arbitrator or arbitrators appointed under paragraph 3 of this article shall be binding on the Contracting Parties in dispute.

Article 16

Reservations

1. Any State may, at the time of signing this Agreement definitively or of depositing its instrument of ratification, acceptance, approval or accession, declare that it does not consider itself bound by Article 15. Other Contracting Parties shall not be bound by Article 15 in respect of any Contracting Party which has entered such a reservation.

2. Any Contracting State having entered a reservation as provided for in paragraph 1 of this article may at any time withdraw such reservation by notifying in writing the Secretary-General of the United Nations.

3. Reservations other than those provided for in this Agreement are not permitted.

Article 17

Administrative Committee

1. An Administrative Committee shall be established to consider the implementation of this Agreement, to consider any amendments proposed thereto and to consider measures to secure uniformity in the interpretation and application thereof.

2. The Contracting Parties shall be members of the Administrative Committee. The Committee may decide that the States referred to in Article 10, paragraph 1 of this Agreement which are not Contracting Parties, any other Member State of the Economic Commission for Europe or of the United Nations or representatives of international intergovernmental or non-governmental organizations may, for questions which interest them, attend the sessions of the Committee as observers.

3. The Secretary-General of the United Nations and the Secretary-General of the Central Commission for the Navigation of the Rhine shall provide the Administrative Committee with secretariat services.

4. The Administrative Committee shall, at the first session of the year, elect a Chairperson and a Vice-Chairperson.

5. The Executive Secretary of the Economic Commission for Europe shall convene the Administrative Committee annually, or at other intervals decided on by the Committee, and also at the request of at least five Contracting Parties.

6. A quorum consisting of not less than one half of the Contracting Parties shall be required for the purpose of taking decisions.

7. Proposals shall be put to the vote. Each Contracting Party represented at the session shall have one vote. The following rules shall apply:

   (a) Proposed amendments to the annexed Regulations and decisions pertaining thereto shall be adopted in accordance with the provisions of Article 19, paragraph 2;

   (b) Proposed amendment to the annexed Regulations and decisions pertaining thereto shall be adopted in accordance with the provisions of Article 20, paragraph 4;

   (c) Proposals and decisions relating to the recommendation of agreed classification societies, or to the withdrawal of such recommendation, shall be adopted in accordance with the procedure of the provisions of Article 20, paragraph 4;

   (d) Any proposal or decision other than those referred to in paragraphs (a) to (c) above shall be adopted by a majority of the Administrative Committee members present and voting.

8. The Administrative Committee may set up such working groups as it may deem necessary to assist it in carrying out its duties.

9. In the absence of relevant provisions in this Agreement, the Rules of Procedure of the Economic Commission for Europe shall be applicable unless the Administrative Committee decides otherwise.

Article 18

Safety Committee

A Safety Committee shall be established to consider all proposals for the amendment of the Regulations annexed to the Agreement, particularly as regards safety of navigation in relation to the construction, equipment and crews of vessels. The Safety Committee shall function within the framework of the activities of the bodies of the Economic Commission for Europe, of the Central Commission for the Navigation of the Rhine and of the Danube Commission which are competent in the transport of dangerous goods by inland waterways.

Article 19

Procedure for amending the Agreement, excluding the annexed Regulations

1. This Agreement, excluding its annexed Regulations, may be amended upon the proposal of a Contracting Party by the procedure specified in this article.

2. Any proposed amendment to this Agreement, excluding the annexed Regulations, shall be considered by the Administrative Committee. Any such amendment considered or prepared during the meeting of the Administrative Committee and adopted by it by a two-thirds majority of the members present and voting shall be communicated by the Secretary-General of the United Nations to the Contracting Parties for their acceptance.

3. Any proposed amendments communicated for acceptance in accordance with paragraph 2 shall come into force with respect to all Contracting Parties six months after the expiry of a period of twenty-four months following the date of communication of the proposed amendment if, during that period, no objection to the amendment in question has been communicated in writing to the Secretary-General of the United Nations by a Contracting Party.

Article 20

Procedure for amending the annexed Regulations

1. The annexed Regulations may be amended upon the proposal of a Contracting Party.

    The Secretary-General of the United Nations may also propose amendments with a view to bringing the annexed Regulations into line with other international agreements concerning the transport of dangerous goods and the United Nations Recommendations on the Transport of Dangerous Goods, as well as amendments proposed by a subsidiary body of the Economic Commission for Europe with competence in the area of the transport of dangerous goods.

2. Any proposed amendment to the annexed Regulations shall in principle be submitted to the Safety Committee, which shall submit the draft amendments it adopts to the Administrative Committee.

3. At the specific request of a Contracting Party, or if the secretariat of the Administrative Committee considers it appropriate, amendments may also be proposed directly to the Administrative Committee. They shall be examined at a first session and if they are deemed to be acceptable, they shall be reviewed at the following session of the Committee at the same time as any related proposal, unless otherwise decided by the Committee.

4. Decisions on proposed amendments and proposed draft amendments submitted to the Administrative Committee in accordance with paragraphs 2 and 3 shall be made by a majority of the members present and voting. However, a draft amendment shall not be deemed adopted if, immediately after the vote, five members present declare their objection to it. Adopted draft amendments shall be communicated by the Secretary-General of the United Nations to the Contracting Parties for acceptance.

5. Any draft amendment to the annexed Regulations communicated for acceptance in accordance with paragraph 4 shall be deemed to be accepted unless, within three months from the date on which the Secretary-General circulates it, at least one-third of the Contracting Parties, or five of them if one-third exceeds that figure, have given the Secretary-General written notification of their objection to the proposed amendment. If the amendment is deemed to be accepted, it shall enter into force for all the Contracting Parties, on the expiry of a further period of three months, except in the following cases:

(a) In cases where similar amendments to other international agreements governing the carriage of dangerous goods have already entered into force, or will enter into force at a different date, the Secretary-General may decide, upon written request by the Executive Secretary of the Economic Commission for Europe, that the amendment shall enter into force on the expiry of a different period so as to allow the simultaneous entry into force of these amendments with those to be made to such other agreements or, if not possible, the quickest entry into force of this amendment after the entry into force of such amendments to other agreements; such period shall not, however, be of less than one month's duration.

(b) The Administrative Committee may specify, when adopting a draft amendment, for the purpose of entry into force of the amendment, should it be accepted, a period of more than three months= duration.

Article 21

Requests, communications and objections

The Secretary-General of the United Nations shall inform all Contracting Parties and all States referred to in Article 10, paragraph 1 of this Agreement of any request, communication or objection under Articles 19 and 20 above and of the date on which any amendment enters into force.

Article 22

Review conference

1. Notwithstanding the procedure provided for in Articles 19 and 20, any Contracting Party may, by notification in writing to the Secretary-General of the United Nations, request that a conference be convened for the purpose of reviewing this Agreement.

A review conference to which all Contracting Parties and all States referred to in Article 10, paragraph 1, shall be invited, shall be convened by the Executive Secretary of the Economic Commission for Europe if, within a period of six months following the date of notification by the Secretary-General, not less than one fourth of the Contracting Parties notify him of their concurrence with the request.

2. Notwithstanding the procedure provided for in Articles 19 and 20, a review conference to which all Contracting Parties and all States referred to in Article 10, paragraph 1, shall be invited, shall also be convened by the Executive Secretary of the Economic Commission for Europe upon notification in writing by the Administrative Committee. The Administrative Committee shall make a request if agreed to by a majority of those present and voting in the Committee.

3.   If a conference is convened in pursuance of paragraphs 1 or 2 of this article, the Executive Secretary of the Economic Commission for Europe shall invite the Contracting Parties to submit, within a period of three months, the proposals which they wish the conference to consider.

4.   The Executive Secretary of the Economic Commission for Europe shall circulate to all the Contracting Parties and to all the States referred to in Article 10, paragraph 1, the provisional agenda for the conference, together with the texts of such proposals, at least six months before the date on which the conference is to meet.

Article 23

Depositary

The Secretary-General of the United Nations shall be the depositary of this Agreement.

IN WITNESS WHEREOF the undersigned, being duly authorized thereto, have signed this Agreement.

DONE at Geneva, this twenty-sixth day of May two thousand, in a single copy, in the English, French, German and Russian languages for the text of the Agreement proper, and in the French language for the annexed Regulations, each text being equally authentic for the Agreement proper.

The Secretary-General of the United Nations is requested to prepare a translation of the annexed Regulations in the English and Russian languages.

The Secretary-General of the Central Commission for the Navigation of the Rhine is requested to prepare a translation of the annexed Regulations in the German language.

———————

PART I

General provisions

CHAPTER 1.1

SCOPE AND APPLICABILITY

1.1.1   **Structure**

The Regulations annexed to ADN are grouped into nine parts. Each part is subdivided into chapters and each chapter into sections and subsections (see table of contents). Within each part the number of the part is included with the numbers of the chapters, sections and subsections, for example Part 2, Chapter 2, section 1 is numbered "2.2.1".

1.1.2   **Scope**

1.1.2.1   For the purposes of Article 2 paragraph 2 (a) and Article 4 of ADN, the annexed Regulations specify:

(a)   dangerous goods which are barred from international carriage;

(b)   dangerous goods which are authorized for international carriage and the conditions attaching to them (including exemptions) particularly with regard to:

–   classification of goods, including classification criteria and relevant test methods;

–   use of packagings (including mixed packing);

–   use of tanks (including filling);

–   consignment procedures (including marking and labelling of packages and placarding and marking of means of transport embarked, the marking of vessels as well as documentation and information required);

–   provisions concerning the construction, testing and approval of packagings and tanks;

–   use of means of transport (including loading, mixed loading and unloading).

1.1.2.2   For the purposes of Article 5 of ADN, section 1.1.3 of this chapter specifies the cases in which the carriage of dangerous goods is partially or totally exempted from the conditions of carriage established by ADN.

1.1.2.3   For the purposes of Article 7 of ADN, Chapter 1.5 of this part specifies the rules concerning the derogations, special authorizations and equivalences for which that article provides.

1.1.2.4   For the purposes of Article 8 of ADN, Chapter 1.6 of this part specifies the transitional measures concerning the application of the Regulations annexed to ADN.

1.1.2.5   The provisions of this part also apply to empty vessels or vessels which have been unloaded as long as the holds, cargo tanks or receptacles or tanks accepted on board are not free from dangerous substances or gases, except for the exemptions for which section 1.1.3 of this chapter provides.

1.1.3 Exemptions

1.1.3.1 *Exemptions related to the nature of the transport operation*

The provisions laid down in ADN do not apply to:

(a)   the carriage of dangerous goods by private individuals where the goods in question are packaged for retail sale and are intended for their personal or domestic use or for their leisure or sporting activities provided that measures have been taken to prevent any leakage of contents in normal conditions of carriage. Dangerous goods in IBCs, large packagings or tanks are not considered to be packaged for retail sale;

(b)   the carriage of machinery or equipment not specified in these annexed Regulations and which happen to contain dangerous goods in their internal or operational equipment, provided that measures have been taken to prevent any leakage of contents in normal conditions of carriage;

(c)   the carriage undertaken by enterprises which is ancillary to their main activity, such as deliveries to or returns from building or civil engineering sites, or in relation to surveying, repairs and maintenance, in quantities of not more than 450 litres per packaging and within the maximum quantities specified in 1.1.3.6. Measures shall be taken to prevent any leakage of contents in normal conditions of carriage. These exemptions do not apply to Class 7.

Carriage undertaken by such enterprises for their supply or external or internal distribution does not fall within the scope of this exemption;

(d)   the carriage undertaken by, or under the supervision of, the emergency services;

(e)   emergency transport under the supervision of the competent authorities intended to save human lives or protect the environment provided that all measures are taken to ensure that such transport is carried out in complete safety.

NOTE: For radioactive material see 2.2.7.1.2.

1.1.3.2 *Exemptions related to the carriage of gases*

The provisions laid down in ADN do not apply to the carriage of:

(a)   *(reserved)*;

(b)   *(reserved)*;

(c)   gases of Groups A and O (according to 2.2.2.1), if the pressure of the gas in the receptacle or tank at a temperature of 15° C does not exceed 200 kPa (2 bar) and if the gas is completely in the gaseous state during carriage. This includes every kind of receptacle or tank, e.g. also parts of machinery and apparatus;

(d)   *(reserved)*;

(e)   *(reserved)*;

(f)   uncleaned empty static pressure vessels which are carried, on condition that all openings with the exception of pressure relief devices (when fitted) are hermetically closed; and

(g)   gases contained in foodstuffs or beverages.

1.1.3.3   ***Exemptions related to substances used for the propulsion of vessels, vehicles or wagons carried, for the operation of their special equipment, for their upkeep or for the safety.***

The requirements of ADN do not apply to substances used for the propulsion of vessels or the vehicles carried, for the operation of their special equipment, for their upkeep or to ensure safety, which are carried on board in the packaging, receptacle or tanks intended for use for this purpose.

1.1.3.4   ***Exemptions related to special provisions or to dangerous goods packed in limited quantities***

NOTE: For radioactive material see 2.2.7.1.2.

1.1.3.4.1   Certain special provisions of Chapter 3.3 exempt partially or totally the carriage of specific dangerous goods from the requirements of ADN. The exemption applies when the special provision is referred to in Column (6) of Table A of Chapter 3.2 against the dangerous goods entry concerned.

1.1.3.4.2   Certain dangerous goods packed in limited quantities may be subject to exemptions provided that the conditions of Chapter 3.4 are met.

1.1.3.5   ***Exemptions related to empty uncleaned packagings***

Empty uncleaned packagings (including IBCs and large packagings) which have contained substances of Classes 2, 3, 4.1, 5.1, 6.1, 8 and 9 are not subject to the conditions of ADN if adequate measures have been taken to nullify any hazards. Hazards are nullified if adequate measures have been taken to nullify all hazards of Classes 1 to 9.

1.1.3.6   ***Exemptions related to quantities carried on board vessels***

1.1.3.6.1   *Exemptions in this subsection apply when the following conditions are met:*

(a)   The total gross mass of the packages does not exceed 3,000 kg and when the goods concerned are other than:

(i)   substances and articles of Class 1;

(ii)   substances of Class 2, groups T, F, TF, TC, TO, TFC or TOC, according to 2.2.2.1.3 and aerosols of groups C, CO, F, FC, T, TF, TC, TO, TFC and TOC according to 2.2.2.1.6;

(iii)   substances of Classes 4.1 or 5.2. for which a danger label of model No. 1 is required in column (5) of Table A of Chapter 3.2;

(iv)   substances of Class 6.2, Group A;

(v)   substances of Class 7 other than UN Nos. 2908, 2909, 2910 and 2911;

(vi)   substances assigned to Packing Group I;

(vii)   substances carried in tanks;

(b)   The gross mass of the packages does not exceed 300 kg in the case of

(i)   substances of Class 2 of group F in accordance with 2.2.2.1.3 or aerosols of group F according to 2.2.2.1.6; or

(ii)   substances assigned to Packing Group I, except substances of Class 6.1.

For the purposes of this paragraph, the dangerous goods exempted in accordance with 1.1.3.2 to 1.1.3.5 and 1.1.3.7 shall not be taken into account.

1.1.3.6.2   When the conditions of 1.1.3.6.1 are met, the requirements of Part 7 (with the exception of those relating to the loading plan of 7.2.4.11) and those of Parts 8 and 9 are not applicable.

The following requirements shall, however, be complied with:

(a)   Packages shall be stowed in the holds, except in the case of containers with complete spray-proof walls, vehicles or wagons with complete spray-proof walls or tank-containers, portable tanks (MEGCs, vehicles with demountable tanks, tank-vehicles or battery-vehicles);

(b)   Goods of different classes shall be separated by a minimum horizontal distance of 3 m. They shall not be stowed on top of each other.

This requirement does not apply to:

(i)   stowage of packages and separation between packages loaded in a vehicle, a wagon or a container, provided that the requirements of ADR applicable to mixed loading and separation or the requirements of the IMDG Code regarding packing and separation are complied with;

(ii)   the separation between

–   containers with complete metal walls;

–   vehicles or wagons with bodies with complete metal walls;

–   tank-containers, portable tanks and MEGCs; or

–   vehicles with demountable tanks, tank-vehicles, battery-vehicles, tank wagons or battery wagons.

NOTE: For seagoing and inland navigation vessels, where the latter carry only containers, tank-containers, portable tanks or MEGCs, the requirements of (a) and (b) above shall be considered to have been met if the requirements of the IMDG Code regarding stowage and separation are met and if this particular is recorded in the transport document.

1.1.4   Applicability of other regulations

1.1.4.1   *General*

The following requirements are applicable to packages:

(a)   in the case of packagings (including large packagings and intermediate bulk containers (IBCs), the applicable requirements of one of the international regulations shall be met (see also Part 4 and Part 6 of these Regulations);

(b) in the case of containers, tank-containers, portable tanks and multiple element gas containers (MEGCs), the applicable requirements of ADR, RID or the IMDG Code shall be met (see also Part 4 and Part 6 of these Regulations);

c) in the case of vehicles or wagons, the vehicles or wagons and their load shall meet the applicable requirements of ADR or of RID, as relevant.

NOTE: For the marking, labelling, placarding and orange plate marking, see also Chapters 5.2 and 5.3.

1.1.4.2 *Carriage in a transport chain including maritime, road, rail or air carriage*

1.1.4.2.1 Packages, containers, portable tanks and tank-containers, which do not entirely meet the requirements for packing, mixed packing, marking, labelling of packages or placarding and orange plate marking, of ADN, but are in conformity with the requirements of the IMDG Code or the ICAO Technical Instructions shall be accepted for carriage in a transport chain including maritime or air carriage subject to the following conditions:

(a) If the packages are not marked and labelled in accordance with ADR, they shall bear markings and danger labels in accordance with the requirements of the IMDG Code or the ICAO Technical Instructions;

(b) The requirements of the IMDG Code or the ICAO Technical Instructions shall be applicable to mixed packing within a package;

(c) For carriage in a transport chain including maritime carriage, if the containers, portable tanks or tank-containers are not marked and placarded in accordance with Chapter 5.3 of this Annex, they shall be marked and placarded in accordance with Chapter 5.3 of the IMDG Code. In such case, only 5.3.2.1.1 of this Annex is applicable to the marking of the vehicle itself. For empty, uncleaned portable tanks and tank-containers, this requirement shall apply up to and including the subsequent transfer to a cleaning station.

This derogation does not apply in the case of goods classified as dangerous goods in classes 1 to 8 of ADN and considered as non-dangerous goods according to the applicable requirements of the IMDG Code or the ICAO Technical Instructions.

1.1.4.2.2 When a maritime, road, rail or air transport operation follows or precedes carriage by inland waterway, the transport document used or to be used for the maritime, road, rail or air transport operation may be used in place of the transport document prescribed in 5.4.1 provided that the particulars it contains are in conformity with the applicable requirements of the IMDG Code, ADR, RID or the ICAO Technical Instructions, respectively except that, when additional information is required by ADN, it shall be added or entered at the appropriate place.

NOTE: For carriage in accordance with 1.1.4.2.1, see also 5.4.1.1.7. For carriage in containers, see also 5.4.2.

1.1.4.3 *(Reserved)*

1.1.4.4 *(Reserved)*

1.1.4.5 *(Reserved).*

1.1.4.6 *Other regulations applicable to carriage by inland waterway*

1.1.4.6.1 In accordance with article 9 of the Agreement, transport operations shall remain subject to the local, regional or international requirements generally applicable to the carriage of goods by inland waterway.

1.1.4.6.2 Where the requirements of these Regulations are in contradiction with the requirements referred to in 1.1.4.6.1, the requirements referred to in 1.1.4.6.1 shall not apply.

CHAPTER 1.2

DEFINITIONS AND UNITS OF MEASUREMENT

1.2.1   **Definitions**

NOTE: This section contains all general or specific definitions.

For the purposes of these regulations:

A

Accommodation means spaces intended for the use of persons normally living on board, including galleys, food stores, lavatories, washrooms, bathrooms, laundries, halls, alleyways, etc., but excluding the wheelhouse;

ADR means the European Agreement concerning the International Carriage of Dangerous Goods by Road;

Aerosol, see *Aerosol dispenser*;

Aerosol dispenser means any non-refillable receptacle meeting the requirements of 6.2.4 of ADR or of RID made of metal, glass or plastics, and containing a gas, compressed, liquefied or dissolved, with or without a liquid, paste or powder, and fitted with a release device allowing the contents to be ejected as solid or liquid particles in suspension in a gas, as a foam, paste or powder or in a liquid state or in a gaseous state;

Auto-ignition temperature (EN 1127-1:1997, No. 331) means the lowest temperature determined under prescribed test conditions of a hot surface on which a flammable substance in the form of a gas/air or vapour/air mixture ignites.

B

Bag means a flexible packaging made of paper, plastics film, textiles, woven material or other suitable material;

Battery-vehicle means a vehicle containing elements which are linked to each other by a manifold and permanently fixed to a transport unit. The following elements are considered to be elements of a battery-vehicle: cylinders, tubes, bundles of cylinders (also known as frames), pressure drums as well as tanks destined for the carriage of gases of Class 2 with a capacity of more than 450 litres;

Battery wagon means a wagon containing elements which are linked to each other by a manifold and permanently fixed to a wagon. The following elements are considered to be elements of a battery wagon: cylinders, tubes, bundles of cylinders (also known as frames), pressure drums as well as tanks intended for gases of Class 2 with a capacity greater than 450 litres;

BC Code means the Code of Safe Practice for Solid Bulk Cargoes of the International Maritime Organization (IMO);

Bilge water means oily water from the engine room bilges, the peak, the cofferdams and the double-hull spaces;

Biological/technical name means a name currently used in scientific and technical handbooks, journals and texts. Trade names shall not be used for this purpose;

Body (for all categories of IBC other than composite IBCs) means the receptacle proper, including openings and closures, but does not include service equipment;

Box means a packaging with complete rectangular or polygonal faces, made of metal, wood, plywood, reconstituted wood, fibreboard, plastics or other suitable material. Small holes for purposes of ease of handling or opening or to meet classification requirements, are permitted as long as they do not compromise the integrity of the packaging during carriage;

Breathing apparatus (ambient air-dependent) means an apparatus which protects the person wearing it when working in a dangerous atmosphere by means of a suitable filter;

Bulk containers means containment systems (including any liner or coating) intended for the carriage of solid substances which are in direct contact with the containment system. Packagings, intermediate bulk containers (IBCs), large packagings and tanks are not included.

Bulk containers are:

-      of a permanent character and accordingly strong enough to be suitable for repeated use;

-      specially designed to facilitate the carriage of goods by one or more modes of carriage without intermediate reloading;

-      fitted with devices permitting its ready handling;

-      of a capacity of not less than 1.0 m³.

Examples of bulk containers are containers, offshore bulk containers, skips, bulk bins, swap bodies, trough-shaped containers, roller containers, load compartments of wagons/vehicles;

Bulkhead means a metal wall, generally vertical, inside the vessel and which is bounded by the bottom, the side plating, a deck, the hatchway covers or by another bulkhead;

Bulkhead (watertight) means

—   in a tank vessel: a bulkhead constructed to withstand a water pressure of 1.00 metre above the deck;

—   in a dry cargo vessel: a bulkhead constructed so that it can withstand water pressure with a head of 1.00 metre above the deck but at least to the top of the hatchway coaming;

Bundle of cylinders (frame) means an assembly of cylinders that are fastened together and are interconnected by a manifold and carried as a unit. The total water capacity shall not exceed 3,000 litres except that bundles intended for the carriage of toxic gases of Class 2 (groups starting with letter T according to 2.2.2.1.3) shall be limited to 1,000 litres water capacity.

C

Cargo area means the whole of the following spaces (see figures below);

Cargo area

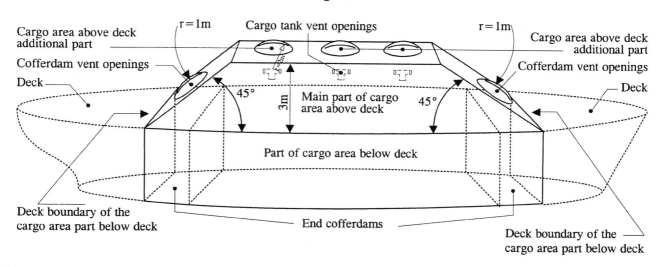

Above deck cargo area for various tank vessel

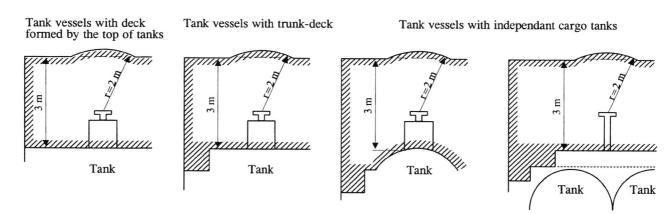

Cargo area (additional part above deck) (When anti-explosion protection is required, comparable to zone 1) means the spaces not included in the main part of cargo area above deck comprising 1.00 m radius spherical segments centred over the ventilation openings of the cofferdams and the service spaces located in the cargo area part below the deck and 2.00 m spherical segments centred over the ventilation openings of the cargo tanks and the opening of the pump-rooms;

Cargo area (main part above deck) (When anti-explosion protection is required - comparable to zone 1) means the space which is bounded:

–   at the sides, by the shell plating extending upwards from the decks sides;

–   fore and aft, by planes inclined at 45° towards the cargo area, starting at the boundary of the cargo area part below deck;

–   vertically, 3.00 m above the deck;

Cargo area (part below deck) means the space between two vertical planes perpendicular to the centre-line plane of the vessel, which comprises cargo tanks, hold spaces, cofferdams, double-hull spaces and double bottoms; these planes normally coincide with the outer cofferdam bulkheads or hold end bulkheads. Their intersection line with the deck is referred to as the boundary of the cargo area part below deck;

Cargo piping, see *Pipes for loading and unloading*;

Cargo pump-room (When anti-explosion protection is required, comparable to zone 1 - see *Classification of zones*) means a service space where the cargo pumps and stripping pumps are installed together with their operational equipment;

Cargo residues means liquid cargo which remain in the cargo tank or cargo piping after discharging or stripping;

Cargo tank (When anti-explosion protection is required, comparable to zone 0) means a tank which is permanently attached to the vessel and the boundaries of which are either formed by the hull itself or by walls separate from the hull and which is intended for the carriage of dangerous goods;

Cargo tank (condition)

discharged : empty, but containing residual cargo;
empty : dry, but not gas-free;
gas-free : not containing any measurable concentration of dangerous gases or vapours;

Carriage means the change of place of dangerous goods, including stops made necessary by transport conditions and including any period spent by the dangerous goods in vessels, vehicles, tanks and containers made necessary by traffic conditions before, during and after the change of place.

This definition also covers the intermediate temporary storage of dangerous goods in order to change the mode or means of transport (transshipment). This shall apply provided that transport documents showing the place of dispatch and the place of reception are presented on request and provided that packages and tanks are not opened during intermediate storage, except to be checked by the competent authorities;

Carriage in bulk means the carriage of an unpackaged solid which can be discharged;

NOTE: *Within the meaning of ADN, the carriage in bulk referred to in ADR is considered as carriage in packages.*

Carrier means the enterprise which carries out the transport operation with or without a transport contract;

Certified safe type electrical apparatus means an electrical apparatus which has been tested and approved by the competent authority regarding its safety of operation in an explosive atmosphere, e.g.

– intrinsically safe apparatus;

– flameproof enclosure apparatus;

– apparatus protected by pressurization;

– powder filling apparatus;

–   apparatus protected by encapsulation;

–   increased safety apparatus.

NOTE: Limited explosion risk apparatus is not covered by this definition.

CEVNI means the UN/ECE European Code for Inland Waterways.

Classification society (recognized) means a classification society which is recognized by the competent authorities in accordance with Chapter 1.15;

Classification of zones (see IEC publication 79-10)

Zone 0:   areas in which dangerous explosive atmospheres of gases, vapours or sprays exist permanently or during long periods;

Zone 1:   areas in which dangerous explosive atmospheres of gases, vapours or sprays are likely to occur occasionally;

Zone 2:   areas in which dangerous explosive atmospheres of gases, vapours or sprays are likely to occur rarely and if so for short periods only.

Closed container means a totally enclosed container having a rigid roof, rigid side walls, rigid end walls and a floor. The term includes containers with an opening roof where the roof can be closed during transport;

Closed vehicle means a vehicle having a body capable of being closed;

Closure means a device which closes an opening in a receptacle;

Cofferdam (when anti-explosion protection is required, comparable to zone 1) means an athwartship compartment which is bounded by watertight bulkheads and which can be inspected. The cofferdam shall extend over the whole area of the end bulkheads of the cargo tanks. The bulkhead not facing the cargo area shall extend from one side of the vessel to the other and from the bottom to the deck in one frame plane;

Collective entry means an entry for a well-defined group of substances or articles (see 2.1.1.2, B, C and D);

Combination packaging means a combination of packagings for transport purposes, consisting of one or more inner packagings secured in an outer packing in accordance with 4.1.1.5 of ADR;

NOTE: The "inners" of "Combination packagings" are always termed "inner packagings" and not "inner receptacles". A glass bottle is an example of such an "inner packaging".

Common vapour piping means a pipe connecting two or more cargo tanks. This pipe is fitted with safety valves which protect cargo tanks against unacceptable internal overpressures or vacuums; it is intended to evacuate gases and vapours to the shore facility;

Compensation piping means a pipe of the shore facility which is connected during the unloading to the vessel's common vapour pipe or gas return piping. This pipe is designed so as to protect the vessel against detonations or the passage of flames from the shore side;

Competent authority means the authority or authorities or any other body or bodies designated as such in each State and in each specific case in accordance with domestic law;

Compliance assurance (radioactive material) means a systematic programme of measures applied by a competent authority which is aimed at ensuring that the requirements of ADN are met in practice;

Composite IBC with plastics inner receptacle means an IBC comprising structural equipment in the form of a rigid outer casing encasing a plastics inner receptacle together with any service or other structural equipment. It is so constructed that the inner receptacle and outer casing once assembled form, and are used as, an integrated single unit to be filled, stored, transported or emptied as such;

NOTE: *Plastics, when used in connection with inner receptacles for composite IBCs, is taken to include other polymeric materials such as rubber, etc.*

Composite packaging (plastics material) is a packaging consisting of an inner plastics receptacle and an outer packaging (made of metal, fibreboard, plywood, etc.). Once assembled such a packaging remains thereafter an inseparable unit; it is filled, stored, despatched and emptied as such;

NOTE: *See NOTE under Composite packagings (glass, porcelain or stoneware).*

Composite packaging (glass, porcelain or stoneware) is a packaging consisting of an inner glass, porcelain or stoneware receptacle and an outer packaging (made of metal, wood, fibreboard, plastics material, expanded plastics material, etc.). Once assembled, such a packaging remains thereafter an inseparable unit; it is filled, stored, despatched and emptied as such;

NOTE: *The "inners" of "composite packagings" are normally termed "inner receptacles". For example, the "inner" of a 6HA1 (composite packaging, plastics material) is such an "inner receptacle" since it is normally not designed to perform a containment function without its "outer packaging" and is not therefore an "inner packaging".*

Consignee means the consignee according to the contract for carriage. If the consignee designates a third party in accordance with the provisions applicable to the contract for carriage, this person shall be deemed to be the consignee within the meaning of ADN. If the transport operation takes place without a contract for carriage, the enterprise which takes charge of the dangerous goods on arrival shall be deemed to be the consignee;

Consignment means any package or packages, or load of dangerous goods, presented by a consignor for carriage;

Consignor means the enterprise which consigns dangerous goods either on its own behalf or for a third party. If the transport operation is carried out under a contract for carriage, consignor means the consignor according to the contract for carriage. In the case of a tank vessel, when the cargo tanks are empty or have just been unloaded, the master is considered to be the consignor for the purpose of the transport document;

Construction pressure means the pressure on the basis of which the cargo tank or the residual cargo tank has been designed and built. This pressure generally equals the maximum working pressure;

Container means an article of transport equipment (lift van or other similar structure):

– of a permanent character and accordingly strong enough to be suitable for repeated use;

– specially designed to facilitate the carriage of goods, by one or more means of transport, without breakage of load;

– fitted with devices permitting its ready stowage and handling, particularly when being transloaded from one means of transport to another;

– so designed as to be easy to fill and empty (see also *Closed container, Large container, Open container, Sheeted container* and *Small container*);

A swap body is a container which, in accordance with European Standard EN 283 (1991 edition) has the following characteristics:

– from the point of view of mechanical strength, it is only built for carriage on a wagon or a vehicle on land or by roll-on roll-off ship;

– it cannot be stacked;

– it can be removed from vehicles by means of equipment on board the vehicle and on its own supports, and can be reloaded;

NOTE: *The term "container" does not cover conventional packagings, IBCs, tank-containers or vehicles.*

Control temperature means the maximum temperature at which an organic peroxide or a self-reactive substance can be safely carried;

Conveyance means, with respect to the carriage by inland waterway, any vessel, hold or defined deck area of any vessel; for carriage by road or by rail, it means a vehicle or a wagon;

Crate means an outer packaging with incomplete surfaces;

Critical temperature means the temperature above which the substance cannot exist in the liquid state;

Cryogenic receptacle means a transportable thermally insulated receptacle for refrigerated liquefied gases of a water capacity of not more than 1,000 litres;

CSC means the International Convention for Safe Containers (Geneva, 1972) as amended and published by the International Maritime Organization (IMO), London;

Cylinder means a transportable pressure receptacle of a water capacity not exceeding 150 litres (see also *Bundle of cylinders (frame)*);

D

Damage control plan means the plan indicating the boundaries of the watertight compartments serving as the basis for the stability calculations, in the event of a leak, the trimming arrangements for the correction of any list due to flooding and the means of closure which are to be kept closed when the vessel is under way;

Damage stability plan means a plan indicating the water-tight subdivisions serving as the basis for the stability calculations, the arrangements necessary to offset a list caused by water penetration and all closing appliances which are to be kept closed during the voyage. These closing appliances shall be appropriately indicated;

Dangerous goods means those substances and articles the carriage of which is prohibited by ADN, or authorized only under the conditions prescribed therein;

Dangerous reaction means:

(a) combustion or evolution of considerable heat;

(b) evolution of flammable, asphyxiate, oxidizing or toxic gases;

(c) the formation of corrosive substances;

(d) the formation of unstable substances; or

(e) dangerous rise in pressure (for tanks only);

Deflagration means an explosion which propagates at subsonic speed (see EN 1127-1:1997);

Demountable tank means a tank, other than a fixed tank, a portable tank, a tank-container or an element of a battery-vehicle or a MEGC which has a capacity of more than 450 litres, is not designed for the carriage of goods without breakage of load, and normally can only be handled when it is empty;

Detonation means an explosion which propagates at supersonic speed and is characterized by a shock-wave (see EN 1127-1:1997);

Drum means a flat-ended or convex-ended cylindrical packaging made out of metal, fibreboard, plastics, plywood or other suitable materials. This definition also includes packagings of other shapes, e.g. round, taper-necked packagings or pail-shaped packagings. *Wooden barrels* and *jerricans* are not covered by this definition.

E

EC Directive means provisions decided by the competent institutions of the European Community and which are binding, as to the result to be achieved, upon each Member State to which it is addressed, but shall leave to the national authorities the choice of form and methods;

Emergency temperature means the temperature at which emergency procedures shall be implemented in the event of loss of temperature control;

Electrical apparatus protected against water jets means an electrical apparatus so designed that water, projected by a nozzle on the enclosure from any direction, has no damaging effects. The test conditions are specified in the IEC publication 529, minimum degree of protection IP55;

EN (standard) means a European standard published by the European Committee for Standardization (CEN) (CEN – 36 rue de Stassart B-1050 Brussels);

Enterprise means any natural person, any legal person, whether profit-making or not, any association or group of persons without legal personality, whether profit-making or not, or any official body, whether it has legal personality itself or is dependent upon an authority that has such personality;

Escape device (suitable) means a respiratory protection device, designed to cover the wearer's mouth, nose and eyes, which can be easily put on and which serves to escape from a danger area;

Explosion means a sudden reaction of oxidation or decomposition with an increase in temperature or in pressure or both simultaneously (see EN 1127-1:1997);

Explosion group (see IEC publication 79 and EN 50 014) means a grouping of flammable gases and vapours according to their maximum experimental safe gaps and minimum ignition currents, and of electrical apparatus which may be used in the corresponding potentially explosive atmosphere.

F

Fibreboard IBC means a fibreboard body with or without separate top and bottom caps, if necessary an inner liner (but no inner packagings), and appropriate service and structural equipment;

Filler means any enterprise

(a) which fills dangerous goods into a tank (tank-vehicle, demountable tank, portable tank or tank-container) or into a battery-vehicle or MEGC; or

(b) which fills dangerous goods into a cargo tank; or

(c) which fills dangerous goods into a vessel, a vehicle, a large container or small container for carriage in bulk;

Filling pressure means the maximum pressure actually built up in the tank when it is being filled under pressure; (see also *Calculation pressure*, *Discharge pressure*, *Maximum working pressure (gauge pressure)* and *Test pressure*);

Filling ratio: Where a filling ratio is given for a cargo tank, it refers to a percentage of the volume at a temperature of the substance of 15° C, except where a different temperature is indicated;

Fixed tank means a tank having a capacity of more than 1,000 litres which is permanently attached to a vehicle (which then becomes a tank-vehicle) or is an integral part of the frame of such vehicle;

Flame arrester means a device mounted in the vent of part of an installation or in the interconnecting piping of a system of installations, the purpose of which is to permit flow but prevent the propagation of a flame front. This device shall be tested according to the European standard EN 12 874 (1999);

Flame arrester plate stack means the part of the flame arrester the main purpose of which is to prevent the passage of a flame front;

Flame arrester housing means the part of a flame arrester the main purpose of which is to form a suitable casing for the flame arrester plate stack and ensure a mechanical connection with other systems;

Flammable component (for aerosols and gas cartridges) means a gas which is flammable in air at normal pressure or a substance or a preparation in liquid form which has a flash-point less than or equal to 100 °C;

Flammable gas detector means a device allowing measuring of any significant concentration of flammable gases given off by the cargo below the lower explosive limit and which clearly indicates the presence of higher concentrations of such gases. Flammable gas detectors may be designed for measuring flammable gases only but also for measuring both flammable gases and oxygen.

This device shall be so designed that measurements are possible without the necessity of entering the spaces to be checked;

Flash-point means the lowest temperature of a liquid at which its vapours form a flammable mixture with air;

Flexible IBC means a body constituted of film, woven fabric or any other flexible material or combinations thereof, and if necessary, an inner coating or liner, together with any appropriate service equipment and handling devices;

Frame (Class 2), see *Bundle of cylinders*;

Full load means any load originating from one consignor for which the use of a vehicle or of a large container is exclusively reserved and all operations for the loading and unloading of which are carried out in conformity with the instructions of the consignor or of the consignee;

NOTE: *The corresponding term for Class 7 is "exclusive use", see 2.2.7.2.*

G

Gas (for the purposes of Class 2) means a substance which:

(a)   at 50° C has a vapour pressure greater than 300 kPa (3 bar); or

(b)   is completely gaseous at 20° C under standard pressure of 101.3 kPa;

Otherwise, *Gases* means gases or vapours;

Gas cartridge means any non-refillable receptacle containing, under pressure, a gas or a mixture of gases. It may be fitted with a valve;

Gas detection system means a fixed system capable of detecting in time significant concentrations of flammable gases given off by the cargoes at concentrations below the lower explosion limit and capable of activating the alarms;

Gas return piping means a pipe connecting a cargo tank to the shore facility during loading. This pipe is fitted with safety valves protecting the cargo tank against unacceptable internal overpressures or vacuums; it is intended to evacuate gases and vapours to the shore facility;

GHS means the Globally Harmonized System of Classification and Labelling of Chemicals, published by the United Nations as document ST/SG/AC.10/30;

H

Handling device (for flexible IBCs) means any sling, loop, eye or frame attached to the body of the IBC or formed from the continuation of the IBC body material;

Hermetically closed tank means a tank intended for the carriage of liquid substances with a calculation pressure of at least 4 bar or intended for the carriage of solid substances (powdery or granular) regardless of its calculation pressure, the openings of which are hermetically closed and which:

- is not equipped with safety valves, bursting discs, other similar safety devices or vacuum valves, or

- is not equipped with safety valves, bursting discs or other similar safety devices, but is equipped with vacuum valves, as allowed by special provision TE15 of 6.8.4 of ADR; or

- is equipped with safety valves preceded by a bursting disc according to 6.8.2.2.10 of ADR, but is not equipped with vacuum valves; or

- is equipped with safety valves preceded by a bursting disc according to 6.8.2.2.10 of ADR and vacuum valves, as allowed by special provision TE15 of 6.8.4 of ADR.;

Highest class may be assigned to a vessel when:

- the hull, inclusive of rudder and steering gear and equipment of anchors and chains, complies with the rules and regulations of a recognized classification society and has been built and tested under its supervision;

- the propulsion plant, together with the essential auxiliary engines mechanical and electrical installations, have been made and tested in conformity with the rules and regulations of this classification society, and the installation has been carried out under its supervision, and the complete plant was tested to its satisfaction on completion;

High velocity vent valve means a pressure-reducing valve with a nominal ejection speed greater than the speed of propagation of a flame, thus preventing the passage of a flame front. This type of installation shall be tested in accordance with European standard EN 12 874 (1999);

Hold (when anti-explosion protection is required, comparable to zone 1 - see *Classification of zones*) means a part of the vessel which, whether covered by hatchway covers or not, is bounded fore and aft by bulkheads and which is intended to carry goods in packages or in bulk. The upper boundary of the hold is the upper edge of the hatchway coaming. Cargo extending above the hatchway coaming shall be considered as loaded on deck;

Hold (condition)

discharged: empty, but containing residual cargo
empty: without residual cargo (swept clean);

Hold space (when anti-explosion protection is required, comparable to zone 1) means an enclosed part of the vessel which is bounded fore and aft by watertight bulkheads and which is intended only to carry cargo tanks independent of the vessel's hull.

I

IAEA means the International Atomic Energy Agency (IAEA), (IAEA, P.O. Box 100 – A-1400 Vienna);

IBC see *Intermediate bulk container*;

ICAO Technical Instructions means the Technical Instructions for the Safe Transport of Dangerous Goods by Air, which complement Annex 18 to the Chicago Convention on

International Civil Aviation (Chicago 1944) published by the International Civil Aviation Organization (ICAO) in Montreal;

Identification number means the number for identifying a substance to which no UN number has been assigned or which cannot be classified under a collective entry with a UN number.

These numbers have four figures beginning with 9;

IEC means The International Electro technical Commission;

IMDG Code means the International Maritime Dangerous Goods Code, for the implementation of Chapter VII, Part A, of the International Convention for the Safety of Life at Sea, 1974 (SOLAS Convention), published by the International Maritime Organization (IMO), London;

Independent cargo tank (when anti-explosion protection is required, comparable to zone 0) means a cargo tank which is permanently built in, but which is independent of the vessel's structure;

Inner packaging means a packaging for which an outer packaging is required for carriage;

Inner receptacle means a receptacle which requires an outer packaging in order to perform its containment function;

Instruction means transmitting know-how or teaching how to do something or how to act. This transmission or teaching may be dispensed internally by the personnel;

Intermediate bulk container (IBC) means a rigid, or flexible portable packaging, other than those specified in Chapter 6.1, that:

(a)   has a capacity of:

    (i)   not more than 3 m^3 for solids and liquids of packing groups II and III;

    (ii)   not more than 1.5 m^3 for solids of packing group I when packed in flexible, rigid plastics, composite, fibreboard and wooden IBCs;

    (iii)   not more than 3 m^3 for solids of packing group I when packed in metal IBCs;

    (iv)   not more than 3 m^3 for radioactive material of Class 7;

(b)   is designed for mechanical handling;

(c)   is resistant to the stresses produced in handling and transport as determined by the tests specified in Chapter 6.5 of ADR (see also *Composite IBC with plastics inter receptacle*, *Fibreboard IBC*, *Flexible IBC*, *Metal IBC*, *Rigid plastics IBC* and *Wooden IBC*);

NOTE 1: *Portable tanks or tank-containers that meet the requirements of Chapter 6.7 or 6.8 of ADR respectively are not considered to be intermediate bulk containers (IBCs).*

NOTE 2: *Intermediate bulk containers (IBCs) which meet the requirements of Chapter 6.5 of ADR are not considered to be containers for the purposes of ADR.*

Intermediate packaging means a packaging placed between inner packagings or articles and an outer packaging;

International regulations means ADR, BC Code, ICAO-TI, IMDG Code or RID.

ISO (standard) means an international standard published by the International Organization for Standardization (ISO) (ISO-1, rue de Varembé – CH-1204 Geneva 20);

J

Jerrican means a metal or plastics packaging of rectangular or polygonal cross-section with one or more orifices.

L

Large container means:

(a) a container having an internal volume of more than 3 m^3;

(b) in the meaning of the CSC, a container of a size such that the area enclosed by the four outer bottom corners is either

   (i) at least 14 m^2 (150 square feet) or

   (ii) at least 7 m^2 (75 square feet) if fitted with top corner fittings;

NOTE: *For radioactive material see 2.2.7.1.2.*

Large packaging means a packaging consisting of an outer packaging which contains articles or inner packagings and which:

(a) is designed for mechanical handling;

(b) exceeds 400 kg net mass or 450 litres capacity but has a volume of not more than 3 m^3;

Light-gauge metal packaging means a packaging of circular, elliptical, rectangular or polygonal cross-section (also conical) and taper-necked and pail-shaped packaging made of metal, having a wall thickness of less than 0.5 mm (e.g. tinplate), flat or convex bottomed and with one or more orifices, which is not covered by the definitions for drums or jerricans;

Limited explosion risk electrical apparatus means an electrical apparatus which, during normal operation, does not cause sparks or exhibits surface temperatures which are above the required temperature class, including e.g.:

– three-phase squirrel cage rotor motors;

– brushless generators with contactless excitation;

– fuses with an enclosed fuse element;

– contactless electronic apparatus;

or means an electrical apparatus with an enclosure protected against water jets (degree of protection IP55) which during normal operation does not exhibit surface temperatures which are above the required temperature class;

Liner means a tube or bag inserted into a packaging, including large packagings or IBCs, but not forming an integral part of it, including the closures of its openings;

Liquid means a substance which at 50° C has a vapour pressure of not more than 300 kPa (3 bar) which is not completely gaseous at 20° C and 101.3 kPa, and which:

—   has a melting point or initial melting point of 20° C or less at a pressure of 101.3 kPa, or

—   is liquid according to the ASTM D 4359-90 test method or

—   is not pasty according to the criteria applicable to the test for determining fluidity (penetrometer test) described in 2.3.4;

NOTE: "Carriage in the liquid state" for the purpose of tank requirements means:

—   Carriage of liquids according to the above definition, or

—   Solids handed over for carriage in the molten state;

Loader means any enterprise which loads dangerous goods into a vessel;

Loading journal means a journal where all activities relating to loading, unloading, cleaning, gas-freeing, delivering washing water and taking in and discharging ballast water (in cargo tanks) are recorded.

M

Manual of Tests and Criteria means the fourth revised edition of the United Nations Model Regulations on the Transport of Dangerous Goods, Manual of Tests and Criteria, published by the United Nations Organization (ST/SG/AC.10/11/Rev.4);

Mass of package means gross mass of the package unless otherwise stated. The mass of containers and tanks used for the carriage of goods is not included in the gross mass;

Master means a person as defined in Article 1.02 of the European Code for Inland Waterways (CEVNI);

Maximum capacity means the maximum inner volume of receptacles or packagings including intermediate bulk containers (IBCs) and large packagings expressed in cubic metres or litres;

Maximum net mass means the maximum net mass of contents in a single packaging or maximum combined mass of inner packagings and the contents thereof expressed in kilograms;

Maximum permissible gross mass, means

(a)   (for all categories of IBCs other than flexible IBCs) means the mass of the IBC and any service or structural equipment together with the maximum net mass;

(b)   (for tanks) means the tare of the tank and the heaviest load authorized for carriage;

NOTE: For portable tanks, see Chapter 6.7 of ADR.

Maximum permissible load (for flexible IBCs) means the maximum net mass for which the IBC is intended and which it is authorized to carry;

Maximum working pressure means the maximum pressure occurring in a cargo tank or a residual cargo tank during operation. This pressure equals the opening pressure of high velocity vent valves;

MEGC, see *Multiple-element gas container*;

Metal IBC means a metal body together with appropriate service and structural equipment;

Multiple-element gas container (MEGC) means a unit containing elements which are linked to each other by a manifold and mounted on a frame. The following elements are considered to be elements of a multiple-element gas container: cylinders, tubes, pressure drums and bundles of cylinders as well as tanks for the carriage of gases of Class 2 having a capacity of more than 450 litres.

N

Naked light means a source of light using a flame which is not enclosed in a flameproof enclosure.

Nominal capacity of the receptacle means the nominal volume of the dangerous substance contained in the receptacle expressed in litres. For compressed gas cylinders the nominal capacity shall be the water capacity of the cylinder;

N.O.S. entry (not otherwise specified entry) means a collective entry to which substances, mixtures, solutions or articles may be assigned if they:

(a)   are not mentioned by name in Table A of Chapter 3.2, and

(b)   exhibit chemical, physical and/or dangerous properties corresponding to the Class, classification code, packing group and the name and description of the n.o.s. entry;

Not readily flammable means a material which is not in itself readily flammable or whose outer surface at least is not readily flammable and limits the propagation of a fire to an appropriate degree.

In order to determine flammability, the IMO procedure, Resolution A.653(16), or any equivalent requirements of a Contracting State are recognized;

O

Offshore bulk container means a bulk container specially designed for repeated use for carriage to, from and between offshore facilities. An offshore bulk container is designed and constructed in accordance with the guidelines for the approval of offshore containers handled in open seas specified by the International Maritime Organization (IMO) in document MSC/Circ.860;

Oil separator vessel means an open type N tank-vessel with a dead weight of up to 300 tonnes, constructed and fitted to accept and carry oily and greasy wastes from the operation of vessels. Vessels without cargo tanks are considered to be subject to Chapters 9.1 or 9.2;

Oily and greasy wastes from the operation of the vessel means used oils, bilge water and other oily or greasy wastes, such as used grease, used filters, used rags, and receptacles and packagings for such wastes;

Open container means an open top container or a platform based container;

Open vehicle means a vehicle the platform of which has no superstructure or is merely provided with side boards and a tailboard;

Opening pressure means the pressure referred to in a list of substances at which the high velocity vent valves open. For pressure tanks the opening pressure of the safety valve shall be established in accordance with the requirements of the competent authority or a recognized classification society;

Outer packaging means the outer protection of the composite or combination packaging together with any absorbent materials, cushioning and any other components necessary to contain and protect inner receptacles or inner packagings;

Overpack means an enclosure used by a single consignor to contain one or more packages, consolidated into a single unit easier to handle and stow during carriage;

Examples of overpacks:

(a)   a loading tray such as a pallet, on which several packages are placed or stacked and secured by a plastic strip, shrink or stretch wrapping or other appropriate means; or

(b)   an outer protective packaging such as a box or a crate;

NOTE: For radioactive material, see the definition of containment system in 2.2.7.2.

Oxygen meter means a device allowing measuring of any significant reduction of the oxygen content of the air. Oxygen meters may either be a device for measuring oxygen only or part of a combination device for measuring both flammable gas and oxygen.

This device shall be so designed that measurements are possible without the necessity of entering the spaces to be checked.

P

Package means the complete product of the packing operation, consisting of the packaging or large packaging or IBC and its contents prepared for dispatch. The term includes receptacles for gases as defined in this section as well as articles which, because of their size, mass or configuration may be carried unpackaged or carried in cradles, crates or handling devices.

On board vessels, the term also includes vehicles, containers (including swap bodies), tank-containers, portable tanks, battery-vehicles, tank vehicles and multiple element gas containers (MECGs).

The term does not apply to goods which are carried in bulk in the holds of vessels, nor to substances carried in tanks in tank vessels.

NOTE: For radioactive material, see 2.2.7.2.

Packaging means the receptacle and any other components or materials necessary for the receptacle to perform its containment function (see also *Combination packaging, Composite packaging (plastics material), Composite packaging (glass, porcelain or stoneware), Inner packaging, Intermediate bulk container (IBC), Intermediate packaging, Large packaging,*

Light-gauge metal packaging, Outer packaging, Reconditioned packaging, Remanufactured packaging, Reused packaging, Salvage packaging and *Sift-proof packaging)*;

NOTE: *For radioactive material, see 2.2.7.2.*

Packer means any enterprise which puts dangerous goods into packagings, including large packagings and intermediate bulk containers (IBCs) and, where necessary, prepares packages for carriage;

Packing group means a group to which, for packing purposes, certain substances may be assigned in accordance with their degree of danger. The packing groups have the following meanings which are explained more fully in Part 2:

Packing group I : Substances presenting high danger;
Packing group II : Substances presenting medium danger; and
Packing group III : Substances presenting low danger;

NOTE: *Certain articles containing dangerous goods are assigned to a packing group.*

Pipes for loading or unloading (cargo piping) means all pipes which may contain liquid or gaseous cargo, including the connected pumps, filters and closure devices;

Portable tank means a multimodal tank having, when used for the carriage of Class 2 substances, a capacity of more than 450 litres in accordance with the definitions in Chapter 6.7 of ADR or the IMDG Code and indicated by a portable tank instruction (T-Code) in Column (10) of Table A of Chapter 3.2 of ADR;

Portable tank operator, see *Tank-container/portable tank operator*;

Pressure drum means a welded, transportable pressure receptacle of a water capacity exceeding 150 litres and of not more than 1,000 litres (e.g. cylindrical receptacles equipped with rolling hoops, spheres on skids);

Pressure relief device means a spring-loaded device which is activated automatically by pressure the purpose of which is to protect the cargo tank against unacceptable excess internal pressure;

Pressure receptacle means a collective term that includes cylinders, tubes, pressure drums, closed cryogenic receptacles and bundles of cylinders;

Pressures For tanks, all kinds of pressures (e.g. working pressure, opening pressure of the high velocity vent valves, test pressure) shall be expressed as gauge pressures in kPa (bar); the vapour pressure of substances, however, shall be expressed as an absolute pressure in kPa (bar);

Pressure tank means a tank designated and approved for a working pressure $\geq$ 400 kPa (4 bar).

Pressurized gas cartridge, see *Aerosol dispenser*;

Protected area means

(a) the hold or holds (when anti-explosion protection is required, comparable to zone 1);

(b) the space situated above the deck (when anti-explosion protection is required, comparable to zone 2), bounded:

(i) athwartships, by vertical planes corresponding to the side plating;

(ii) fore and aft, by vertical planes corresponding to the end bulkheads of the hold; and

(iii) upwards, by a horizontal plane 2.00 m above the upper level of the load, but at least by a horizontal plane 3.00 m above the deck.

Protected IBC (for metal IBCs) means an IBC provided with additional protection against impact, the protection taking the form of, for example, a multi-layer (sandwich) or double-wall construction, or a frame with a metal lattice-work casing.

Q

Quality assurance means a systematic programme of controls and inspections applied by any organization or body which is aimed at providing confidence that the safety prescriptions in ADN are met in practice.

R

Receptacle (Class 1) includes boxes, cylinders, cans, drums, jars and tubes, including any means of closure used in the inner or intermediate packaging;

Receptacle means a containment vessel for receiving and holding substances or articles, including any means of closing. This definition does not apply to shells (see also *Cryogenic receptacle, Inner receptacle, Rigid inner receptacle* and *Gas cartridge*);

NOTE: *Receptacles for gases of Class 2 are cylinders, tubes, pressure drums, cryogenic receptacles and bundles of cylinders (frames).*

Recycled plastics material means material recovered from used industrial packagings that has been cleaned and prepared for processing into new packagings;

Reel (Class 1) means a device made of plastics, wood, fibreboard, metal or other suitable material comprising a central spindle with, or without, side walls at each end of the spindle. Articles and substances can be wound on to the spindle and may be retained by side walls;

Rescue winch means a device for hoisting persons from spaces such as cargo tanks, cofferdams and double-hull spaces. The device shall be operable by one person;

Residual cargo means liquid cargo remaining in the cargo tank or cargo piping after unloading without the use of the stripping system;

RID means Regulations concerning the International Carriage of Dangerous Goods by Rail, Annex 1 to Appendix B (Uniform Rules Concerning the Contract for International Carriage of Goods by Rail) (CIM) of COTIF (Convention concerning International Carriage by Rail);

Rigid inner receptacle (for composite IBCs) means a receptacle which retains its general shape when empty without its closures in place and without benefit of the outer casing. Any inner receptacle that is not rigid is considered to be flexible;

Rigid plastics IBC means a rigid plastics body, which may have structural equipment together with appropriate service equipment;

S

Safety valve means a spring-loaded device which is activated automatically by pressure the purpose of which is to protect the cargo tank against unacceptable excess internal pressure or negative internal pressure (see also *Pressure-relief device* and *Vacuum valve*);

SADT see *Self-accelerating decomposition temperature*;

Salvage packaging means a special packaging into which damaged, defective or leaking dangerous goods packages, or dangerous goods that have spilled or leaked are placed for purposes of carriage for recovery or disposal;

Self-accelerating decomposition temperature (SADT), means the lowest temperature at which self-accelerating decomposition may occur with substance in the packaging as used during carriage. Provisions for determining the SADT and the effects of heating under confinement are contained in Part II of the Manual of Tests and Criteria;

Service space means a space which is accessible during the operation of the vessel and which is neither part of the accommodation nor of the cargo tanks, with the exception of the forepeak and after peak, provided no machinery has been installed in these latter spaces;

Settled pressure means the pressure of the contents of a pressure receptacle in thermal and diffusive equilibrium;

Sheeted container means an open container equipped with a sheet to protect the goods loaded;

Sheeted vehicle means an open vehicle provided with a sheet to protect the load;

Sheeted wagon means an open wagon provided with a sheet to protect the load;

Sift-proof packaging means a packaging impermeable to dry contents, including fine solid material produced during carriage;

Slops means liquid cargo residues which cannot be removed from the cargo tank or cargo piping by discharging, draining or stripping; by extension, a mixture of cargo residues and washing water, rust, etc., which is either suitable or not suitable for pumping;

Small container means a container having an internal volume of not less than 1 m^3 and not more than 3 m^3;

NOTE: *For radioactive material, see 2.2.7.2.*

Small receptacle containing gas, see *Gas cartridge*;

SOLAS means the International Convention for the Safety of Life at Sea, 1974, as amended;

Solid means:

(a)   a substance with a melting point or initial melting point of more than 20 °C at a pressure of 101.3 kPa; or

(b)   a substance which is not liquid according to the ASTM D 4359-90 test method or which is pasty according to the criteria applicable to the test for determining fluidity (penetrometer test) described in 2.3.4;

Steady burning means combustion stabilized for an indeterminate period (see EN 12 874:1999);

Stripping system (efficient) means a system for draining the cargo tanks and stripping the cargo piping except for the cargo residues;

Supply installation (bunkering system) means an installation for the supply of vessels with liquid fuels;

Supply vessel means an open type N tank vessel with a dead weight of up to 300 tonnes, constructed and fitted for the carriage and delivery to other vessels of products intended for the operation of vessels;

Swap-body, see *Container*.

T

Tank means a shell, including its service and structural equipment. When used alone, the term tank means a tank-container, portable tank, demountable tank or fixed tank as defined in this part, including tanks forming elements of battery-vehicles or MEGCs (see also *Demountable tank, Fixed tank, Portable tank and Multiple-element gas container)*;

NOTE: *For portable tanks, see 6.7.4.1 of ADR.*

Tank-container means an article of transport equipment meeting the definition of a container, and comprising a shell and items of equipment, including the equipment to facilitate movement of the tank-container without significant change of attitude, used for the carriage of gases, liquid, powdery or granular substances and, when used for the carriage of Class 2 substances having a capacity of more than 0.45 m^3 (450 litres);

NOTE: *IBCs which meet the requirements of Chapter 6.5 of ADR are not considered to be tank-containers.*

Tank-container/portable tank operator means any enterprise in whose name the tank-container/portable tank is registered;

Tank swap body is considered to be a tank-container;

Tank-vehicle means a vehicle built to carry liquids, gases or powdery or granular substances and comprising one or more fixed tanks. In addition to the vehicle proper, or the units of running gear used in its stead, a tank-vehicle comprises one or more shells, their items of equipment and the fittings for attaching them to the vehicle or to the running-gear units;

Tank vessel means a vessel intended for the carriage of substances in cargo tanks;

Tank wagon means a wagon intended for the carriage of liquids, gases, powdery or granular substances, comprising a superstructure, consisting of one or more tanks and their equipment and an underframe fitted with its own items of equipment (running gear, suspension, buffing, traction, braking gear and inscriptions).

NOTE: *Tank wagon also includes wagons with demountable tanks.*

Technical name means a recognized chemical name, or a recognized biological name where relevant, or another name currently used in scientific and technical handbooks, journals and texts (see 3.1.2.8.1.1);

Temperature class (*see IEC publication 79 and EN 50 014*) means a grouping of flammable gases and vapours of flammable liquids according to their ignition temperature; and of the electrical apparatus intended to be used in the corresponding potentially explosive atmosphere according to their maximum surface temperature;

Test pressure means the pressure at which a cargo tank, a residual cargo tank, a cofferdam or the loading and unloading pipes shall be tested prior to being brought into service for the first time and subsequently regularly within prescribed times;

Toximeter means a device allowing measuring of any significant concentration of toxic gases given off by the cargo.

This device shall be so designed that such measurements are possible without the necessity of entering the spaced to be checked.

Training means teaching instruction, courses or apprenticeships dispensed by an organizer approved by the competent authority;

Transport unit means a vehicle according to article 1 (a) of ADR, a wagon according to the RID definition, a container, a tank-container, a portable tank or an MEGC;

Transport unit means a motor vehicle without an attached trailer, or a combination consisting of a motor vehicle and an attached trailer;

Transport unit (inland waterways) means, in carriage by inland waterways, a vessel, a hold, or a specific part of a vessel's deck;

Tray (Class 1) means a sheet of metal, plastics, fibreboard or other suitable material which is placed in the inner, intermediate or outer packaging and achieves a close-fit in such packaging. The surface of the tray may be shaped so that packagings or articles can be inserted, held secure and separated from each other;

Tube means a seamless transportable pressure receptacle of a water capacity exceeding 150 litres and of not more than 3,000 litres;

Types of protection (see IEC Publication 79 and EN 50 014)

EEx (d)	:	flameproof enclosure (EN 50 018);
EEx (e)	:	increased safety (EN 50 019);
EEx (ia) and EEx (ib)	:	intrinsic safety (EN 50 020);
EEx (m)	:	encapsulation (EN 50 028);
EEx (p)	:	pressurized apparatus (EN 50 016);
EEx (q)	:	powder filling (EN 50 017).

Type of vessel

Type G	:	means a tank vessel intended for the carriage of gases. Carriage may be under pressure or under refrigeration.
Type C	:	means a tank vessel intended for the carriage of liquids. The vessel shall be of the flush-deck/double-hull type with double-hull spaces, double bottoms, but without trunk. The cargo tanks may be formed by the vessel's inner hull or may be installed in the hold spaces as independent tanks.

Type N   :   means a tank vessel intended for the carriage of liquids.

Sketches (as example)

Type G :

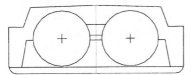

Type G Condition of cargo tank 1,
        Type of cargo tanks 1
        (also by flush-deck)

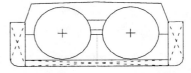

Type G Condition of cargo tank 1,
        Type of cargo tanks 1
        (also by flush-deck)

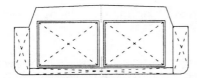

Type G Condition of cargo tank 2,
        Type of cargo tank 1
        (also by flush-deck)

Type C :

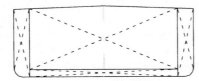

Type C Condition of cargo tank 2,
        Type of cargo tank 2

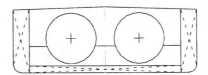

Type C Condition of cargo tank 1,
        Type of cargo tank 1

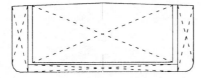

Type C Condition of cargo tank 2
        Type of cargo tank 1

Type N :

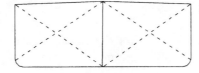

Type N Condition of cargo tank 2, 3 or 4
        Type of cargo tank 2

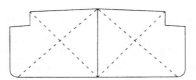

Type N Condition of cargo tank 2, 3 or 4
        Type of cargo tank 2

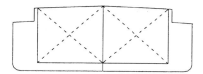

Type N Condition of cargo tank 2, 3 or 4
Type of cargo tanks 1
(also by flush-deck)

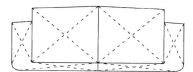

Type N Condition of cargo tank 2, 3 or 4
Type of cargo tank 3
(also by flush-deck)

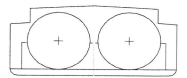

Type N Condition of cargo tank 2, 3 or 4
Type of cargo tank 1
(also by flush-deck)

U

Undertaking, see *Enterprise;*

UN Model Regulations means the Model Regulations annexed to the thirteenth revised edition of the Recommendations on the Transport of Dangerous Goods published by the United Nations (ST/SG/AC.10/1/Rev.13);

UN number means the four-figure identification number of the substance or article taken from the United Nations Model Regulations.

V

Vacuum-operated waste tank means a fixed or demountable tank primarily used for the carriage of dangerous wastes, with special constructional features and/or equipment to facilitate the loading and unloading of wastes as specified in Chapter 6.10 of ADR. A tank which fully complies with the requirements of Chapter 6.7 or 6.8 of ADR is not considered to be a vacuum-operated waste tank;

Vacuum valve means a spring-loaded device which is activated automatically by pressure the purpose of which is to protect the cargo tank against unacceptable negative internal pressure;

Vehicle means any vehicle covered by the definition of the term vehicle in the ADR or wagon in RID (see *Battery-vehicle, Closed vehicle, Open vehicle, Sheeted vehicle* and *Tank-vehicle);*

Venting piping means a pipe of the shore facility which is connected during the loading to the vessel's common vapour pipe or gas return piping. This pipe is designed so as to protect the vessel against detonations or the passage of flames from the shoreside;

Vessel means an inland navigation vessel or a seagoing vessel.

W

Wagon means a rail vehicle without its own means of propulsion that runs on its own wheels on railway tracks and is used for the carriage of goods;

Wastes means substances, solutions, mixtures or articles for which no direct use is envisaged but which are transported for reprocessing, dumping, elimination by incineration or other methods of disposal;

Wooden barrel means a packaging made of natural wood, of round cross-section, having convex walls, consisting of staves and heads and fitted with hoops;

Wooden IBC means a rigid or collapsible wooden body, together with an inner liner (but no inner packaging) and appropriate service and structural equipment;

Working pressure means the settled pressure of a compressed gas at a reference temperature of 15° C in a full pressure receptacle.

NOTE: *For tanks, see Maximum working pressure.*

1.2.2   Units of measurement

1.2.2.1   The following units of measurement [a] are applicable in ADN:

Measurement of	SI Unit[b]	Acceptable alternative unit	Relationship between units
Length	m (metre)	-	-
Area	m² (square metre)	-	-
Volume	m³ (cubic metre)	l [c] (litre)	$1\,l = 10^{-3}\,m^3$
Time	s (second)	min. (minute)	1 min. = 60 s
		h (hour)	1 h = 3 600 s
		d (day)	1 d = 86 400 s
Mass	kg (kilogram)	g (gramme)	$1 g = 10^{-3}\,kg$
		t (ton)	$1\,t = 10^3\,kg$
Mass density	kg/m³	kg/l	$1\,kg/l = 10^3\,kg/m^3$
Temperature	K (kelvin)	°C (degree Celsius)	0° C = 273.15 K
Temperature difference	K (kelvin)	°C (degree Celsius)	1° C = 1 K
Force	N (newton)	-	$1\,N = 1\,kg.m/s^2$
Pressure	Pa (pascal)		$1\,Pa = 1\,N/m^2$
		bar (bar)	$1\,bar = 10^5\,Pa$
Stress	N/m²	N/mm²	$1\,N/mm^2 = 1\,MPa$
Work		kWh (kilowatt hours)	1 kWh = 3.6 MJ
Energy	J (joule)		1 J = 1 N.m = 1 W.s
Quantity of heat		eV (electronvolt)	$1\,eV = 0.1602\,H\,10^{-18}J$
Power	W (watt)	-	1 W = 1 J/s = 1 N.m/s
Kinematic viscosity	m²/s	mm²/s	$1\,mm^2/s = 10^{-6}\,m^2/s$
Dynamic viscosity	Pa.s	mPa.s	$1\,mPa.s = 10^{-3}\,Pa.s$
Activity	Bq (becquerel)		
Dose equivalent	Sv (sievert)		

[a] *The following round figures are applicable for the conversion of the units hitherto used into SI Units.*

Force			*Stress*	
1 kg	=	*9.807 N*	*1 kg/mm²*	*= 9.807 N/mm²*
1 N	=	*0.102 kg*	*1 N/mm²*	*= 0.102 kg/mm²*

Pressure
1 Pa	=	*1 N/m²*	=	*10⁻⁵ bar*	=	*1.02 H 10⁻⁵ kg/cm²*	*= 0.75 H 10⁻² torr*
1 bar	=	*10⁵ Pa*	=	*1.02 kg/cm²*	=	*750 torr*	
1 kg/cm²	=	*9.807 H 10⁴ Pa*	=	*0.9807 bar*	=	*736 torr*	
1 torr	=	*1.33 H 10² Pa*	=	*1.33 H 10⁻³ bar*	=	*1.36 H 10⁻³ kg/cm²*	

Energy, Work, Quantity of heat

1 J	=	1 N.m	=	0.278×10^{-6} kWh	=	0.102 kgm		= 0.239×10^{-3} kcal
1 kWh	=	3.6×10^6 J	=	367×10^3 kgm	=	860 kcal		
1 kgm	=	9.807 J	=	2.72×10^{-6} kWh	=	2.34×10^{-3} kcal		
1 kcal	=	4.19×10^3 J	=	1.16×10^{-3} kWh	=	427 kgm		

Power

1 W	=	0.102 kgm/s	=	0.86 kcal/h
1 kgm/s	=	9.807 W	=	8.43 kcal/h
1 kcal/h	=	1.16 W	=	0.119 kgm/s

Kinematic viscosity

1 m^2/s	=	10^4 St (Stokes)
1 St	=	10^{-4} m^2/s

Dynamic viscosity

1 Pa.s	=	1 N.s/m^2	=	10 P (poise)	=	0.102 kg.s/m^2
1 P	=	0.1 Pa.s	=	0.1 N.s/m^2	=	1.02×10^{-2} kg.s/m^2
1 kg.s/m^2	=	9.807 Pa.s	=	9.807 N.s/m^2	=	98.07 P

[b] *The International System of Units (SI) is the result of decisions taken at the General Conference on Weights and Measures (Address: Pavillon de Breteuil, Parc de St-Cloud, F-92 310 Sèvres).*

[c] *The abbreviation "L" for litre may also be used in place of the abbreviation "l" when a typewriter cannot distinguish between figure "1" and letter "l".*

The decimal multiples and sub-multiples of a unit may be formed by prefixes or symbols, having the following meanings, placed before the name or symbol of the unit:

Factor		Prefix	Symbol
1 000 000 000 000 000 000	= 10^{18}	quintillion	exa	E
1 000 000 000 000 000	= 10^{15}	quadrillion	peta	P
1 000 000 000 000	= 10^{12}	trillion	tera	T
1 000 000 000	= 10^9	billion	giga	G
1 000 000	= 10^6	million	mega	M
1 000	= 10^3	thousand	kilo	k
100	= 10^2	hundred	hecto	h
10	= 10^1	ten	deca	da
0.1	= 10^{-1}	tenth	deci	d
0.01	= 10^{-2}	hundredth	centi	c
0.001	= 10^{-3}	thousandth	milli	m
0.000 001	= 10^{-6}	millionth	micro	μ
0.000 000 001	= 10^{-9}	billionth	nano	n
0.000 000 000 001	= 10^{-12}	trillionth	pico	p
0.000 000 000 000 001	= 10^{-15}	quadrillionth	femto	f
0.000 000 000 000 000 001	= 10^{-18}	quintillionth	atto	a

NOTE: *10^9 = 1 billion is United Nations usage in English. By analogy, so is 10^{-9} = 1 billionth.*

1.2.2.2   Unless expressly stated otherwise, the sign "%" in ADN represents:

(a)   In the case of mixtures of solids or of liquids, and also in the case of solutions and of solids wetted by a liquid, a percentage mass based on the total mass of the mixture, the solution or the wetted solid;

(b)   In the case of mixtures of compressed gases, when filled by pressure, the proportion of the volume indicated as a percentage of the total volume of the gaseous mixture, or, when filled by mass, the proportion of the mass indicated as a percentage of the total mass of the mixture;

(c)   In the case of mixtures of liquefied gases and dissolved gases, the proportion of the mass indicated as a percentage of the total mass of the mixture.

1.2.2.3   Pressures of all kinds relating to receptacles (such as test pressure, internal pressure, safety valve opening pressure) are always indicated in gauge pressure (pressure in excess of atmospheric pressure); however, the vapour pressure of substances is always expressed in absolute pressure.

1.2.2.4   Where ADN specifies a degree of filling for receptacles, this is always related to a reference temperature of the substances of 15° C, unless some other temperature is indicated.

CHAPTER 1.3

TRAINING OF PERSONS INVOLVED IN THE CARRIAGE OF DANGEROUS GOODS

1.3.1   **Scope and applicability**

Persons employed by the participants referred to in Chapter 1.4, whose duties concern the carriage of dangerous goods, shall receive training in the requirements governing the carriage of such goods appropriate to their responsibilities and duties. Training requirements specific to security of dangerous goods in Chapter 1.10 shall also be addressed.

NOTE 1: With regard to the training for the safety adviser, see 1.8.3.

NOTE 2: With regard to expert training, see Chapter 8.2.

1.3.2   **Nature of the training**

The training shall take the following form, appropriate to the responsibility and duties of the individual concerned.

1.3.2.1   *General awareness training*

Personnel shall be familiar with the general requirements of the provisions for the carriage of dangerous goods.

1.3.2.2   *Function-specific training*

1.3.2.2.1   Personnel shall receive detailed training, commensurate directly with their duties and responsibilities in the requirements of the regulations concerning the carriage of dangerous goods. Where the carriage of dangerous goods involves a multimodal transport operation, the personnel shall be made aware of the requirements concerning other transport modes.

1.3.2.2.2   The crew shall be familiarized with the handling of fire-extinguishing systems and fire-extinguishers.

1.3.2.2.3   The crew shall be familiarized with the handling of the fire-extinguishing systems and fire-extinguishers with the special equipment referred to in 8.1.5.

1.3.2.2.4   Persons wearing self-contained breathing apparatus shall be physically able to bear the additional constraints.

They shall:

-    in the case of devices operating with pressurized air, be trained in their handling and maintenance;

-    in the case of devices supplied with pressurized air through a hose, be trained in their handling and maintenance.

1.3.2.3.5   The master shall bring the instructions in writing to the attention of the other persons on board to ensure that they are capable of applying them.

1.3.2.3   *Safety training*

Commensurate with the degree of risk of injury or exposure arising from an incident involving the carriage of dangerous goods, including loading and unloading, personnel shall receive training covering the hazards and dangers presented by dangerous goods.

The training provided shall aim to make personnel aware of the safe handling and emergency response procedures.

1.3.2.4   *Training for Class 7*

For the purpose of Class 7, personnel shall receive appropriate training concerning the radiation hazards involved and the precautions to be observed in order to ensure restriction of their exposure and that of other persons who might be affected by their actions.

1.3.3   **Documentation**

Details of all the training undertaken shall be kept by both the employer and the employee and shall be verified upon commencing a new employment. The training shall be periodically supplemented with refresher training to take account of changes in regulations.

CHAPTER 1.4

SAFETY OBLIGATIONS OF THE PARTICIPANTS

1.4.1   General safety measures

1.4.1.1   The participants in the carriage of dangerous goods shall take appropriate measures according to the nature and the extent of foreseeable dangers, so as to avoid damage or injury and, if necessary, to minimize their effects. They shall, in all events, comply with the requirements of ADN in their respective fields.

1.4.1.2   When there is an immediate risk that public safety may be jeopardized, the participants shall immediately notify the emergency services and shall make available to them the information they require to take action.

1.4.1.3   ADN may specify certain of the obligations falling to the various participants.

If a Contracting Party considers that no lessening of safety is involved, it may in its domestic legislation transfer the obligations falling to a specific participant to one or several other participants, provided that the obligations of 1.4.2 and 1.4.3 are met. These derogations shall be communicated by the Contracting Party to the secretariat of the United Nations Economic Commission for Europe which will bring them to the attention of the Contracting Parties.

The requirements of 1.2.1, 1.4.2 and 1.4.3 concerning the definitions of participants and their respective obligations shall not affect the provisions of domestic law concerning the legal consequences (criminal nature, liability, etc.) stemming from the fact that the participant in question is e.g. a legal entity, a self-employed worker, an employer or an employee.

1.4.2   Obligations of the main participants

> *NOTE: For radioactive material see also 1.7.6.*

1.4.2.1   *Consignor*

1.4.2.1.1   The consignor of dangerous goods is required to hand over for carriage only consignments which conform to the requirements of ADN. In the context of 1.4.1, he shall in particular:

(a)   ascertain that the dangerous goods are classified and authorized for carriage in accordance with ADN;

(b)   furnish the carrier with information and data and, if necessary, the required transport documents and accompanying documents (authorizations, approvals, notifications, certificates, etc.), taking into account in particular the requirements of Chapter 5.4 and of the tables in Part 3;

(c)   use only packagings, large packagings, intermediate bulk containers (IBCs) and tanks (tank-vehicles, demountable tanks, battery-vehicles, MEGCs, portable tanks, tank-containers, tank wagons and battery wagons) approved for and suited to the carriage of the substances concerned and bearing the markings prescribed by one of the international Regulations, and to use only approved vessels or tank-vessels suitable for the carriage of the goods in question;

(d)   comply with the requirements on the means of dispatch and on forwarding restrictions;

(e)   ensure that even empty uncleaned and not degassed tanks (tank-vehicles, demountable tanks, battery-vehicles, MEGCs, portable tanks, tank-containers, tank wagons and tank vehicles) or empty uncleaned vehicles, wagons and large and small bulk containers are appropriately marked and labelled and that empty uncleaned tanks are closed and present the same degree of leakproofness as if they were full.

1.4.2.1.2   If the consignor uses the services of other participants (packer, loader, filler, etc.), he shall take appropriate measures to ensure that the consignment meets the requirements of ADN. He may, however, in the case of 1.4.2.1.1 (a), (b), (c) and (e), rely on the information and data made available to him by other participants.

1.4.2.1.3   When the consignor acts on behalf of a third party, the latter shall inform the consignor in writing that dangerous goods are involved and make available to him all the information and documents he needs to perform his obligations.

1.4.2.2   *Carrier*

1.4.2.2.1   In the context of 1.4.1, where appropriate, the carrier shall in particular:

(a)   ascertain that the dangerous goods to be carried are authorized for carriage in accordance with ADN;

(b)   ascertain that the prescribed documentation is on board the vessel;

(c)   ascertain visually that the vessels and loads have no obvious defects, leakages or cracks, missing equipment, etc.;

(d)   *(reserved)*;

(e)   verify that the vessels are not overloaded;

(f)   *(reserved)*;

(g)   ascertain that the equipment prescribed in the written instructions for the master is on board the vessel;

(h)   ascertain that the marking requirements for the vessel have been met;

(i)   ascertain that during loading, carriage, unloading and any other handling of the dangerous goods in the holds or cargo tanks, special requirements are complied with.

Where appropriate, this shall be done on the basis of the transport documents and accompanying documents, by a visual inspection of the vessel or the containers and, where appropriate, the load.

1.4.2.2.2   The carrier may, however, in the case of 1.4.2.2.1 (a), (b) and (i), rely on information and data made available to him by other participants.

1.4.2.2.3   If the carrier observes an infringement of the requirements of ADN, in accordance with 1.4.2.2.1, he shall not forward the consignment until the matter has been rectified.

1.4.2.2.4   *(Reserved)*.

1.4.2.3   *Consignee*

1.4.2.3.1   The consignee has the obligation not to defer acceptance of the goods without compelling reasons and to verify, before, during or after unloading, that the requirements of ADN concerning him have been complied with.

In the context of 1.4.1, he shall in particular:

(a)   carry out in the cases provided for by ADN the prescribed operations for the unloading of vessels;

(b)   carry out in the cases provided for by ADN the prescribed cleaning and decontamination of the vessels;

(c)   ensure that the containers, vehicles and wagons, once completely unloaded, cleaned and decontaminated, no longer bear danger markings conforming to Chapter 5.3;

(d)   ascertain that provision has been made in the fore and aft sections of the vessel for its evacuation in the event of an emergency;

(e)   ascertain that in the cases provided for by ADN a flame-arrester is installed in the gas discharge pipe or the compensation pipe to protect the vessel against detonations and flame-fronts from the landward side;

(f)   ascertain that the seals he has put in place to ensure that the connections between the vessel's loading and discharging hoses are leakproof are made of a material which is not attacked by the cargo, which does not cause the decomposition of the cargo and does not cause a harmful or dangerous reaction with the cargo;

(g)   ascertain that permanent and appropriate surveillance is ensured for the entire duration of loading or discharging.

1.4.2.3.2   If the consignee makes use of the services of other participants (unloader, cleaner, decontamination facility, etc.) he shall take appropriate measures to ensure that the requirements of ADN have been complied with.

1.4.2.3.3   If these verifications bring to light an infringement of the requirements of ADN, the consignee shall return a container or a vehicle to the carrier only after the infringement has been remedied.

1.4.3   **Obligations of the other participants**

A non-exhaustive list of the other participants and their respective obligations is given below. The obligations of the other participants flow from section 1.4.1 above insofar as they know or should have known that their duties are performed as part of a transport operation subject to ADN;

1.4.3.1   *Loader*

1.4.3.1.1   In the context of 1.4.1, the loader has the following obligations in particular:

(a)   He shall hand the dangerous goods over to the carrier only if they are authorized for carriage in accordance with ADN;

(b)   He shall, when handing over for carriage packed dangerous goods or uncleaned empty packagings, check whether the packaging is damaged. He shall not hand over a package the packaging of which is damaged, especially if it is not leakproof, and there are leakages or the possibility of leakages of the dangerous substance, until the damage has been repaired; this obligation also applies to empty uncleaned packagings;

(c)   He shall, when loading dangerous goods in a vessel, a vehicle, a wagon, or a large or small container, comply with the special requirements concerning loading and handling;

(d)   He shall, after loading dangerous goods into a container comply with the requirements concerning danger markings conforming to Chapter 5.3;

(e)   He shall, when loading packages, comply with the prohibitions on mixed loading taking into account dangerous goods already in the vessel, vehicle, wagon or large container and requirements concerning the separation of foodstuffs, other articles of consumption or animal feedstuffs;

(f)   He shall ascertain that provision has been made in the fore and aft sections of the vessel for its evacuation in the event of an emergency;

(g)   He shall furnish the masters with the additional protection material and equipment required in the instructions in writing.

1.4.3.1.2   The loader may, however, in the case of 1.4.3.1.1 (a), (d) and (e), rely on information and data made available to him by other participants.

1.4.3.2   *Packer*

In the context of 1.4.1, the packer shall comply with in particular:

(a)   the requirements concerning packing conditions, or mixed packing conditions and,

(b)   when he prepares packages for carriage, the requirements concerning marking and labelling of the packages.

1.4.3.3   *Filler*

In the context of 1.4.1, the filler has the following obligations in particular:

Obligations concerning the filling of tanks (tank-vehicles, battery-vehicles, demountable tanks, portable tanks, tank-containers, MEGCs, tank wagons and battery wagons):

(a)   He shall ascertain prior to the filling of tanks that both they and their equipment are technically in a satisfactory condition;

(b)   He shall ascertain that the date of the next test for tank-vehicles, battery-vehicles, demountable tanks, portable tanks, tank-containers, MEGCs, tank wagons and battery wagons has not expired;

(c)   He shall only fill tanks with the dangerous goods authorized for carriage in those tanks;

(d)   He shall, in filling the tank, comply with the requirements concerning dangerous goods in adjoining compartments;

(e)   He shall, during the filling of the tank, observe the maximum permissible degree of filling or the maximum permissible mass of contents per litre of capacity for the substance being filled;

(f)   He shall, after filling the tank, check the leakproofness of the closing devices;

(g)   He shall ensure that no dangerous residue of the filling substance adheres to the outside of the tanks filled by him;

(h)   He shall, in preparing the dangerous goods for carriage, ensure that the orange plates and placards or labels prescribed are affixed in accordance with the requirements of chapter 5.3 concerning tanks.

Obligations concerning the bulk loading of dangerous solids in vehicles, wagons or containers:

(i)   He shall ascertain, prior to loading, that the vehicles, wagons and containers, and if necessary their equipment, are technically in a satisfactory condition and that the carriage in bulk of the dangerous goods in question is authorized in these vehicles or containers;

(j)   He shall ensure after loading that the orange plates and placards or labels prescribed are affixed in accordance with the requirements of Chapter 5.3 applicable to such vehicles, wagons or containers;

Obligations concerning the filling of cargo tanks:

(k)   He shall ascertain, prior to filling, that the additional protection material and equipment required in the instructions in writing have been provided to the master;

(l)   He shall complete his section of the check list referred to in 7.2.4.10 prior to the loading of the cargo tanks of a tank vessel;

(m)   He shall only fill cargo tanks with the dangerous goods accepted in such tanks;

(n)   He shall, when necessary, issue a heating instruction in the case of the carriage of substances whose melting point is 0 °C or higher;

(o)   He shall ascertain that during loading the trigger for the automatic device for the prevention of overfilling switches off the electric line established and supplied by the on-shore installation and that he can take steps against overfilling;

(p)   He shall ascertain that provision has been made in the fore and aft sections of the vessel for appropriate means for its evacuation in the event of an emergency;

(q)   He shall ascertain that, when prescribed in 7.2.4.25.5. there is a flame-arrester in the gas discharge pipe or the compensation pipe to protect the vessel against detonations and flame-fronts from the landward side;

(r)   He shall ascertain that the loading flows conform to the loading instructions referred to in 9.3.2.25.9 or 9.3.3.25.9 and that the pressure at the crossing-point of the gas discharge pipe or the compensation pipe is not greater than the opening pressure of the high velocity vent valve;

(s)   He shall, after filling the tank, check the leakproofness of the closing devices;

(t) He shall ensure that no dangerous residue of the filling substance adheres to the outside of the tanks filled by him.

Obligations concerning the bulk loading of dangerous solids in vessels:

(u) He shall ascertain, prior to loading, that the additional protection material and equipment required in the instructions in writing have been provided to the master;

(v) He shall only load the vessel with dangerous goods the bulk carriage of which is authorized in that vessel;

(w) He shall ascertain that provision has been made in the fore and aft sections of the vessel for appropriate means for its evacuation in the event of an emergency.

1.4.3.4 *Tank-container/portable tank operator*

In the context of 1.4.1, the tank-container/portable tank operator shall in particular:

(a) ensure compliance with the requirements for construction, equipment, tests and marking;

(b) ensure that the maintenance of shells and their equipment is carried out in such a way as to ensure that, under normal operating conditions, the tank-container/portable tank satisfies the requirements of ADR, RID or the IMDG Code until the next inspection;

(c) have an exceptional check made when the safety of the shell or its equipment is liable to be impaired by a repair, an alteration or an accident.

1.4.3.5 *(Reserved)*

CHAPTER 1.5

SPECIAL RULES, DEROGATIONS

1.5.1   **Bilateral and multilateral agreements**

1.5.1.1   In accordance with Article 7, paragraph 1 of ADN, for the purpose of adapting the requirements of the annexed Regulations to technological and industrial developments, the competent authorities of the Contracting Parties may agree directly among themselves to authorize certain transport operations in their territories by temporary derogation from the requirements of ADN, provided that safety is not compromised thereby. The authority which has taken the initiative with respect to the temporary derogation shall notify such derogations to the Secretariat of the United Nations Economic Commission for Europe which shall bring them to the attention of the Contracting Parties.

> *NOTE: "Special arrangement" in accordance with 1.7.4 is not considered to be a temporary derogation in accordance with this section.*

1.5.1.2   The period of validity of the temporary derogation shall not be more than five years from the date of its entry into force. The temporary derogation shall automatically cease as from the date of the entry into force of a relevant amendment to these annexed Regulations.

1.5.1.3   Transport operations on the basis of these agreements shall constitute transport operations in the sense of ADN.

1.5.2   **Special authorizations concerning transport in tank vessels**

1.5.2.1   *Special authorizations*

1.5.2.1.1   In accordance with paragraph 2 of Article 7, the competent authority shall have the right to issue special authorizations to a carrier or a consignor for the international carriage in tank vessels of dangerous substances, including mixtures, the carriage of which in tank vessels is not authorized under these Regulations, in accordance with the procedure set out below.

1.5.2.1.2   The special authorization shall be valid, due account being taken of the restrictions specified therein, for the Contracting Parties and on whose territory the transport operation will take place, for not more than two years but unless it is repealed at an earlier date. With the approval of the competent authorities of these Contracting Parties, the special authorization may be renewed for a period of not more than one year.

1.5.2.1.3   The special authorization shall include a statement concerning its repeal at an earlier date and shall conform to the model established by the Administrative Committee.

1.5.2.2   *Procedure*

1.5.2.2.1   The carrier or the consignor shall apply to the competent authority of a Contracting Party on whose territory the transport operation takes place for the issue of a special authorization.

The application shall include the particulars mentioned in these Regulations. The applicant shall be responsible for the accuracy of the particulars.

1.5.2.2.2   The competent authority shall consider the application from the technical and safety point of view. If it has no reservations, it shall draw up a special authorization in accordance with the criteria established by the Administrative Committee and immediately inform the other competent authorities involved in the carriage in question. The special authorization shall be issued only when the authorities concerned agree to it or have not expressed opposition within a period of two months after receiving the information. The applicant shall receive the original of the special authorization and keep a copy of it on board the vessel(s) involved in the carriage in question. The competent authorities shall immediately communicate to the Administrative Committee the applications for special authorizations, the applications rejected and the special authorizations granted.

1.5.2.2.3   If the special authorization is not issued because doubts or opposition have been expressed, the Administrative Committee shall decide whether or not to issue a special authorization.

1.5.2.3   *Update of the list of substances authorized for carriage in tank vessels*

1.5.2.3.1   The Administrative Committee shall consider all the special authorizations and applications communicated to it and decide whether the substance is to be included in the list of substances in these Regulations, authorized for carriage in tank vessels.

1.5.2.3.2   If the Administrative Committee enters technical or safety reservations concerning the inclusion of the substance in the list of substances of these Regulations authorized for carriage in tank vessels or concerning certain conditions, the competent authority shall be so informed. The competent authority shall immediately withdraw or, if necessary, modify the special authorization.

1.5.3   Equivalents and derogations (Article 7, paragraph 3 of ADN)

1.5.3.1   *Procedure for equivalents*

When the provisions of these Regulations prescribe for a vessel the use or the presence on board of certain materials, installations or equipment or the adoption of certain construction measures or certain fixtures, the competent authority may agree to the use or the presence on board of other materials, installations or equipment or the adoption of other construction measures or other fixtures for this vessel if, in line with recommendations established by the Administrative Committee, they are accepted as equivalent.

1.5.3.2   *Derogations on a trial basis*

The competent authority may, on the basis of a recommendation by the Administrative Committee, issue a trial certificate of approval for a limited period for a specific vessel having new technical characteristics departing from the requirements of these Regulations, provided that these characteristics are sufficiently safe.

1.5.3.3   *Particulars of equivalents and derogations*

The equivalents and derogations referred to in 1.5.3.1 and 1.5.3.2 shall be entered in the certificate of approval.

CHAPTER 1.6

TRANSITIONAL MEASURES

1.6.1   **General**

1.6.1.1   Unless otherwise provided, the substances and articles of ADN may be carried until 30 June 2005 in accordance with the requirements of ADN applicable up to 31 December 2004.

1.6.1.2   The danger labels which until 31 December 1998 conformed to the models prescribed up to that date may be used until stocks are exhausted.

1.6.1.3   The transitional measures of 1.6.1.3 and 1.6.1.4 of ADR and RID, or falling within the scope of 4.1.5.19 of IMDG Code, concerning the packaging of substances and articles of Class 1, are also valid for carriage subject to ADN.

1.6.1.4-1.6.1.7 *(Reserved)*

1.6.1.8   Existing orange-coloured plates which meet the requirements of sub-section 5.3.2.2 applicable up to 31 December 2004 may continue to be used.

1.6.1.9   *(Reserved).*

1.6.1.10   Lithium cells and batteries manufactured before 1 July 2003 which had been tested in accordance with the requirements applicable until 31 December 2002 but which had not been tested in accordance with the requirements applicable as from 1 January 2003, and appliances containing such lithium cells or batteries, may continue to be carried up to 30 June 2013 if all the other applicable requirements are fulfilled.

1.6.2   **Receptacles for Class 2**

The transitional measures of sections 1.6.2 of ADR and RID are also valid for transport operations subject to ADN.

1.6.3   **Fixed tanks (tank-vehicles and tank wagons), demountable tanks, battery vehicles and battery wagons**

The transitional measures of sections 1.6.3 of ADR and RID are also valid for transport operations subject to ADN.

1.6.4   **Tank-containers, portable tanks and MEGCs**

The transitional measures of sections 1.6.4 of ADR and RID or of section 4.2.0 of the IMDG Code, depending on the case, are also valid for transport operations subject to ADN.

1.6.5   **Vehicles and wagons**

The transitional measures of sections 1.6.5 of ADR and RID are also valid for transport operations subject to ADN.

1.6.6   **Class 7**

The transitional measures of sections 1.6.6 of ADR and RID or of section 6.4.24 of the IMDG Code are also valid for transport operations subject to ADN.

1.6.7   **Transitional provisions concerning vessels**

1.6.7.1   *General*

1.6.7.1.1   For the purposes of Article 8 of ADN, section 1.6.7 sets out general transitional provisions in 1.6.7.2 (see Article 8, paragraphs 1, 2 and 4) and specific transitional provisions in 1.6.7.3 (see Article 8, paragraph 3).

1.6.7.1.2   In this section 1.6.7:

(a)   "Vessel in service" means a vessel according to Article 8, paragraph 2 of the Agreement;

(b)   "N.R.M." means that the requirement does not apply to vessels in service except where the parts concerned are replaced or modified, i.e. it applies only to vessels which are **n**ew (as from the date indicated), or to parts which are **r**eplaced or **m**odified after the date indicated; where existing parts are replaced by spare or replacement parts of the same type and manufacture, this shall not be considered a replacement 'R' as defined in these transitional provisions.

Modification shall also be taken to mean the conversion of an existing type of tank vessel, a type of cargo tank or a cargo tank design to another type or design at a higher level.

(c)   "Renewal of the certificate of approval after the ..." means that the requirement shall be met at the next renewal of the certificate of approval following the date indicated. If the certificate of approval expires during the first year after the date of application of these Regulations, the requirement shall be mandatory only after the expiry of this first year.

1.6.7.2   *General transitional provisions*

1.6.7.2.1   *General transitional provisions for dry cargo vessels*

1.6.7.2.1.1   Vessels in service shall meet:

(a)   the requirements of paragraphs mentioned in the table below within the period established therein;

(b)   the requirements of paragraphs not mentioned in the table below at the date of application of these Regulations.

The construction and equipment of vessels in service shall be maintained at least at the previous standard of safety.

1.6.7.2.1.1	Table of general transitional provisions: Dry cargo	
Paragraphs	Subject	Time limit and comments
9.1.0.12.1	Ventilation of holds	N.R.M. The following requirements apply on board vessels in service: Each hold shall have appropriate natural or artificial ventilation; for the carriage of substances of Class 4.3, each hold shall be equipped with forced-air ventilation; the appliances used for this purpose must be so constructed that water cannot enter the hold.
9.1.0.12.3	Ventilation of service spaces	N.R.M.
9.1.0.17.2	Gas-tight openings facing holds	N.R.M. The following requirements apply on board vessels in service: Openings of accommodation and the wheelhouse facing the holds must be capable of being tightly closed.
9.1.0.17.3	Entrances and openings in the protected area	N.R.M. The following requirements apply on board vessels in service: Openings of accommodation and the wheelhouse facing holds shall be capable of being tightly closed.
9.1.0.31.2	Air intakes of engines	N.R.M.
9.1.0.32.2	Air pipes 50 cm above the deck	N.R.M.
9.1.0.34.1	Exhaust pipes	N.R.M.
9.1.0.35	Stripping pumps in the protected area	N.R.M. The following requirements apply on board vessels in service: In the event of the carriage of substances of Class 4.1, 52°, of all substances of Class 4.3 in bulk or unpackaged and polymeric beads, expandable, of Class 9, 4° (c), the stripping of the holds may only be effected using a stripping installation located in the protected area. The stripping installation located above the engine room must be clamped.
9.1.0.40.1	Fire extinguishers, two pumps, etc.	N.R.M.
9.1.0.40.2	Fire extinguishing systems permanently fixed in engine rooms	N.R.M.

1.6.7.2.1.1	Table of general transitional provisions: Dry cargo	
Paragraphs	Subject	Time limit and comments
9.1.0.41 in conjunction with 7.1.3.41	Fire and naked light	N.R.M. The following requirements apply on board vessels in service: The outlets of funnels shall be located not less than 2.00 m from the nearest point on hold hatchways. Heating and cooking appliances shall be permitted only in metal-based accommodation and wheelhouses. However: Heating appliances fuelled with liquid fuels having a flashpoint above 55 °C shall be permitted in engine rooms; Central-heating boilers fuelled with solid fuels shall be permitted in spaces situated below deck and accessible only from the deck.
9.2.0.31.2	Air intakes of engines	N.R.M.
9.2.0.34.1	Position of exhaust pipes	N.R.M.
9.2.0.41 in conjunction with 7.1.3.4.1	Fire and naked light	N.R.M. The following requirements apply on board vessels in service: Outlets of funnels shall be located not less than 2.00 m from the nearest point on hold hatchways. Heating and cooking appliances shall be permitted only in metal-based accommodation and wheelhouses. However: Heating appliances fuelled with liquid fuels having a flashpoint above 55° C shall be permitted in engine rooms; Central-heating boilers fuelled by solid fuels shall be permitted in spaces situated below the deck and accessible only from the deck.

1.6.7.2.1.2 Vessels carrying only the dangerous goods referred to below in bulk are only required to meet the requirements of ADN as from 1 January 2005:

Class 4.1 1350 SULPHUR:
3175 SOLIDS or mixtures of solids (such as preparations and wastes) CONTAINING FLAMMABLE LIQUID N.O.S., having a flash point up to 61° C;

Class 4.2 1364 COTTON WASTE, OILY, in bulk;
1365 COTTON, WET
1373 FIBRES or FABRICS, ANIMAL or VEGETABLE or SYNTHETIC, N.O.S. with oil;
1376 IRON OXIDE, SPENT or IRON SPONGE, SPENT obtained from coal gas purification;
1379 PAPER, UNSATURATED OIL TREATED, incompletely dried (including carbon paper);
2210 MANEB or MANEB PREPARATION with not less than 60% maneb;
3190 SELF-HEATING SOLID, INORGANIC, N.O.S., Packing Group III;

Class 9   2969   CASTOR BEANS

Vessels shall, however, meet the requirements of the following paragraphs of Part 7 below: 7.1.1.11 and 7.1.3.5.1.4

1.6.7.2.2   *General transitional provisions for tank vessels*

1.6.7.2.2.1   Vessels in service shall meet:

(a)   the requirements of paragraphs mentioned in the table below within the period established therein;

(b)   the requirements of paragraphs not mentioned in the table below at the date of application of these Regulations.

The construction and equipment of vessels in service shall be maintained at least at the previous standard of safety.

1.6.7.2.3   *General transitional provisions for tank vessels*

1.6.7.2.3.1   Table of general transitional provisions for tank vessels

1.6.7.2.3.1 Table of general transitional provisions: Tank vessels		
Paragraphs	Subject	Time limit and comments
1.2.1	Limited explosion risk electrical apparatus	N.R.M. The following requirements apply on board vessels in service: Limited explosion risk electrical apparatus is: – Electrical apparatus which, during normal operation, does not cause sparks or exhibit surface temperatures exceeding 200 °C; or – Electrical apparatus with a spray-water protected housing which, during normal operation, does not exhibit surface temperatures above 200 °C.
1.2.1	Hold space	Not applicable to Type N open vessels whose hold spaces contain auxiliary appliances and which are carrying only substances of Class 8, with remark 30 in column (20) of Table C of Chapter 3.2.
1.2.1	Flame arrester High velocity vent valve according to standard EN 12 874 (1999)	N.R.M. The following requirements are applicable on board vessels in service: Flame arresters and high velocity vent valves shall be of a type approved by the competent authority for the use prescribed.
7.2.2.6	Approved gas detection system	N.R.M.
7.2.2.19.3	Vessels used for propulsion	N.R.M.
7.2.3.20	Use of cofferdams for ballasting	On board vessels in service, cofferdams may be filled with water during unloading to provide trim and to permit residue-free drainage if possible.

1.6.7.2.3.1	Table of general transitional provisions: Tank vessels	
Paragraphs	Subject	Time limit and comments
7.2.3.20.1	Ballast water Prohibition against filling cofferdams with water	N.R.M. The following requirements apply on board vessels in service: Cofferdams may be filled with ballast water only when cargo tanks are empty.
7.2.3.20.1	Proof of stabilization in the event of a leak connected with ballast water for Type G vessels	N.R.M.
7.2.3.25.1 (c)	Connections prohibited between pipes for loading and unloading and pipes located outside the cargo area	N.R.M. for oil-separator vessels
7.2.3.31.2	Motor vehicles only outside the cargo area: Type N open	N.R.M. The following requirements apply on board vessels in service: The vehicle shall not be started on board.
7.2.3.42.3	Use of the cargo heating system	Not applicable to vessels in service of Type N open.
7.2.3.51.3	Live sockets for Type G and Type N vessels	N.R.M.
7.2.4.16.15	Start of loading flow	N.R.M.
7.2.4.22.1	Opening of openings Type N open	N.R.M. On board vessels in service cargo tank hatches may be opened during loading for control and sampling.
8.1.2.3 (c)	Damage control plan: Type G	N.R.M.
8.1.2.3 (c)	Documents concerning intact stability	N.R.M.
8.1.2.3 (i)	Loading and unloading instructions	N.R.M.
9.3.2.0.1 (c) 9.3.3.0.1 (c)	Protection of vapour pipes against corrosion	N.R.M.
9.3.1.0.3 (d) 9.3.2.0.3 (d) 9.3.3.0.3 (d)	Fire-resistant materials of accommodation and wheelhouse	N.R.M.
9.3.3.8.1	Classification of Type N open vessels with flame arresters and Type N open vessels	N.R.M.
9.3.3.8.1 in conjunction with 7.2.2.8	Continuation of class for Type N open vessels with flame arresters and Type N open vessels	N.R.M. The following requirements apply on board vessels in service: Except where otherwise provided, the type of construction, the strength, the subdivision, the equipment and the gear of the vessel shall conform or be equivalent to the construction requirements for classification in the highest class of a recognized classification society.

1.6.7.2.3.1	Table of general transitional provisions: Tank vessels	
Paragraphs	Subject	Time limit and comments
9.3.1.10.2 9.3.2.10.2 9.3.3.10.2	Door coamings, etc.	N.R.M. The following requirements apply on board vessels in service, with the exception of Type N open vessels: This requirement may be met by fitting vertical protection walls not less than 0.50 m in height; On board vessels in service less than 50.00 m long, the height of 0.50 m may be reduced to 0.30 m in passageways leading to the deck.
9.3.1.11.1 (b)	Ratio of length to diameter of pressure cargo tanks	Not applicable to Type G vessels whose keels were laid before 1 January 1977.
9.3.3.11.1 (d)	Limitation of length of cargo tanks	N.R.M.
9.3.1.11.2 (a)	Arrangement of cargo tanks Distance between cargo tanks and side walls Height of saddles, spacers	N.R.M. Not applicable to Type G vessels whose keels were laid before 1 January 1977. N.R.M. The following requirements apply on board vessels in service: Where tank volume is more than 200 m³ or where the ratio of length to diameter is less than 7 but more than 5, the hull in the tank area shall be such that, in the event of a collision, the tanks remain intact as far as possible. This requirement shall be considered as having been met where, in the tank area, the vessel: – is double-hulled with a distance of at least 80 cm between the side plating and the longitudinal bulkhead, – or is designed as follows: (a) Between the gangboard and the top of the floorplates there shall be side stringers at regular intervals of not more than 60 cm; (b) The side stringers shall be supported by web frames spaced at intervals of not more than 2.00 m. The height of the web frames shall be not less than 10% of the depth and in any event not less than 30 cm. They shall be fitted with a face plate made of flat steel having a cross section of not less than 15 cm²; (c) The side stringers referred to in (a) shall have the same height as the web frames and be fitted with a face plate made of flat steel having a cross section of not less than 7.5 cm².
9.3.1.11.2 (b) 9.3.2.11.2 (b) 9.3.3.11.2 (a)	Cargo tank fastenings	N.R.M.
9.3.1.11.2 (c) 9.3.2.11.2 (c) 9.3.3.11.2 (b)	Capacity of suction well	N.R.M.

1.6.7.2.3.1	Table of general transitional provisions: Tank vessels	
Paragraphs	Subject	Time limit and comments
9.3.1.11.2 (d) 9.3.2.11.2 (d)	Side stringers between the hull and the cargo tanks	N.R.M.
9.3.1.11.3 (a)	End bulkheads of cargo area with "A-60" insulation. Distance of 0.50 m from cargo tanks in hold spaces	N.R.M.
9.3.2.11.3 (a) 9.3.3.11.3 (a)	Width of cofferdams of 0.60 m Hold spaces with cofferdams or "A-60" insulated bulkheads Distance of 0.50 m from cargo tanks in hold spaces	N.R.M. The following requirements apply on board vessels in service: Type C: minimum width of cofferdams: 0.50 m; Type N: minimum width of cofferdams: 0.50 m, on board vessels with a deadweight of up to 150 t: 0.40 m; Type N open: cofferdams shall not be required with deadweight up to 150 t: The distance between cargo tanks and end bulkheads of hold spaces shall be at least 0.40 m.
9.3.3.11.4	Passages through the end bulkheads of hold spaces	Shall not apply to Type N open vessels whose keels were laid before 1 January 1977.
9.3.3.11.6 (a)	Form of cofferdam arranged as a pump room	Shall not apply to Type N vessels whose keels were laid before 1 January 1977.
9.3.1.11.7 9.3.3.11.8	Arrangement of service spaces located in the cargo area below decks	N.R.M.
9.3.3.11.7	Distances in relation to the outer wall	N.R.M.
9.3.1.11.8 9.3.3.11.9	Dimensions of openings for access to spaces within the cargo area	N.R.M.
9.3.1.11.8 9.3.2.11.10 9.3.3.11.9	Interval between reinforcing elements	N.R.M.
9.3.2.12.1 9.3.3.12.1	Ventilation opening in hold spaces	N.R.M.
9.3.1.12.2 9.3.3.12.2	Ventilation systems in double-hull spaces and double bottoms	N.R.M.
9.3.1.12.3 9.3.2.12.3 9.3.3.12.3	Height above the deck of the air intake for service spaces located below deck	N.R.M.
9.3.1.12.6 9.3.2.12.6 9.3.3.12.6	Distance of ventilation inlets from cargo area	N.R.M.
9.3.1.12.6 9.3.2.12.6 9.3.3.12.6	Permanently installed flame screens	N.R.M.
9.3.3.12.7	Approval of flame arresters	Shall not apply to Type N vessels whose keels were laid before 1 January 1977.
9.3.1.13 9.3.3.13	General stability	N.R.M.
9.3.1.14 9.3.3.14	Intact stability	N.R.M.

1.6.7.2.3.1	Table of general transitional provisions: Tank vessels	
Paragraphs	Subject	Time limit and comments
9.3.3.15	Stability after damage	N.R.M.
9.3.1.16.1 9.3.3.16.1	Distance of openings of engine rooms from the cargo area	N.R.M.
9.3.3.16.1	Internal combustion engines outside the cargo area for Type N open vessels	N.R.M.
9.3.1.16.2 9.3.3.16.2	Hinges of doors facing the cargo area Engine rooms accessible from the deck for Type N open vessels	Shall not apply to vessels whose keels were laid before 1 January 1977 where alterations would obstruct other major openings. N.R.M.
9.3.1.17.1 9.3.3.17.1	Accommodation and wheelhouse outside the cargo area Type N open	Shall not apply to vessels whose keels were laid before 1 January 1977, provided that there is no connection between the wheelhouse and other enclosed spaces. Shall not apply to vessels up to 50 m in length whose keels were laid before 1 January 1977 and whose wheelhouses are located in the cargo area even if it provides access to another enclosed space, provided that safety is ensured by appropriate service requirements of the competent authority. N.R.M.
9.3.1.17.2 9.3.2.17.2 9.3.3.17.2	Arrangement of entrances and openings of forward superstructures Entrances facing the cargo area Entrances and openings on Type N open vessels	N.R.M. Shall not apply to vessels up to 50.00 m in length whose keels were laid before 1 January 1977, provided that gas screens are installed. N.R.M.
9.3.1.17.3	Entrances and openings must be capable of being closed Type N open	N.R.M.
9.3.1.17.4 9.3.3.17.4	Distance of openings from the cargo area	N.R.M.
9.3.3.17.5 (b), (c)	Approval of shaft passages and displaying of instructions Type N open	N.R.M.
9.3.1.17.6 9.3.3.17.6	Pump-room below deck	N.R.M. The following requirements apply on board vessels in service: Pump-rooms below deck shall meet the requirements for service spaces: for Type G vessels: 9.3.1.12.3 for Type N vessels: 9.3.3.12.3

1.6.7.2.3.1	Table of general transitional provisions: Tank vessels	
Paragraphs	Subject	Time limit and comments
9.3.2.20.1 9.3.3.20.1	Access and ventilation openings 0.50 m above the deck	N.R.M.
9.3.2.20.2 9.3.3.20.2	Intake valve	N.R.M.
9.3.3.20.2	Filling of cofferdams with pump Type N open	N.R.M.
9.3.2.20.2 9.3.3.20.2	Filling of cofferdams within 30 minutes	N.R.M.
9.3.3.21.1 (b)	Liquid level gauge Type N open with flame arrester Type N open	N.R.M.
9.3.3.21.1 (c)	Level alarm device	Not applicable to open Type N vessels in service permitted only to carry SULPHUR, MOLTEN, UN No. 2448.
9.3.1.21.1.(d) 9.3.2.21.1 (d) 9.3.3.21.1 (d)	Sensor for actuating the facility against overflowing	Applicable only to vessels to be loaded in a Contracting Party where the shore installation is equipped accordingly.
9.3.2.21.1 (e)	Alarm of the instrument for measuring the pressure in each cargo tank in the event of the carriage of substances for which deck spraying is required	Renewal of certificate of approval after 1 January 1999.
9.3.2.21.1.(e) 9.3.3.21.1.(e)	Instrument for measuring pressure in the cargo tank	Renewal of the certificate of approval after 1 January 2001. Up to 31 December 2010 on board vessels in service which do not carry substances for which remarks 5, 6 or 7 are included in column (20) of Table C of Chapter 3.2, the instrument for measuring pressure in the cargo tank conforms to requirements when the vapour pipe is equipped with such an instrument at its front and rear extremities.
9.3.2.21.1 (f) 9.3.3.21.1 (f)	Installation of the instrument for measuring the temperature	Renewal of certificate of approval after 1 January 1999.
9.3.3.21.1 (g)	Sampling opening Type N open	N.R.M.
9.3.1.21.4 9.3.2.21.4 9.3.3.21.4	Independent liquid-level alarm device	N.R.M.
9.3.1.21.5 9.3.2.21.5 9.3.3.21.5	Socket close to the shore connections and cut-out of vessel's pump	N.R.M.
9.3.3.21.5 (b)	Sensor according to 9.3.3.21.1 (d)	Renewal of the certificate of approval after 1 January 1999.
9.3.3.21.5 (c)	Connecting nozzle according to standard EN 12827	Renewal of the certificate of approval after 31 December 2002
9.3.3.21.5 (c)	Device for rapid shutting off of supply	Renewal of the certificate of approval after 31 December 2003

1.6.7.2.3.1	Table of general transitional provisions: Tank vessels	
Paragraphs	Subject	Time limit and comments
9.3.1.21.7 9.3.2.21.7 9.3.3.21.7	Vacuum or over-pressure alarms in cargo tanks for the carriage of substances **without** remark 5 in column (20) of Table C of Chapter 3.2.	N.R.M.
9.3.2.21.7 9.3.3.21.7	Vacuum or over-pressure alarms in cargo tanks for the carriage of substances **with** remark 5 in column (20) of Table C of Chapter 3.2.	N.R.M. Vessels furnished with a certificate of approval valid at 31 December 2000 shall meet these requirements no later than 31 December 2010.
9.3.1.21.7 9.3.2.21.7 9.3.3.21.7	Temperature alarms in cargo tanks	N.R.M.
9.3.3.21.12	Self-closing lid	N.R.M.
9.3.3.22.1 (b)	Cargo tank openings 0.50 m above the deck	Shall not apply to vessels whose keels were laid before 1 January 1977.
9.3.1.22.4	Prevention of spark-formation by closure devices	N.R.M.
9.3.1.22.3 9.3.2.22.4 (b) 9.3.3.22.4 (b)	Position of outlets of valves above the deck	N.R.M.
9.3.2.22.4 (b) 9.3.3.22.4 (b)	Pressure setting of high velocity vent valves	N.R.M.
9.3.2.22.5 9.3.3.22.5	Flame arrester or Valves or Individual gas discharge pipe or Shut-off devices	N.R.M. Vessels furnished with a certificate of approval valid at 31 December 1998 shall meet these requirements no later than 31 December 2010
9.3.2.22.5 (a)	Fire-fighting installation	31 December 2010
9.3.3.23.2	Test pressure for cargo tanks	Shall not apply to vessels whose keels were laid before 1 January 1977, for which a test pressure of 15 kPa (0.15 bar) is required. A test pressure of 10 kPa (0.10 bar) shall be sufficient.
9.3.3.23.3	Test pressure for pipes for loading and unloading	On board oil-separator vessels in service before 1 January 1999 a test pressure of 400 kPa is sufficient.
9.3.2.25.1 9.3.3.25.1	Shut-down of cargo pumps	N.R.M.
9.3.1.25.1 9.3.2.25.1 9.3.3.25.1	Distance of pumps, etc. from accommodation, etc.	N.R.M.
9.3.3.25.2 (a)	Pipes for loading and unloading located in the below-deck area	N.R.M. for oil-separator vessels
9.3.1.25.2 (d) 9.3.2.25.2 (d)	Position of loading and unloading pipes on deck	N.R.M.
9.3.1.25.2 (e) 9.3.2.25.2 (e) 9.3.3.25.2 (e)	Distance of shore connections from accommodation, etc.	N.R.M.
9.3.1.25.2 (i) 9.3.2.25.2.(j) 9.3.3.25.2 (k)	Position of cargo piping	N.R.M.
9.3.2.25.8 (a)	Ballasting suction pipes located within the cargo area but outside the cargo tanks	N.R.M.

1.6.7.2.3.1	Table of general transitional provisions: Tank vessels	
Paragraphs	Subject	Time limit and comments
9.3.2.25.9 9.3.3.25.9	Loading and unloading flow	N.R.M. As from 1 January 2003, the loading flows mentioned in the certificate of approval shall be checked if necessary when the certificate of approval is renewed.
9.3.3.25.12	9.3.3.25.1 (a) and (c), 9.3.3.25.2 (e), 9.3.3.25.3 and 9.3.3.25.4 (a) are not applicable with the exception of Type N open carrying corrosive substances (see Chapter 3.2, Table C, column (5), hazard 8)	N.R.M. This time limit concerns only Type N open vessels carrying corrosive substances (see Chapter 3.2, Table C, column (5), hazard 8).
9.3.1.27.2	Refrigeration system List of 12° instead of 10°	N.R.M.
9.3.2.28	Water-spray installation required in Table C of Chapter 3.2	This transitional requirement is valid only for substances accepted for carriage in tank vessels before 1 January 1995.
9.3.1.31.2 9.3.2.31.2 9.3.3.31.2	Distance of engine air intakes from the cargo area	N.R.M.
9.3.1.31.4 9.3.2.31.4 9.3.3.31.4	Temperature of outer parts of engines, etc.	N.R.M. The following requirements apply on board vessels in service: The temperature of outer parts shall not exceed 300° C.
9.3.1.31.5 9.3.2.31.5 9.3.3.31.5	Temperature in the engine room	N.R.M. The following requirements apply on board vessels in service: The temperature in the engine room shall not exceed 45 °C.
9.3.1.32.2 9.3.2.32.2 9.3.3.32.2	Openings of air pipes 0.50 m above the deck	N.R.M.
9.3.3.34.1	Exhaust pipes	N.R.M.
9.3.1.35.1 9.3.3.35.1	Stripping and ballast pumps in the cargo area	N.R.M.
9.3.3.35.3	Suction pipes for ballasting located within the cargo area but outside the cargo tanks	N.R.M.
9.3.1.35.4	Stripping installation of the pump-room outside the pump-room	N.R.M.
9.3.1.40.1 9.3.2.40.1 9.3.3.40.1	Fire extinguishing systems, two pumps, etc.	N.R.M.
9.3.1.40.2 9.3.2.40.2 9.3.3.40.2	Fixed fire extinguishing system in engine room	N.R.M.
9.3.1.41.1 9.3.3.41.1	Outlets of funnels located not less than 2 m from the cargo area	Not applicable to vessels whose keels were laid before 1 January 1977.

1.6.7.2.3.1	Table of general transitional provisions: Tank vessels	
Paragraphs	Subject	Time limit and comments
9.3.3.41.1	Outlets of funnels	N.R.M. for oil-separator vessels
9.3.1.41.2 9.3.2.41.3 9.3.3.41.2 in conjunction with 7.2.3.41	Heating, cooking and refrigerating appliances	N.R.M.
9.3.3.42.2	Cargo heating system: Type N open	N.R.M. The following requirements apply on board vessels in service: This can be achieved by an oil separator fitted to the condensed water return pipe.
9.3.1.51.2 9.3.2.51.2 9.3.3.51.2	Visual and audible alarm	N.R.M.
9.3.1.51.3 9.3.2.51.3 9.3.3.51.3	Temperature class and explosion group	N.R.M.
9.3.3.52.1 (b), (c), (d) and (e)	Electrical installations: Type N open	N.R.M.
9.3.1.52.1 (e) 9.3.3.52.1 (e)	Electrical installations of the "certified safe" type in the cargo area	Shall not apply to vessels whose keels were laid before 1 January 1977. The following conditions shall be met during loading, unloading and gas-freeing on board vessels having non-gastight wheelhouse openings (e.g. doors, windows, etc.) giving on to the cargo area: (a) All electrical installations designed to be used shall be of a limited explosion-risk type, i.e. they shall be so designed that there is no sparking under normal operating conditions and the temperature of their outer surfaces does not rise above 200° C, or be of a type protected against water spray the temperature of whose outer surfaces does not exceed 200° C under normal operating conditions; (b) Electrical installations which do not meet the requirements of (a) above shall be marked in red and it shall be possible to switch them off by means of a central switch.
9.3.3.52.2	Accumulators located outside the cargo area	N.R.M.

1.6.7.2.3.1	Table of general transitional provisions: Tank vessels	
Paragraphs	Subject	Time limit and comments

9.3.1.52.3 (a)
9.3.1.52.3 (b)
9.3.3.52.3 (a)
9.3.3.52.3 (b)
	Electrical installations used during loading, unloading or gas-freeing	Shall not apply to the following installations on vessels whose keels were laid before 1 January 1977:
		Lighting installations in accommodation, with the exception of switches near the entrances to accommodation;
		Radio telephone installations in accommodation and wheelhouses and combustion engine control appliances.
		All other electrical installations shall meet the following requirements:
		(a) Generators, engines, etc.
		       P13 protection mode
		(b) Control panels, lamps, etc.
		       IP23 protection mode
		(c) Appliances, etc.
		       IP55 protection mode.

	Type N open	N.R.M.
9.3.1.52.3 (b) 9.3.2.52.3 (b) 9.3.3.52.3 (b) in conjunction with 3 (a)	Electrical installations used during loading, unloading and gas-freeing	N.R.M. On board vessels in service, paragraph (3) (a) shall not apply to: – Lighting installations in accommodation, with the exception of switches near entrances to accommodation; – Radiotelephone installations in accommodation and wheelhouses.
9.3.1.52.4 9.3.2.52.4 9.3.3.52.4 last sentence	Disconnection of such installations from a centralized location	N.R.M.
9.3.3.52.4	Red mark on electrical installations Type N open	N.R.M.
9.3.3.52.5	Cut-out switch for continuously driven generator: Type N open	N.R.M.
9.3.3.52.6	Permanently fitted sockets: Type N open	N.R.M.
9.3.1.56.1 9.3.3.56.1	Metallic sheaths for all cables	Shall not apply to vessels whose keels were laid before 1 January 1977.
9.3.3.56.1	Metallic sheath	N.R.M. for oil-separator vessels
9.3.1.56.3 9.3.2.56.3 9.3.3.56.3	Movable cables in the cargo area	N.R.M.

1.6.7.2.3.2   Transitional provisions concerning the application of the requirements of Table C of Chapter 3.2 to the carriage of goods in tank vessels.

1.6.7.2.3.2.1   The goods for which Type N closed with a minimum valve setting of 10 kPa (0.10 bar) is required in Table C of Chapter 3.2, may be carried in tank-vessels in service of Type N closed with a minimum valve setting of 6 kPa (0.06 bar) (cargo tank test pressure of 10 kPa (0.10 bar)).

1.6.7.2.3.2.2 (Remark 5)

On board tank vessels in service, the dismantling of the fixed plate stacks of flame arresters is permitted in the event of the carriage of substances for which remark 5 is included in column (20) of Table C of Chapter 3.2. This transitional provision is valid until 31 December 2010.

1.6.7.2.3.2.3 (Remarks 6 and 7)

On board tank vessels in service vapour pipes and pressure/vacuum valves do not need to be heated in the event of the carriage of substances for which remarks 6 or 7 are included in column (20) of Table C of Chapter 3.2. This transitional provision is valid until 30 December 2010.

On board vessels equipped with flame arresters with fixed plate stacks, the latter may be dismantled in the event of the carriage of the above-mentioned substances. This transitional provision is valid until 31 December 2010.

1.6.7.3 *Supplementary transitional provisions applicable to specific inland waterways*

1.6.7.3.1 Vessels in service to which the transitional provisions of this subsection are applied shall meet:

- the requirements of paragraphs and subparagraphs mentioned in the table below and in the table of general transitional provisions (see 1.6.7.2.1.1 and 1.6.7.2.3.1) within the period established therein;

- the requirements of paragraphs and subparagraphs not mentioned in the table below or in the table of general transitional provisions at the date of application of these Regulations.

The construction and equipment of vessels in service shall be maintained at least at the previous standard of safety.

Table of supplementary transitional provisions		
Paragraph	Subject	Time limit and comments
9.1.0.11.1 (b)	Holds, common bulkheads with oil fuel tanks	N.R.M. The following requirements apply on board vessels in service: Holds may share a common bulkhead with the oil fuel tanks, provided that the cargo or its packaging does not react chemically with the fuel.
9.1.0.92	Emergency exit	N.R.M. The following requirements apply on board vessels in service: Spaces the entrances or exits of which are partly or fully immersed in damaged condition shall be provided with an emergency exit not less than 0.075 m above the damage waterline.

Table of supplementary transitional provisions		
Paragraph	Subject	Time limit and comments
9.1.0.95.1 (c)	Height of openings above damage waterline	N.R.M. The following requirements apply on board vessels in service: The lower edge of any non-watertight openings (e.g. doors, windows, access hatchways) shall, at the final stage of flooding, be not less than 0.075 m above the damage waterline.
9.1.0.95.2 9.3.2.15.2	Extent of the stability diagram (damaged condition)	N.R.M. The following requirements apply on board vessels in service: At the final stage of flooding the angle of heel shall not exceed: 20° before measures to right the vessel; 12° following measures to right the vessel.
9.3.3.8.1	Classification of Type N open vessels	N.R.M.
9.3.1.11.1 (a) 9.3.2.11.1 (a) 9.3.3.11.1 (a)	Maximum capacity of cargo tanks.	N.R.M. The following requirements apply on board vessels in service: The maximum permissible capacity of a cargo tank shall be 760 m^3.
9.3.1.12.3 9.3.2.12.3 9.3.3.12.3	Position of air inlets	N.R.M. The following requirements apply on board vessels in service: The air inlets to be positioned at least 5.00 m from the safety-valve outlets
9.3.2.11.1 (d)	Length of cargo tanks	N.R.M. The following requirements apply on board vessels in service: The length of a cargo tank may exceed 10 m and 0.2 L.
9.3.3.8.1	Classification of Type N open vessels	N.R.M.
9.3.2.15.1 (c)	Height of openings above damage waterline	N.R.M. The following requirements apply on board vessels in service: The lower edge of any non-watertight openings (e.g. doors, windows, access hatchways) shall, at the final stage of flooding, be not less than 0.075 m above the damage waterline.
9.3.2.20.2 9.3.3.20.2	Filling of cofferdams with water	N.R.M. The following requirements apply on board vessels in service: Cofferdams shall be fitted with a system for filling with water or inert gas.

Table of supplementary transitional provisions		
Paragraph	Subject	Time limit and comments
9.3.1.92 9.3.2.92	Emergency Exit	N.R.M. The following requirements apply on board vessels in service: Spaces the entrances or exits of which are partly or fully immersed in damaged condition shall be provided with an emergency exit not less than 0.075 m above the damage waterline.

CHAPTER 1.7

GENERAL REQUIREMENTS CONCERNING CLASS 7

1.7.1   **General**

1.7.1.1   ADN establishes standards of safety which provide an acceptable level of control of the radiation, criticality and thermal hazards to persons, property and the environment that are associated with the carriage of radioactive material. These standards are based on the IAEA Regulations for the Safe Transport of Radioactive Material (1996 Edition, Revised) [TS-R-1 (ST-1, Revised)], IAEA, Vienna (2000) with the amendments adopted by the IAEA up to 2002. Explanatory material on TS-R-1 (ST-1, Revised) can be found in the "Advisory Material for the IAEA Regulations for the Safe Transport of Radioactive Material", Safety Guide No. TS-G-1.1 (ST-2) IAEA, Vienna (2002).

1.7.1.2   The objective of ADN is to protect persons, property and the environment from the effects of radiation during the carriage of radioactive material. This protection is achieved by requiring:

     (a)   Containment of the radioactive contents;

     (b)   Control of external radiation levels;

     (c)   Prevention of criticality; and

     (d)   Prevention of damage caused by heat.

These requirements are satisfied firstly by applying a graded approach to contents limits for packages and vehicles and to performance standards applied to package designs depending upon the hazard of the radioactive contents. Secondly, they are satisfied by imposing requirements on the design and operation of packages and on the maintenance of packagings, including a consideration of the nature of the radioactive contents. Finally, they are satisfied by requiring administrative controls including, where appropriate, approval by competent authorities.

1.7.1.3   ADN applies to the carriage of radioactive material by inland waterways including carriage which is incidental to the use of the radioactive material. Carriage comprises all operations and conditions associated with and involved in the movement of radioactive material; these include the design, manufacture, maintenance and repair of packaging, and the preparation, consigning, loading, carriage including in-transit storage, unloading and receipt at the final destination of loads of radioactive material and packages. A graded approach is applied to the performance standards in ADN that is characterized by three general severity levels:

     (a)   Routine conditions of carriage (incident free);

     (b)   Normal conditions of carriage (minor mishaps);

     (c)   Accident conditions of carriage.

1.7.2   **Radiation protection programme**

1.7.2.1   The carriage of radioactive material shall be subject to a Radiation protection programme which shall consist of systematic arrangements aimed at providing adequate consideration of radiation protection measures.

1.7.2.2	The nature and extent of the measures to be employed in the programme shall be related to the magnitude and likelihood of radiation exposures. The programme shall incorporate the requirements in 1.7.2.3, and 1.7.2.4, CV33 (1.1) and (1.4) of 7.5.11 of ADR and applicable emergency response procedures. Programme documents shall be available, on request, for inspection by the relevant competent authority.

1.7.2.2   The nature and extent of the measures to be employed in the programme shall be related to the magnitude and likelihood of radiation exposures. The programme shall incorporate the requirements in 1.7.2.3, and 1.7.2.4, CV33 (1.1) and (1.4) of 7.5.11 of ADR and applicable emergency response procedures. Programme documents shall be available, on request, for inspection by the relevant competent authority.

1.7.2.3   Protection and safety shall be optimized in order that the magnitude of individual doses, the number of persons exposed, and the likelihood of incurring exposure shall be kept as low as reasonably achievable, economic and social factors being taken into account, and doses to persons shall be below the relevant dose limits. A structured and systematic approach shall be adopted and shall include consideration of the interfaces between carriage and other activities.

1.7.2.4   For occupational exposures arising from transport activities, where it is assessed that the effective dose:

(a)   is most unlikely to exceed 1 mSv in a year, no special work patterns, detailed monitoring, dose assessment programmes or individual record keeping shall be required;

(b)   is likely to be between 1 mSv and 6 mSv in a year, a dose assessment programme via work place monitoring or individual monitoring shall be conducted;

(c)   is likely to exceed 6 mSv in a year, individual monitoring shall be conducted.

When individual monitoring or work place monitoring is conducted, appropriate records shall be kept.

1.7.3   **Quality assurance**

Quality assurance programmes based on international, national or other standards acceptable to the competent authority shall be established and implemented for the design, manufacture, testing, documentation, use, maintenance and inspection of all special form radioactive material, low dispersible radioactive material and packages and for carriage and in-transit storage operations to ensure compliance with the relevant provisions of ADN. Certification that the design specification has been fully implemented shall be available to the competent authority. The manufacturer, consignor or user shall be prepared to provide facilities for competent authority inspection during manufacture and use and to demonstrate to any cognizant competent authority that:

(a)   the manufacturing methods and materials used are in accordance with the approved design specifications; and

(b)   all packagings are periodically inspected and, as necessary, repaired and maintained in good condition so that they continue to comply with all relevant requirements and specifications, even after repeated use.

Where competent authority approval is required, such approval shall take into account and be contingent upon the adequacy of the quality assurance programme.

1.7.4   **Special arrangement**

1.7.4.1   Special arrangement shall mean those provisions, approved by the competent authority, under which consignments which do not satisfy all the requirements of ADN applicable to radioactive material may be transported.

NOTE: Special arrangement is not considered to be a temporary derogation in accordance with 1.5.1.

1.7.4.2   Consignments for which conformity with any provision applicable to Class 7 is impracticable shall not be transported except under special arrangement. Provided the competent authority is satisfied that conformity with the Class 7 provisions of ADN is impracticable and that the requisite standards of safety established by ADN have been demonstrated through alternative means the competent authority may approve special arrangement transport operations for single or a planned series of multiple consignments. The overall level of safety in carriage shall be at least equivalent to that which would be provided if all the applicable requirements had been met. For international consignments of this type, multilateral approval shall be required.

1.7.5   Radioactive material possessing other dangerous properties

In addition to the radioactive and fissile properties, any subsidiary risk of the contents of the package, such as explosiveness, flammability, pyrophoricity, chemical toxicity and corrosiveness, shall also be taken into account in the documentation, packing, labelling, marking, placarding, stowage, segregation and carriage, in order to be in compliance with all relevant provisions for dangerous goods of ADN.

1.7.6   Non-compliance

1.7.6.1   In the event of a non-compliance with any limit in ADN applicable to radiation level or contamination,

(a)   The consignor shall be informed of the non-compliance

(i)   by the carrier if the non-compliance is identified during carriage; or

(ii)   by the consignee if the non-compliance is identified at receipt;

(b)   The carrier, consignor or consignee, as appropriate shall:

(i)   take immediate steps to mitigate the consequences of the non-compliance;

(ii)   investigate the non-compliance and its causes, circumstances and consequences;

(iii)   take appropriate action to remedy the causes and circumstances that led to the non-compliance and to prevent a recurrence of similar circumstances that led to the non-compliance; and

(iv)   communicate to the competent authority(ies) on the causes of the non-compliance and on corrective or preventive actions taken or to be taken; and

(c)   The communication of the non-compliance to the consignor and competent authority(ies), respectively, shall be made as soon as practicable and it shall be immediate whenever an emergency exposure situation has developed or is developing.

CHAPTER 1.8

CHECKS AND OTHER SUPPORT MEASURES TO ENSURE COMPLIANCE WITH SAFETY REQUIREMENTS

1.8.1   **Monitoring compliance with requirements**

1.8.1.1   *General*

1.8.1.1.1   In accordance with Article 4, paragraph 3 of ADN, Contracting Parties shall ensure that a representative proportion of consignments of dangerous goods carried by inland waterways is subject to monitoring in accordance with the provisions of this Chapter.

1.8.1.1.2   Participants in the carriage of dangerous goods (see Chapter 1.4) shall, without delay, in the context of their respective obligations, provide the competent authorities and their agents with the necessary information for carrying out the checks.

1.8.1.2   *Monitoring procedure*

1.8.1.2.1   In order to carry out the checks provided for in Article 4, paragraph 3 of ADN, the Contracting Parties shall use the checklist to be developed by the Administrative Committee. A copy of this checklist or a certificate showing the result of the check drawn up by the competent authority which carried it out shall be given to the master of the vessel and presented on request in order to simplify or avoid, where possible, subsequent checks. This paragraph shall not prejudice Contracting Parties' right to carry out specific measures for detailed checks.

1.8.1.2.2   The checks shall be random and shall as far as possible cover an extensive portion of the inland waterway network.

1.8.1.2.3   When exercising the right to monitor, the authorities shall make all possible efforts to avoid unduly detaining or delaying a vessel.

1.8.1.3   *Infringements of the requirements*

Without prejudice to other penalties which may be imposed, vessels in respect of which one or more infringements of the rules on the transport of dangerous goods by inland waterways are established may be detained at a place designated for this purpose by the authorities carrying out the check and required to be brought into conformity before continuing their journey or may be subject to other appropriate measures, depending on the circumstances or the requirements of safety.

1.8.1.4   *Checks in companies and at places of loading and unloading*

1.8.1.4.1   Checks may be carried out at the premises of undertakings, as a preventive measure or where infringements which jeopardize safety in the transport of dangerous goods have been recorded during the voyage.

1.8.1.4.2   The purpose of such checks shall be to ensure that safety conditions for the transport of dangerous goods by inland waterways comply with the relevant laws.

1.8.1.4.3   *Sampling*

Where appropriate and provided that this does not constitute a safety hazard, samples of the goods transported may be taken for examination by laboratories recognized by the competent authority.

1.8.1.4.4 *Cooperation of the competent authorities*

1.8.1.4.4.1 Contracting Parties shall assist one another in order to give proper effect to these requirements.

1.8.1.4.4.2 Serious or repeated infringements jeopardizing the safety of the transport of dangerous goods committed by a foreign vessel or undertaking shall be reported to the competent authority in the Contracting Party where the certificate of approval of the vessel was issued or where the undertaking is established.

1.8.1.4.4.3 The competent authority of the Contracting Party where serious or repeated infringements have been recorded may ask the competent authority of the Contracting Party where the certificate of approval of the vessel was issued or where the undertaking is established for appropriate measures to be taken with regard to the offender or offenders.

1.8.1.4.4.4 The latter competent authority shall notify the competent authorities of the Contracting Party where the infringements were recorded of any measures taken with regard to the offender or offenders.

1.8.2 Administrative assistance during the checking of a foreign vessel

If the findings of a check on a foreign vessel give grounds for believing that serious or repeated infringements have been committed which cannot be detected in the course of that check in the absence of the necessary data, the competent authorities of the Contracting Parties concerned shall assist one another in order to clarify the situation.

1.8.3 Safety adviser

1.8.3.1 Each undertaking, the activities of which include the carriage, or the related packing, loading, filling or unloading, of dangerous goods by inland waterways shall appoint one or more safety advisers, hereinafter referred to as "advisers", for the carriage of dangerous goods, responsible for helping to prevent the risks inherent in such activities with regard to persons, property and the environment.

1.8.3.2 The competent authorities of the Contracting Parties may provide that these requirements shall not apply to undertakings:

(a) the activities of which concern quantities in each transport unit smaller than those referred to in 1.1.3.6, 2.2.7.1.2 and in Chapters 3.3 and 3.4; or

(b) the main or secondary activities of which are not the carriage or the related loading or unloading of dangerous goods but which occasionally engage in the national carriage or the related loading or unloading of dangerous goods posing little danger or risk of pollution.

1.8.3.3 The main task of the adviser shall be, under the responsibility of the head of the undertaking, to seek by all appropriate means and by all appropriate action, within the limits of the relevant activities of that undertaking, to facilitate the conduct of those activities in accordance with the requirements applicable and in the safest possible way.

With regard to the undertaking's activities, the adviser has the following duties in particular:

– monitoring compliance with the requirements governing the carriage of dangerous goods;

–   advising his undertaking on the carriage of dangerous goods;

–   preparing an annual report to the management of his undertaking or a local public authority, as appropriate, on the undertaking's activities in the carriage of dangerous goods. Such annual reports shall be preserved for five years and made available to the national authorities at their request.

The adviser's duties also include monitoring the following practices and procedures relating to the relevant activities of the undertaking:

–   the procedures for compliance with the requirements governing the identification of dangerous goods being transported;

–   the undertaking's practice in taking account, when purchasing means of transport, of any special requirements in connection with the dangerous goods being transported;

–   the procedures for checking the equipment used in connection with the carriage, loading or unloading of dangerous goods;

–   the proper training of the undertaking's employees and the maintenance of records of such training;

–   the implementation of proper emergency procedures in the event of any accident or incident that may affect safety during the carriage, loading or unloading of dangerous goods;

–   investigating and, where appropriate, preparing reports on serious accidents, incidents or serious infringements recorded during the carriage, loading or unloading of dangerous goods;

–   the implementation of appropriate measures to avoid the recurrence of accidents, incidents or serious infringements;

–   the account taken of the legal prescriptions and special requirements associated with the carriage of dangerous goods in the choice and use of sub-contractors or third parties;

–   verification that employees involved in the carriage, loading or unloading of dangerous goods have detailed operational procedures and instructions,

–   the introduction of measures to increase awareness of the risks inherent in the carriage, loading and unloading of dangerous goods;

–   the implementation of verification procedures to ensure the presence on board, means of transport of the documents and safety equipment which must accompany transport and the compliance of such documents and equipment with the regulations;

–   the implementation of verification procedures to ensure compliance with the requirements governing loading and unloading;

-   the existence of the security plan indicated in 1.10.3.2.

1.8.3.4   The safety adviser may also be the head of the undertaking, a person with other duties in the undertaking, or a person not directly employed by that undertaking, provided that that person is capable of performing the duties of adviser.

| 1.8.3.5 | Each undertaking concerned shall, on request, inform the competent authority or the body designated for that purpose by each Contracting Party of the identity of its adviser. |

| 1.8.3.6 | Whenever an accident affects persons, property or the environment or results in damage to property or the environment during carriage, loading or unloading carried out by the undertaking concerned, the safety adviser shall, after collecting all the relevant information, prepare an accident report to the management of the undertaking or to a local public authority, as appropriate. That report shall not replace any report by the management of the undertaking which might be required under any other international or national legislation. |

| 1.8.3.7 | A safety adviser shall hold a vocational training certificate, valid for transport by inland waterways. That certificate shall be issued by the competent authority or the body designated for that purpose by each Contracting Party. |

| 1.8.3.8 | To obtain a certificate, a candidate shall undergo training and pass an examination approved by the competent authority of the Contracting Party. |

| 1.8.3.9 | The main aims of the training shall be to provide candidates with sufficient knowledge of the risks inherent in the carriage of dangerous goods, of the laws, regulations and administrative provisions applicable to the modes of transport concerned and of the duties listed in 1.8.3.3. |

| 1.8.3.10 | The examination shall be organized by the competent authority or by an examining body designated by the competent authority. |

The examining body shall be designated in writing. This approval may be of limited duration and shall be based on the following criteria:

–   competence of the examining body;

–   specifications of the form of the examinations the examining body is proposing;

–   measures intended to ensure that examinations are impartial;

–   independence of the body from all natural or legal persons employing safety advisers.

| 1.8.3.11 | The aim of the examination is to ascertain whether candidates possess the necessary level of knowledge to carry out the duties incumbent upon a safety adviser as listed in 1.8.3.3, for the purpose of obtaining the certificate prescribed in subsection 1.8.3.7, and it shall cover at least the following subjects: |

(a)   Knowledge of the types of consequences which may be caused by an accident involving dangerous goods and knowledge of the main causes of accidents;

(b)   Requirements under national law, international conventions and agreements, with regard to the following in particular:

–   classification of dangerous goods (procedure for classifying solutions and mixtures, structure of the list of substances, classes of dangerous goods and principles for their classification, nature of dangerous goods transported, physical, chemical and toxicological properties of dangerous goods);

–   general packing provisions, provisions for tanks and tank-containers (types, code, marking, construction, initial and periodic inspection and testing);

–   marking and labelling, placarding and orange plates marking (marking and labelling of packages, placing and removal of placards and orange plates);

- particulars in transport documents (information required);

- method of consignment and restrictions on dispatch (full load, carriage in bulk, carriage in intermediate bulk containers, carriage in containers, carriage in fixed or demountable tanks);

- transport of passengers;

- prohibitions and precautions relating to mixed loading;

- segregation of goods;

- limitation of the quantities carried and quantities exempted;

- handling and stowage (loading and unloading - filling ratios -, stowage and segregation);

- cleaning and/or degassing before loading and after unloading;

- crews, vocational training;

- vehicle documents (transport document, instructions in writing, vessel approval certificate, ADN dangerous goods training certificate, copies of any derogations, other documents);

- instructions in writing (implementation of the instructions and crew protection equipment);

- supervision requirements (parking);

- traffic regulations and restrictions;

- operational discharges or accidental leaks of pollutants;

- requirements relating to equipment for transport by vessel.

1.8.3.12   The examination shall consist of a written test which may be supplemented by an oral examination.

The written examination shall consist of two parts:

(a)   Candidates shall receive a questionnaire. It shall include at least 20 open questions covering at least the subjects mentioned in the list in 1.8.3.11. However, multiple choice questions may be used. In this case, two multiple choice questions count as one open question. Amongst these subjects particular attention shall be paid to the following subjects:

- general preventive and safety measures;

- classification of dangerous goods;

- general packing provisions, including tanks, tank-containers, tank-vehicles, etc.;

- danger markings and labels;

- information in transport document;

- handling and stowage;

- crew, vocational training;

- vehicle documents and transport certificates;

- instructions in writing;

- requirements concerning equipment for transport by vessel;

(b) Candidates shall undertake a case study in keeping with the duties of the adviser referred to in 1.8.3.3, in order to demonstrate that they have the necessary qualifications to fulfil the task of adviser.

1.8.3.13 The Contracting Parties may decide that candidates who intend working for undertakings specializing in the carriage of certain types of dangerous goods need only be questioned on the substances relating to their activities. These types of goods are:

- Class 1;

- Class 2;

- Class 7;

- Classes 3, 4.1, 4.2, 4.3, 5.1, 5.2, 6.1, 6.2, 8 and 9;

- UN Nos. 1202, 1203 and 1223.

The certificate prescribed in 1.8.3.7 shall clearly indicate that it is only valid for one type of the dangerous goods referred to in this subsection and on which the adviser has been questioned under the conditions defined in 1.8.3.12.

1.8.3.14 The competent authority or the examining body shall keep a running list of the questions that have been included in the examination.

1.8.3.15 The certificate prescribed in 1.8.3.7 shall take the form laid down in 1.8.3.18 and shall be recognized by all Contracting Parties.

1.8.3.16 *Validity and renewal of certificates*

1.8.3.16.1 The certificate shall be valid for five years. The period of the validity of a certificate shall be extended from the date of its expiry for five years at a time where, during the year before its expiry, its holder has passed an examination. The examination shall be approved by the competent authority.

1.8.3.16.2 The aim of the examination is to ascertain that the holder has the necessary knowledge to carry out the duties set out in 1.8.3.3. The knowledge required is set out in 1.8.3.11 (b) and shall include the amendments to the regulations introduced since the award of the last certificate. The examination shall be held and supervised on the same basis as in 1.8.3.10 and 1.8.3.12 to 1.8.3.14. However, holders need not undertake the case study specified in 1.8.3.12 (b).

1.8.3.17 The requirements set out in 1.8.3.1 to 1.8.3.16 shall be considered to have been fulfilled if the relevant conditions of Council Directive 96/35/EC of 3 June 1996 on the appointment and vocational qualification of safety advisers for the transport of dangerous goods by road, rail and inland waterway [1] and of Directive 2000/18/EC of the European Parliament and of the Council of 17 April 2000 on minimum examination requirements for safety advisers for the transport of dangerous goods by road, rail or inland waterway [2] are applied.

---

[1]   *Official Journal of the European Communities, No. L145 of 19 June 1996, page 10.*

[2]   *Official Journal of the European Communities, No. L118 of 19 May 2000, page 41.*

1.8.3.18   *Form of certificate*

Certificate of training as safety adviser for the transport of dangerous goods

Certificate No: ....

Distinguishing sign of the State issuing the certificate: ....

Surname: ....

Forename(s): ....

Date and place of birth: ....

Nationality: ....

Signature of holder: ....

Valid until .... for undertakings which transport dangerous goods and for undertakings which carry out related loading or unloading:

☐ by road   ☐ by rail   ☐ by inland waterway

Issued by: ....

   Date:..   Signature: ....

   Extended until: : ....   By: ....

   Date: ....   Signature: ....

1.8.4   **List of competent authorities and bodies designated by them**

The Contracting Parties shall communicate to the Secretariat of the United Nations Economic Commission for Europe the addresses of the authorities and bodies designated by them which are competent in accordance with national law to implement ADN, referring in each case to the relevant requirement of ADN and giving the addresses to which the relevant applications should be made.

The secretariat of the United Nations Economic Commission for Europe shall establish a list on the basis of the information received and shall keep it up-to-date. It shall communicate this list and the amendments thereto to the Contracting Parties.

1.8.5   **Notifications of occurrences involving dangerous goods**

1.8.5.1   If a serious accident or incident takes place during the carriage of dangerous goods on the territory of a Contracting Party, the carrier is required to make a report to the competent authority of the Contracting Party concerned.

1.8.5.2   The Contracting Party shall in turn, if necessary, make a report to the secretariat of the United Nations Economic Commission for Europe with a view to informing the other Contracting Parties.

1.8.5.3   *An occurrence subject to report* in accordance with 1.8.5.1 has occurred if dangerous goods were released or if there was an imminent risk of loss of product, if personal injury, material or environmental damage occurred, or if the authorities were involved and one or more of the following criteria has/have been met:

Personal injury means an occurrence in which death or injury directly relating to the dangerous goods carried has occurred, and where the injury

(a)   requires intensive medical treatment,

(b)   requires a stay in hospital of at least one day, or

(c)   results in the inability to work for at least three consecutive days.

Loss of product means the release of dangerous goods

(a)   substances of Classes 1 or 2 or packing group I in quantities of 50 kg or 50 litres or more, or other substances not assigned to a packing group;

(b)   substances of packing group II in quantities of 333 kg or 333 litres or more; or

(c)   substances of packing group III in quantities of 1,000 kg or 1,000 litres or more.

The loss of product criterion also applies if there was an imminent risk of loss of product in the above-mentioned quantities. As a rule, this has to be assumed if, owing to structural damage, the means of containment is no longer suitable for further carriage or if, for any other reason, a sufficient level of safety is no longer ensured (e.g. owing to distortion of tanks or containers, overturning of a tank or fire in the immediate vicinity).
If dangerous goods of Class 6.2 are involved, the obligation to report applies without quantity limitation.

In occurrences involving Class 7 material, the criteria for loss of product are:

(a)   Any release of radioactive material from the packages;

(b)   Exposure leading to a breach of the limits set out in the regulations for protection of workers and members of the public against ionizing radiation (Schedule II of IAEA Safety Series No. 115 – "International Basic Safety Standards for Protection Against Ionizing Radiation and for Safety of Radiation Sources"); or

(c)   Where there is reason to believe that there has been a significant degradation in any package safety function (containment, shielding, thermal protection or criticality) that may have rendered the package unsuitable for continued carriage without additional safety measures.

NOTE: *See the provisions of 7.5.11 CV33 (6) of ADR or of 7.5.11 CW33 (6) of RID for undeliverable consignments.*

Material damage or *environmental damage* means the release of dangerous goods, irrespective of the quantity, where the estimated amount of damage exceeds 50,000 Euros. Damage to any directly involved means of carriage containing dangerous goods and to the modal infrastructure shall not be taken into account for this purpose.

Involvement of authorities means the direct involvement of the authorities or emergency services during the occurrence involving dangerous goods and the evacuation of persons or closure of public traffic routes (roads/railways) for at least three hours owing to the danger posed by the dangerous goods.

If necessary, the competent authority may request further relevant information.

1.8.5.4   The Contracting Parties may establish a standard format for these reports.

CHAPTER 1.9

TRANSPORT RESTRICTIONS BY THE COMPETENT AUTHORITIES

1.9.1   In accordance with Article 6, paragraph 1 of ADN, the entry of dangerous goods into the territory of Contracting Parties may be subject to regulations or prohibitions imposed for reasons other than safety during carriage. Such regulations or prohibitions shall be published in an appropriate form.

1.9.2   Subject to the provisions of 1.9.3, a Contracting Party may apply to vessels engaged in the international carriage of dangerous goods by inland waterways on its territory certain additional provisions not included in ADN, provided that those provisions do not conflict with Article 4, paragraph 2 of the Agreement, and are contained in its domestic legislation applying equally to vessels engaged in the domestic carriage of dangerous goods by inland waterways on the territory of that Contracting Party.

1.9.3   Additional provisions falling within the scope of 1.9.2 are as follows:

(a)   Additional safety requirements or restrictions concerning vessels using certain structures such as bridges or tunnels, or vessels entering or leaving ports or other transport terminals;

(b)   Requirements for vessels to follow prescribed routes to avoid commercial or residential areas, environmentally sensitive areas, industrial zones containing hazardous installations or inland waterways presenting severe physical hazards;

(c)   Emergency requirements regarding routeing or parking of vessels carrying dangerous goods resulting from extreme weather conditions, earthquake, accident, industrial action, civil disorder or military hostilities;

(d)   Restrictions on movement of vessels carrying dangerous goods on certain days of the week or year.

1.9.4   The competent authority of the Contracting Party applying on its territory any additional provisions within the scope of 1.9.3 (a) and (d) above shall notify the secretariat of the United Nations Economic Commission for Europe of the additional provisions, which secretariat shall bring them to the attention of the Contracting Parties.

CHAPTER 1.10

SECURITY PROVISIONS

NOTE: *For the purposes of this Chapter, "security" means measures or precautions to be taken to minimise theft or misuse of dangerous goods that may endanger persons, property or the environment.*

1.10.1   General provisions

1.10.1.1   All persons engaged in the carriage of dangerous goods shall consider the security requirements set out in this Chapter commensurate with their responsibilities.

1.10.1.2   Dangerous goods shall only be offered for carriage to carriers that have been appropriately identified.

1.10.1.3   Areas within temporary storage terminals, temporary storage sites, vehicle depots, berthing areas and marshalling yards used for the temporary storage during carriage of dangerous goods shall be properly secured, well lit and, where possible and appropriate, not accessible to the general public.

1.10.1.4   Each crew member of a vessel carrying dangerous goods shall carry with them means of identification, which includes their photograph, during carriage.

1.10.1.5   (Reserved)

1.10.1.6   The competent authority shall maintain up-to-date registers of all valid training certificates for experts stipulated in 8.2.1 issued by it or by any recognized organization.

1.10.2   Security training

1.10.2.1   The training and the refresher training specified in Chapter 1.3 shall also include elements of security awareness. The security refresher training need not be linked to regulatory changes only.

1.10.2.2   Security awareness training shall address the nature of security risks, recognising security risks, methods to address and reduce such risks and actions to be taken in the event of a security breach. It shall include awareness of security plans (if appropriate) commensurate with the responsibilities and duties of individuals and their part in implementing security plans.

1.10.3   Provisions for high consequence dangerous goods

1.10.3.1   "High consequence dangerous goods" are those which have the potential for misuse in a terrorist incident and which may, as a result, produce serious consequences such as mass casualties or mass destruction. The list of high consequence dangerous goods is provided in Table 1.10.5.

1.10.3.2   *Security plans*

1.10.3.2.1   Carriers, consignors and other participants specified in 1.4.2 and 1.4.3 engaged in the carriage of high consequence dangerous goods (see Table 1.10.5) shall adopt, implement and comply with a security plan that addresses at least the elements specified in 1.10.3.2.2.

1.10.3.2.2   The security plan shall comprise at least the following elements:

(a) specific allocation of responsibilities for security to competent and qualified persons with appropriate authority to carry out their responsibilities;

(b) records of dangerous goods or types of dangerous goods concerned;

(c) review of current operations and assessment of security risks, including any stops necessary to the transport operation, the keeping of dangerous goods in the vessel, tank or container before, during and after the journey and the intermediate temporary storage of dangerous goods during the course of intermodal transfer or transshipment between units;

(d) clear statement of measures that are to be taken to reduce security risks, commensurate with the responsibilities and duties of the participant, including:

- training;

- security policies (e.g. response to higher threat conditions, new employee/employment verification, etc.);

- operating practices (e.g. choice/use of routes where known, access to dangerous goods in intermediate temporary storage (as defined in (c)), proximity to vulnerable infrastructure etc.);

- equipment and resources that are to be used to reduce security risks;

(e) effective and up to date procedures for reporting and dealing with security threats, breaches of security or security incidents;

(f) procedures for the evaluation and testing of security plans and procedures for periodic review and update of the plans;

(g) measures to ensure the physical security of transport information contained in the security plan; and

(h) measures to ensure that the distribution of information relating to the transport operation contained in the security plan is limited to those who need to have it. Such measures shall not preclude the provision of information required elsewhere in ADN.

NOTE: Carriers, consignors and consignees should co-operate with each other and with competent authorities to exchange threat information, apply appropriate security measures and respond to security incidents.

1.10.3.3   Devices, equipment or arrangements to prevent the theft of the vessel carrying high consequence dangerous goods (see Table 1.10.5) or its cargo, shall be applied and measures taken to ensure that these are operational and effective at all times. The application of these protective measures shall not jeopardize emergency response.

NOTE: When appropriate and already fitted, the use of transport telemetry or other tracking methods or devices should be used to monitor the movement of high consequence dangerous goods (see Table 1.10.5).

1.10.4   The requirements of 1.10.1, 1.10.2 and 1.10.3 do not apply when the quantities carried in packages on a vessel do not exceed those referred to in 1.1.3.6.1.

1.10.5   High consequence dangerous goods are those listed in the table below and carried in quantities greater than those indicated therein.

Table 1.10.5: List of high consequence dangerous goods

Class	Division	Substance or article	Quantity		
			Tank (*l*)	Bulk (kg)	Packages (kg)
1	1.1	Explosives	a	a	0
	1.2	Explosives	a	a	0
	1.3	Compatibility group C explosives	a	a	0
	1.5	Explosives	0	a	0
2		Flammable gases (classification codes including only letter F)	3000	a	b
		Toxic gases (classification codes including letters T, TF, TC, TO, TFC or TOC) excluding aerosols	0	a	0
3		Flammable liquids of packing groups I and II	3000	a	b
		Desensitized explosives	a	a	0
4.1		Desensitized explosives	a	a	0
4.2		Packing group I substances	3000	a	b
4.3		Packing group I substances	3000	a	b
5.1		Oxidizing liquids of packing group I	3000	a	b
		Perchlorates, ammonium nitrate and ammonium nitrate fertilizers	3000	3000	b
6.1		Toxic substances of packing group I	0	a	0
6.2		Infectious substances of Category A	a	a	0
7		Radioactive material	3000 A_1 (special form) or 3000 A_2, as applicable, in Type B or Type C packages		
8		Corrosive substances of packing group I	3000	a	b

a   *Not relevant.*

b   *The provisions of 1.10.3 do not apply, whatever the quantity is.*

NOTE: *For purposes of non-proliferation of nuclear material the Convention on Physical Protection of Nuclear Material applies to international transport supported by IAEA INFCIRC/225 (Rev.4).*

CHAPTERS 1.11 to 1.14

(Reserved)

CHAPTER 1.15

RECOGNITION OF CLASSIFICATION SOCIETIES

1.15.1　　**General**

In the event of the conclusion of an international agreement concerning more general regulations or the navigation of vessels on inland waterways and containing provisions relating to the full range of activities of classification societies and their recognition, any provision of this Chapter in contradiction with any of the provisions of the said international agreement would, in the relations among Parties to this Agreement which had become parties to the international agreement and as from the day of the entry into force of the latter, automatically be deleted and replaced ipso facto by the relevant provision of the international agreement. This Chapter would become null and void once the international agreement came into force if all Parties to this Agreement became Parties to the international agreement.

1.15.2　　**Procedure for the recognition of classification societies**

1.15.2.1　　A classification society which wishes to be recommended for recognition under this Agreement shall submit its application for recognition, in accordance with the provisions of this Chapter, to the competent authority of a Contracting Party.

The classification society shall prepare the relevant information in accordance with the provisions of this Chapter. It shall produce it in, at least, an official language of the State where the application is submitted and in English.

The Contracting Party shall forward the application to the Administrative Committee unless in its opinion the conditions and criteria referred to in 1.15.3 have manifestly not been met.

1.15.2.2　　The Administrative Committee shall appoint a Committee of Experts and determine its composition and its rules of procedure. This Committee of Experts shall consider the proposal; it shall determine whether the classification society meets the criteria set out in 1.15.3 and shall make a recommendation to the Administrative Committee within a period of six months.

1.15.2.3　　The Administrative Committee shall examine the report of the experts. It shall decide in accordance with the procedure set out in Article 17, 7(c), within one year maximum, whether or not to recommend to the Contracting Parties that they should recognize the classification society in question. The Administrative Committee shall establish a list of the classification societies recommended for recognition by the Contracting Parties.

1.15.2.4　　Each Contracting Party may or may not decide to recognize the classification societies in question, only on the basis of the list referred to in 1.15.2.3. The Contracting Party shall inform the Administrative Committee and the other Contracting Parties of its decision.

The Administrative Committee shall update the list of recognitions issued by Contracting Parties.

1.15.2.5　　If a Contracting Party considers that a classification society no longer meets the conditions and criteria set out in 1.15.3, it may submit a proposal to the Administrative Committee for withdrawal from the list of recommended societies. Such a proposal shall be substantiated by convincing evidence of a failure to meet the conditions and criteria.

1.15.2.6	The Administrative Committee shall set up a new Committee of Experts following the procedure set out under 1.15.2.2 which shall report to the Administrative Committee within a period of six months.

1.15.2.7	The Administrative Committee may decide, according to Article 17, 7 (c), to withdraw the name of the society in question from the list of societies recommended for recognition.

In such a case the society in question shall immediately be so informed. The Administrative Committee shall also inform all the Contracting Parties that the classification society in question no longer meets the requirements to act as a recognized classification society in the context of the Agreement and shall invite them to take the necessary steps in order to remain in conformity with the requirements of the Agreement.

1.15.3 **Conditions and criteria for the recognition of a classification society applying for recognition under this Agreement**

A classification society applying for recognition under this Agreement shall meet all the following conditions and criteria:

1.15.3.1	A classification society shall be able to demonstrate extensive knowledge of and experience in the assessment of the design and construction of inland navigation vessels. The society should have comprehensive rules and regulations for the design, construction and periodical inspection of vessels. These rules and regulations shall be published and continuously updated and improved through research and development programmes.

1.15.3.2	Registers of the vessels classified by the classification society shall be published annually.

1.15.3.3	The classification society shall not be controlled by shipowners or shipbuilders, or by others engaged commercially in the manufacture, fitting out, repair or operation of ships. The classification society shall not be substantially dependent on a single commercial enterprise for its revenue.

1.15.3.4	The headquarters or a branch of the classification society authorized and entitled to give a ruling and to act in all areas incumbent on it under the regulations governing inland navigation shall be located in one of the Contracting Parties.

1.15.3.5	The classification society and its experts shall have a good reputation in inland navigation; the experts shall be able to provide proof of their professional abilities.

1.15.3.6	The classification society:

– shall have sufficient professional staff and engineers for the technical tasks of monitoring and inspection and for the tasks of management, support and research, in proportion to the tasks and the number of vessels classified and sufficient to keep regulations up to date and develop them in the light of quality requirements;

– shall have experts in at least two Contracting Parties.

1.15.3.7	The classification society shall be governed by a code of ethics.

1.15.3.8	The classification society shall have prepared and implemented and shall maintain an effective system of internal quality based on the relevant aspects of internationally recognized quality standards and conforming to the standards EN: 45004:1995 (control mechanisms) and ISO 9001 or EN 29001:1997. The classification society is subject to certification of its quality system by an independent body of auditors recognized by the administration of the State in which it is located.

1.15.4 Obligations of recommended classification societies

1.15.4.1   Recommended classification societies shall undertake to cooperate with each other so as to guarantee the equivalence of their technical standards and their implementation.

1.15.4.2   Recommended classification societies shall undertake to bring their requirements into line with the present and future provisions of this Agreement.

CHAPTER 1.16

PROCEDURE FOR THE ISSUE OF THE CERTIFICATE OF APPROVAL

1.16.1   **Certificate of approval**

1.16.1.1   *General*

1.16.1.1.1   Dry cargo vessels carrying dangerous goods in quantities greater than exempted quantities, the vessels referred to in 7.1.2.19.1, tank vessels carrying dangerous goods and the vessels referred to in 7.2.2.19.3 shall be provided with an appropriate certificate of approval.

1.16.1.1.2   The certificate of approval shall be valid for not more than five years, subject to the provisions of 1.16.11.

1.16.1.2   **Format of the certificate of approval, particulars to be included**

1.16.1.2.1   The certificate of approval shall conform to the model 8.6.1.1 or 8.6.1.3 and include the required particulars, as appropriate. It shall include the date of expiry of the period of validity.

1.16.1.2.2   The certificate of approval shall attest that the vessel has been inspected and has its construction and equipment comply with the applicable provisions of Part 9 of ADN.

1.16.1.2.3   All particulars for amendments to the certificate of approval provided for in these Regulations and in the other regulations drawn up by mutual agreement by the Contracting Parties may be entered in the certificate by the competent authority.

1.16.1.2.4   The competent authority shall include the following particulars in the certificate of approval of double-hull vessels meeting the additional requirements of 9.1.0.80 to 9.1.0.95 or 9.2.0.80 to 9.2.0.95:

"The vessel meets the additional requirements for double-hull vessels of 9.1.0.80 to 9.1.0.95" or "The vessel meets the additional requirements for double-hull vessels of 9.2.0.80 to 9.2.0.95."

1.16.1.2.5   For tank vessels, the certificate of approval must be supplemented by a list of all the dangerous goods accepted for carriage in the tank vessel, drawn up by the recognized classification society which has classified the vessel.

1.16.1.2.6   When the competent authority issues a certificate of approval for tank vessels, it shall also issue a first loading journal.

1.16.1.3   **Provisional certificate of approval**

1.16.1.3.1   For a vessel which is not provided with a certificate of approval, a provisional certificate of approval of limited duration may be issued in the following cases, subject to the following conditions:

(a)   The vessel complies with the applicable provisions of these Regulations, but the normal certificate of approval could not be issued in time. The provisional certificate of approval shall be valid for an appropriate period but not exceeding three months;

(b)   The vessel does not comply with every applicable provision of these Regulations after sustaining damage. In this case the provisional certificate of approval shall be valid only for a single specified voyage and for a specified cargo. The competent authority may impose additional conditions.

1.16.1.3.2 The provisional certificate of approval shall conform to the model in 8.6.1.2 or 8.6.1.4 or a single model certificate combining a provisional certificate of inspection and the provisional certificate of approval provided that the single model certificate contains the same information as the model in 8.6.1.2 or 8.6.1.4 and is approved by the competent authority.

1.16.2 Issue and recognition of certificates of approval

1.16.2.1 The certificate of approval referred to in 1.16.1 shall be issued by the competent authority of the Contracting Party where the vessel is registered, or in its absence, of the Contracting Party where it has its home port or, in its absence, of the Contracting Party where the owner is domiciled or in its absence, by the competent authority selected by the owner or his representative.

The other Contracting Parties shall recognize such certificates of approval.

The period of validity shall not exceed five years subject to the provisions of 1.16.10.

1.16.2.2 The competent authority of any of the Contracting Parties may request the competent authority of any other Contracting Party to issue a certificate of approval in its stead.

1.16.2.3 The competent authority of any of the Contracting Parties may delegate the authority to issue the certificate of approval to an inspection body as defined in 1.16.4.

1.16.2.4 The provisional certificate of approval referred to in 1.16.1.3 shall be issued by the competent authority of one of the Contracting Parties for the cases and under the conditions referred to in these Regulations.

The other Contracting Parties shall recognize such provisional certificates of approval.

1.16.3 Inspection procedure

1.16.3.1 The competent authority of the Contracting Party shall supervise the inspection of the vessel. Under this procedure, the inspection may be performed by an inspection body designated by the Contracting Party or by a recognized classification society. The inspection body or the recognized classification society shall issue an inspection report certifying that the vessel conforms partially or completely to the provisions of these Regulations.

1.16.3.2 This inspection report shall be drawn up in a language accepted by the competent authority and shall contain all the necessary information to enable the certificate to be drawn up.

1.16.4 Inspection body

1.16.4.1 Inspection bodies shall be subject to recognition by the Contracting Party administration as expert bodies on the construction and inspection of inland navigation vessels and as expert bodies on the transport of dangerous goods by inland waterway. They shall meet the following criteria:

– Compliance by the body with the requirements of impartiality;

– Existence of a structure and personnel that provide objective evidence of the professional ability and experience of the body;

–	Compliance with the material contents of standard EN 45004:1995 supported by detailed inspection procedures.

1.16.4.2   Inspection bodies may be assisted by experts (e.g. an expert in electrical installations) or specialized bodies according to the national provisions applicable (e.g. classification societies).

1.16.4.3   The Administrative Committee shall maintain an up-to-date list of the inspection bodies appointed.

1.16.5   Application for the issue of a certificate of approval

The owner of a vessel, or his representative, who requests a certificate of approval, shall deposit an application with the competent authority referred to in 1.16.2.1. The competent authority shall specify the documents to be submitted to it. In order to obtain a certificate of approval a valid vessel certificate shall accompany the request.

1.16.6   Particulars entered in the certificate of approval and amendments thereto

1.16.6.1   The owner of a vessel, or his representative, shall inform the competent authority of any change in the name of the vessel or change of official number or registration number and shall transmit to it the certificate of approval for amendment.

1.16.6.2   All amendments to the certificate of approval provided for in these Regulations and in the other regulations drawn up by mutual agreement by the Contracting Parties may be entered in the certificate by the competent authority.

1.16.6.3   When the owner of the vessel, or his representative, has the vessel registered in another Contracting Party, he shall request a new certificate of approval from the competent authority of that Contracting Party. The competent authority may issue the new certificate for the remaining period of validity of the existing certificate without making a new inspection of the vessel, provided that the state and the technical specifications of the vessel have not undergone any modification.

1.16.7   Presentation of the vessel for inspection

1.16.7.1   The owner, or his representative, shall present the vessel for inspection unladen, cleaned and equipped; he shall be required to provide such assistance as may be necessary for the inspection, such as providing a suitable launch and personnel, and uncovering those parts of the hull or installations which are not directly accessible or visible.

1.16.7.2   In the case of a first, special or periodical inspection, the inspection body or the recognized classification society may require a dry-land inspection.

1.16.8   First inspection

If a vessel does not yet have a certificate of approval or if the validity of the certificate of approval expired more than six months ago, the vessel shall undergo a first inspection.

1.16.9   Special inspection

If the vessel's hull or equipment has undergone alterations liable to diminish safety in respect of the carriage of dangerous goods, or has sustained damage affecting such safety, the vessel shall be presented without delay by the owner or his representative for further inspection.

1.16.10   **Periodic inspection and renewal of the certificate of approval**

1.16.10.1   To renew the certificate of approval, the owner of the vessel, or his representative, shall present the vessel for a periodic inspection. The owner of the vessel or his representative may request an inspection at any time.

1.16.10.2   If the request for a periodic inspection is made during the last year preceding the expiry of the validity of the certificate of approval, the period of validity of the new certificate shall commence when the validity of the preceding certificate of approval expires.

1.16.10.3   A periodic inspection may also be requested during a period of six months after the expiry of the certificate of approval.

1.16.10.4   The competent authority shall establish the period of validity of the new certificate of approval on the basis of the results of the inspection.

1.16.11   **Extension of the certificate of approval without an inspection**

By derogation from 1.16.10, at the substantiated request of the owner or his representative, the competent authority may grant an extension of the validity of the certificate of approval of not more than one year without an inspection. This extension shall be granted in writing and shall be kept on board the vessel. Such extensions may be granted only once every two validity periods.

1.16.12   **Official inspection**

1.16.12.1   If the competent authority of a Contracting Party has reason to assume that a vessel which is in its territory may constitute a danger in relation to the transport of dangerous goods, for the persons on board or for shipping or for the environment, it may order an inspection of the vessel in accordance with 1.16.3.

1.16.12.2   When exercising this right to inspect, the authorities will make all possible efforts to avoid unduly detaining or delaying a vessel. Nothing in this Agreement affects rights relating to compensation for undue detention or delay. In any instance of alleged undue detention or delay the burden of proof shall lie with the owner or operator of the vessel.

1.16.13   **Withholding and return of the certificate of approval**

1.16.13.1   The certificate of approval may be withdrawn if the vessel is not properly maintained or if the vessel's construction or equipment no longer complies with the applicable provisions of these Regulations.

1.16.13.2   The certificate of approval may only be withdrawn by the authority by which it has been issued.

Nevertheless, in the cases referred to in 1.16.2.1 to 1.16.9 above, the competent authority of the State in which the vessel is staying may prohibit its use for the carriage of those dangerous goods for which the certificate is required. For this purpose it may withdraw the certificate until such time as the vessel again complies with the applicable provisions of these Regulations. In that case it shall notify the competent authority which issued the certificate.

1.16.13.3   Notwithstanding 1.16.2.2 above, any competent authority may amend or withdraw the certificate of approval at the request of the vessel's owner, provided that it so notifies the competent authority which issued the certificate.

1.16.13.4   When an inspection body or a classification society observes, in the course of an inspection, that a vessel or its equipment suffers from serious defects in relation to dangerous goods which might jeopardize the safety of the persons on board or the safety of shipping, or constitute a hazard for the environment, it shall immediately notify the competent authority to which it answers with a view to a decision to withhold the certificate.

If this authority which decided to withdraw the certificate is not the authority which issued the certificate, it shall immediately inform the latter and, where necessary, return the certificate to it if it presumes that the defects cannot be eliminated in the near future.

1.16.13.5   When the inspection body or the classification society referred to in 1.16.13.1 above ascertains, by means of a special inspection according to 1.16.9, that these defects have been remedied, the certificate of approval shall be returned by the competent authority to the owner or to his representative.

This inspection may be made at the request of the owner or his representative by another inspection body or another classification society. In this case, the certificate of approval shall be retuned through the competent authority to which the inspection body or the classification society answers.

1.16.13.6   When a vessel is finally immobilized or scrapped, the owner shall send the certificate of approval back to the competent authority which issued it.

1.16.14   Duplicate copy

In the event of the loss, theft or destruction of the certificate of approval or when it becomes unusable for other reasons, an application for a duplicate copy, accompanied by appropriate supporting documents, shall be made to the competent authority which issued the certificate.

This authority shall issue a duplicate copy of the certificate of approval, which shall be designated as such.

1.16.15   Register of certificates of approval

1.16.15.1   The competent authorities shall assign a serial number to the certificates of approval which they issue. They shall keep a register of all the certificates issued.

1.16.15.2   The competent authorities shall keep copies of all the certificates which they have issued and enter all particulars and amendments in them, as well as cancellations and replacements of certificates.

PART 2

Classification

(See Volume II)

PART 3

Dangerous goods list, special provisions and exemptions related to dangerous goods packed in limited quantities

CHAPTER 3.1

GENERAL

(See Volume II)

CHAPTER 3.2

LIST OF DANGEROUS GOODS

3.2.1   **Table A: List of dangerous goods in numerical order**

See Volume II

3.2.1   **Table B: List of dangerous goods in alphabetical order**

See Volume II

3.2.3   **Table C: List of dangerous goods accepted for carriage in tank vessels in numerical order**

Explanations concerning Table C:

As a rule, each row of Table C of this Chapter deals with the substance(s) covered by a specific UN number or identification number. However, when substances belonging to the same UN number or identification number have different chemical properties, physical properties and/or carriage conditions, several consecutive rows may be used for that UN number or identification number.

Each column of Table C is dedicated to a specific subject as indicated in the explanatory notes below. The intersection of columns and rows (cell) contains information concerning the subject treated in that column, for the substance(s) of that row:

–   The first four cells identify the substance(s) belonging to that row;

–   The following cells give the applicable special provisions, either in the form of complete information or in coded form. The codes cross-refer to detailed information that is to be found in the numbers indicated in the explanatory notes below. An empty cell means either that there is no special provision and that only the general requirements apply, or that the carriage restriction indicated in the explanatory notes is in force.

The applicable general requirements are not referred to in the corresponding cells.

Explanatory notes for each column:

Column (1)   "UN number/identification number"

Contains the UN number or identification number:

–   of the dangerous substance if the substance has been assigned its own specific UN number or identification number, or

–   of the generic or n.o.s. entry to which the dangerous substances not mentioned by name shall be assigned in accordance with the criteria ("decision trees") of Part 2.

Column (2)   "Name and description"

Contains, in upper case characters, the name of the substance, if the substance has been assigned its own specific UN number or identification number or of the generic or n.o.s. entry to which the dangerous substances have been assigned in accordance with the criteria ("decision trees") of Part 2. This name shall be used as the proper shipping name or, when applicable, as part of the proper shipping name (see 3.1.2 for further details on the proper shipping name).

A descriptive text in lower case characters is added after the proper shipping name to clarify the scope of the entry if the classification or carriage conditions of the substance may be different under certain conditions.

Column (3a) "Class"

Contains the number of the Class, whose heading covers the dangerous substance. This Class number is assigned in accordance with the procedures and criteria of Part 2.

Column (3b) "Classification code"

Contains the classification code of the dangerous substance.

– For dangerous substances of Class 2, the code consists of a number and one or more letters representing the hazardous property group, which are explained in 2.2.2.1.2 and 2.2.2.1.3.

– For dangerous substances or articles of Classes 3, 4.1, 4.2, 4.3, 5.1, 5.2, 6.1, 6.2, 8 and 9, the codes are explained in 2.2.x.1.2. [1]

Column (4) "Packing group"

Contains the packing group number(s) (I, II or III) assigned to the dangerous substance. These packing group numbers are assigned on the basis of the procedures and criteria of Part 2. Certain substances are not assigned to packing groups.

Column (5) "Labels"

This column contains information concerning the hazards inherent in the dangerous substance. They are included on the basis of the danger labels of Table A, column (5). In the case of a chemically unstable substance the code "unst." is added to the information.

Column (6) "Type of tank vessel"

Contains the type of tank vessel: G, C or N.

Column (7) "Cargo tank design"

Contains information concerning the design of the cargo tank:

1 Pressure cargo tank

2 Closed cargo tank

---

[1] x = *the Class number of the dangerous substance or article, without dividing point if applicable.*

	3	Open cargo tank with flame arrester
	4	Open cargo tank

Column (8)   "Cargo tank type"

Contains information concerning the cargo tank type.

1   Independent cargo tank

2   Integral cargo tank

3   Cargo tank with walls distinct from the outer hull

Column (9)   "Cargo tank equipment"

Contains information concerning the cargo tank equipment.

1   Refrigeration system

2   Heating system

3   Water-spray system

Column (10)   "Opening pressure of high-velocity vent valve in kPa"

Contains information concerning the opening pressure of the high-velocity vent valve in kPa.

Column (11)   "Maximum degree of filling (%)"

Contains information concerning the maximum degree of filling of cargo tanks as a percentage.

Column (12)   "Relative density"

Contains information concerning the relative density of the substance at 20° C. Data concerning the density are for information only.

Column (13)   "Type of sampling device"

Contains information concerning the prescribed type of sampling device.

1   Closed sampling device

2   Partly closed sampling device

3   Open sampling device

Column (14)	"Pump-room below deck permitted"

Contains an indication of whether a pump-room is permitted below deck.

Yes   pump-room below deck permitted

No   pump-room below deck not permitted

Column (15)	"Temperature class"

Contains the temperature class of the substance.

Column (16)	"Explosion group"

Contains the explosion group of the substance.

Column (17)	"Anti-explosion protection required"

Contains a code referring to protection against explosions.

Yes   anti-explosion protection required

No   anti-explosion protection not required

Column (18)	"Equipment required"

This column contains the alphanumeric codes for the equipment required for the carriage of the dangerous substance (see 8.1.5).

Column (19)	"Number of cones/blue lights"

This column contains the number of cones/lights which should constitute the marking of the vessel during the carriage of this dangerous substance or article.

Column (20)	"Additional requirements/Remarks"

This column contains the additional requirements or remarks applicable to the vessel.

These additional requirements or remarks are:

1. Anhydrous ammonia is liable to cause stress crack corrosion in cargo tanks and cooling systems constructed of carbon-manganese steel or nickel steel.

    In order to minimize the risk of stress crack corrosion the following measures shall be taken:

    (a) Where carbon-manganese steel is used, cargo tanks, pressure vessels of cargo refrigeration systems and cargo piping shall be constructed of fine-grained steel having a specified minimum yield stress of not more than 355 N/mm^2. The actual yield stress shall not exceed 440 N/mm^2. In addition, one of the following construction or operational measures shall be taken:

.1 Material with a low tensile strength ($R_m < 410$ N/mm^2) shall be used; or

.2 Cargo tanks, etc., shall undergo a post-weld heat treatment for the purpose of stress relieving; or

.3 The transport temperature shall preferably be maintained close to the evaporation temperature of the cargo of -33° C, but in no case above -20° C; or

.4 Ammonia shall contain not less than 0.1 % water, by mass.

(b) When carbon-manganese steel with yield stress values higher than those referred to in (a) above is used, the completed tanks, pipe sections, etc., shall undergo a post-weld heat treatment for the purpose of stress relieving.

(c) Pressure vessels of the cargo refrigeration systems and the piping systems of the condenser of the cargo refrigeration system constructed of carbon-manganese steel or nickel steel shall undergo a post-weld heat treatment for the purpose of stress relieving.

(d) The yield stress and the tensile strength of welding consumables may exceed only by the smallest value possible the corresponding values of the tank and piping material.

(e) Nickel steels containing more than 5 % nickel and carbon-manganese steel which are not in compliance with the requirements of (a) and (b) above may not be used for cargo tanks and piping systems intended for the transport of this substance.

(f) Nickel steels containing not more than 5 % nickel may be used if the transport temperature is within the limits referred to in (a) above.

(g) The concentration of oxygen dissolved in the ammonia shall not exceed the values given in the table below:

t in °C	O$_2$ in %, by volume
-30 and below	0.90
-20	0.50
-10	0.28
0	0.16
10	0.10
20	0.05
30	0.03

2. Before loading, air shall be removed and subsequently kept away to a sufficient extent from the cargo tanks and the accessory cargo piping by the means of inert gas (see also 7.2.4.18).

3.	Arrangements shall be made to ensure that the cargo is sufficiently stabilized in order to prevent a reaction at any time during carriage. The transport document shall contain the following additional particulars:

(a)	Name and amount of inhibitor added;

(b)	Date on which inhibitor was added and expected duration of effectiveness under normal conditions;

(c)	Any temperature limits having an effect on the inhibitor.

When stabilization is ensured solely by blanketing with an inert gas it is sufficient to mention the name of the inert gas used in the transport document.

When stabilization is ensured by another measurement, e.g. the special purity of the substance, this measurement shall be mentioned in the transport document.

4.	The substance shall not be allowed to solidify; the transport temperature shall be maintained above the melting point. In instances where cargo heating installations are required, they must be so designed that polymerisation through heating is not possible in any part of the cargo tank. Where the temperature of steam-heated coils could give rise to overheating, lower-temperature indirect heating systems shall be provided.

5.	This substance is liable to clog the vapour pipe and its fittings. Careful surveillance should be ensured. If a close-type tank vessel is required for the carriage of this substance the vapour pipe shall conform to 9.3.2.22.5 (a) (i), (ii), (iv), (v), (b), (c) or (d) or to 9.3.3.22.5 (a) (i), (ii), (iv), (b), (c) or (d). This requirement does not apply when the cargo tanks are inerted in accordance with 7.2.4.18 nor when protection against explosions is not required in column (17) and when flame-arresters have not been installed.

6.	When external temperatures are below or equal to that indicated in column (20), the substance may only be carried in tank vessels meeting the following conditions:

The tank vessels shall be equipped with a cargo heating system conforming to 9.3.2.42 or 9.3.3.2. The arrangement of heating coils inside the cargo tanks instead of a cargo heating system may be sufficient (possibility of heating the cargo).

In addition, in the event of carriage in a closed-type vessel, if the tank vessel:

–	is fitted out in accordance with 9.3.2.22.5 (a) (i) or (d) or 9.3.3.22.5 (a) (i) or (d), it shall be equipped with pressure/vacuum valves capable of being heated; or

–	is fitted out in accordance with 9.3.2.22.5 (a) (ii), (v), (b) or (c) or 9.3.3.22.5 (a) (ii), (v), (b) or (c), it shall be equipped with heatable vapour pipes and heatable pressure/vacuum valves; or

— is fitted out in accordance with 9.3.2.22.5 (a) (iii) or (iv) or 9.3.3.22.5 (a) (iii) or (iv), it shall be equipped with heatable vapour pipes and with heatable pressure/vacuum valves and heatable flame-arresters.

The temperature of the vapour pipes, pressure/vacuum valves and flame-arresters shall be kept at least above the melting point of the substance.

7. If a closed-type tank vessel is required to carry this substance or if the substance is carried in a closed-type tank vessel, if this vessel:

— is fitted out in accordance with 9.3.2.22.5 (a) (i) or (d) or 9.3.3.22.5 (a) (i) or (d), it shall be equipped with heatable pressure/vacuum valves, or

— is fitted out in accordance with 9.3.2.22.5 (a) (ii), (v), (b) or (c) or 9.3.3.22.5 (a) (ii), (v), (b) or (c), it shall be equipped with heatable vapour pipes and heatable pressure/vacuum valves, or

— is fitted out in accordance with 9.3.2.22.5 (a) (iii) or (iv) or 9.3.3.22.5 (a) (iii) or (iv), it shall be equipped with heatable vapour pipes and with heatable pressure/vacuum valves and heatable flame-arresters.

The temperature of the vapour pipes, pressure/vacuum valves and flame-arresters shall be kept at least above the melting point of the substance.

8. Double-hull spaces, double bottoms and heating coils shall not contain any water.

9. (a) While the vessel is underway, an inert-gas pad shall be maintained in the ullage space above the liquid level.

(b) Cargo piping and vent lines shall be independent of the corresponding piping used for other cargoes.

(c) Safety valves shall be made of stainless steel.

10. *(Reserved)*

11. (a) Stainless steel of type 416 or 442 and cast iron shall not be used for cargo tanks and pipes for loading and unloading.

(b) The cargo may be discharged only by deep-well pumps or pressure inert gas displacement. Each cargo pump shall be arranged to ensure that the substance does not heat significantly if the pressure discharge line from the pump is shut off or otherwise blocked.

(c)   The cargo shall be cooled and maintained at temperatures below 30° C.

(d)   The safety valves shall be set at a pressure of not less than 550 kPa (5.5 bar) gauge pressure. Special authorization is required for the maximum setting pressure.

(e)   While the vessel is underway, a nitrogen pad shall be maintained in the ullage space above the cargo (see also 7.2.4.18). An automatic nitrogen supply system shall be installed to prevent the pressure from falling below 7 kPa (0.07 bar) gauge within the cargo tank in the event of a cargo temperature fall due to ambient temperature conditions or to some other reason. In order to satisfy the demand of the automatic pressure control a sufficient amount of nitrogen shall be available on board. Nitrogen of a commercially pure quality of 99.9 %, by volume, shall be used for padding. A battery of nitrogen cylinders connected to the cargo tanks through a pressure reduction valve satisfies the intention of the expression "automatic" in this context.

The required nitrogen pad shall be such that the nitrogen concentration in the vapour space of the cargo tank is not less than 45 % at any time.

(f)   Before loading and while the cargo tank contains this substance in a liquid or gaseous form, it shall be inerted with nitrogen.

(g)   The water-spray system shall be fitted with remote-control devices which can be operated from the wheelhouse or from the control station, if any.

(h)   Transfer arrangements shall be provided for emergency transfer of ethylene oxide in the event of an uncontrollable self-reaction.

12.   (a)   The substance shall be acetylene free.

(b)   Cargo tanks which have not undergone appropriate cleaning shall not be used for the carriage of these substances if one of the previous three cargoes consisted of a substance known to promote polymerisation, such as:

.1   mineral acids (e.g. sulphuric acid, hydrochloric acid, nitric acid);

.2   carboxylic acids and anhydrides (e.g. formic acid, acetic acid);

.3   halogenated carboxylic acids (e.g. chloroacetic acid);

.4   sulphonic acids (e.g. benzen sulphonic acid);

.5   caustic alkalis (e.g. sodium hydroxide, potassium hydroxide);

.6   ammonia and ammonia solutions;

.7   amines and amine solutions;

.8   oxidizing substances.

(c)   Before loading, cargo tanks and their piping shall be efficiently and thoroughly cleaned so as to eliminate all traces of previous cargoes, except when the last cargo was constituted of propylene oxide or a mixture of ethylene oxide and propylene oxide. Special precautions shall be taken in the case of ammonia in cargo tanks built of steel other than stainless steel.

(d)   In all cases the efficiency of the cleaning of cargo tanks and their piping shall be monitored by means of appropriate tests or inspections to check that no trace of acid or alkaline substance remains that could present a danger in the presence of these substances.

(e)   The cargo tanks shall be entered and inspected prior to each loading of these substances to ensure freedom from contamination, heavy rust deposits or visible structural defects.

When these cargo tanks are in continuous service for these substances, such inspections shall be performed at intervals of not more than two and a half years.

(f)   Cargo tanks which have contained these substances may be reused for other cargoes once they and their piping have been thoroughly cleaned by washing and flushing with an inert gas.

(g)   Substances shall be loaded and unloaded in such a way that there is no release of gas into the atmosphere. If gas is returned to the shore installation during loading, the gas return system connected to the tank containing that substance shall be independent from all other cargo tanks.

(h)   During discharge operations, the pressure in the cargo tanks shall be maintained above 7 kPa (0.07 bar) gauge.

(i)   The cargo shall be discharged only by deep-well pumps, hydraulically operated submerged pumps or pressure inert gas displacement. Each cargo pump shall be arranged to ensure that the substance does not heat significantly if the pressure discharge line from the pump is shut off or otherwise blocked.

(j)   Each cargo tank carrying these substances shall be ventilated by a system independent from the ventilation systems of other cargo tanks carrying other substances.

(k)   Loading pipes used for these substances shall be marked as follows:

"To be used only for the transfer of alkylene oxide."

(l)   Cargo tanks, cofferdams, double-hull spaces, double bottoms, cargo tank spaces adjacent to a cargo tank carrying this substance shall either contain compatible cargo (the substances mentioned under (b) are examples of substances considered to be incompatible) or be inerted with an appropriate inert gas. Spaces so inerted shall be monitored for these substances and oxygen. The oxygen content shall be maintained below 2 %, by volume. Portable measuring devices are permitted.

(m)   No air shall be allowed to enter the cargo pumps and cargo piping system while these substances are contained within the system.

(n)   Before the shore connections are disconnected, piping containing liquids or gas shall be depressurised at the shore link by means of appropriate devices.

(o)   The piping system for cargo tanks to be loaded with these substances shall be separate from piping system for all other cargo tanks, including empty cargo tanks. If the piping system for the cargo tanks to be loaded is not independent, separation shall be accomplished by the removal of spool pieces, shut-off valves, other pipe sections and by fitting blank flanges at these locations. The required separation applies to all liquid pipes and vapour vent lines and any other connections which may exist such as common inert gas supply lines.

(p)   These substances may be carried only in accordance with cargo handling plans that have been approved by a competent authority.

Each loading arrangement shall be shown on a separate cargo handling plan. Cargo handling plans shall show the entire cargo piping system and the locations for installations of blank flanges needed to meet the above piping separation requirements. A copy of each cargo handling plan shall be kept on board. Reference to the approved cargo handling plans shall be included in the certificate of approval.

(q)   Before loading of these substances and before carriage is resumed a qualified person approved by the competent authority shall certify that the prescribed separation of the piping has been effected; this certificate shall be kept on board. Each connection between a blank flange and a shut-off valve in the piping shall be fitted with a sealed wire to prevent the flange from being disassembled inadvertently.

(r)   During the voyage, the cargo shall be covered with nitrogen. An automatic nitrogen make-up system shall be installed to prevent the cargo tank pressure from falling below 7 kPa (0.07 bar) gauge in the event of a cargo temperature fall due to ambient temperature conditions or to some other reason. Sufficient nitrogen shall be available on board to satisfy the demand of automatic pressure control. Nitrogen of commercially pure quality of 99.9 %, by volume, shall be used for padding. A battery of nitrogen cylinders connected to the cargo tanks through a pressure reduction valve satisfies the intention of the expression "automatic" in this context.

(s) The vapour space of the cargo tanks shall be checked before and after each loading operation to ensure that the oxygen content is 2 %, by volume, or less.

(t) Loading flow

The loading flow (L_R) of cargo tank shall not exceed the following value:

$$L_R = 3600 \times U/t \ (m^3/h)$$

In this formula:

U = the free volume (m^3) during loading for the activation of the overflow prevention system;

T = the time (s) required between the activation of the overflow prevention system and the complete stop of the flow of cargo into the cargo tank;

The time is the sum of the partial times needed for successive operations, e.g. reaction time of the service personnel, the time needed to stop the pumps and the time needed to close the shut-off valves;

The loading flow shall also take account of the design pressure of the piping system.

13. If no stabilizer is supplied or if the supply is inadequate, the oxygen content in the vapour phase shall not exceed 0.1 %. Overpressure must be constantly maintained in cargo tanks. This requirement applies also to voyages on ballast or empty with uncleaned cargo tanks between cargo transport operations.

14. The following substances may not be carried under these conditions:

– substances with self-ignition temperatures $\leq$200 °C;

– mixtures containing halogenated hydrocarbons;

– mixtures containing more than 10 % benzene;

– substances and mixtures carried in a stabilized state.

15. Provision shall be made to ensure that alkaline or acidic substances such as sodium hydroxide solution or sulphuric acid do not contaminate this cargo.

16. If there is a possibility of a dangerous reaction such as polymerisation, decomposition, thermal instability or evolution of gases resulting from local overheating of the cargo in either the cargo tank or associated piping system, this cargo shall be loaded and carried adequately segregated from other substances the temperature of which is sufficiently high to initiate such reaction. Heating coils inside cargo tanks carrying this substance shall be blanked off or secured by equivalent means.

17. The melting point of the cargo shall be shown in the transport documents.

18. *(Reserved)*

19. Provision shall be made to ensure that the cargo does not come into contact with water. The following additional requirements apply:

    Carriage of the cargo is not permitted in cargo tanks adjacent to slop tanks or cargo tanks containing ballast water, slops or any other cargo containing water. Pumps, piping and vent lines connected to such tanks shall be separated from similar equipment of tanks carrying these substances. Pipes from slop tanks or ballast water pipes shall not pass through cargo tanks containing this cargo unless they are encased in a tunnel.

20. The maximum permitted transport temperature given in column (20) shall not be exceeded.

21. *(Reserved)*

22. The relative density of the cargo shall be shown in the transport document.

23. The instrument for measuring the pressure of the vapour phase in the cargo tank shall activate the alarm when the internal pressure reaches 40 kPa. The water-spray system shall immediately be activated and remain in operation until the internal pressure drops to 30 kPa.

24. Substances having a flash-point above 61 °C which are handed over for carriage or which are carried heated within a limiting range of 15 K below their flash-point shall be carried under the conditions of substance number 9001.

25. Type 3 cargo tank may be used for the carriage of this substance provided that the construction of the cargo tank has been accepted by a recognized classification society for the maximum permitted transport temperature.

26. Type 2 cargo tank may be used for the carriage of this substance provided that the construction of the cargo tank has been accepted

by a recognized classification society for the maximum permitted transport temperature.

27. The requirements of 3.1.2.8.1 are applicable.

28. (a) When this substance is carried, the forced ventilation of the cargo tanks shall be brought into service at latest when the concentration of hydrogen sulphide reaches 1.0 %, by volume.

    (b) When during the carriage of this substance, the concentration of hydrogen sulphide exceeds 1.85 %, the boat master shall immediately notify the nearest competent authority.

    When a significant increase in the concentration of hydrogen sulphide in a hold space leads it to be supposed that the sulphur has leaked, the cargo tanks shall be unloaded as rapidly as possible. A new load may only be taken on board once the authority which issued the certificate of approval has carried out a further inspection.

    (c) When this substance is carried, the concentration of hydrogen sulphide shall be measured in the vapour phase of the cargo tanks and concentrations of sulphur dioxide and hydrogen sulphide in the hold spaces.

    (d) The measurements prescribed in (c) shall be made every eight hours. The results of the measurements shall be recorded in writing.

29. When particulars concerning the vapour pressure or the boiling point are given in column (2), the relevant information shall be added to the proper shipping name in the transport document, e.g.

    UN 1224 KETONES, LIQUID, N.O.S.,
    110 kPa < vp 50 < 175 kPa or

    UN 2929 TOXIC LIQUID, FLAMMABLE, ORGANIC, N.O.S.,
    boiling point < 60° C

30. When these substances are carried, the hold spaces of open type N tank vessels may contain auxiliary equipment.

31. When these substances are carried, the vessel shall be equipped with a rapid blocking valve placed directly on the shore connection.

32. In the case of transport of this substance, the following additional requirements are applicable:

    (a) The outside of the cargo tanks should be equipped with insulation of low flammability. This insulation should be strong enough to resist shocks and vibration. Above deck, the insulation should be protected by a covering.

The outside temperature of this covering should not exceed 70 °C.

(b)   The spaces containing the cargo tanks should be provided with ventilation. Connections for forced ventilation should be fitted.

(c)   The cargo tanks should be equipped with forced ventilation installations which, in all transport conditions, will reliably keep the concentration of hydrogen sulphide above the liquid phase below 1.85 % by volume.

The ventilation installations should be fitted in such a way as to prevent the deposit of the goods to be transported.

The exhaust line of the ventilation should be fitted in such a way as not to present a risk to personnel.

(d)   The cargo tank and the hold spaces should be fitted with outlets and piping to allow gas sampling.

(e)   The outlets of the cargo tanks should be situated at a height such that for a trim of 2° and a list of 10°, no sulphur can escape. All the outlets should be situated above the deck in the open air. Each outlet should be equipped with a satisfactory fixed closing mechanism.

One of these mechanisms should be capable of being opened for slight overpressure within the tank.

(f)   The pipes for loading and unloading should be equipped with adequate insulation. They should be capable of being heated.

(g)   The heat transfer fluid should be such that in the event of a leak into a tank, there is no risk of a dangerous reaction with the sulphur.

33.   The following provisions are applicable to transport of this substance:

Construction requirements:

(a)   Hydrogen peroxide solutions may be transported only in cargo tanks equipped with deep-well pumps.

(b)   Cargo tanks and their equipment should be constructed of solid stainless steel of a type appropriate to hydrogen peroxide solutions (for example, 304, 304L, 316, 316L or 316 Ti). None of the non-metallic materials used for the system of cargo tanks should be attacked by hydrogen peroxide solutions or cause the decomposition of the substance.

(c)   The temperature sensors should be installed in the cargo tanks directly under the deck and at the bottom. Remote temperature read-outs and monitoring should be provided for in the wheelhouse.

(d) Fixed oxygen monitors (or gas-sampling lines) should be provided in the areas adjacent to the cargo tanks so that leaks in such areas can be detected. Account should be taken of the increased flammability arising from the increased presence of oxygen. Remote read-outs, continuous monitoring (if the sampling lines are used, intermittent monitoring will suffice) and visible and audible alarms similar to those for the temperature sensors should also be located in the wheelhouse. The visible and audible alarms should be activated if the oxygen concentration in these void spaces exceeds 30 % by volume. Two additional oxygen monitors should also be available.

(e) The cargo tank venting systems which are equipped with filters should be fitted with pressure/vacuum relief valves appropriate to closed-circuit ventilation and with an extraction installation should cargo tank pressure rise rapidly as a result of an uncontrolled breakdown (see under m). These air supply and extraction systems should be so designed that water cannot enter the cargo tanks. In designing the emergency extraction installation account should be taken of the design pressure and the size of the cargo tanks.

(f) A fixed water-spray system should be provided for diluting and washing away any hydrogen peroxide solutions spilled onto the deck. The area covered by the jet of water should include the shore connections and the deck containing the cargo tanks designated for carrying hydrogen peroxide solutions.

The following minimum requirements should be complied with:

.1 The product should be diluted from the original concentration to a 35 % concentration within five minutes from the spillage on the deck;

.2 The rate and estimated size of the spill should be determined in the light of the maximum permissible loading or unloading rates, the time required to halt the spillage in the event of tank overfill or a piping/hose failure, and the time necessary to begin application of dilution water with actuation at the cargo control location or in the wheelhouse.

(g) The outlets of the pressure valves should be situated at least 2.00 metres from the walkways if they are less than 4.00 metres from the walkway.

(h) A temperature sensor should be installed by each pump to make it possible to monitor the temperature of the cargo during unloading and detect any overheating due to defective operation of the pump.

Servicing requirements:

Shipper

(i) Hydrogen peroxide solutions may only be carried in cargo tanks which have been thoroughly cleaned and passivated, in accordance with the procedure described under (j), of all traces of previous cargoes, their vapours or their ballast waters. A certificate stating that the procedure described under (j) has been duly complied with must be carried on board.

Particular care in this respect is essential to ensure the safe carriage of hydrogen peroxide solutions:

.1 When a hydrogen peroxide solution is being carried, no other cargo may be carried simultaneously;

.2 Tanks which have contained hydrogen peroxide solutions may be reused for other cargoes after they have been cleaned by persons or companies approved for this purpose by the competent authority;

.3 In the design of the cargo tanks, efforts must be made to keep to a minimum any internal tank structure, to ensure free draining, no entrapment and ease of visual inspection.

(j) Procedures for inspection, cleaning, passivation and loading for the transport of hydrogen peroxide solutions with a concentration of 8-60 per cent in cargo tanks which have previously carried other cargoes.

Before their reuse for the transport of hydrogen peroxide solutions, cargo tanks which have previously carried cargoes other than hydrogen peroxide must be inspected, cleaned and passivated. The procedures described in paragraphs .1 to .7 below for inspection and cleaning apply to stainless steel cargo tanks. The procedure for passivating stainless steel is described in paragraph .8. Failing any other instructions, all the measures apply to cargo tanks and to all their structures which have been in contact with other cargoes.

.1 After offloading of the previous cargo, the cargo tank must be degassed and inspected for any remaining traces, carbon residues and rust.

.2 The cargo tanks and their equipment must be washed with clear filtered water. The water used must be at least of the same quality as drinking water and have a low chlorine content.

.3 Traces of the residues and vapours of the previous cargo must be removed by the steam cleaning of the cargo tanks and their equipment.

.4 The cargo tanks and their equipment must then be rewashed with clear water of the quality specified in paragraph 2 above and dried in filtered, oil-free air.

.5 Samples must be taken of the atmosphere in the cargo tanks and these must be analysed for their content of organic gases and oxygen.

.6 The cargo tank must be reinspected for any traces of the previous cargo, carbon residues or rust or odours of the previous cargo.

.7 If the inspection and the other measures point to the presence of traces of the previous cargo or of its gases, the measures described in paragraphs .2 to .4 above must be repeated.

.8 Stainless steel cargo tanks and their structures which have contained cargoes other than hydrogen peroxide solutions and which have been repaired must, regardless whether or not they have previously been passivated, be cleaned and passivated in accordance with the following procedure:

.8.1 The new weld seams and other repaired parts must be cleaned and scrubbed with stainless steel brushes, graving tools, sandpaper and polishers. Rough surfaces must be made smooth and a final polishing must be carried out;

.8.2 Fatty and oily residues must be removed with the use of organic solvents or appropriate cleaning products diluted with water. The use of chlorinated products should be avoided because these might seriously interfere with the passivation procedure;

.8.3 Any residues of the product that have been removed must be eliminated and the tanks must then be washed.

(k) During the transfer of the hydrogen peroxide solutions, the related piping system must be separated from all other systems. Cargo hoses used for the transfer of hydrogen peroxide solutions must be marked as follows:

"Uniquement pour le transbordement de peroxydes d'hydrogène en solution"
"For Hydrogen Peroxide Solution Transfer only"

(l)   If the temperature in the cargo tanks rises above 35 °C, visible and audible alarms should activate on the navigating bridge.

Master

(m)   If the temperature rise exceeds 4 °C for 2 hours or if the temperature in the cargo tanks exceeds 40 °C, the master must contact the consignor directly, with a view to taking any action that might be necessary.

Filler

(n)   Hydrogen peroxide solutions must be stabilized to prevent decomposition. The manufacturer must provide a stabilization certificate which must be carried on board and must specify:

.1   The disintegration date of the stabilizer and the duration of its effectiveness;

.2   Actions to be taken should the product become unstable during the voyage.

(o)   Only those hydrogen peroxide solutions which have a maximum decomposition rate of 1.0 per cent per year at 25 °C may be carried. A certificate from the shipper stating that the product meets this standard must be presented to the master and kept on board.

An authorized representative of the manufacturer must be on board to monitor the transfer operations and to test the stability of the hydrogen peroxide solutions to be transported. He should certify to the master that the cargo has been loaded in a stable condition.

34.   The flanges and stuffing boxes of the loading and unloading hoses must be fitted with a protection device to protect against splashing.

(1) UN No. or substance identification No.	(2) Name and description	(3a) Class	(3b) Classification code	(4) Packing group	(5) Labels	(6) Type of tank vessel	(7) Cargo tank design	(8) Cargo tank type	(9) Cargo tank equipment	(10) Opening pressure of the high-velocity vent valve in kPa	(11) Maximum degree of filling in %	(12) Relative density at 20 °C	(13) Type of sampling device	(14) Pump room below deck permitted	(15) Temperature class	(16) Explosion group	(17) Anti-explosion protection required	(18) Equipment required	(19) Number of cones/blue lights	(20) Additional requirements/Remarks
1005	AMMONIA, ANHYDROUS	2	2TC		2.3+8	G	1	1	3		91		1		T1	II A	yes	PP, EP, EX, TOX, A	2	1; 31
1010	1,2-BUTADIENE, STABILIZED, having a vapour pressure at 70 °C not exceeding 1.1 MPa (11 bar) and a density at 50 °C not lower than 0.525 kg/l	2	2F		2.1+unst.	G	1	1			91		1	yes	T2	II B[4]	yes	PP, EX, A	1	2; 3; 31
1010	1,3-BUTADIENE, STABILIZED, having a vapour pressure at 70 °C not exceeding 1.1 MPa (11 bar) and a density at 50 °C not lower than 0.525 kg/l	2	2F		2.1+unst.	G	1	1			91		1	yes	T2	II B	yes	PP, EX, A	1	2; 3; 31
1010	MIXTURES OF 1,3-BUTADIENE AND HYDROCARBONS, STABILIZED, having a vapour pressure at 70 °C not exceeding 1.1 MPa (11 bar) and a density at 50 °C not lower than 0.525 kg/l	2	2F		2.1+unst.	G	1	1			91		1	yes	T2	II B	yes	PP, EX, A	1	2; 3; 31
1011	BUTANE	2	2F		2.1	G	1	1			91		1	yes	T2	II A	yes	PP, EX, A	1	31
1012	1-BUTYLENE	2	2F		2.1	G	1	1			91		1	yes	T2	II A	yes	PP, EX, A	1	31
1020	CHLOROPENTAFLUORO-ETHANE (REFRIGERANT GAS R 115)	2	2A		2.2	G	1	1			91		1	yes			no	PP	0	31
1030	1,1-DIFLUOROETHANE (REFRIGERANT GAS R 152a)	2	2F		2.1	G	1	1			91		1	yes	T1	II A	yes	PP, EX, A	1	31
1033	DIMETHYL ETHER	2	2F		2.1	G	1	1			91		1	yes	T3	II B	yes	PP, EX, A	1	31
1038	ETHYLENE, REFRIGERATED LIQUID	2	3F		2.1	G	1	1	1		95	0.57	1	no	T1	II B	yes	PP, EX, A	1	31
1040	ETHYLENE OXIDE WITH NITROGEN up to a total pressure of 1 MPa (10 bar) at 50 °C	2	2TF		2.3+2.1	G	1	1			91		1	no	T2	II B	yes	PP, EP, EX, TOX, A	2	2; 3; 11; 31
1055	ISOBUTYLENE	2	2F		2.1	G	1	1			91		1	yes	T2[1]	II A	yes	PP, EX, A	1	31

(1) UN No. or substance identification No.	(2) Name and description	(3a) Class	(3b) Classification code	(4) Packing group	(5) Labels	(6) Type of tank vessel	(7) Cargo tank design	(8) Cargo tank type	(9) Cargo tank equipment	(10) Opening pressure of the high-velocity vent valve in kPa	(11) Maximum degree of filling in %	(12) Relative density at 20 °C	(13) Type of sampling device	(14) Pump room below deck permitted	(15) Temperature class	(16) Explosion group	(17) Anti-explosion protection required	(18) Equipment required	(19) Number of cones/blue lights	(20) Additional requirements/Remarks
1063	METHYL CHLORIDE (REFRIGERANT GAS R 40)	2	2F		2.1	G	1	1			91		1	yes	T1	II A	yes	PP, EX, A	1	31
1077	PROPYLENE	2	2F		2.1	G	1	1			91		1	yes	T1	II A	yes	PP, EX, A	1	31
1083	TRIMETHYLAMINE, ANHYDROUS	2	2F		2.1	G	1	1			91		1	yes	T4	II A	yes	PP, EX, A	1	31
1086	VINYL CHLORIDE, STABILIZED	2	2F		2.1+unst.	G	1	1			91		1	yes	T2	II A	yes	PP, EX, A	1	2; 3; 13; 31
1088	ACETAL	3	F1	II	3	N	2	2		10	97	0.83	3	yes	T3	II B[4]	yes	PP, EX, A	1	
1089	ACETALDEHYDE (ethanal)	3	F1	I	3	C	1	1			95	0.78	1	yes	T4	II A	yes	PP, EX, A	1	
1090	ACETONE	3	F1	II	3	N	2	2		10	97	0.79	3	yes	T1	II A	yes	PP, EX, A	1	
1092	ACROLEINE, STABILIZED	6.1	TF1	I	6.1+3+unst.	C	2	2	3	50	95	0.84	1	no	T3[2]	II B	yes	PP, EP, EX, TOX, A	2	2; 3; 5; 23
1093	ACRYLONITRILE, STABILIZED	3	FT1	I	3+6.1+unst.	C	2	2	3	50	95	0.8	1	no	T1	II B	yes	PP, EP, EX, TOX, A	2	3; 5; 23
1098	ALLYL ALCOHOL	6.1	TF1	I	6.1+3	C	2	2		40	95	0.85	1	no	T2	II B	yes	PP, EP, EX, TOX, A	2	
1100	ALLYL CHLORIDE	3	FT1	I	3+6.1	C	2	2	3	50	95	0.94	1	no	T2	II A	yes	PP, EP, EX, TOX, A	2	23
1105	PENTANOLS (n-pentanol)	3	F1	III	3	N	3	2			97	0.81	3	yes	T2	II A	yes	PP, EX, A	0	
1106	AMYLAMINE (n-amylamine)	3	FC	II	3+8	C	2	2		40	95	0.76	2	yes	T4[3]	II A[7]	yes	PP, EP, EX, A	1	
1107	AMYL CHLORIDES (1-chloropentane)	3	F1	II	3	C	2	2		40	95	0.88	2	yes	T3	II A	yes	PP, EX, A	1	
1107	AMYL CHLORIDES (1-chloro-3-methylbutane)	3	F1	II	3	C	2	2		45	95	0.89	2	yes	T3	II A	yes	PP, EX, A	1	
1107	AMYL CHLORIDES (2-chloro-2-methylbutane)	3	F1	II	3	C	2	2		50	95	0.87	2	yes	T2	II A	yes	PP, EX, A	1	

(1)	(2)	3 (a)	3 (b)	(4)	(5)	(6)	(7)	(8)	(9)	(10)	(11)	(12)	(13)	(14)	(15)	(16)	(17)	(18)	(19)	(20)
1107	AMYL CHLORIDES (1-chloro-2,2-dimethylpropane)	3	F1	II	3	C	2	2		50	95	0.87	2	yes	T3[2]	II A	yes	PP, EX, A	1	
1107	AMYL CHLORIDES	3	F1	II	3	C	1	1			95	0.9	1	yes	T3[2]	II A	yes	PP, EX, A	1	27
1108	1-PENTENE (n-AMYLENE)	3	F1	I	3	N	1	1			97	0.64	1	yes	T3	II B[4]	yes	PP, EX, A	1	
1114	BENZENE	3	F1	II	3	C	2	2	3	50	95	0.88	2	yes	T1	II A	yes	PP, EP, EX, TOX, A	1	6: +10 °C; 17; 23
1120	BUTANOLS (tert-butyl alcohol)	3	F1	II	3	N	2	2	2	10	97	0.79	3	yes	T1	II A[7]	yes	PP, EX, A	1	7; 17
1120	BUTANOLS (sec-butyl alcohol)	3	F1	III	3	N	3	2			97	0.81	3	yes	T2	II B[7]	yes	PP, EX, A	0	
1120	BUTANOLS (n-butyl alcohol)	3	F1	III	3	N	3	2		10	97	0.81	3	yes	T2	II B	yes	PP, EX, A	0	
1123	BUTYL ACETATES (sec-butyl acetate)	3	F1	II	3	N	2	2			97	0.86	3	yes	T2	II A[7]	yes	PP, EX, A	1	
1123	BUTYL ACETATES (sec-butyl acetate)	3	F1	III	3	N	3	2			97	0.86	3	yes	T2	II A	yes	PP, EX, A	0	
1125	n-BUTYLAMINE	3	FC	II	3+8	C	2	2	3	50	95	0.75	2	yes	T2	II A	yes	PP, EP, EX, A	1	23
1127	CHLOROBUTANES (1-chlorobutane)	3	F1	II	3	C	2	2	3	50	95	0.89	2	yes	T3	II A	yes	PP, EX, A	1	23
1127	CHLOROBUTANES (2-chlorobutane)	3	F1	II	3	C	2	2	3	50	95	0.87	2	yes	T4[3]	II A	yes	PP, EX, A	1	23
1127	CHLOROBUTANES (1-chloro-2-methylpropane)	3	F1	II	3	C	2	2	3	50	95	0.88	2	yes	T4[3]	II A	yes	PP, EX, A	1	23
1127	CHLOROBUTANES (2-chloro-2-methylpropane)	3	F1	II	3	C	2	2	3	50	95	0.84	2	yes	T1	II A	yes	PP, EX, A	1	23
1127	CHLOROBUTANES	3	F1	II	3	C	1	1			95	0.89	1	yes	T4[3]	II A	yes	PP, EX, A	1	27
1129	BUTYRALDEHYDE (n-butyraldehyde)	3	F1	II	3	C	2	2	3	50	95	0.8	2	yes	T4	II A	yes	PP, EX, A	1	15; 23
1131	CARBON DISULPHIDE (carbon sulphide)	3	FT1	I	3+6.1	C	2	2	3	50	95	1.26	1	no	T6	II C	yes	PP, EP, EX, TOX, A	2	2; 9; 23

(1) UN No. or substance identification No.	(2) Name and description	(3a) Class	(3b) Classification code	(4) Packing group	(5) Labels	(6) Type of tank vessel	(7) Cargo tank design	(8) Cargo tank type	(9) Cargo tank equipment	(10) Opening pressure of the high-velocity vent valve in kPa	(11) Maximum degree of filling in %	(12) Relative density at 20 °C	(13) Type of sampling device	(14) Pump room below deck permitted	(15) Temperature class	(16) Explosion group	(17) Anti-explosion protection required	(18) Equipment required	(19) Number of cones/blue lights	(20) Additional requirements/Remarks
1134	CHLOROBENZENE (phenyl chloride)	3	F1	III	3	C	2	2		30	95	1.11	2	yes	T1	II A[8]	yes	PP, EX, A	0	
1135	ETHYLENE CHLOROHYDRIN (2-chloroethanol)	6.1	TFI	I	6.1+3	C	2	2		30	95	1.21	1	no	T2	II A[8]	yes	PP, EP, EX, TOX, A	2	
1143	CROTONALDEHYDE, STABILIZED	6.1	TFI	I	6.1+3+unst.	C	2	2		40	95	0.85	1	no	T3	II B	yes	PP, EP, EX, TOX, A	2	3; 5; 15
1145	CYCLOHEXANE	3	F1	II	3	N	2	2		10	97	0.78	3	yes	T3	II A	yes	PP, EX, A	1	6: +11 °C; 17
1146	CYCLOPENTANE	3	F1	II	3	N	2	2		10	97	0.75	3	yes	T2	II A	yes	PP, EX, A	1	
1150	1,2-DICHLOROETHYLENE (cis)	3	F1	II	3	C	2	2	3	50	95	1.28	2	yes	T2[1]	II A	yes	PP, EX, A	1	23
1150	1,2-DICHLOROETHYLENE (trans)	3	F1	II	3	C	2	2	3	50	95	1.26	2	yes	T2	II A	yes	PP, EX, A	1	23
1153	ETHYLENE GLYCOL DIETHYL ETHER	3	F1	III	3	N	3	2			97	0.84	3	yes	T4[3]	II B[8]	yes	PP, EX, A	0	
1154	DIETHYLAMINE	3	FC	II	3+8	C	2	2	3	50	95	0.7	2	yes	T2	II A	yes	PP, EP, EX, A	1	23
1155	DIETHYL ETHER (ETHYL ETHER)	3	F1	I	3	C	1	1			95	0.71	1	yes	T4	II B	yes	PP, EX, A	1	
1157	DIISOBUTYL KETONE	3	F1	III	3	N	3	2			97	0.81	3	yes	T4[3]	II B[8]	yes	PP, EX, A	0	
1159	DIISOPROPYL ETHER	3	F1	II	3	N	2	2		10	97	0.72	3	yes	T2	II A	yes	PP, EX, A	1	
1160	DIMETHYLAMINE AQUEOUS SOLUTION	3	FC	II	3+8	C	2	2	3	50	95	0.82	2	yes	T2	II B[8]	yes	PP, EP, EX, A	1	23
1163	DIMETHYLHYDRAZINE, UNSYMMETRICAL	6.1	TFC	I	6.1+3+8	C	2	2	3	50	95	0.78	1	no	T3	II B[4]	yes	PP, EP, EX, TOX, A	2	23
1165	DIOXANE	3	F1	II	3	N	2	2		10	97	1.03	3	yes	T2	II B	yes	PP, EX, A	1	6: +14 °C; 17
1167	DIVINYL ETHER, STABILIZED	3	F1	I	3+unst.	C	1	1			95	0.77	1	yes	T2	II B[7]	yes	PP, EX, A	1	2; 3
1170	ETHANOL (ETHYL ALCOHOL)	3	F1	II	3	N	2	2		10	97	0.79 - 0.87	3	yes	T2	II B	yes	PP, EX, A	1	

(1) UN No. or substance identification No.	(2) Name and description	(3)(a) Class	(3)(b) Classification code	(4) Packing group	(5) Labels	(6) Type of tank vessel	(7) Cargo tank design	(8) Cargo tank type	(9) Cargo tank equipment	(10) Opening pressure of the high-velocity vent valve in kPa	(11) Maximum degree of filling in %	(12) Relative density at 20 °C	(13) Type of sampling device	(14) Pump room below deck permitted	(15) Temperature class	(16) Explosion group	(17) Anti-explosion protection required	(18) Equipment required	(19) Number of cones/blue lights	(20) Additional requirements/Remarks
1170	ETHANOL SOLUTION (ETHYL ALCOHOL SOLUTION) aqueous solution with more than 70 % alcohol by volume	3	F1	II	3	N	2	2		10	97	0.79 - 0.87	3	yes	T2	II B	yes	PP, EX, A	1	
1170	ETHANOL SOLUTION (ETHYL ALCOHOL SOLUTION) aqueous solution with more than 24 % and not more than 70 % alcohol by volume	3	F1	III	3	N	3	2			97	0.87 - 0.96	3	yes	T2	II B	yes	PP, EX, A	0	
1171	ETHYLENE GLYCOL MONOETHYL ETHER	3	F1	III	3	N	3	2			97	0.93	3	yes	T3	II B	yes	PP, EX, A	0	
1172	ETHYLENE GLYCOL MONOETHYL ETHER ACETATE	3	F1	III	3	N	3	2			97	0.98	3	yes	T2	II A	yes	PP, EX, A	0	
1173	ETHYL ACETATE	3	F1	II	3	N	2	2		10	97	0.9	3	yes	T1	II A	yes	PP, EX, A	1	
1175	ETHYLBENZENE	3	F1	II	3	N	2	2		10	97	0.87	3	yes	T2	II B	yes	PP, EX, A	1	
1177	2-ETHYLBUTYL ACETATE	3	F1	III	3	N	3	2			97	0.88	3	yes	T3	II A	yes	PP, EX, A	0	
1184	ETHYLENE DICHLORIDE (1,2-dichloroethane)	3	FT1	II	3+6.1	C	2	2		50	95	1.25	2	no	T2	II A	yes	PP, EP, EX, TOX, A	2	
1188	ETHYLENE GLYCOL MONOMETHYL ETHER	3	F1	III	3	N	3	2			97	0.97	3	yes	T3	II B	yes	PP, EX, A	0	
1191	OCTYL ALDEHYDES (2-ethylcapronaldehyde)	3	F1	III	3	C	2	2		30	95	0.82	2	yes	T4	II A	yes	PP, EX, A	0	
1191	OCTYL ALDEHYDES (n-octaldehyde)	3	F1	III	3	N	3	2			97	0.82	3	yes	T3	II B [4]	yes	PP, EX, A	0	
1193	ETHYL METHYL KETONE (METHYL ETHYL KETONE)	3	F1	II	3	N	2	2		10	97	0.8	3	yes	T1	II A	yes	PP, EX, A	1	
1198	FORMALDEHYDE SOLUTION, FLAMMABLE	3	FC	III	3+8	N	3	2			97	1.09	3	yes	T2	II B	yes	PP, EP, EX, A	0	34
1199	FURALDEHYDES (a-furfuraldehyde) or furfuraldehydes (a-furfurylaldehyde)	6.1	TF1	II	6.1+3	C	2	2		25	95	1.16	2	no	T3 [2]	II B	yes	PP, EP, EX, TOX, A	2	15

(1) UN No. or substance identification No.	(2) Name and description	3(a) Class	3(b) Classification code	(4) Packing group	(5) Labels	(6) Type of tank vessel	(7) Cargo tank design	(8) Cargo tank type	(9) Cargo tank equipment	(10) Opening pressure of the high-velocity vent valve in kPa	(11) Maximum degree of filling in %	(12) Relative density at 20 °C	(13) Type of sampling device	(14) Pump room below deck permitted	(15) Temperature class	(16) Explosion group	(17) Anti-explosion protection required	(18) Equipment required	(19) Number of cones/blue lights	(20) Additional requirements/Remarks
1202	GAS OIL or DIESEL FUEL or HEATING OIL, LIGHT	3	F1	III	3	N	4	2			97	0.74	3	yes			no	PP	0	
1203	MOTOR SPIRIT or GASOLINE or PETROL	3	F1	II	3	N	2	2		10	97	0.68 - 0.72[10]	3	yes	T3	II A	yes	PP, EX, A	1	14
1203	MOTOR SPIRIT or GASOLINE or PETROL, with more than 10 % benzene boiling point ≤ 60 °C	3	F1	II	3	C	1	1			95		1	yes	T3	II A	yes	PP, EX, A	1	29
1203	MOTOR SPIRIT or GASOLINE or PETROL with more than 10 % benzene 60 °C < boiling point ≤ 85 °C	3	F1	II	3	C	2	2	3	50	95		2	yes	T3	II A	yes	PP, EX, A	1	23; 29
1203	MOTOR SPIRIT or GASOLINE or PETROL with more than 10 % benzene 85 °C < boiling point ≤ 115 °C	3	F1	II	3	C	2	2		50	95		2	yes	T3	II A	yes	PP, EX, A	1	29
1203	MOTOR SPIRIT or GASOLINE or PETROL with more than 10 % benzene boiling point > 115 °C	3	F1	II	3	C	2	2		35	95		2	yes	T3	II A	yes	PP, EX, A	1	29
1206	HEPTANES (n-heptane)	3	F1	II	3	N	2	2		10	97	0.68	3	yes	T3	II A	yes	PP, EX, A	1	
1208	HEXANES (n-hexane)	3	F1	II	3	N	2	2		10	97	0.66	3	yes	T3	II A	yes	PP, EX, A	1	
1212	ISOBUTANOL (ISOBUTYL ALCOHOL)	3	F1	III	3	N	3	2			97	0.8	3	yes	T2	II A	yes	PP, EX, A	0	
1213	ISOBUTYL ACETATE	3	F1	II	3	N	2	2		10	97	0.87	3	yes	T2	II A[7]	yes	PP, EX, A	1	
1214	ISOBUTYLAMINE	3	FC	II	3+8	C	2	2	3	50	95	0.73	2	yes	T2	II A	yes	PP, EP, EX, A	1	23
1216	ISOOCTENE	3	F1	II	3	N	2	2		10	97	0.73	3	yes	T3	II B[4]	yes	PP, EX, A	1	
1218	ISOPRENE, STABILIZED	3	F1	I	3+unst.	N	1	1			95	0.68	1	yes	T3	II B	yes	PP, EX, A	1	2; 3; 5; 16
1219	ISOPROPANOL (ISOPROPYL ALCOHOL)	3	F1	II	3	N	2	2		10	97	0.78	3	yes	T2	II A	yes	PP, EX, A	1	

(1) UN No. or substance identification No.	(2) Name and description	3(a) Class	3(b) Classification code	(4) Packing group	(5) Labels	(6) Type of tank vessel	(7) Cargo tank design	(8) Cargo tank type	(9) Cargo tank equipment	(10) Opening pressure of the high-velocity vent valve in kPa	(11) Maximum degree of filling in %	(12) Relative density at 20 °C	(13) Type of sampling device	(14) Pump room below deck permitted	(15) Temperature class	(16) Explosion group	(17) Anti-explosion protection required	(18) Equipment required	(19) Number of cones/blue lights	(20) Additional requirements/Remarks
1220	ISOPROPYLE ACETATE	3	F1	II	3	N	2	2		10	97	0.88	3	yes	T2	II A	yes	PP, EX, A	1	
1221	ISOPROPYLAMINE	3	FC	I	3+8	C	1	1			95	0.69	1	yes	T2	II A[7)]	yes	PP, EP, EX, A	1	
1223	KEROSENE	3	F1	III	3	N	3	2			97	≤ 0.83	3	yes	T3	II A	yes	PP, EX, A	0	14
1224	KETONES, LIQUID, N.O.S. 110 kPa < vp50 ≤ 175 kPa	3	F1	II	3	N	2	2		50	97		3	yes	T4[3)]	II B[4)]	yes	PP, EX, A	1	14; 27; 29
1224	KETONES, LIQUID, N.O.S. 110 kPa < vp50 ≤ 150 kPa	3	F1	II	3	N	2	2	3	10	97		3	yes	T4[3)]	II B[4)]	yes	PP, EX, A	1	14; 27; 29
1224	KETONES, LIQUID, N.O.S. vp50 ≤ 110 kPa	3	F1	II	3	N	2	2		10	97		3	yes	T4[3)]	II B[4)]	yes	PP, EX, A	1	14; 27; 29
1224	KETONES, LIQUID, N.O.S.	3	F1	III	3	N	3	2			97		3	yes	T4[3)]	II B[4)]	yes	PP, EX, A	0	14; 27
1229	MESITYL OXYDE	3	F1	III	3	N	3	2			97	0.85	3	yes	T2	II B[4)]	yes	PP, EX, A	0	
1230	METHANOL	3	FT1	II	3+6.1	N	2	2	3	50	95	0.79	2	yes	T2	II A	yes	PP, EP, EX, TOX, A	1	23
1231	METHYL ACETATE	3	F1	II	3	N	2	2		10	97	0.93	3	yes	T1	II A	yes	PP, EX, A	1	
1235	METHYLAMINE, AQUEOUS SOLUTION	3	FC	II	3+8	C	2	2		50	95		2	yes	T2	II A	yes	PP, EP, EX, A	1	
1243	METHYLE FORMATE	3	F1	I	3	N	1	1			97	0.97	1	yes	T2	II A	yes	PP, EX, A	1	
1244	METHYLHYDRAZINE	6.1	TFC	I	6.1+3+8	C	2	2		45	95	0.88	1	no	T4	II C[5)]	yes	PP, EP, EX, TOX, A	2	
1245	METHYL ISOBUTYL KETONE	3	F1	II	3	N	2	2		10	97	0.8	3	yes	T1	II A	yes	PP, EX, A	1	
1247	METHYL METHACRYLATE MONOMER, STABILIZED	3	F1	II	3+unst.	C	2	2		40	95	0.94	1	yes	T2	II A	yes	PP, EX, A	1	3; 5; 16
1262	OCTANES (n-octane)	3	F1	II	3	N	2	2		10	97	0.7	3	yes	T3	II A	yes	PP, EX, A	1	
1264	PARALDEHYDE	3	F1	III	3	N	3	2			97	0.99	3	yes	T3	II A[7)]	yes	PP, EX, A	0	6: +16 °C; 17

(1) UN No. or substance identification No.	(2) Name and description	(3a) Class	(3b) Classification code	(4) Packing group	(5) Labels	(6) Type of tank vessel	(7) Cargo tank design	(8) Cargo tank type	(9) Cargo tank equipment	(10) Opening pressure of the high-velocity vent valve in kPa	(11) Maximum degree of filling in %	(12) Relative density at 20 °C	(13) Type of sampling device	(14) Pump room below deck permitted	(15) Temperature class	(16) Explosion group	(17) Anti-explosion protection required	(18) Equipment required	(19) Number of cones/blue lights	(20) Additional requirements/Remarks
1265	PENTANES, liquid (2-methylbutane)	3	F1	I	3	N	1	1			97	0.62	1	yes	T2	II A	yes	PP, EX, A	1	
1265	PENTANES, liquid (n-pentane)	3	F1	II	3	N	2	2	3	50	97	0.63	3	yes	T3	II A	yes	PP, EX, A	1	
1265	PENTANES, liquid (n-pentane)	3	F1	II	3	N	2	2	3	10	97	0.63	3	yes	T3	II A	yes	PP, EX, A	1	
1267	PETROLEUM CRUDE OIL vp50 > 175 kPa	3	F1	I	3	N	1	1			97		1	yes	T4[3]	II B[4]	yes	PP, EX, A	1	14; 29
1267	PETROLEUM CRUDE OIL vp50 > 175 kPa	3	F1	I	3	N	2	2	1	50	97		2	yes	T4[3]	II B[4]	yes	PP, EX, A	1	14; 29
1267	PETROLEUM CRUDE OIL with more than 10 % benzene vp50 > 175 kPa	3	F1	I	3	C	1	1			95		1	yes	T4[3]	II B[4]	yes	PP, EX, A	1	29
1267	PETROLOLEUM CRUDE OIL 110 kPa < vp50 ≤ 175 kPa	3	F1	II	3	N	2	2	3	50	97		3	yes	T4[3]	II B[4]	yes	PP, EX, A	1	14; 29
1267	PETROLEUM CRUDE OIL 110 kPa < vp50 ≤ 150 kPa	3	F1	II	3	N	2	2		10	97		3	yes	T4[3]	II B[4]	yes	PP, EX, A	1	14; 29
1267	PETROLEUM CRUDE OIL with more than 10 % benzene 110 kPa < vp50 ≤ 175 kPa	3	F1	II	3	C	1	1			95		1	yes	T4[3]	II B[4]	yes	PP, EX, A	1	29
1267	PETROLEUM CRUDE OIL vp50 ≤ 110 kPa	3	F1	II	3	N	2	2		10	97		3	yes	T4[3]	II B[4]	yes	PP, EX, A	1	14; 29
1267	PETROLEUM CRUDE OIL with more than 10 % benzene vp50 ≤ 110 kPa boiling point ≤ 60 °C	3	F1	II	3	C	1	1			95		1	yes	T4[3]	II B[4]	yes	PP, EX, A	1	29
1267	PETROLEUM CRUDE OIL with more than 10 % benzene vp50 ≤ 110 kPa 60 °C < boiling point ≤ 85 °C	3	F1	II	3	C	2	2	3	50	95		2	yes	T4[3]	II B[4]	yes	PP, EX, A	1	23; 29
1267	PETROLEUM CRUDE OIL with more than 10 % benzene vp50 ≤ 110 kPa 85 °C < boiling point ≤ 115 °C	3	F1	II	3	C	2	2		50	95		2	yes	T4[3]	II B[4]	yes	PP, EX, A	1	29
1267	PETROLEUM CRUDE OIL with more than 10 % benzene vp50 ≤ 110 kPa boiling point > 115 °C	3	F1	II	3	C	2	2		35	95		2	yes	T4[3]	II B[4]	yes	PP, EX, A	1	29

(1) UN No. or substance identification No.	(2) Name and description	3 (a) Class	3 (b) Classification code	(4) Packing group	(5) Labels	(6) Type of tank vessel	(7) Cargo tank design	(8) Cargo tank type	(9) Cargo tank equipment	(10) Opening pressure of the high-velocity vent valve in kPa	(11) Maximum degree of filling in %	(12) Relative density at 20 °C	(13) Type of sampling device	(14) Pump room below deck permitted	(15) Temperature class	(16) Explosion group	(17) Anti-explosion protection required	(18) Equipment required	(19) Number of cones/blue lights	(20) Additional requirements/Remarks
1267	PETROLEUM CRUDE OIL	3	F1	III	3	N	3	2			97		3	yes	T4[3]	II B[4]	yes	PP, EX, A	0	14
1268	PETROLEUM DISTILLATES, N.O.S. or PETROLEUM PRODUCTS, N.O.S. vp50 > 175 kPa	3	F1	I	3	N	1	1			97		1	yes	T4[3]	II B[4]	yes	PP, EX, A	1	14; 27; 29
1268	PETROLEUM DISTILLATES, N.O.S. or PETROLEUM PRODUCTS, N.O.S vp50 > 175 kPa	3	F1	I	3	N	2	2	1	50	97		2	yes	T4[3]	II B[4]	yes	PP, EX, A	1	14; 27; 29
1268	PETROLEUM DISTILLATES, N.O.S. with more than 10 % benzene or PETROLEUM PRODUCTS, N.O.S. with more than 10 % benzene vp50 > 175 kPa	3	F1	I	3	C	1	1			95		1	yes	T4[3]	II B[4]	yes	PP, EX, A	1	27; 29
1268	PETROLEUM DISTILLATES, N.O.S. or PETROLEUM PRODUCTS, N.O.S. 110 kPa < vp50 ≤ 175 kPa	3	F1	II	3	N	2	2	3	50	97		3	yes	T4[3]	II B[4]	yes	PP, EX, A	1	14; 27; 29
1268	PETROLEUM DISTILLATES, N.O.S. with more than 10 % benzene or PETROLEUM PRODUCTS, N.O.S. with more than 10 % benzene 110 kPa < vp50 ≤ 175 kPa	3	F1	II	3	C	1	1			95		1	yes	T4[3]	II B[4]	yes	PP, EX, A	1	27; 29
1268	PETROLEUM DISTILLATES, N.O.S. or PETROLEUM PRODUCTS, N.O.S. 110 kPa < vp50 ≤ 150 kPa	3	F1	II	3	N	2	2		10	97		3	yes	T4[3]	II B[4]	yes	PP, EX, A	1	14; 27; 29
1268	PETROLEUM DISTILLATES, N.O.S. or PETROLEUM PRODUCTS, N.O.S. vp50 ≤ 110 kPa	3	F1	II	3	N	2	2		10	97		3	yes	T4[3]	II B[4]	yes	PP, EX, A	1	14; 27; 29

(1) UN No. or substance identification No.	(2) Name and description	3(a) Class	3(b) Classification code	(4) Packing group	(5) Labels	(6) Type of tank vessel	(7) Cargo tank design	(8) Cargo tank type	(9) Cargo tank equipment	(10) Opening pressure of the high-velocity vent valve in kPa	(11) Maximum degree of filling in %	(12) Relative density at 20 °C	(13) Type of sampling device	(14) Pump room below deck permitted	(15) Temperature class	(16) Explosion group	(17) Anti-explosion protection required	(18) Equipment required	(19) Number of cones/blue lights	(20) Additional requirements/Remarks
1268	PETROLEUM DISTILLATES, N.O.S. with more than 10 % benzene or PETROLEUM PRODUCTS, N.O.S. with more than 10 % benzene vp50 ≤ 110 kPa boiling point ≤ 60 °C	3	F1	II	3	C	1	1			95		1	yes	$T4^{3)}$	$II\,B^{4)}$	yes	PP, EX, A	1	27; 29
1268	PETROLEUM DISTILLATES, N.O.S. with more than 10 % benzene or PETROLEUM PRODUCTS, N.O.S. with more than 10 % benzene vp50 ≤ 110 kPa 60 °C < boiling point ≤ 85 °C	3	F1	II	3	C	2	2	3	50	95	0.765	2	yes	$T4^{3)}$	$II\,B^{4)}$	yes	PP, EX, A	1	23; 27; 29
1268	PETROLEUM DISTILLATES, N.O.S. with more than 10 % benzene or PETROLEUM PRODUCTS, N.O.S., benzene heart cut with more than 10 % benzene vp50 ≤ 110 kPa 60 °C < boiling point ≤ 85 °C	3	F1	II	3	C	2	2	3	50	95		2	yes	T3	II A	yes	PP, EX, A	1	23; 27; 29
1268	PETROLEUM DISTILLATES, N.O.S. with more than 10 % benzene or PETROLEUM PRODUCTS, N.O.S. with more than 10 % benzene, vp50 ≤ 110 kPa 85 °C < boiling point ≤ 115 °C	3	F1	II	3	C	2	2	2	50	95		2	yes	$T4^{3)}$	$II\,B^{4)}$	yes	PP, EX, A	1	27; 29
1268	PETROLEUM DISTILLATES, N.O.S. with more than 10 % benzene or PETROLEUM PRODUCTS, N.O.S with more than 10 % benzene vp50 ≤ 110 kPa boiling point > 115 °C	3	F1	II	3	C	2	2		35	95		2	yes	$T4^{3)}$	$II\,B^{4)}$	yes	PP, EX, A	1	27; 29
1268	PETROLEUM DISTILLATES, N.O.S. or PETROLEUM PRODUCTS, N.O.S.	3	F1	III	3	N	3	2			97		3	yes	$T4^{3)}$	$II\,B^{4)}$	yes	PP, EX, A	0	14; 27

(1)	(2)	3(a)	3(b)	(4)	(5)	(6)	(7)	(8)	(9)	(10)	(11)	(12)	(13)	(14)	(15)	(16)	(17)	(18)	(19)	(20)
UN No. or substance identification No.	Name and description	Class	Classification code	Packing group	Labels	Type of tank vessel	Cargo tank design	Cargo tank type	Cargo tank equipment	Opening pressure of the high-velocity vent valve in kPa	Maximum degree of filling in %	Relative density at 20 °C	Type of sampling device	Pump room below deck permitted	Temperature class	Explosion group	Anti-explosion protection required	Equipment required	Number of cones/blue lights	Additional requirements/Remarks
1268	PETROLEUM DISTILLATES, N.O.S or PETROLEUM PRODUCTS, N.O.S. (naphtha) 110 kPa < vp50 ≤ 175 kPa	3	F1	II	3	N	2	2		50	97	0.735	3	yes	T3	II A	yes	PP, EX, A	1	14; 27; 29
1268	PETROLEUM DISTILLATES, N.O.S or PETROLEUM PRODUCTS, N.O.S. (naphtha) 110 kPa < vp50 ≤ 150 kPa	3	F1	II	3	N	2	2	3	10	97	0.735	3	yes	T3	II A	yes	PP, EX, A	1	14; 29
1268	PETROLEUM DISTILLATES, N.O.S or PETROLEUM PRODUCTS, N.O.S. (naphtha) vp50 ≤ 110 kPa	3	F1	II	3	N	2	2		10	97	0.735	3	yes	T3	II A	yes	PP, EX, A	1	14; 29
1268	PETROLEUM DISTILLATES, N.O.S. (benzene heart cut) vp50 ≤ 110 kPa	3	F1	II	3	N	2	2		10	97	0.765	3	yes	T3	II A	yes	PP, EX, A	1	14; 29
1274	n-PROPANOL (PROPYL ALCOHOL, NORMAL)	3	F1	II	3	N	2	2		10	97	0.8	3	yes	T2	II B	yes	PP, EX, A	1	
1274	n-PROPANOL (PROPYL ALCOHOL, NORMAL)	3	F1	III	3	N	3	2			97	0.8	3	yes	T2	II B	yes	PP, EX, A	0	
1275	PROPIONALDEHYDE	3	F1	II	3	C	2	2	3	50	95	0.81	2	yes	T4	II B	yes	PP, EX, A	1	15; 23
1276	n-PROPYL ACETATE	3	F1	II	3	N	2	2		10	97	0.88	3	yes	T1	II A	yes	PP, EX, A	1	
1277	PROPYLAMINE (1-aminopropane)	3	FC	II	3+8	C	2	2	3	50	95	0.72	2	yes	T3[2)]	II A	yes	PP, EP, EX, A	1	23
1278	1-CHLOROPROPANE (propyl chloride)	3	F1	II	3	C	2	2	3	50	95	0.89	2	yes	T1	II A	yes	PP, EX, A	1	23
1279	1,2-DICHLOROPROPANE (propyl dichloride)	3	F1	II	3	C	2	2		45	95	1.16	2	yes	T1	II A[8)]	yes	PP, EX, A	1	
1280	PROPYLENE OXIDE	3	F1	I	3+unst.	C	1	1			95	0.83	1	yes	T2	II B	yes	PP, EX, A	1	2; 12; 31
1282	PYRIDINE	3	F1	II	3	N	2	2		10	97	0.98	3	yes	T1	II A[8)]	yes	PP, EX, A	1	
1289	SODIUM METHYLATE SOLUTION in alcohol	3	FC	III	3+8	N	3	2			97	0.969	3	yes	T2	II A	yes	PP, EP, EX, A	0	34

(1) UN No. or substance identification No.	(2) Name and description	(3a) Class	(3b) Classification code	(4) Packing group	(5) Labels	(6) Type of tank vessel	(7) Cargo tank design	(8) Cargo tank type	(9) Cargo tank equipment	(10) Opening pressure of the high-velocity vent valve in kPa	(11) Maximum degree of filling in %	(12) Relative density at 20 °C	(13) Type of sampling device	(14) Pump room below deck permitted	(15) Temperature class	(16) Explosion group	(17) Anti-explosion protection required	(18) Equipment required	(19) Number of cones/blue lights	(20) Additional requirements/Remarks
1294	TOLUENE	3	F1	II	3	N	2	2		10	97	0.87	3	yes	T1	II A[8]	yes	PP, EX, A	1	
1296	TRIETHYLAMINE	3	FC	II	3+8	C	2	2		50	95	0.73	2	yes	T3	II A[8]	yes	PP, EP, EX, A	1	
1300	TURPENTINE SUBSTITUTE (white spirit)	3	F1	III	3	N	3	2			97	0.78	3	yes	T3	II B[4]	yes	PP, EX, A	0	
1301	VINYL ACETATE, STABILIZED	3	F1	II	3+unst.	N	2	2		10	97	0.93	2	yes	T2	II A	yes	PP, EX, A	1	3; 5; 16
1307	XYLENES (o-xylene)	3	F1	II	3	N	3	2			97	0.88	3	yes	T1	II A	yes	PP, EX, A	1	
1307	XYLENES (m-xylene)	3	F1	III	3	N	3	2			97	0.86	3	yes	T1	II A	yes	PP, EX, A	0	
1307	XYLENES (p-xylene)	3	F1	III	3	N	3	2			97	0.86	3	yes	T1	II A	yes	PP, EX, A	0	6: +17 °C; 17
1541	ACETONE CYANOHYDRIN, STABILIZED	6.1	T1	I	6.1+unst.	C	2	2		50	95	0.932	1	no			no	PP, EP, TOX, A	2	3
1545	ALLYL ISOTHIOCYANATE, STABILIZED	6.1	TF1	II	6.1+3+unst.	C	2	2	2	30	95	1.02	1	no	T4[3]	II B[4]	yes	PP, EP, EX, TOX, A	2	2; 3
1547	ANILINE	6.1	T1	II	6.1	C	2	2	2	25	95	1.02	2	no			no	PP, EP, TOX, A	2	
1578	CHLORONITROBENZENES, SOLID (p-chloronitrobenzene)	6.1	T2	II	6.1	C	2	1		25	95	1.37	2	no	T4[3]	II B[4]	yes	PP, EP, EX, TOX, A	2	7; 17; 26
1578	CHLORONITROBENZENES, SOLID (p-chloronitrobenzene)	6.1	T2	II	6.1	C	2	1	3	25	95	1.37	2	no			no	PP, EP, TOX, A	2	7; 17; 20: +112 °C; 26
1591	o-DICHLOROBENZENE	6.1	T1	III	6.1	C	2	2		25	95	1.32	2	no			no	PP, EP, TOX, A	0	
1593	DICHLOROMETHANE (methyl chloride)	6.1	T1	III	6.1	C	2	2		50	95	1.33	2	no			no	PP, EP, TOX, A	0	23
1594	DIETHYLSULPHATE	6.1	T1	II	6.1	C	2	2		25	95	1.18	2	no			no	PP, EP, TOX, A	2	
1595	DIMETHYL SULPHATE	6.1	TC1	I	6.1+8	C	2	2		25	95	1.33	2	no			no	PP, EP, TOX, A	2	
1604	ETHYLENEDIAMINE	8	CF1	II	8+3	N	3	2			97	0.9	3	yes	T2	II A	yes	PP, EP, EX, A	1	6: +12 °C; 17; 34

(1) UN No.	(2) Name and description	3(a) Class	3(b) Classification code	(4) Packing group	(5) Labels	(6) Type of tank vessel	(7) Cargo tank design	(8) Cargo tank type	(9) Cargo tank equipment	(10) Opening pressure of the high-velocity vent valve in kPa	(11) Maximum degree of filling in %	(12) Relative density at 20 °C	(13) Type of sampling device	(14) Pump room below deck permitted	(15) Temperature class	(16) Explosion group	(17) Anti-explosion protection required	(18) Equipment required	(19) Number of cones/blue lights	(20) Additional requirements/Remarks
1605	ETHYLENE DIBROMIDE	6.1	T1	I	6.1	C	2	2		30	95	2.18	1	no			no	PP, EP, TOX, A	2	6: +14 °C; 17
1648	ACETONITRILE (methyl cyanide)	3	F1	II	3	N	2	2		10	97	0.78	3	yes	T1	II A	yes	PP, EX, A	1	
1662	NITROBENZENE	6.1	T1	II	6.1	C	2	2		25	95	1.21	2	no	T1	II B	yes	PP, EP, EX, TOX, A	2	17
1662	NITROBENZENE	6.1	T1	II	6.1	C	2	2	2	25	95	1.21	2	no			no	PP, EP, TOX, A	2	17; 20: +73 °C
1663	NITROPHENOLS (o-, m-, p-)	6.1	T2	III	6.1	C	2	2	2	25	95		2	no	T1	II B[3]	yes	PP, EP, EX, TOX, A	0	7; 17
1663	NITROPHENOLS (o-, m-, p-)	6.1	T2	III	6.1	C	2	2		25	95	1.16	2	no			no	PP, EP, TOX, A	0	7; 17; 20: +65 °C
1664	NITROTOLUENES, LIQUID (o-nitrotoluene)	6.1	T1	II	6.1	C	2	2		25	95	1	2	no			no	PP, EP, TOX, A	2	17
1708	TOLUIDINES, LIQUID (o-toluidine)	6.1	T1	II	6.1	C	2	2		25	95	1.03	2	no			no	PP, EP, TOX, A	2	
1708	TOLUIDINES, LIQUID (m-toluidine)	6.1	T1	III	6.1	C	2	2		25	95	1.46	2	no			no	PP, EP, TOX, A	2	
1710	TRICHLOROETHYLENE	6.1	T1	III	6.1	C	2	2		50	95	1.46	2	no			no	PP, EP, TOX, A	0	15
1715	ACETIC ANHYDRIDE	8	CF1	II	8+3	N	2	3		10	97	1.08	3	yes	T2	II A	yes	PP, EP, EX, A	1	34
1717	ACETYL CHLORIDE	3	FC	II	3+8	C	2	2	3	50	95	1.1	2	yes	T2	II A[8]	yes	PP, EP, EX, A	1	23
1718	BUTYL ACIDE PHOSPHATE	8	C3	III	8	N	4	3			97	0.98	3	yes			no	PP, EP	0	34
1719	CAUSTIC ALKALI LIQUID, N.O.S.	8	C5	II	8	N	4	2	3		97		3	yes			no	PP, EP	0	27; 30; 34
1719	CAUSTIC ALKALI LIQUID, N.O.S.	8	C5	III	8	N	4	2			97		3	yes			no	PP, EP	0	27; 30; 34
1738	BENZYL CHLORIDE	6.1	TC1	II	6.1+8+3	C	2	2		25	95	1.1	2	no	T1	II A[8]	yes	PP, EP, EX, TOX, A	2	
1742	BORON TRIFLUORIDE ACETIC ACID COMPLEX, LIQUID	8	C3	II	8	N	4	2		25	97	1.35	3	yes			no	PP, EP	0	34

(1) UN No. or substance identification No.	(2) Name and description	(3a) Class	(3b) Classification code	(4) Packing group	(5) Labels	(6) Type of tank vessel	(7) Cargo tank design	(8) Cargo tank type	(9) Cargo tank equipment	(10) Opening pressure of the high-velocity vent valve in kPa	(11) Maximum degree of filling in %	(12) Relative density at 20 °C	(13) Type of sampling device	(14) Pump room below deck permitted	(15) Temperature class	(16) Explosion group	(17) Anti-explosion protection required	(18) Equipment required	(19) Number of cones/blue lights	(20) Additional requirements/Remarks
1750	CHLORACETIC ACID SOLUTION	6.1	TC1	II	6.1+8	C	2	2	2	25	95	1.58	2	no	T1	II A	yes	PP, EP, EX, TOX, A	2	7; 17
1750	CHLORACETIC ACID SOLUTION	6.1	TC1	II	6.1+8	C	2	2	2	25	95	1.58	2	no			no	PP, EP, EX, TOX, A	2	7; 17; 20: +111 °C
1760	CORROSIVE LIQUID, N.O.S.	8	C9	I	8	N	2	3		10	97		3	yes			no	PP, EP	0	27; 34
1760	CORROSIVE LIQUID, N.O.S.	8	C9	II	8	N	2	3		10	97		3	yes			no	PP, EP	0	27; 34
1760	CORROSIVE LIQUID, N.O.S.	8	C9	III	8	N	4	3			97		3	yes			no	PP, EP	0	27; 34
1760	CORROSIVE LIQUID, N.O.S. (sodium mercaptobenzothiazole, 50 % aqueous solution)	8	C9	II	8	N	4	2			97	1.25	3	yes			no	PP, EP	0	34
1760	CORROSIVE LIQUID, N.O.S. (fatty alcohol, C$_{12}$-C$_{14}$)	8	C9	III	8	N	4	2			97	0.89	3	yes			no	PP, EP	0	34
1760	CORROSIVE LIQUID, N.O.S. (ethylene diaminetetraacetic acid, tetrasodium salt, 40 % aqueous solution)	8	C9	III	8	N	4	2			97	1.28	3	yes			no	PP, EP	0	34
1764	DICHLOROACETIC ACID	8	C3	II	8	N	3	3			97	1.56	3	yes	T1	II A	yes	PP, EP, EX, A	0	17; 34
1778	FLUOROSILICIC ACID	8	C1	II	8	N	2	3		10	97		3	yes			no	PP, EP	0	34
1779	FORMIC ACID	8	C3	II	8	N	2	3		10	97	1.22	3	yes	T1	II A	yes	PP, EP, EX, A	1	6: +12 °C; 17; 34
1780	FUMARYL CHLORIDE	8	C3	II	8	N	2	3		10	97	1.41	3	yes			no	PP, EP	0	8; 34
1783	HEXAMETHYLENEDIAMINE SOLUTION	8	C7	II	8	N	3	2	2		97		3	yes	T4[3]	II B[4]	yes	PP, EP, EX, A	0	7; 17; 34
1783	HEXAMETHYLENEDIAMINE SOLUTION	8	C7	III	8	N	3	2	2		97		3	yes	T3	II B[4]	yes	PP, EP, EX, A	0	7; 17; 34
1789	HYDROCHLORIC ACID	8	C1	II	8	N	2	3		10	97		3	yes			no	PP, EP	0	34
1789	HYDROCHLORIC ACID	8	C1	III	8	N	4	3			97		3	yes			no	PP, EP	0	34
1805	PHOSPHORIC ACID, with more than 80 % (volume) acid	8	C1	III	8	N	4	3	2		95		3	yes			no	PP, EP	0	7; 17; 22; 34
1805	PHOSPHORIC ACID, SOLUTION, with 80 % (volume) acid, or less	8	C1	III	8	N	4	3			97	1.00 - 1.6	3	yes			no	PP, EP	0	22; 34
1814	POTASSIUM HYDROXIDE SOLUTION	8	C5	II	8	N	4	2			97		3	yes			no	PP, EP	0	30; 34

(1) UN No. or substance identification No.	(2) Name and description	(3a) Class	(3b) Classification code	(4) Packing group	(5) Labels	(6) Type of tank vessel	(7) Cargo tank design	(8) Cargo tank type	(9) Cargo tank equipment	(10) Opening pressure of the high-velocity vent valve in kPa	(11) Maximum degree of filling in %	(12) Relative density at 20 °C	(13) Type of sampling device	(14) Pump room below deck permitted	(15) Temperature class	(16) Explosion group	(17) Anti-explosion protection required	(18) Equipment required	(19) Number of cones/blue lights	(20) Additional requirements/Remarks
1814	POTASSIUM HYDROXIDE SOLUTION	8	C5	III	8	N	4	2			97		3	yes			no	PP, EP	0	30; 34
1823	SODIUM HYDROXIDE, SOLID, molten	8	C6	II	8	N	4	1	2		95	2.13	3	yes			no	PP, EP	0	7; 17; 34
1824	SODIUM HYDROXIDE SOLUTION	8	C5	II	8	N	4	2			97		3	yes			no	PP, EP	0	30; 34
1824	SODIUM HYDROXIDE SOLUTION	8	C5	III	8	N	4	2			97		3	yes			no	PP, EP	0	30; 34
1830	SULPHURIC ACID with more than 51 % acid	8	C1	II	8	N	4	3			97	1.4 - 1.84	3	yes			no	PP, EP	0	8; 22; 30; 34
1831	SULPHURIC ACID, FUMING (oleum)	8	CT1	I	8+6.1	C	2	2		50	95	1.94	1	no			no	PP, EP, TOX, A	2	8
1832	SULPHURIC ACID, SPENT	8	C1	II	8	N	4	3			97		3	yes			no	PP, EP	0	8; 30; 34
1846	CARBON TETRACHLORIDE	6.1	T1	II	6.1	C	2	2	3	50	95	1.59	2	no			no	PP, EP, TOX, A	2	23
1848	PROPIONIC ACID	8	C3	III	8	N	3	3			97	0.99	3	yes	T1	II A[7]	yes	PP, EP, EX, A	0	34
1863	FUEL, AVIATION, TURBINE ENGINE vp50 > 175 kPa	3	F1	I	3	N	1	1			97		1	yes	T4[3]	II B[4]	yes	PP, EX, A	1	14; 29
1863	FUEL, AVIATION, TURBINE ENGINE vp50 > 175 kPa	3	F1	I	3	N	2	2	1	50	97		2	yes	T4[3]	II B[4]	yes	PP, EX, A	1	14; 29
1863	FUEL, AVIATION, TURBINE ENGINE with more than 10 % benzene vp50 > 175 kPa	3	F1	I	3	C	1	1			95		1	yes	T4[3]	II B[4]	yes	PP, EX, A	1	29
1863	FUEL, AVIATION, TURBINE ENGINE 110 kPa < vp50 ≤ 175 kPa	3	F1	II	3	N	2	2		50	97		3	yes	T4[3]	II B[4]	yes	PP, EX, A	1	14; 29
1863	FUEL, AVIATION, TURBINE ENGINE 110 kPa < vp50 ≤ 150 kPa	3	F1	II	3	N	2	2	3	10	97		3	yes	T4[3]	II B[4]	yes	PP, EX, A	1	14; 29
1863	FUEL, AVIATION, TURBINE ENGINE with more than 10 % benzene 110 kPa < vp50 ≤ 175 kPa	3	F1	II	3	C	1	1			95		1	yes	T4[3]	II B[4]	yes	PP, EX, A	1	29

(1) UN No. or substance identification No.	(2) Name and description	(3a) Class	(3b) Classification code	(4) Packing group	(5) Labels	(6) Type of tank vessel	(7) Cargo tank design	(8) Cargo tank type	(9) Cargo tank equipment	(10) Opening pressure of the high-velocity vent valve in kPa	(11) Maximum degree of filling in %	(12) Relative density at 20 °C	(13) Type of sampling device	(14) Pump room below deck permitted	(15) Temperature class	(16) Explosion group	(17) Anti-explosion protection required	(18) Equipment required	(19) Number of cones/blue lights	(20) Additional requirements/Remarks
1863	FUEL, AVIATION, TURBINE ENGINE vp50 ≤ 110 kPa	3	F1	II	3	N	2	2		10	97		3	yes	T4³⁾	II B⁴⁾	yes	PP, EX, A	1	14; 29
1863	FUEL, AVIATION, TURBINE ENGINE with more than 10 % benzene vp50 ≤ 110 kPa boiling point ≤ 60 °C	3	F1	II	3	C	1	1			95		1	yes	T4³⁾	II B⁴⁾	yes	PP, EX, A	1	29
1863	FUEL, AVIATION, TURBINE ENGINE with more than 10 % benzene vp50 ≤ 110 kPa 60 °C < boiling point ≤ 85 °C	3	F1	II	3	C	2	2	3	50	95		2	yes	T4³⁾	II B⁴⁾	yes	PP, EX, A	1	29
1863	FUEL, AVIATION, TURBINE ENGINE with more than 10 % benzene vp50 ≤ 110 kPa 85 °C < boiling point ≤ 115 °C	3	F1	II	3	C	2	2		50	95		2	yes	T4³⁾	II B⁴⁾	yes	PP, EX, A	1	29
1863	FUEL, AVIATION, TURBINE ENGINE with more than 10 % benzene vp50 ≤ 110 kPa boiling point ≥ 115 °C	3	F1	II	3	C	2	2	3	35	95		2	yes	T4³⁾	II B⁴⁾	yes	PP, EX, A	1	29
1863	FUEL, AVIATION, TURBINE ENGINE	3	F1	III	3	N	3	2		50	97		3	yes	T4³⁾	II B⁴⁾	yes	PP, EX, A	1	14
1888	CHLOROFORM	6.1	T1	III	6.1	C	2	2		50	95	1.48	2	no			no	PP, EP, TOX, A	0	23
1897	TETRACHLOROETHYLENE	6.1	T1	III	6.1	C	2	2		50	95	1.62	2	no			no	PP, EP, TOX, A	0	
1912	METHYL CHLORIDE AND METHYLENE CHLORIDE MIXTURE (liquefied gas)	2	2F		2.1	G	1	1			91		1	yes	T1	II A⁸⁾	yes	PP, EX, A	1	31
1915	CYCLOHEXANONE	3	F1	III	3	N	3	2			97	0.95	3	yes	T2	II A	yes	PP, EX, A	0	
1917	ETHYL ACRYLATE, STABILIZED	3	F1	II	3+unst.	C	2	2		40	95	0.92	1	yes	T2	II B	yes	PP, EX, A	1	3; 5
1918	ISOPROPYLBENZENE (cumene)	3	F1	III	3	N	3	2			97	0.86	3	yes	T2	II A⁵⁾	yes	PP, EX, A	0	

(1) UN No. or substance identification No.	(2) Name and description	(3a) Class	(3b) Classification code	(4) Packing group	(5) Labels	(6) Type of tank vessel	(7) Cargo tank design	(8) Cargo tank type	(9) Cargo tank equipment	(10) Opening pressure of the high-velocity vent valve in kPa	(11) Maximum degree of filling in %	(12) Relative density at 20 °C	(13) Type of sampling device	(14) Pump room below deck permitted	(15) Temperature class	(16) Explosion group	(17) Anti-explosion protection required	(18) Equipment required	(19) Number of cones/blue lights	(20) Additional requirements/Remarks
1919	METHYL ACRYLATE, STABILIZED	3	F1	II	3+unst.	C	2	2	3	50	95	0.95	1	yes	T2	II B	yes	PP, EX, A	1	3; 5; 23
1920	NONANES	3	F1	III	3	N	3	2			97	0.70 - 0.75	3	yes	T3	II A	yes	PP, EX, A	0	
1922	PYRROLIDINE	3	FC	II	3+8	C	2	2		50	95	0.86	2	yes	T2	II A	yes	PP, EP, EX, A	1	
1965	HYDROCARBON GAS MIXTURE, LIQUEFIED, N.O.S., (mixture A)	2	2F		2.1	G	1	1			91		1	yes	T4[3]	II B[4]	yes	PP, EX, A	1	31
1965	HYDROCARBON GAS MIXTURE, LIQUEFIED, N.O.S., (mixture A0)	2	2F		2.1	G	1	1			91		1	yes	T4[3]	II B[4]	yes	PP, EX, A	1	31
1965	HYDROCARBON GAS MIXTURE, LIQUEFIED, N.O.S., (mixture A01)	2	2F		2.1	G	1	1			91		1	yes	T4[3]	II B[4]	yes	PP, EX, A	1	31
1965	HYDROCARBON GAS MIXTURE, LIQUEFIED, N.O.S., (mixture A02)	2	2F		2.1	G	1	1			91		1	yes	T4[3]	II B[4]	yes	PP, EX, A	1	31
1965	HYDROCARBON GAS MIXTURE, LIQUEFIED, N.O.S., (mixture A1)	2	2F		2.1	G	1	1			91		1	yes	T4[3]	II B[4]	yes	PP, EX, A	1	31
1965	HYDROCARBON GAS MIXTURE, LIQUEFIED, N.O.S., (mixture B)	2	2F		2.1	G	1	1			91		1	yes	T4[3]	II B[4]	yes	PP, EX, A	1	31
1965	HYDROCARBON GAS MIXTURE, LIQUEFIED, N.O.S., (mixture B1)	2	2F		2.1	G	1	1			91		1	yes	T4[3]	II B[4]	yes	PP, EX, A	1	31
1965	HYDROCARBON GAS MIXTURE, LIQUEFIED, N.O.S., (mixture B2)	2	2F		2.1	G	1	1			91		1	yes	T4[3]	II B[4]	yes	PP, EX, A	1	31
1965	HYDROCARBON GAS MIXTURE, LIQUEFIED, N.O.S., (mixture C)	2	2F		2.1	G	1	1			91		1	yes	T4[3]	II B[4]	yes	PP, EX, A	1	31
1969	ISOBUTANE	2	2F		2.1	G	1	1			91		1	yes	T2[1]	II A	yes	PP, EX, A	1	31
1978	PROPANE	2	2F		2.1	G	1	1			91		1	yes	T1	II A	yes	PP, EX, A	1	31

(1) UN No. or substance identification No.	(2) Name and description	(3)(a) Class	(3)(b) Classification code	(4) Packing group	(5) Labels	(6) Type of tank vessel	(7) Cargo tank design	(8) Cargo tank type	(9) Cargo tank equipment	(10) Opening pressure of the high-velocity vent valve in kPa	(11) Maximum degree of filling in %	(12) Relative density at 20 °C	(13) Type of sampling device	(14) Pump room below deck permitted	(15) Temperature class	(16) Explosion group	(17) Anti-explosion protection required	(18) Equipment required	(19) Number of cones/blue lights	(20) Additional requirements/Remarks
1986	ALCOHOLS, FLAMMABLE, TOXIC, N.O.S. boiling point < 60 °C	3	FT1	I	3+6.1	C	1	1			95		1	no	T4³⁾	II B⁴⁾	yes	PP, EP, EX, TOX, A	2	27; 29
1986	ALCOHOLS, FLAMMABLE, TOXIC, N.O.S. 60 °C < boiling point ≤ 85 °C	3	FT1	II	3+6.1	C	2	2	3	50	95		2	no	T4³⁾	II B⁴⁾	yes	PP, EP, EX, TOX, A	2	23; 27; 29
1986	ALCOHOLS, FLAMMABLE, TOXIC, N.O.S. 85 °C < boiling point ≤ 115 °C	3	FT1	II	3+6.1	C	2	2		50	95		2	no	T4³⁾	II B⁴⁾	yes	PP, EP, EX, TOX, A	2	27; 29
1986	ALCOHOLS, FLAMMABLE, TOXIC, N.O.S. boiling point > 115 °C	3	FT1	II	3+6.1	C	2	2	3	35	95		2	no	T4³⁾	II B⁴⁾	yes	PP, EP, EX, TOX, A	2	27; 29
1986	ALCOHOLS, FLAMMABLE, TOXIC, N.O.S. 60 °C < boiling point ≤ 85 °C	3	FT1	III	3+6.1	C	2	2		50	95		2	no	T4³⁾	II B⁴⁾	yes	PP, EP, EX, TOX, A	0	23; 27; 29
1986	ALCOHOLS, FLAMMABLE, TOXIC, N.O.S. 85 °C < boiling point ≤ 115 °C	3	FT1	III	3+6.1	C	2	2		50	95		2	no	T4³⁾	II B⁴⁾	yes	PP, EP, EX, TOX, A	0	27; 29
1986	ALCOHOLS, FLAMMABLE, TOXIC, N.O.S. boiling point > 115 °C	3	FT1	III	3+6.1	C	2	2		35	95		2	no	T4³⁾	II B⁴⁾	yes	PP, EP, EX, TOX, A	0	27; 29
1987	ALCOHOLS, N.O.S. 110 kPa < vp50 ≤ 175 kPa	3	F1	II	3	N	2	2	3	50	97		3	yes	T4³⁾	II B⁴⁾	yes	PP, EX, A	1	14; 27; 29
1987	ALCOHOLS, N.O.S. 110 kPa < vp50 ≤ 150 kPa	3	F1	II	3	N	2	2		10	97		3	yes	T4³⁾	II B⁴⁾	yes	PP, EX, A	1	14; 27; 29
1987	ALCOHOLS, N.O.S. vp50 ≤ 110 kPa	3	F1	II	3	N	2	2	2	10	97		3	yes	T4³⁾	II B⁴⁾	yes	PP, EX, A	1	14; 27; 29
1987	ALCOHOLS, N.O.S. (tert-butanol 90 % (mass)/methanol 10 % (mass) mixture)	3	F1	II	3	N	2	2	2	10	97		3	yes	T1	II A	yes	PP, EX, A	1	
1987	ALCOHOLS, N.O.S.	3	F1	III	3	N	3	2			97		3	yes	T4³⁾	II B⁴⁾	yes	PP, EX, A	0	14; 27
1987	ALCOHOLS, N.O.S.	3	F1	III	3	N	3	2	2		95	0.95	3	yes	T3	II A	yes	PP, EX, A	0	7; 17
1987	ALCOHOLS, N.O.S.	3	F1	III	3	N	3	2	2		95	0.95	3	yes			no	PP	0	7; 17; 20: +46 °C

(1) UN No. or substance identification No.	(2) Name and description	(3a) Class	(3b) Classification code	(4) Packing group	(5) Labels	(6) Type of tank vessel	(7) Cargo tank design	(8) Cargo tank type	(9) Cargo tank equipment	(10) Opening pressure of the high-velocity vent valve in kPa	(11) Maximum degree of filling in %	(12) Relative density at 20 °C	(13) Type of sampling device	(14) Pump room below deck permitted	(15) Temperature class	(16) Explosion group	(17) Anti-explosion protection required	(18) Equipment required	(19) Number of cones/blue lights	(20) Additional requirements/Remarks
1989	ALDEHYDES, N.O.S. 110 kPa < vp50 ≤ 175 kPa	3	F1	II	3	N	2	2		50	97		3	yes	T4 [3]	II B [4]	yes	PP, EX, A	1	14; 27; 29
1989	ALDEHYDES, N.O.S. 110 kPa < vp50 ≤ 150 kPa	3	F1	II	3	N	2	2	3	10	97		3	yes	T4 [3]	II B [4]	yes	PP, EX, A	1	14; 27; 29
1989	ALDEHYDES, N.O.S. vp50 ≤ 110 kPa	3	F1	II	3	N	2	2		10	97		3	yes	T4 [3]	II B [4]	yes	PP, EX, A	1	14; 27; 29
1989	ALDEHYDES, N.O.S.	3	F1	III	3	N	3	2	3		97		3	yes	T4 [3]	II B [4]	yes	PP, EX, A	0	14; 27
1991	CHLOROPRENE, STABILIZED	3	FT1	I	3+6.1+unst.	C	2	2		50	95	0.96	1	no	T2	II B [4]	yes	PP, EP, EX, TOX, A	2	3; 5; 23
1992	FLAMMABLE LIQUID, TOXIC, N.O.S. boiling point ≤ 60 °C	3	FT1	I	3+6.1	C	1	1			95		1	no	T4 [3]	II B [4]	yes	PP, EP, EX, TOX, A	2	27; 29
1992	FLAMMABLE LIQUID, TOXIC, N.O.S. boiling point ≤ 60 °C	3	FT1	II	3+6.1	C	1	1			95		1	no	T4 [3]	II B [4]	yes	PP, EP, EX, TOX, A	2	27; 29
1992	FLAMMABLE LIQUID, TOXIC, N.O.S. 60 °C < boiling point ≤ 85 °C	3	FT1	II	3+6.1	C	2	2	3	50	95		2	no	T4 [3]	II B [4]	yes	PP, EP, EX, TOX, A	2	23; 27; 29
1992	FLAMMABLE LIQUID, TOXIC, N.O.S. 85 °C < boiling point ≤ 115 °C	3	FT1	II	3+6.1	C	2	2		50	95		2	no	T4 [3]	II B [4]	yes	PP, EP, EX, TOX, A	2	27; 29
1992	FLAMMABLE LIQUID, TOXIC, N.O.S. boiling point > 115 °C	3	FT1	II	3+6.1	C	2	2		35	95		2	no	T4 [3]	II B [4]	yes	PP, EP, EX, TOX, A	2	27; 29
1992	FLAMMABLE LIQUID, TOXIC, N.O.S. boiling point ≤ 60 °C	3	FT1	III	3+6.1	C	1	1			95		1	no	T4 [3]	II B [4]	yes	PP, EP, EX, TOX, A	0	27; 29
1992	FLAMMABLE LIQUID, TOXIC, N.O.S. 60 °C < boiling point ≤ 85 °C	3	FT1	III	3+6.1	C	2	2	3	50	95		2	no	T4 [3]	II B [4]	yes	PP, EP, EX, TOX, A	0	23; 27; 29
1992	FLAMMABLE LIQUID, TOXIC, N.O.S. 85 °C < boiling point ≤ 115 °C	3	FT1	III	3+6.1	C	2	2		50	95		2	no	T4 [3]	II B [4]	yes	PP, EP, EX, TOX, A	0	27; 29
1992	FLAMMABLE LIQUID, TOXIC, N.O.S. boiling point > 115 °C	3	FT1	III	3+6.1	C	2	2		35	95		2	no	T4 [3]	II B [4]	yes	PP, EP, EX, TOX, A	0	27; 29

(1) UN No. or substance identification No.	(2) Name and description	(3a) Class	(3b) Classification code	(4) Packing group	(5) Labels	(6) Type of tank vessel	(7) Cargo tank design	(8) Cargo tank type	(9) Cargo tank equipment	(10) Opening pressure of the high-velocity vent valve in kPa	(11) Maximum degree of filling in %	(12) Relative density at 20 °C	(13) Type of sampling device	(14) Pump room below deck permitted	(15) Temperature class	(16) Explosion group	(17) Anti-explosion protection required	(18) Equipment required	(19) Number of cones/blue lights	(20) Additional requirements/Remarks
1993	FLAMMABLE LIQUID, N.O.S. vp50 >175 kPa	3	F1	I	3	N	1	1	1		97		1	yes	T4[3]	IIB[4]	yes	PP, EX, A	1	14; 27; 29
1993	FLAMMABLE LIQUID, N.O.S. vp50 >175 kPa	3	F1	I	3	N	2	2		50	97		2	yes	T4[3]	IIB[4]	yes	PP, EX, A	1	14; 27; 29
1993	FLAMMABLE LIQUID, N.O.S. (..., with more than 10 % benzene) vp50 >175 kPa	3	F1	I	3	C	1	1			95		1	yes	T4[3]	IIB[4]	yes	PP, EX, A	1	27; 29
1993	FLAMMABLE LIQUID, N.O.S. 110 kPa < vp50 ≤ 175 kPa	3	F1	I	3	N	2	2		50	97		3	yes	T4[3]	IIB[4]	yes	PP, EX, A	1	14; 27; 29
1993	FLAMMABLE LIQUID, N.O.S. 110 kPa < vp50 ≤ 175 kPa	3	F1	II	3	N	2	2		50	97		3	yes	T4[3]	IIB[4]	yes	PP, EX, A	1	14; 27; 29
1993	FLAMMABLE LIQUID, N.O.S. 110 kPa < vp50 ≤ 150 kPa	3	F1	I	3	N	2	2	3	10	97		3	yes	T4[3]	IIB[4]	yes	PP, EX, A	1	14; 27; 29
1993	FLAMMABLE LIQUID, N.O.S. 110 kPa < vp50 ≤ 150 kPa	3	F1	II	3	N	2	2	3	10	97		3	yes	T4[3]	IIB[4]	yes	PP, EX, A	1	14; 27; 29
1993	FLAMMABLE LIQUID, N.O.S. (..., with more than 10 % benzene) 110 kPa < vp50 ≤ 175 kPa	3	F1	I	3	C	1	1			95		1	yes	T4[3]	IIB[4]	yes	PP, EX, A	1	27; 29
1993	FLAMMABLE LIQUID, N.O.S. (..., with more than 10 % benzene) 110 kPa < vp50 ≤ 175 kPa	3	F1	II	3	C	1	1			95		1	yes	T4[3]	IIB[4]	yes	PP, EX, A	1	27; 29
1993	FLAMMABLE LIQUID, N.O.S. vp50 ≤ 110 kPa	3	F1	II	3	N	2	2		10	97		3	yes	T4[3]	IIB[4]	yes	PP, EX, A	1	14; 27; 29
1993	FLAMMABLE LIQUID, N.O.S. (..., with more than 10 % benzene) vp50 ≤ 110 kPa boiling point ≤ 60 °C	3	F1	II	3	C	1	1	3		95		1	yes	T4[3]	IIB[4]	yes	PP, EX, A	1	27; 29
1993	FLAMMABLE LIQUID, N.O.S. (..., with more than 10 % benzene) vp50 ≤ 110 kPa 60 °C < boiling point ≤ 85 °C	3	F1	II	3	C	2	2		50	95		2	yes	T4[3]	IIB[4]	yes	PP, EX, A	1	23; 27; 29
1993	FLAMMABLE LIQUID, N.O.S. (..., with more than 10 % benzene) vp50 ≤ 110 kPa 85 °C < boiling point ≤ 115 °C	3	F1	II	3	C	2	2		50	95		2	yes	T4[3]	IIB[4]	yes	PP, EX, A	1	27; 29

(1) UN No. or substance identification No.	(2) Name and description	(3a) Class	(3b) Classification code	(4) Packing group	(5) Labels	(6) Type of tank vessel	(7) Cargo tank design	(8) Cargo tank type	(9) Cargo tank equipment	(10) Opening pressure of the high-velocity vent valve in kPa	(11) Maximum degree of filling in %	(12) Relative density at 20 °C	(13) Type of sampling device	(14) Pump room below deck permitted	(15) Temperature class	(16) Explosion group	(17) Anti-explosion protection required	(18) Equipment required	(19) Number of cones/blue lights	(20) Additional requirements/Remarks
1993	FLAMMABLE LIQUID, N.O.S. (..., with more than 10 % benzene) vp50 ≤ 110 kPa boiling point > 115 °C	3	F1	II	3	C	2	2		35	95		2	yes	T4[3]	II B[4]	yes	PP, EX, A	1	27; 29
1993	FLAMMABLE LIQUID, N.O.S.	3	F1	III	3	N	3	2	3		97		3	yes	T4[3]	II B[4]	yes	PP, EX, A	0	14; 27
1993	FLAMMABLE LIQUID, N.O.S. (..., with more than 10 % benzene) 60 °C < boiling point ≤ 85 °C	3	F1	III	3	C	2	2		50	95		2	yes	T4[3]	II B[4]	yes	PP, EX, A	0	23; 27; 29
1993	FLAMMABLE LIQUID, N.O.S. (..., with more than 10 % benzene) 85 °C < boiling point ≤ 115 °C	3	F1	III	3	C	2	2		50	95		2	yes	T4[3]	II B[4]	yes	PP, EX, A	0	27; 29
1993	FLAMMABLE LIQUID, N.O.S. (..., with more than 10 % benzene) boiling point > 115 °C	3	F1	III	3	C	2	2		35	95		2	yes	T4[3]	II B[4]	yes	PP, EX, A	0	27; 29
1993	FLAMMABLE LIQUID, N.O.S. (cyclohexanone/cyclohexanol mixture)	3	F1	III	3	N	3	2			97	0.95	3	yes	T3	II A[7]	yes	PP, EX, A	0	
1999	TARS, LIQUID 23 °C ≤ flash-point ≤ 61 °C	3	F1	III	3	N	4	2	2	35	97		3	yes	T3	II A[7]	yes	PP, EX, A	0	
2014	HYDROGEN PEROXIDE, AQUEOUS SOLUTION with not less than 20 % but not more than 60 % hydrogen peroxide (stabilized as necessary)	5.1	OC1	II	5.1+8+unst.	C	2	2		35	95	1.2	2	yes			no	PP, EP	0	3; 33
2021	CHLOROPHENOLS, LIQUID (2-chlorophenol)	6.1	T1	III	6.1	C	2	2		25	95	1.23	2	no	T1	II A[7]	yes	PP, EP, EX, TOX, A	0	6: +10 °C; 17
2022	CRESILIC ACID	6.1	TC1	II	6.1+8	C	2	2		25	95	1.03	2	no	T1	II A	yes	PP, EP, EX, TOX, A	2	6: +16 °C; 17
2023	EPICHLORHYDRINE	6.1	TF1	II	6.1+3	C	2	2		35	95	1.18	2	no	T2	II B	yes	PP, EP, EX, TOX, A	2	5
2031	NITRIC ACID, other than red fuming, with more than 70 % acid	8	CO1	I	8+5.1	N	2	3		10	97	1.41 (at 68 % HNO3)	3	yes			no	PP, EP	0	34

(1)	(2)	(3a)	(3b)	(4)	(5)	(6)	(7)	(8)	(9)	(10)	(11)	(12)	(13)	(14)	(15)	(16)	(17)	(18)	(19)	(20)
UN No. or substance identification No.	Name and description	Class	Classification code	Packing group	Labels	Type of tank vessel	Cargo tank design	Cargo tank type	Cargo tank equipment	Opening pressure of the high-velocity vent valve in kPa	Maximum degree of filling in %	Relative density at 20 °C	Type of sampling device	Pump room below deck permitted	Temperature class	Explosion group	Anti-explosion protection required	Equipment required	Number of cones/blue lights	Additional requirements/Remarks
2031	NITRIC ACID, other than red fuming, with not more than 70 % acid	8	CO1	II	8	N	2	3		10	97	1.51[1] (at 68 % HNO$_3$)	3	yes			no	PP, EP	0	34
2032	NITRIC ACID, RED FUMING	8	COT	I	8+5.1+6.1	C	2	2		50	95	1.51	1	no			no	PP, EP, TOX, A	2	
2045	ISOBUTYRALDEHYDE (ISOBUTYL ALDEHYDE)	3	F1	II	3	C	2	2		50	95	0.79	2	yes	T4	II A[7]	yes	PP, EX, A	1	7
2046	CYMENES	3	F1	III	3	N	3	2			97	0.88	3	yes	T2	II A	yes	PP, EX, A	0	
2047	DICHLOROPROPENES (2,3-dichloroprop-1-ene)	3	F1	II	3	C	2	2		45	95	1.2	2	yes	T1	II A	yes	PP, EX, A	1	
2047	DICHLOROPROPENES (mixtures of 2,3-dichloroprop-1-ene and 1,3-dichloroprop-1-ene)	3	F1	II	3	C	2	2		45	95	1.23	2	yes	T2[1]	II A	yes	PP, EX, A	1	
2047	DICHLOROPROPENES (mixtures of 2,3-dichloroprop-1-ene and 1,3-dichloroprop-1-ene)	3	F1	III	3	C	2	2		45	95	1.23	2	yes	T2[1]	II A	yes	PP, EX, A	0	
2047	DICHLOROPROPENES (1,3-dichloroprop-1-ene)	3	F1	III	3	C	2	2		40	95	1.23	2	yes	T2[1]	II A[7]	yes	PP, EX, A	0	
2048	DICYCLOPENTADIENE	3	F1	III	3	N	3	2			95	0.94	3	yes	T1	II B[4]	yes	PP, EX, A	0	7; 17
2050	DIISOBUTYLENE, ISOMERIC COMPOUNDS	3	F1	II	3	N	2	2	2	10	97	0.72	3	yes	T3[2]	II A[7]	yes	PP, EX, A	1	
2051	2-DIMETHYLAMINOETHANOL	8	CF1	II	8+3	N	3	2			97	0.89	3	yes	T3	II A	yes	PP, EP, EX, A	1	34
2053	METHYL ISOBUTIL CARBINOL	3	F1	III	3	N	3	2			97	0.81	3	yes	T2	II B[4]	yes	PP, EX, A	0	
2054	MORPHOLINE	8	CF1	I	8+3	N	3	2			97	1	3	yes	T3	II A	yes	PP, EP, EX, A	1	34
2055	STYRENE MONOMER, STABILIZED (vinylbenzene monomer, stabilized)	3	F1	III	3+unst.	N	3	2			97	0.91	3	yes	T1	II A	yes	PP, EX, A	0	3; 5; 16
2056	TETRAHYDROFURAN	3	F1	II	3	N	2	2		10	97	0.89	3	yes	T3	II B	yes	PP, EX, A	1	
2057	TRIPROPYLENE (propylentrimer)	3	F1	III	3	N	3	2			97	0.73	3	yes	T3	II B[4]	yes	PP, EX, A	0	

(1)	(2)	(3)(a)	(3)(b)	(4)	(5)	(6)	(7)	(8)	(9)	(10)	(11)	(12)	(13)	(14)	(15)	(16)	(17)	(18)	(19)	(20)
UN No. or substance identification No.	Name and description	Class	Classification code	Packing group	Labels	Type of tank vessel	Cargo tank design	Cargo tank type	Cargo tank equipment	Opening pressure of the high-velocity vent valve in kPa	Maximum degree of filling in %	Relative density at 20 °C	Type of sampling device	Pump room below deck permitted	Temperature class	Explosion group	Anti-explosion protection required	Equipment required	Number of cones/blue lights	Additional requirements/Remarks
2078	TOLUENE DIISOCYANATE and isomeric mixtures (2,4-toluene diisocyanate)	6.1	T1	II	6.1	C	2	2	2	25	95	1.22	2	no	T1	II B[4]	yes	PP, EP, EX, TOX, A	2	2; 7; 8; 17
2078	TOLUENE DIISOCYANATE and isomeric mixtures (2,4-toluene diisocyanate)	6.1	T1	II	6.1	C	2	2	2	25	95	1.22	2	no			no	PP, EP, TOX, A	2	2; 7; 8; 17; 20: +112 °C
2079	DIETHYLENETRIAMINE	8	C7	II	8	N	4	2			97	0.96	3	yes			no	PP, EP	0	34
2205	ADIPONITRILE	6.1	T1	III	6.1	C	2	2	2	25	95	0.96	2	no	T4[3]	II B[4]	yes	PP, EP, EX, TOX, A	0	17
2206	ISOCYANATES, TOXIC, N.O.S. (4-chlorophenyl isocyanate)	6.1	T1	II	6.1	C	2	2	2	25	95	1.25	2	no			no	PP, EP, TOX, A	2	7; 17
2209	FORMALDEHYDE SOLUTION with not less than 25 % formaldehyde	8	C9	III	8	N	4	2			97	1.09	3	yes			no	PP, EP	0	15; 34
2215	MALEIC ANHYDRIDE, MOLTEN	8	C3	III	8	N	3	3	2		95	0.93	3	yes	T2	II B[4]	yes	PP, EP, EX, A	0	7; 17; 34
2215	MALEIC ANHYDRIDE, MOLTEN	8	C3	III	8	N	3	3	2		95	0.93	3	yes			no	PP, EP	0	7; 17; 34; 20: +88 °C
2218	ACRYLIC ACID, STABILIZED	8	CF1	II	8+3+unst.	C	2	2		30	95	1.05	1	yes	T2	II A[7]	yes	PP, EP, EX, A	1	3; 4; 5; 17
2227	n-BUTYL METHACRYLATE, STABILIZED	3	F1	III	3+unst.	C	2	2		25	95	0.9	1	yes	T3	II A	yes	PP, EX, A	0	3; 5
2238	CHLOROTOLUENES (m-chlorotoluene)	3	F1	III	3	C	2	2		30	95	1.08	2	yes	T1	II A[7]	yes	PP, EX, A	0	
2238	CHLOROTOLUENES (o-chlorotoluene)	3	F1	III	3	C	2	2		30	95	1.08	2	yes	T1	II A[7]	yes	PP, EX, A	0	
2238	CHLOROTOLUENES (p-chlorotoluene)	3	F1	III	3	C	2	2		30	95	1.07	2	yes	T1	II A[7]	yes	PP, EX, A	0	6: +11 °C; 17
2241	CYCLOHEPTANE	3	F1	II	3	N	2	2		10	97	0.81	3	yes	T4[3]	II A	yes	PP, EX, A	1	
2247	n-DECANE	3	F1	III	3	N	3	2			97	0.73	3	yes	T4	II A	yes	PP, EX, A	0	
2248	DI-n-BUTYLAMINE	8	CF1	II	8+3	N	3	2			97	0.76	3	yes	T3	II A[7]	yes	PP, EP, EX, A	1	34
2259	TRIETHYLENETETRAMINE	8	C7	II	8	N	3	2			97	0.98	3	yes	T2	II B[4]	yes	PP, EP, EX, A	1	34

(1) UN No. or substance identification No.	(2) Name and description	(3)(a) Class	(3)(b) Classification code	(4) Packing group	(5) Labels	(6) Type of tank vessel	(7) Cargo tank design	(8) Cargo tank type	(9) Cargo tank equipment	(10) Opening pressure of the high-velocity vent valve in kPa	(11) Maximum degree of filling in %	(12) Relative density at 20 °C	(13) Type of sampling device	(14) Pump room below deck permitted	(15) Temperature class	(16) Explosion group	(17) Anti-explosion protection required	(18) Equipment required	(19) Number of cones/blue lights	(20) Additional requirements/Remarks
2263	DIMETHYLCYCLOHEXANES (cis-1,4-dimethylcyclohexane)	3	F1	II	3	C	2	2		35	95	0.78	2	yes	T4[3]	II A[7]	yes	PP, EX, A	1	
2263	DIMETHYLCYCLOHEXANES (trans-1,4-dimethylcyclohexane)	3	F1	II	3	C	2	2		35	95	0.76	2	yes	T4[3]	II A[7]	yes	PP, EX, A	1	34
2264	N,N-DIMETHYLCYCLO-HEXYLAMINE	8	CF1	II	8+3	N	3	2			97	0.85	3	yes	T3	II B[4]	yes	PP, EP, EX, A	1	
2265	N,N-DIMETHYLFORMAMIDE	3	F1	III	3	N	3	2	3		97	0.95	3	yes	T2	II A	yes	PP, EX, A	0	
2266	DIMETHYL-N-PROPYLAMINE	3	FC	II	3+8	C	2	2		50	95	0.72	2	yes	T4	II A	yes	PP, EP, EX, A	1	23
2276	2-ETHYLHEXYLAMINE	3	FC	III	3+8	N	3	2			97	0.79	3	yes	T3	II A[7]	yes	PP, EP, EX, A	0	34
2278	n-HEPTENE	3	F1	II	3	N	2	2		10	97	0.7	3	yes	T3	II B[4]	yes	PP, EX, A	1	
2280	HEXAMETHYLENEDIAMINE, SOLID, molten	8	C8	III	8	N	3	3	2		95	0.83	3	yes	T3	II B[4]	yes	PP, EP, EX, A	0	7; 17; 34
2280	HEXAMETHYLENEDIAMINE, SOLID, molten	8	C8	III	8	N	3	3	2		95	0.83	3	yes			no	PP, EP	0	7; 17; 34; 20: +66 °C
2282	HEXANOLS	3	F1	III	3	N	3	2			97	0.83	3	yes	T3	II A	yes	PP, EX, A	0	
2286	PENTAMETHYLHEPTANE (isododecane)	3	F1	III	3	N	3	2			97	0.75	3	yes	T2	II A[7]	yes	PP, EX, A	0	
2288	ISOHEXENES	3	F1	II	3+unst.	C	2	2	3	50	95	0.735	2	yes	T2	II B[4]	yes	PP, EX, A	1	3
2289	ISOPHORONEDIAMINE	8	C7	III	8	N	3	2			97	0.92	3	yes	T2	II A	yes	PP, EP, EX, A	0	17; 34
2303	ISOPROPENYLBENZENE	3	F1	III	3	N	3	2			97	0.91	3	yes	T2	II B	yes	PP, EX, A	0	16
2309	OCTADIENE (1,7-octadiene)	3	F1	II	3	N	2	2		10	97	0.75	3	yes	T3	II B[4]	yes	PP, EX, A	1	
2311	PHENETIDINES	6.1	T1	III	6.1	C	2	2	2	25	95	1.07	2	no			no	PP, EP, TOX, A	0	6: +7 °C; 17
2312	PHENOL, MOLTEN	6.1	T1	II	6.1	C	2	2	2	25	95	1.07	2	no	T1	II A[8]	yes	PP, EP, EX, TOX, A	2	7; 17
2312	PHENOL, MOLTEN	6.1	T1	II	6.1	C	2	2	2	25	95	1.07	2	no			no	PP, EP, TOX, A	2	7; 17; 20: +67 °C

(1) UN No. or substance identification No.	(2) Name and description	(3a) Class	(3b) Classification code	(4) Packing group	(5) Labels	(6) Type of tank vessel	(7) Cargo tank design	(8) Cargo tank type	(9) Cargo tank equipment	(10) Opening pressure of the high-velocity vent valve in kPa	(11) Maximum degree of filling in %	(12) Relative density at 20 °C	(13) Type of sampling device	(14) Pump room below deck permitted	(15) Temperature class	(16) Explosion group	(17) Anti-explosion protection required	(18) Equipment required	(19) Number of cones/blue lights	(20) Additional requirements/Remarks
2320	TETRAETHYLENEPENTAMINE	8	C7	III	8	N	4	2	2		97	1	3	yes			no	PP, EP	0	34
2321	TRICHLOROBENZENES, LIQUID (1,2,4-trichlorobenzene)	6.1	T1	III	6.1	C	2	2	2	25	95	1.45	2	no	T1	II A	yes	PP, EP, EX, TOX, A	0	7; 17
2321	TRICHLOROBENZENES, LIQUID (1,2,4-trichlorobenzene)	6.1	T1	III	6.1	C	2	2		25	95	1.45	2	no			no	PP, EP, TOX, A	0	7; 17; 20: +95 °C
2323	TRIETHYL PHOSPHITE	3	F1	III	3	N	3	2			97	0.8	3	yes	T3	II B[4]	yes	PP, EX, A	0	
2324	TRIISOBUTYLENE	3	F1	III	3	N	3	2			97	0.76	3	yes	T2	II B[4]	yes	PP, EX, A	0	
2325	1,3,5-TRIMETHYLBENZENE	3	F1	III	3	N	3	2			97	0.87	3	yes	T1	II A	yes	PP, EX, A	0	
2333	ALLYL ACETATE	3	FT1	II	3+6.1	C	2	2	3	40	95	0.93	2	no	T2	II A[7]	yes	PP, EP, EX, TOX, A	2	
2348	BUTYL ACRYLATES, STABILIZED (n-butylacrylate, stabilized)	3	F1	III	3+unst.	C	2	2		30	95	0.9	1	yes	T3	II B	yes	PP, EX, A	0	3; 5
2350	BUTYL METHYL ETHER	3	F1	II	3	N	2	2	3	10	97	0.74	3	yes	T4[3]	II B[4]	yes	PP, EX, A	1	23
2356	2-CHLOROPROPANE	3	F1	I	3	C	2	2		50	95	0.86	2	yes	T1	II A	yes	PP, EX, A	1	23
2357	CYCLOHEXYLAMINE	8	CF1	II	8+3	N	3	2			97	0.86	3	yes	T3	II A[8]	yes	PP, EP, EX, A	1	34
2362	1,1-DICHLOROETHANE	3	F1	II	3	C	2	2	3	50	95	1.17	2	yes	T2	II A	yes	PP, EX, A	1	23
2370	1-HEXENE	3	F1	II	3	N	2	2		10	97	0.67	3	yes	T3	II B[4]	yes	PP, EX, A	1	
2382	DIMETHYLHYDRAZINE, SYMMETRICAL	6.1	TF1	I	6.1+3	C	2	2		50	95	0.83	1	yes	T4[3]	II C	yes	PP, EP, EX, TOX, A	2	
2383	DIPROPYLAMINE	3	FC	II	3+8	C	2	2		35	95	0.74	2	no	T3	II A	yes	PP, EP, EX, A	1	23
2397	3-METHYLBUTAN-2-ONE	3	F1	II	3	N	2	2		10	97	0.81	3	yes	T1	II A	yes	PP, EX, A	1	

- 143 -

(1) UN No. or substance identification No.	(2) Name and description	(3)(a) Class	(3)(b) Classification code	(4) Packing group	(5) Labels	(6) Type of tank vessel	(7) Cargo tank design	(8) Cargo tank type	(9) Cargo tank equipment	(10) Opening pressure of the high-velocity vent valve in kPa	(11) Maximum degree of filling in %	(12) Relative density at 20 °C	(13) Type of sampling device	(14) Pump room below deck permitted	(15) Temperature class	(16) Explosion group	(17) Anti-explosion protection required	(18) Equipment required	(19) Number of cones/blue lights	(20) Additional requirements/Remarks
2398	METHYL tert-BUTYL ETHER	3	F1	II	3	N	2	2		10	97	0.74	3	yes	T1	II A	yes	PP, EX, A	1	
2404	PROPIONITRILE	3	FT1	II	3+6.1	C	2	2		45	95	0.78	2	no	T1[9]	II A	yes	PP, EP, EX, TOX, A	2	
2414	THIOPHENE	3	F1	II	3	N	2	2		10	97	1.06	3	yes	T2	II A	yes	PP, EX, A	1	
2430	ALKYLPHENOLS, SOLID, N.O.S. (nonylphenol, isomeric mixture, molten)	8	C4	II	8	N	3	3	2		95	95	3	yes	T2	II A[7]	yes	PP, EP, EX, A	0	7; 17; 34
2430	ALKYLPHENOLS, SOLID, N.O.S. (nonylphenol, isomeric mixture, molten)	8	C4	II	8	N	3	3	2		95	95	3	yes			no	PP, EP	0	7; 17; 34; 20: +125 °C
2432	N,N-DIETHYLANILINE	6.1	T1	III	6.1	C	2	2		25	95	0.93	2	no			no	PP, EP, TOX, A	0	
2448	SULPHUR, MOLTEN	4.1	F3	III	4.1	N	4	1	2		95	2.07	3	yes			no	PP, EP, TOX*, A	0	*Toximeter for H₂S; 7; 20: +150 °C; 32
2458	HEXADIENES	3	F1	II	3	N	2	2		10	97	0.72	3	yes	T4[3]	II B[4]	yes	PP, EX, A	1	
2477	METHYL ISOTHIOCYANATE	6.1	TF1	I	6.1+3	C	2	2	2	35	95	1.07[11]	2	no	T4[3]	II B[4]	yes	PP, EP, EX, TOX, A	2	7; 17
2485	n-BUTYL ISOCYANATE	6.1	TF1	I	6.1+3	C	2	2		35	95	0.89	1	no	T2	II B[4]	yes	PP, EP, EX, TOX, A	2	
2486	ISOBUTYL ISOCYANATE	3	FT1	II	3+6.1	C	2	2		40	95		2	no	T4[3]	II B[4]	yes	PP, EP, EX, TOX, A	2	
2487	PHENYL ISOCYANATE	6.1	TF1	I	6.1+3	C	2	2		25	95	1.1	1	no	T1	II A	yes	PP, EP, EX, TOX, A	2	
2490	DICHLOROISOPROPYL ETHER	6.1	T1	II	6.1	C	2	2		25	95	1.11	2	no			no	PP, EP, TOX, A	2	
2491	ETHANOLAMINE or ETHANOLAMINE SOLUTION	8	C7	III	8	N	3	2			97	1.02	3	yes	T2	II B[4]	yes	PP, EP, EX, A	0	17

- 144 -

(1)	(2)	(3a)	(3b)	(4)	(5)	(6)	(7)	(8)	(9)	(10)	(11)	(12)	(13)	(14)	(15)	(16)	(17)	(18)	(19)	(20)
UN No. or substance identification No.	Name and description	Class	Classification code	Packing group	Labels	Type of tank vessel	Cargo tank design	Cargo tank type	Cargo tank equipment	Opening pressure of the high-velocity vent valve in kPa	Maximum degree of filling in %	Relative density at 20 °C	Type of sampling device	Pump room below deck permitted	Temperature class	Explosion group	Anti-explosion protection required	Equipment required	Number of cones/blue lights	Additional requirements/Remarks
2493	HEXAMETHYLENEIMINE	3	FC	II	3+8	N	3	2			97	0.88	3	yes	T3[2]	II A	yes	PP, EP, EX, A	1	34
2496	PROPIONIC ANHYDRIDE	8	C3	III	8	N	4	3			97	1.02	3	yes			no	PP, EP	0	34
2518	1,5,9-CYCLODODECATRIENE	6.1	T1	III	6.1	C	2	2		25	95	0.9	2	no			no	PP, EP, TOX, A	0	
2527	ISOBUTYL ACRYLATE, STABILIZED	3	F1	III	3+unst.	C	2	2		30	95	0.89	1	yes	T2	II B[9]	yes	PP, EX, A	0	3; 5
2528	ISOBUTYL ISOBUTYRATE	3	F1	III	3	N	3	2			97	0.86	3	yes	T2	II A	yes	PP, EX, A	0	
2531	METHACRYLIC ACID, STABILIZED	8	C3	II	8+unst.	C	2	2	2	25	95	1.02	1	yes	T2	II B[4]	yes	PP, EP, EX, A	0	3; 4; 5; 17
2564	TRICHLOROACETIC ACID SOLUTION	8	C3	II	8	N	3	3	2		95	1.62[1]	3	yes	T1	II A[7]	yes	PP, EP, EX, A	0	7; 17; 22; 34
2564	TRICHLOROACETIC ACID SOLUTION	8	C3	III	8	N	4	3			97	1.62[1]	3	yes	T1	II A[7]	yes	PP, EP, EX, A	0	22; 34
2574	TRICRESYL PHOSPHATE with more than 3 % ortho isomer	6.1	T1	II	6.1	C	2	2		25	95	1.18	2	no			no	PP, EP, TOX, A	2	
2579	PIPERAZINE, molten (diethylenediamine)	8	C8	III	8	N	3	3	2		95	0.9	3	yes			no	PP, EP	0	7; 17; 34
2586	ALKYLSULFONIC ACIDS, LIQUID with not more than 5 % free sulphuric acid	8	C3	III	8	N	4	3			97		3	yes			no	PP, EP	0	34
2608	NITROPROPANES	3	F1	III	3	N	3	2			97	1	3	yes	T2	II B[7]	yes	PP, EX, A	0	
2615	ETHYL PROPYL ETHER	3	F1	II	3	N	2	2		10	97	0.73	3	yes	T4[3]	II A[7]	yes	PP, EX, A	1	
2618	VINYLTOLUENES, STABILIZED	3	F1	III	3+unst.	C	2	2		25	95	0.92	1	yes	T1	II B[4]	yes	PP, EX, A	0	3; 5
2651	4,4'-DIAMINODIPHENYL-METHANE	6.1	T2	III	6.1	C	2	2		25	95	1	2	no			no	PP, EP, TOX, A	0	7; 17
2672	AMMONIA SOLUTION (relative density between 0.880 and 0.957 at 15 °C in water, with more than 10 % but not more than 35 % ammonia)	8	C5	III	8	N	2	2	2	10	97	0.88[10] - 0.96[10]	3	yes			no	PP, EP	0	34

(1) UN No. or substance identification No.	(2) Name and description	(3a) Class	(3b) Classification code	(4) Packing group	(5) Labels	(6) Type of tank vessel	(7) Cargo tank design	(8) Cargo tank type	(9) Cargo tank equipment	(10) Opening pressure of the high-velocity vent valve in kPa	(11) Maximum degree of filling in %	(12) Relative density at 20 °C	(13) Type of sampling device	(14) Pump room below deck permitted	(15) Temperature class	(16) Explosion group	(17) Anti-explosion protection required	(18) Equipment required	(19) Number of cones/blue lights	(20) Additional requirements/Remarks
2683	AMMONIUM SULPHIDE SOLUTION	8	CFT	II	8+3+6.1	C	2	2		50	95		2	no	T4³⁾	II B⁴⁾	yes	PP, EP, EX, TOX, A	2	15; 16
2693	BISULPHITES, AQUEOUS SOLUTION, N.O.S.	8	C1	III	8	N	4	3			97		3	yes			no	PP, EP	0	27; 34
2709	BUTYLBENZENES	3	F1	III	3	N	3	2			97	0.87	3	yes	T2	II A	yes	PP, EX, A	0	
2733	AMINES, FLAMMABLE, CORROSIVE, N.O.S. or POLYAMINES, FLAMMABLE, CORROSIVE, N.O.S. (2-aminobutane)	3	FC	II	3+8	C	2	2	3	50	95	0.72	2	yes	T4³⁾	II A	yes	PP, EP, EX, A	1	23
2735	AMINES, LIQUID, CORROSIVE, N.O.S. or POLYAMINES, LIQUID, CORROSIVE, N.O.S.	8	C7	I	8	N	4	2			97		3	yes			no	PP, EP	0	27; 34
2735	AMINES, LIQUID, CORROSIVE, N.O.S. or POLYAMINES, LIQUID, CORROSIVE, N.O.S.	8	C7	II	8	N	4	2			97		3	yes			no	PP, EP	0	27; 34
2735	AMINES, LIQUID, CORROSIVE, N.O.S. or POLYAMINES, LIQUID, CORROSIVE, N.O.S.	8	C7	III	8	N	4	2			97		3	yes			no	PP, EP	0	27; 34
2754	N-ETHYLTOLUIDINES (N-ethyl-o-toluidine)	6.1	T1	II	6.1	C	2	2		25	95	0.94	2	no			no	PP, EP, TOX, A	2	
2754	N-ETHYLTOLUIDINES (N-ethyl-m-toluidine)	6.1	T1	II	6.1	C	2	2		25	95	0.94	2	no			no	PP, EP, TOX, A	2	
2754	N-ETHYLTOLUIDINES (N-ethyl-o-toluidine and N-ethyl-m-toluidine mixtures)	6.1	T1	II	6.1	C	2	2		25	95	0.94	2	no			no	PP, EP, TOX, A	2	
2754	N-ETHYLTOLUIDINES (N-ethyl-p-toluidine)	6.1	T1	II	6.1	C	2	2	2	25	95	0.94	2	no			no	PP, EP, TOX, A	2	7; 17
2789	ACETIC ACID, GLACIAL	8	CF1	II	8+3	N	2	3	2	10	95	1.05 (with 100 % acid)	3	yes	T1	II A	yes	PP, EP, EX, A	1	7; 17; 34
2789	ACETIC ACID SOLUTION, more than 80 % acid, by mass	8	CF1	II	8+3	N	2	3	2	10	95	1.05 (with 100 % acid)	3	yes	T1	II A	yes	PP, EP, EX, A	1	7; 17; 34

(1) UN No. or substance identification No.	(2) Name and description	3(a) Class	3(b) Classification code	(4) Packing group	(5) Labels	(6) Type of tank vessel	(7) Cargo tank design	(8) Cargo tank type	(9) Cargo tank equipment	(10) Opening pressure of the high-velocity vent valve in kPa	(11) Maximum degree of filling in %	(12) Relative density at 20 °C	(13) Type of sampling device	(14) Pump room below deck permitted	(15) Temperature class	(16) Explosion group	(17) Anti-explosion protection required	(18) Equipment required	(19) Number of cones/blue lights	(20) Additional requirements/Remarks
2790	ACETIC ACID SOLUTION, not less than 50 % but not more than 80 % acid, by mass	8	C3	II	8	N	2	3		10	95		3	yes			no	PP, EP	0	34
2790	ACETIC ACID SOLUTION, more than 10 % and less than 50 % acid, by mass	8	C3	III	8	N	2	3		10	95		3	yes			no	PP, EP	0	34
2796	BATTERY FLUID, ACID	8	C1	II	8	N	4	3			97	1.00 - 1.84	3	yes			no	PP, EP	0	8; 22; 30; 34
2796	SULPHURIC ACID with not more than 51 % acid	8	C1	II	8	N	4	3			97	1.00 - 1.41	3	yes			no	PP, EP	0	8; 22; 30; 34
2797	BATTERY FLUID, ALKALI	8	C5	II	8	N	4	3			97	1.00 - 2.13	3	yes			no	PP, EP	0	22; 30; 34
2810	TOXIC LIQUID, ORGANIC, N.O.S. boiling point ≤ 60 °C	6.1	T1	I	6.1	C	1	1	3	50	95		1	no			no	PP, EP, TOX, A	2	27; 29
2810	TOXIC LIQUID, ORGANIC, N.O.S. 60 °C < boiling point ≤ 85 °C	6.1	T1	I	6.1	C	2	2		50	95		1	no			no	PP, EP, TOX, A	2	23; 27; 29
2810	TOXIC LIQUID, ORGANIC, N.O.S. 85 °C < boiling point ≤ 115 °C	6.1	T1	I	6.1	C	2	2			95		1	no			no	PP, EP, TOX, A	2	27; 29
2810	TOXIC LIQUID, ORGANIC, N.O.S. boiling point > 115 °C	6.1	T1	I	6.1	C	2	2		35	95		1	no			no	PP, EP, TOX, A	2	27; 29
2810	TOXIC LIQUID, ORGANIC, N.O.S. boiling point ≤ 60 °C	6.1	T1	II	6.1	C	1	1	3	50	95		1	no			no	PP, EP, TOX, A	2	27; 29
2810	TOXIC LIQUID, ORGANIC, N.O.S. 60 °C < boiling point ≤ 85 °C	6.1	T1	II	6.1	C	2	2		50	95		2	no			no	PP, EP, TOX, A	2	23; 27; 29
2810	TOXIC LIQUID, ORGANIC, N.O.S. 85 °C < boiling point ≤ 115 °C	6.1	T1	II	6.1	C	2	2			95		2	no			no	PP, EP, TOX, A	2	27; 29
2810	TOXIC LIQUID, ORGANIC, N.O.S. boiling point > 115 °C	6.1	T1	II	6.1	C	2	2		35	95		2	no			no	PP, EP, TOX, A	2	27; 29

(1) UN No. or substance identification No.	(2) Name and description	3(a) Class	3(b) Classification code	(4) Packing group	(5) Labels	(6) Type of tank vessel	(7) Cargo tank design	(8) Cargo tank type	(9) Cargo tank equipment	(10) Opening pressure of the high-velocity vent valve in kPa	(11) Maximum degree of filling in %	(12) Relative density at 20 °C	(13) Type of sampling device	(14) Pump room below deck permitted	(15) Temperature class	(16) Explosion group	(17) Anti-explosion protection required	(18) Equipment required	(19) Number of cones/blue lights	(20) Additional requirements/Remarks
2810	TOXIC LIQUID, ORGANIC, N.O.S. boiling point ≤ 60 °C	6.1	T1	III	6.1	C	1	1			95		1	no			no	PP, EP, TOX, A	0	27; 29
2810	TOXIC LIQUID, ORGANIC, N.O.S. 60 °C < boiling point ≤ 85 °C	6.1	T1	III	6.1	C	2	2	3	50	95		2	no			no	PP, EP, TOX, A	0	23; 27; 29
2810	TOXIC LIQUID, ORGANIC, N.O.S. 85 °C < boiling point ≤ 115 °C	6.1	T1	III	6.1	C	2	2		50	95		2	no			no	PP, EP, TOX, A	0	27; 29
2810	TOXIC LIQUID, ORGANIC, N.O.S. boiling point > 115 °C	6.1	T1	III	6.1	C	2	2		35	95		2	no			no	PP, EP, TOX, A	0	27; 29
2811	TOXIC SOLID, ORGANIC, N.O.S. (1,2,3-trichlorobenzene, molten)	6.1	T2	III	6.1	C	2	2	2	25	95		2	no	T4[3]	II B[4]	yes	PP, EP, EX, TOX, A	0	7; 17; 22
2811	TOXIC SOLID, ORGANIC, N.O.S. (1,2,3-trichlorobenzene, molten)	6.1	T2	III	6.1	C	2	2	2	25	95		2	no			no	PP, EP, TOX, A	0	7; 17; 20: +92 °C; 22
2811	TOXIC SOLID, ORGANIC, N.O.S. (1,3,5-trichlorobenzene, molten)	6.1	T2	III	6.1	C	2	2	2	25	95		2	no	T4[3]	II B[4]	yes	PP, EP, EX, TOX, A	0	7; 17; 22
2811	TOXIC SOLID, ORGANIC, N.O.S. (1,3,5-trichlorobenzene, molten)	6.1	T2	III	6.1	C	2	2	2	25	95		2	no			no	PP, EP, TOX, A	0	7; 17; 20: +92 °C; 22
2815	N-AMINOETHYLPIPERAZINE	8	C7	III	8	N	4	2			97	0.98	3	yes			no	PP, EP	0	34
2820	BUTYRIC ACID	8	C3	III	8	N	2	3		10	97	0.96	3	yes			no	PP, EP	0	34
2829	CAPROIC ACID	8	C3	III	8	N	4	3			97	0.92	3	yes			no	PP, EP	0	34
2831	1,1,1-TRICHLOROETHANE	6.1	T1	III	6.1	C	2	2	3	50	95	1.34	2	yes			no	PP, EP, TOX, A	0	23
2850	PROPYLENE TETRAMER (tetrapropylene)	3	F1	III	3	N	4	2			97	0.76	3	yes			no	PP, EX, A	0	
2874	FURFURYL ALCOHOL	6.1	T1	III	6.1	C	2	2		25	95	1.13	2	no			no	PP, EP, TOX, A	0	
2920	CORROSIVE LIQUID, FLAMMABLE, N.O.S. (2-propanol and didecyldimethylammonium chloride, aqueous solution)	8	CF1	II	8+3	N	3	3			95	0.95	3	yes	T3	II A	yes	PP, EP, EX, A	1	34

(1) UN No. or substance identification No.	(2) Name and description	(3a) Class	(3b) Classification code	(4) Packing group	(5) Labels	(6) Type of tank vessel	(7) Cargo tank design	(8) Cargo tank type	(9) Cargo tank equipment	(10) Opening pressure of the high-velocity vent valve in kPa	(11) Maximum degree of filling in %	(12) Relative density at 20 °C	(13) Type of sampling device	(14) Pump room below deck permitted	(15) Temperature class	(16) Explosion group	(17) Anti-explosion protection required	(18) Equipment required	(19) Number of cones/blue lights	(20) Additional requirements/Remarks
2920	CORROSIVE LIQUID, FLAMMABLE, N.O.S. (aqueous solution of hexadecyltrimethyl-ammonium chloride (50 %) and ethanol (35 %))	8	CF1	II	8+3	N	2	3		10	95	0.9	3	yes	T2	II B	yes	PP, EP, EX, A	1	6: +7 °C; 17; 34
2922	CORROSIVE LIQUID, TOXIC, N.O.S. boiling point ≤ 60 °C	8	CT1	I	8+6.1	C	1	1			95		1	no			no	PP, EP, TOX, A	2	27; 29
2922	CORROSIVE LIQUID, TOXIC, N.O.S. 60 °C < boiling point ≤ 85 °C	8	CT1	I	8+6.1	C	2	2	3	50	95		1	no			no	PP, EP, TOX, A	2	23; 27; 29
2922	CORROSIVE LIQUID, TOXIC, N.O.S. 85 °C < boiling point ≤ 115 °C	8	CT1	I	8+6.1	C	2	2		50	95		1	no			no	PP, EP, TOX, A	2	27; 29
2922	CORROSIVE LIQUID, TOXIC, N.O.S. boiling point > 115 °C	8	CT1	I	8+6.1	C	2	2		35	95		1	no			no	PP, EP, TOX, A	2	27; 29
2922	CORROSIVE LIQUID, TOXIC, N.O.S. boiling point ≤ 60 °C	8	CT1	II	8+6.1	C	1	1			95		1	no			no	PP, EP, TOX, A	2	27; 29
2922	CORROSIVE LIQUID, TOXIC, N.O.S. 60 °C < boiling point ≤ 85 °C	8	CT1	II	8+6.1	C	2	2	3	50	95		2	no			no	PP, EP, TOX, A	2	23; 27; 29
2922	CORROSIVE LIQUID, TOXIC, N.O.S. 85 °C < boiling point ≤ 115 °C	8	CT1	II	8+6.1	C	2	2		50	95		2	no			no	PP, EP, TOX, A	2	27; 29
2922	CORROSIVE LIQUID, TOXIC, N.O.S. boiling point > 115 °C	8	CT1	II	8+6.1	C	2	2		35	95		2	no			no	PP, EP, TOX, A	2	27; 29
2922	CORROSIVE LIQUID, TOXIC, N.O.S. boiling point ≤ 60 °C	8	CT1	III	8+6.1	C	1	1			95		1	no			no	PP, EP, TOX, A	0	27; 29
2922	CORROSIVE LIQUID, TOXIC, N.O.S. 60 °C < boiling point ≤ 85 °C	8	CT1	III	8+6.1	C	2	2	3	50	95		2	no			no	PP, EP, TOX, A	0	23; 27; 29
2922	CORROSIVE LIQUID, TOXIC, N.O.S. 85 °C < boiling point ≤ 115 °C	8	CT1	III	8+6.1	C	2	2		50	95		2	no			no	PP, EP, TOX, A	0	27; 29

(1) UN No. or substance identification No.	(2) Name and description	(3a) Class	(3b) Classification code	(4) Packing group	(5) Labels	(6) Type of tank vessel	(7) Cargo tank design	(8) Cargo tank type	(9) Cargo tank equipment	(10) Opening pressure of the high-velocity vent valve in kPa	(11) Maximum degree of filling in %	(12) Relative density at 20 °C	(13) Type of sampling device	(14) Pump room below deck permitted	(15) Temperature class	(16) Explosion group	(17) Anti-explosion protection required	(18) Equipment required	(19) Number of cones/blue lights	(20) Additional requirements/Remarks
2922	CORROSIVE LIQUID, TOXIC, N.O.S. boiling point > 115 °C	8	CT1	III	8+6.1	C	2	2		35	95		2	no			no	PP, EP, TOX, A	0	27; 29
2924	FLAMMABLE LIQUID, CORROSIVE, N.O.S. boiling point ≤ 60 °C	3	FC	I	3+8	C	1	1			95		1	yes	T4[3]	II B[4]	yes	PP, EP, EX, A	1	27; 29
2924	FLAMMABLE LIQUID, CORROSIVE, N.O.S. boiling point ≤ 60 °C	3	FC	II	3+8	C	1	1			95		1	yes	T4[3]	II B[4]	yes	PP, EP, EX, A	1	27; 29
2924	FLAMMABLE LIQUID, CORROSIVE, N.O.S. 60 °C < boiling point ≤ 85 °C	3	FC	II	3+8	C	2	2	3	50	95		2	yes	T4[3]	II B[4]	yes	PP, EP, EX, A	1	23; 27; 29
2924	FLAMMABLE LIQUID, CORROSIVE, N.O.S. 85 °C < boiling point ≤ 115 °C	3	FC	II	3+8	C	2	2		50	95		2	yes	T4[3]	II B[4]	yes	PP, EP, EX, A	1	27; 29
2924	FLAMMABLE LIQUID, CORROSIVE, N.O.S. boiling point > 115 °C	3	FC	II	3+8	C	2	2		35	95		2	yes	T4[3]	II B[4]	yes	PP, EP, EX, A	1	27; 29
2924	FLAMMABLE LIQUID, CORROSIVE, N.O.S. boiling point ≤ 60 °C	3	FC	III	3+8	C	1	1			95		1	yes	T4[3]	II B[4]	yes	PP, EP, EX, A	1	27; 29
2924	FLAMMABLE LIQUID, CORROSIVE, N.O.S. 60 °C < boiling point ≤ 85 °C	3	FC	III	3+8	C	2	2	3	50	95		2	yes	T4[3]	II B[4]	yes	PP, EP, EX, A	0	23; 27; 29
2924	FLAMMABLE LIQUID, CORROSIVE, N.O.S. 85 °C < boiling point ≤ 115 °C	3	FC	III	3+8	C	2	2		50	95		2	yes	T4[3]	II B[4]	yes	PP, EP, EX, A	0	27; 29
2924	FLAMMABLE LIQUID, CORROSIVE, N.O.S. boiling point > 115 °C	3	FC	III	3+8	C	2	2		35	95		2	yes	T4[3]	II B[4]	yes	PP, EP, EX, A	0	27; 29
2924	FLAMMABLE LIQUID, CORROSIVE, N.O.S. (aqueous solution of dialkyl-(C8-C18)-dimethylammonium chloride and 2-propanol)	3	FC	II	3+8	C	2	2		50	95	0.88	2	yes	T2	II A	yes	PP, EP, EX, A	1	
2927	TOXIC LIQUID, CORROSIVE, ORGANIC, N.O.S. boiling point ≤ 60 °C	6.1	TC1	I	6.1+8	C	1	1			95		1	no			no	PP, EP, TOX, A	2	27; 29

(1) UN No. or substance identification No.	(2) Name and description	(3a) Class	(3b) Classification code	(4) Packing group	(5) Labels	(6) Type of tank vessel	(7) Cargo tank design	(8) Cargo tank type	(9) Cargo tank equipment	(10) Opening pressure of the high-velocity vent valve in kPa	(11) Maximum degree of filling in %	(12) Relative density at 20 °C	(13) Type of sampling device	(14) Pump room below deck permitted	(15) Temperature class	(16) Explosion group	(17) Anti-explosion protection required	(18) Equipment required	(19) Number of cones/blue lights	(20) Additional requirements/Remarks
2927	TOXIC LIQUID, CORROSIVE, ORGANIC, N.O.S. 60 °C < boiling point ≤ 85 °C	6.1	TC1	I	6.1+8	C	2	2	3	50	95		1	no			no	PP, EP, TOX, A	2	23; 27; 29
2927	TOXIC LIQUID, CORROSIVE, ORGANIC, N.O.S. 85 °C < boiling point ≤ 115 °C	6.1	TC1	I	6.1+8	C	2	2		50	95		1	no			no	PP, EP, TOX, A	2	27; 29
2927	TOXIC LIQUID, CORROSIVE, ORGANIC, N.O.S. boiling point > 115 °C	6.1	TC1	I	6.1+8	C	2	2		35	95		1	no			no	PP, EP, TOX, A	2	27; 29
2927	TOXIC LIQUID, CORROSIVE, ORGANIC, N.O.S. boiling point ≤ 60 °C	6.1	TC1	II	6.1+8	C	1	1			95		1	no			no	PP, EP, TOX, A	2	27; 29
2927	TOXIC LIQUID, CORROSIVE, ORGANIC, N.O.S. 60 °C < boiling point ≤ 85 °C	6.1	TC1	II	6.1+8	C	2	2	3	50	95		2	no			no	PP, EP, TOX, A	2	23; 27; 29
2927	TOXIC LIQUID, CORROSIVE, ORGANIC, N.O.S. 85 °C < boiling point ≤ 115 °C	6.1	TC1	II	6.1+8	C	2	2		50	95		2	no			no	PP, EP, TOX, A	2	27; 29
2927	TOXIC LIQUID, CORROSIVE, ORGANIC, N.O.S. boiling point > 115 °C	6.1	TC1	II	6.1+8	C	2	2		35	95		2	no			no	PP, EP, TOX, A	2	27; 29
2929	TOXIC LIQUID, FLAMMABLE, ORGANIC, N.O.S.	6.1	TF1	I	6.1+3	C	1	1			95		1	no	T4 [3]	II B [4]	yes	PP, EP, EX, TOX, A	2	27
2929	TOXIC LIQUID, FLAMMABLE, ORGANIC, N.O.S. boiling point ≤ 60 °C	6.1	TF1	I	6.1+3	C	1	1			95		1	no	T4 [3]	II B [4]	yes	PP, EP, EX, TOX, A	2	27; 29
2929	TOXIC LIQUID, FLAMMABLE, ORGANIC, N.O.S. 60 °C < boiling point ≤ 85 °C	6.1	TF1	I	6.1+3	C	2	2	3	50	95		1	no	T4 [3]	II B [4]	yes	PP, EP, EX, TOX, A	2	23; 27; 29
2929	TOXIC LIQUID, FLAMMABLE, ORGANIC, N.O.S. 85 °C < boiling point ≤ 115 °C	6.1	TF1	I	6.1+3	C	2	2		50	95		1	no	T4 [3]	II B [4]	yes	PP, EP, EX, TOX, A	2	27; 29
2929	TOXIC LIQUID, FLAMMABLE, ORGANIC, N.O.S. boiling point > 115 °C	6.1	TF1	I	6.1+3	C	2	2		35	95		1	no	T4 [3]	II B [4]	yes	PP, EP, EX, TOX, A	2	27; 29

(1) UN No.	(2) Name and description	(3a) Class	(3b) Classification code	(4) Packing group	(5) Labels	(6) Type of tank vessel	(7) Cargo tank design	(8) Cargo tank type	(9) Cargo tank equipment	(10) Opening pressure of the high-velocity vent valve in kPa	(11) Max. degree of filling in %	(12) Relative density at 20 °C	(13) Type of sampling device	(14) Pump room below deck permitted	(15) Temperature class	(16) Explosion group	(17) Anti-explosion protection required	(18) Equipment required	(19) Number of cones/blue lights	(20) Additional requirements/Remarks
2929	TOXIC LIQUID, FLAMMABLE, ORGANIC, N.O.S. boiling point ≤ 60 °C	6.1	TF1	II	6.1+3	C	1	1			95		1	no	T4³⁾	II B⁴⁾	yes	PP, EP, EX, TOX, A	2	27; 29
2929	TOXIC LIQUID, FLAMMABLE, ORGANIC, N.O.S. 60 °C < boiling point ≤ 85 °C	6.1	TF1	II	6.1+3	C	2	2	3	50	95		2	no	T4³⁾	II B⁴⁾	yes	PP, EP, EX, TOX, A	2	23; 27; 29
2929	TOXIC LIQUID, FLAMMABLE, ORGANIC, N.O.S. 85 °C < boiling point ≤ 115 °C	6.1	TF1	II	6.1+3	C	2	2		50	95		2	no	T4³⁾	II B⁴⁾	yes	PP, EP, EX, TOX, A	2	27; 29
2929	TOXIC LIQUID, FLAMMABLE, ORGANIC, N.O.S. boiling point > 115 °C	6.1	TF1	II	6.1+3	C	2	2		35	95		2	no	T4³⁾	II B⁴⁾	yes	PP, EP, EX, TOX, A	2	27; 29
2935	ETHYL-2-CHLORO-PROPIONATE	3	F1	III	3	C	2	2		30	95	1.08	2	yes	T4³⁾	II A	yes	PP, EX, A	0	
2947	ISOPROPYL CHLOROACETATE	3	F1	III	3	C	2	2		30	95	1.09	2	yes	T4³⁾	II A	yes	PP, EX, A	0	
2966	THIOGLYCOL	6.1	T1	II	6.1	C	2	2	3	25	95	1.12	2	no			no	PP, EP, TOX, A	2	
2983	ETHYLENE OXIDE AND PROPYLENE OXIDE MIXTURE, with not more than 30 % ethylene oxide	3	FT1	I	3+6.1+unst.	C	1	1	3	45	95	0.85	1	no	T2	II B	yes	PP, EP, EX, TOX, A	2	2; 3; 12; 31
3077	ENVIRONMENTALLY HAZARDOUS SUBSTANCE, SOLID, N.O.S., molten, (alkyl-amine (C₁₂ to C₁₈))	9	M7	III	9	N	4	3	2		95	0.79	3	yes			no	PP	0	7; 17
3079	METHACRYLONITRILE, STABILIZED	3	FT1	I	3+6.1+unst.	C	2	2			95	0.8	1	no	T1	II B⁴⁾	yes	PP, EP, EX, TOX, A	2	3; 5
3082	ENVIRONMENTALLY HAZARDOUS SUBSTANCE, LIQUID, N.O.S.	9	M6	III	9	N	4	3			97		3	yes			no	PP	0	22; 27
3082	ENVIRONMENTALLY HAZARDOUS SUBSTANCE, LIQUID, N.O.S. (bilge water)	9	M6	III	9	N	4	2			97			yes			no	PP	0	
3092	1-METHOXY-2-PROPANOL	3	F1	III	3	N	3	2			97	0.92	3	yes	T3	II B	yes	PP, EX, A	0	

(1)	(2)	(3 a)	(3 b)	(4)	(5)	(6)	(7)	(8)	(9)	(10)	(11)	(12)	(13)	(14)	(15)	(16)	(17)	(18)	(19)	(20)
UN No. or substance identification No.	Name and description	Class	Classification code	Packing group	Labels	Type of tank vessel	Cargo tank design	Cargo tank type	Cargo tank equipment	Opening pressure of the high-velocity vent valve in kPa	Maximum degree of filling in %	Relative density at 20 °C	Type of sampling device	Pump room below deck permitted	Temperature class	Explosion group	Anti-explosion protection required	Equipment required	Number of cones/blue lights	Additional requirements/Remarks
3145	ALKYLPHENOLS, LIQUID, N.O.S. (including C_2-C_{12} homologues)	8	C3	II	8	N	4	3			97	0.95	3	yes			no	PP, EP	0	34
3145	ALKYLPHENOLS, LIQUID, N.O.S. (including C_2-C_{12} homologues)	8	C3	III	8	N	4	3			97	0.95	3	yes			no	PP, EP	0	34
3175	SOLIDS CONTAINING FLAMMABLE LIQUID, N.O.S., molten, having a flash-point up to 61 °C (2-propanol and dialkyl-l(C_{12} to C_{18})-dimethyl-ammonium chloride)	4.1	F1	II	4.1	N	3	3			95	0.86	3	yes	T2	II A	yes	PP, EX, A	1	7;17
3256	ELEVATED TEMPERATURE LIQUID, FLAMMABLE, N.O.S. with flash-point above 61 °C, at or above its flash-point	3	F2	III	3	N	3	2	2		95		3	yes	T4[3]	II B[4]	yes	PP, EX, A	0	7;27
3256	ELEVATED TEMPERATURE LIQUID, FLAMMABLE, N.O.S. with flash-point above 61 °C, at or above its flash-point (carbon black reedstock) (pyrolysis oil)	3	F2	III	3	N	3	2	2		95		3	yes	T1	II B	yes	PP, EX, A	0	7
3256	ELEVATED TEMPERATURE LIQUID, FLAMMABLE, N.O.S. with flash-point above 61 °C, at or above its flash-point (pyrolysis oil A)	3	F2	III	3	N	3	2	2		95		3	yes	T1	II B	yes	PP, EX, A	0	7
3256	ELEVATED TEMPERATURE LIQUID, FLAMMABLE, N.O.S. with flash-point above 61 °C, at or above its flash-point (residual oil)	3	F2	III	3	N	3	2	2		95		3	yes	T1	II B	yes	PP, EX, A	0	7
3256	ELEVATED TEMPERATURE LIQUID, FLAMMABLE, N.O.S. with flash-point above 61 °C, at or above its flash-point (mixture of crude naphthaline)	3	F2	III	3	N	3	2	2		95		3	yes	T1	II B	yes	PP, EX, A	0	7

(1) UN No. or substance identification No.	(2) Name and description	(3a) Class	(3b) Classification code	(4) Packing group	(5) Labels	(6) Type of tank vessel	(7) Cargo tank design	(8) Cargo tank type	(9) Cargo tank equipment	(10) Opening pressure of the high-velocity vent valve in kPa	(11) Maximum degree of filling in %	(12) Relative density at 20 °C	(13) Type of sampling device	(14) Pump room below deck permitted	(15) Temperature class	(16) Explosion group	(17) Anti-explosion protection required	(18) Equipment required	(19) Number of cones/blue lights	(20) Additional requirements/Remarks
3256	ELEVATED TEMPERATURE LIQUID, FLAMMABLE, N.O.S. with flash-point above 61 °C, at or above its flash-point (creosote oil)	3	F2	III	3	N	3	2	2		95		3	yes	T2	II B	yes	PP, EX, A	0	7
3257	ELEVATED TEMPERATURE LIQUID, N.O.S. at or above 100 °C and below its flash-point (including molten metals, molten salts, etc.)	9	M9	III	9	N	4	1	2		95		3	yes			no	PP	0	7; 20: +115 °C; 22; 24; 25; 27
3257	ELEVATED TEMPERATURE LIQUID, N.O.S. at or above 100 °C and below its flash-point (including molten metals, molten salts, etc.)	9	M9	III	9	N	4	1	2		95		3	yes			no	PP	0	7; 20:+225 °C; 22; 24; 27
3259	AMINES, SOLID, CORROSIVE, N.O.S. molten (monoalkyl-(C₁₂ to C₁₈)-amine acetate)	8	C8	III	8	N	4	3	2		95	0.87	3	yes			no	PP, EP	0	7; 17; 34
3264	CORROSIVE LIQUID, ACIDIC, INORGANIC, N.O.S.	8	C1	I	8	N	2	3		10	97		3	yes			no	PP, EP	0	27; 34
3264	CORROSIVE LIQUID, ACIDIC, INORGANIC, N.O.S.	8	C1	II	8	N	2	3		10	97		3	yes			no	PP, EP	0	27; 34
3264	CORROSIVE LIQUID, ACIDIC, INORGANIC, N.O.S.	8	C1	III	8	N	4	3			97		3	yes			no	PP, EP	0	27; 34
3264	CORROSIVE LIQUID, ACIDIC, INORGANIC, N.O.S. (aqueous solution of phosphoric acid and citric acid)	8	C1	I	8	N	2	3		10	97		3	yes			no	PP, EP	0	34
3264	CORROSIVE LIQUID, ACIDIC, INORGANIC, N.O.S. (aqueous solution of phosphoric acid and citric acid)	8	C1	II	8	N	4	3			97		3	yes			no	PP, EP	0	34
3264	CORROSIVE LIQUID, ACIDIC, INORGANIC, N.O.S. (aqueous solution of phosphoric acid and citric acid)	8	C1	III	8	N	4	3			97		3	yes			no	PP, EP	0	34
3265	CORROSIVE LIQUID, ACIDIC, ORGANIC, N.O.S.	8	C3	I	8	N	2	3		10	97		3	yes			no	PP, EP	0	27; 34
3265	CORROSIVE LIQUID, ACIDIC, ORGANIC, N.O.S.	8	C3	II	8	N	2	3		10	97		3	yes			no	PP, EP	0	27; 34

(1) UN No. or substance identification No.	(2) Name and description	(3a) Class	(3b) Classification code	(4) Packing group	(5) Labels	(6) Type of tank vessel	(7) Cargo tank design	(8) Cargo tank type	(9) Cargo tank equipment	(10) Opening pressure of the high-velocity vent valve in kPa	(11) Maximum degree of filling in %	(12) Relative density at 20 °C	(13) Type of sampling device	(14) Pump room below deck permitted	(15) Temperature class	(16) Explosion group	(17) Anti-explosion protection required	(18) Equipment required	(19) Number of cones/blue lights	(20) Additional requirements/Remarks
3265	CORROSIVE LIQUID, ACIDIC, ORGANIC, N.O.S.	8	C3	III	8	N	4	3			97		3	yes			no	PP, EP	0	27; 34
3266	CORROSIVE LIQUID, BASIC, INORGANIC, N.O.S.	8	C5	I	8	N	4	2			97		3	yes			no	PP, EP	0	27; 34
3266	CORROSIVE LIQUID, BASIC, INORGANIC, N.O.S.	8	C5	II	8	N	4	2			97		3	yes			no	PP, EP	0	27; 34
3266	CORROSIVE LIQUID, BASIC, INORGANIC, N.O.S.	8	C5	III	8	N	4	2			97		3	yes			no	PP, EP	0	27; 34
3267	CORROSIVE LIQUID, BASIC, ORGANIC, N.O.S.	8	C7	I	8	N	4	2			97		3	yes			no	PP, EP	0	27; 34
3267	CORROSIVE LIQUID, BASIC, ORGANIC, N.O.S.	8	C7	II	8	N	4	2			97		3	yes			no	PP, EP	0	27; 34
3267	CORROSIVE LIQUID, BASIC, ORGANIC, N.O.S.	8	C7	III	8	N	4	2			97		3	yes			no	PP, EP	0	27; 34
3271	ETHERS, N.O.S. vp50 ≤ 110 kPa	3	F1	II	3	N	2	2		10	97		3	yes	T4[3]	II B[4]	yes	PP, EX, A	1	14, 27, 29
3271	ETHERS, N.O.S. (tert-amylmethyl ether)	3	F1	II	3	N	2	2		10	97	0.77	3	yes	T2	II B[4]	yes	PP, EX, A	1	
3271	ETHERS, N.O.S.	3	F1	III	3	N	3	2			97		3	yes	T4[3]	II B[4]	yes	PP, EX, A	0	14, 27
3272	ESTERS, N.O.S. vp50 ≤ 110 kPa	3	F1	II	3	N	2	2		10	97	0.77	3	yes	T2	II B[4]	yes	PP, EX, A	1	14, 27, 29
3272	ESTERS, N.O.S.	3	F1	III	3	N	3	2			97		3	yes	T4[3]	II B[4]	yes	PP, EX, A	0	14, 27
3276	NITRILES, TOXIC, LIQUID, N.O.S. (2-methylglutaronitrile)	6.1	T1	II	6.1	C	2	2	3	10	97	0.95	2	no			no	PP, EP, TOX, A	2	
3286	FLAMMABLE LIQUID, TOXIC, CORROSIVE, N.O.S. boiling point ≤ 60 °C	3	FTC	I	3+6.1+8	C	1	1			95		1	no	T4[3]	II B[4]	yes	PP, EP, EX, TOX, A	2	27; 29
3286	FLAMMABLE LIQUID, TOXIC, CORROSIVE, N.O.S. boiling point ≤ 60 °C	3	FTC	II	3+6.1+8	C	1	1			95		1	no	T4[3]	II B[4]	yes	PP, EP, EX, TOX, A	2	27; 29
3286	FLAMMABLE LIQUID, TOXIC, CORROSIVE, N.O.S. 60 °C < boiling point ≤ 85 °C	3	FTC	II	3+6.1+8	C	2	2		50	95		2	no	T4[3]	II B[4]	yes	PP, EP, EX, TOX, A	2	23, 27; 29

(1) UN No. or substance identification No.	(2) Name and description	3 (a) Class	3 (b) Classification code	(4) Packing group	(5) Labels	(6) Type of tank vessel	(7) Cargo tank design	(8) Cargo tank type	(9) Cargo tank equipment	(10) Opening pressure of the high-velocity vent valve in kPa	(11) Maximum degree of filling in %	(12) Relative density at 20 °C	(13) Type of sampling device	(14) Pump room below deck permitted	(15) Temperature class	(16) Explosion group	(17) Anti-explosion protection required	(18) Equipment required	(19) Number of cones/blue lights	(20) Additional requirements/Remarks
3286	FLAMMABLE LIQUID, TOXIC, CORROSIVE, N.O.S. 85 °C < boiling point ≤ 115 °C	3	FTC	II	3+6.1+8	C	2	2		50	95		2	no	T4³⁾	II B⁴⁾	yes	PP, EP, EX, TOX, A	2	27; 29
3286	FLAMMABLE LIQUID, TOXIC, CORROSIVE, N.O.S. boiling point > 115 °C	3	FTC	II	3+6.1+8	C	2	2		35	95		2	no	T4³⁾	II B⁴⁾	yes	PP, EP, EX, TOX, A	2	27; 29
3287	TOXIC LIQUID, INORGANIC, N.O.S. boiling point ≤ 60 °C	6.1	T4	I	6.1	C	1	1			95		1	no			no	PP, EP, TOX, A	2	27; 29
3287	TOXIC LIQUID, INORGANIC, N.O.S. 60 °C < boiling point ≤ 85 °C	6.1	T4	I	6.1	C	2	2	3	50	95		1	no			no	PP, EP, TOX, A	2	23; 27; 29
3287	TOXIC LIQUID, INORGANIC, N.O.S. 85 °C < boiling point ≤ 115 °C	6.1	T4	I	6.1	C	2	2		50	95		1	no			no	PP, EP, TOX, A	2	27; 29
3287	TOXIC LIQUID, INORGANIC, N.O.S. boiling point > 115 °C	6.1	T4	I	6.1	C	2	2		35	95		1	no			no	PP, EP, TOX, A	2	27; 29
3287	TOXIC LIQUID, INORGANIC, N.O.S. boiling point ≤ 60 °C	6.1	T4	II	6.1	C	1	1			95		1	no			no	PP, EP, TOX, A	2	27; 29
3287	TOXIC LIQUID, INORGANIC, N.O.S. 60 °C < boiling point ≤ 85 °C	6.1	T4	II	6.1	C	2	2	3	50	95		2	no			no	PP, EP, TOX, A	2	23; 27; 29
3287	TOXIC LIQUID, INORGANIC, N.O.S. 85 °C < boiling point ≤ 115 °C	6.1	T4	II	6.1	C	2	2		50	95		2	no			no	PP, EP, TOX, A	2	27; 29
3287	TOXIC LIQUID, INORGANIC, N.O.S. boiling point > 115 °C	6.1	T4	II	6.1	C	2	2		35	95		2	no			no	PP, EP, TOX, A	2	27; 29
3287	TOXIC LIQUID, INORGANIC, N.O.S. boiling point ≤ 60 °C	6.1	T4	III	6.1	C	1	1			95		1	no			no	PP, EP, TOX, A	0	27; 29
3287	TOXIC LIQUID, INORGANIC, N.O.S. 60 °C < boiling point ≤ 85 °C	6.1	T4	III	6.1	C	2	2	3	50	95		2	no			no	PP, EP, TOX, A	0	23; 27; 29

(1) UN No. or substance identification No.	(2) Name and description	(3a) Class	(3b) Classification code	(4) Packing group	(5) Labels	(6) Type of tank vessel	(7) Cargo tank design	(8) Cargo tank type	(9) Cargo tank equipment	(10) Opening pressure of the high-velocity vent valve in kPa	(11) Maximum degree of filling in %	(12) Relative density at 20 °C	(13) Type of sampling device	(14) Pump room below deck permitted	(15) Temperature class	(16) Explosion group	(17) Anti-explosion protection required	(18) Equipment required	(19) Number of cones/blue lights	(20) Additional requirements/Remarks
3287	TOXIC LIQUID, INORGANIC, N.O.S. 85 °C < boiling point ≤ 115 °C	6.1	T4	III	6.1	C	2	2		50	95		2	no			no	PP, EP, TOX, A	0	27; 29
3287	TOXIC LIQUID, INORGANIC, N.O.S. boiling point > 115 °C	6.1	T4	III	6.1	C	2	2		35	95		2	no			no	PP, EP, TOX, A	0	27; 29
3287	TOXIC LIQUID, INORGANIC, N.O.S. (sodium dichromate solution)	6.1	T4	III	6.1	C	2	2		30	95	1.68	2	no			no	PP, EP, TOX, A	0	
3289	TOXIC LIQUID, CORROSIVE, INORGANIC, N.O.S. boiling point ≤ 60 °C	6.1	TC3	I	6.1+8	C	1	1			95		1	no			no	PP, EP, TOX, A	2	27; 29
3289	TOXIC LIQUID, CORROSIVE, INORGANIC, N.O.S. 60 °C < boiling point ≤ 85 °C	6.1	TC3	I	6.1+8	C	2	2	3	50	95		2	no			no	PP, EP, TOX, A	2	23; 27; 29
3289	TOXIC LIQUID, CORROSIVE, INORGANIC, N.O.S. 85 °C < boiling point ≤ 115 °C	6.1	TC3	I	6.1+8	C	2	2		50	95		2	no			no	PP, EP, TOX, A	2	27; 29
3289	TOXIC LIQUID, CORROSIVE, INORGANIC, N.O.S. boiling point > 115 °C	6.1	TC3	I	6.1+8	C	2	2		35	95		2	no			no	PP, EP, TOX, A	2	27; 29
3289	TOXIC LIQUID, CORROSIVE, INORGANIC, N.O.S. boiling point ≤ 60 °C	6.1	TC3	II	6.1+8	C	1	1			95		1	no			no	PP, EP, TOX, A	2	27; 29
3289	TOXIC LIQUID, CORROSIVE, INORGANIC, N.O.S. 60 °C < boiling point ≤ 85 °C	6.1	TC3	II	6.1+8	C	2	2	3	50	95		2	no			no	PP, EP, TOX, A	2	23; 27; 29
3289	TOXIC LIQUID, CORROSIVE, INORGANIC, N.O.S. 85 °C < boiling point ≤ 115 °C	6.1	TC3	II	6.1+8	C	2	2		50	95		2	no			no	PP, EP, TOX, A	2	27; 29
3289	TOXIC LIQUID, CORROSIVE, INORGANIC, N.O.S. boiling point > 115 °C	6.1	TC3	II	6.1+8	C	2	2		35	95		2	no			no	PP, EP, TOX, A	2	27; 29
3295	HYDROCARBONS, LIQUID, N.O.S. vp50 > 175 kPa	3	F1	I	3	N	1	1			97		1	yes	T4[3]	IIB[4]	yes	PP, EX, A	1	14; 27; 29

(1) UN No. or substance identification No.	(2) Name and description	3(a) Class	3(b) Classification code	(4) Packing group	(5) Labels	(6) Type of tank vessel	(7) Cargo tank design	(8) Cargo tank type	(9) Cargo tank equipment	(10) Opening pressure of the high-velocity vent valve in kPa	(11) Maximum degree of filling in %	(12) Relative density at 20 °C	(13) Type of sampling device	(14) Pump room below deck permitted	(15) Temperature class	(16) Explosion group	(17) Anti-explosion protection required	(18) Equipment required	(19) Number of cones/blue lights	(20) Additional requirements/Remarks
3295	HYDROCARBONS, LIQUID, N.O.S. vp50 > 175 kPa	3	F1	I	3	N	2	2	1	50	97		1	yes	T4³⁾	IIB⁴⁾	yes	PP, EX, A	1	14; 27; 29
3295	HYDROCARBONS, LIQUID, N.O.S. 110 kPa < vp50 ≤ 175 kPa	3	F1	I	3	N	2	2	3	50	97		3	yes	T4³⁾	IIB⁴⁾	yes	PP, EX, A	1	14; 27; 29
3295	HYDROCARBONS, LIQUID, N.O.S. 110 kPa < vp50 ≤ 150 kPa	3	F1	I	3	N	2	2		10	97		3	yes	T4³⁾	IIB⁴⁾	yes	PP, EX, A	1	14; 27; 29
3295	HYDROCARBONS, LIQUID, N.O.S. 110 kPa < vp50 ≤ 175 kPa	3	F1	II	3	N	2	2	3	50	97		3	yes	T4³⁾	IIB⁴⁾	yes	PP, EX, A	1	14; 27; 29
3295	HYDROCARBONS, LIQUID, N.O.S. 110 kPa < vp50 ≤ 150 kPa	3	F1	II	3	N	2	2		10	97		3	yes	T4³⁾	IIB⁴⁾	yes	PP, EX, A	1	14; 27; 29
3295	HYDROCARBONS, LIQUID, N.O.S. vp50 > 110 kPa	3	F1	II	3	N	2	2		10	97		3	yes	T4³⁾	IIB⁴⁾	yes	PP, EX, A	1	14; 27; 29
3295	HYDROCARBONS, LIQUID, N.O.S.	3	F1	III	3	N	3	2			97		3	yes	T4³⁾	IIB⁴⁾	yes	PP, EX, A	0	14; 27
3295	HYDROCARBONS, LIQUID, N.O.S. (1-octen)	3	F1	II	3	N	2	2		10	97	0.71	3	yes	T3	IIB⁴⁾	yes	PP, EX, A	1	14
3295	HYDROCARBONS, LIQUID, N.O.S. (polycyclic aromatic hydrocarbons mixture)	3	F1	III	3	N	3	2			97	1.08	3	yes	T1	II A	yes	PP, EX, A	0	14
3295	HYDROCARBONS, LIQUID, N.O.S. (... with more than 10 % benzene) vp50 > 175 kPa	3	F1	I	3	C	1	1			95		1	yes	T4³⁾	IIB⁴⁾	yes	PP, EX, A	1	27; 29
3295	HYDROCARBONS, LIQUID, N.O.S. (... with more than 10 % benzene) 110 kPa < vp50 ≤ 175 kPa	3	F1	I	3	C	1	1			95		1	yes	T4³⁾	IIB⁴⁾	yes	PP, EX, A	1	27; 29
3295	HYDROCARBONS, LIQUID, N.O.S. (... with more than 10 % benzene) 110 kPa < vp50 ≤ 175 kPa	3	F1	II	3	C	1	1			95		1	yes	T4³⁾	IIB⁴⁾	yes	PP, EX, A	1	27; 29

(1) UN No. or substance identification No.	(2) Name and description	(3a) Class	(3b) Classification code	(4) Packing group	(5) Labels	(6) Type of tank vessel	(7) Cargo tank design	(8) Cargo tank type	(9) Cargo tank equipment	(10) Opening pressure of the high-velocity vent valve in kPa	(11) Maximum degree of filling in %	(12) Relative density at 20 °C	(13) Type of sampling device	(14) Pump room below deck permitted	(15) Temperature class	(16) Explosion group	(17) Anti-explosion protection required	(18) Equipment required	(19) Number of cones/blue lights	(20) Additional requirements/Remarks
3295	HYDROCARBONS, LIQUID, N.O.S. (... with more than 10 % benzene) vp50 ≤ 110 kPa boiling point ≤ 60 °C	3	F1	II	3	C	1	1			95		1	yes	T4³⁾	II B⁴⁾	yes	PP, EX, A	1	27; 29
3295	HYDROCARBONS, LIQUID, N.O.S. (... with more than 10 % benzene) vp50 ≤ 110 kPa 60 °C < boiling point ≤ 85 °C	3	F1	II	3	C	2	2	3	50	95		2	yes	T4³⁾	II B⁴⁾	yes	PP, EX, A	1	23; 27; 29
3295	HYDROCARBONS, LIQUID, N.O.S. (... with more than 10 % benzene) vp50 ≤ 110 kPa 85 °C < boiling point ≤ 115 °C	3	F1	II	3	C	2	2		50	95		2	yes	T4³⁾	II B⁴⁾	yes	PP, EX, A	1	27; 29
3295	HYDROCARBONS, LIQUID, N.O.S. (... with more than 10 % benzene) vp50 ≤ 110 kPa boiling point > 115 °C	3	F1	II	3	C	2	2		35	95		2	yes	T4³⁾	II B⁴⁾	yes	PP, EX, A	1	27; 29
3295	HYDROCARBONS, LIQUID, N.O.S. (... with more than 10 % benzene) vp50 ≤ 110 kPa boiling point ≤ 60 °C	3	F1	III	3	C	2	2	3	50	95		2	yes	T4³⁾	II B⁴⁾	yes	PP, EX, A	0	23; 27; 29
3295	HYDROCARBONS, LIQUID, N.O.S. (... with more than 10 % benzene) vp50 ≤ 110 kPa 85 °C < boiling point ≤ 115 °C	3	F1	III	3	C	2	2		50	95		2	yes	T4³⁾	II B⁴⁾	yes	PP, EX, A	0	27; 29
3295	HYDROCARBONS, LIQUID, N.O.S. (... with more than 10 % benzene) vp50 ≤ 110 kPa boiling point > 115 °C	3	F1	III	3	C	2	2		35	95		2	yes	T4³⁾	II B⁴⁾	yes	PP, EX, A	0	27; 29
3426	ACRYLAMIDE, aqueous SOLUTION	6.1	T2	III	6.1	C	2	2		30	95	1.03	2	no			no	PP, EP, TOX, A	0	3; 5; 16

(1) UN No. or substance identification No.	(2) Name and description	(3)(a) Class	(3)(b) Classification code	(4) Packing group	(5) Labels	(6) Type of tank vessel	(7) Cargo tank design	(8) Cargo tank type	(9) Cargo tank equipment	(10) Opening pressure of the high-velocity vent valve in kPa	(11) Maximum degree of filling in %	(12) Relative density at 20 °C	(13) Type of sampling device	(14) Pump room below deck permitted	(15) Temperature class	(16) Explosion group	(17) Anti-explosion protection required	(18) Equipment required	(19) Number of cones/blue lights	(20) Additional requirements/Remarks
3429	CHLOROTOLUIDINES, LIQUID	6.1	T1	III	6.1	C	2	2		25	95	1.15	2	no	T1	II A[7]	yes	PP, EP, EX, TOX, A	0	6: +6 °C; 17
3446	NITROTOLUENES, SOLID (p-nitrotoluene, molten)	6.1	T2	II	6.1	C	2	2	2	25	95	1.16	2	no	T2	II B[4]	yes	PP, EP, EX, TOX, A	2	7; 17
3446	NITROTOLUENES, SOLID (p-nitrotoluene, molten)	6.1	T2	II	6.1	C	2	2	2	25	95	1.16	2	no			no	PP, EP, TOX, A	2	7; 17; 20: +88 °C
3451	TOLUIDINES. SOLID (p-toluidine, molten)	6.1	T2	II	6.1	C	2	2	2	25	95	1.05	2	no	T1	II A[8]	yes	PP, EP, EX, TOX, A	2	7; 17
3451	TOLUIDINES, SOLID (p-toluidine, molten)	6.1	T2	II	6.1	C	2	2	2	25	95	1.05	2	no			no	PP, EP, TOX, A	2	7; 17; 20: +60 °C
3455	CRESOLS, SOLID, molten	6.1	TC2	II	6.1+8	C	2	2	2	25	95	1.03 - 1.05	2	no	T1	II A[8]	yes	PP, EP, EX, TOX, A	2	7; 17
3455	CRESOLS, SOLID, molten	6.1	TC2	II	6.1+8	C	2	2	2	25	95	1.03 - 1.05	2	no			no	PP, EP, TOX, A	2	7; 17; 20: +66 °C
9000	AMMONIA, heavily refrigerated	2	3TC		2.1+2.3+8	G	1	1	1; 3		95		1	yes	T1	II A	yes	PP, EP, EX, TOX, A	2	1; 31
9001	SUBSTANCES with a flash-point above 61 °C, heated within a limiting range of 15 K below their flash-point, N.O.S.	3	F3			N	3	2			97		3	yes	T4[3]	II B[4]	yes	PP, EX, A	0	27
9002	SUBSTANCES with a self-ignition temperature of 200 °C or below, N.O.S.	3	F4		3	C	1	1			95		1	yes	T4	II B[4]	yes	PP, EX, A	0	
9003	SUBSTANCES with a flash-point above 61 °C but not more than 100 °C, N.O.S.	9				N	4	2			97		3	yes			no	PP	0	27
9003	SUBSTANCES with a flash-point above 61 °C but not more than 100 °C, N.O.S. (ethylene glycol monobutyl ether)	9				N	4	2			97	0.9	3	yes			no	PP	0	

(1)	(2)	(3)(a)	(3)(b)	(4)	(5)	(6)	(7)	(8)	(9)	(10)	(11)	(12)	(13)	(14)	(15)	(16)	(17)	(18)	(19)	(20)
UN No. or substance identification No.	Name and description	Class	Classification code	Packing group	Labels	Type of tank vessel	Cargo tank design	Cargo tank type	Cargo tank equipment	Opening pressure of the high-velocity vent valve in kPa	Maximum degree of filling in %	Relative density at 20 °C	Type of sampling device	Pump room below deck permitted	Temperature class	Explosion group	Anti-explosion protection required	Equipment required	Number of cones/blue lights	Additional requirements/Remarks
9003	SUBSTANCES with a flash-point above 61 °C but not more than 100 °C, N.O.S. (2-ethylhexyl-acrylate)	9				N	4	2			97	0.89	3	yes			no	PP	0	3; 5; 16
9004	DIPHENYLMETHANE-4,4'-DIISOCYANATE	9				N	2	3	2	10	95	1.21[1]	3	yes			no	PP	0	7; 8; 17; 19

Footnotes related to the list of substances

1) The ignition temperature has not been determined in accordance with IEC 79-4; therefore, provisional assignment has been made to temperature class T2 which is considered safe.

2) The ignition temperature has not been determined in accordance with IEC 79-4; therefore, provisional assignment has been made to temperature class T3 which is considered safe.

3) The ignition temperature has not been determined in accordance with IEC 79-1A; therefore, provisional assignment has been made to temperature class T4 which is considered safe.

4) No maximum experimental safe gap (MESG) has been measured in accordance with IEC 79-1A; therefore, provisional assignment has been made to explosion group IIB which is considered safe.

5) No maximum experimental safe gap (MESG) has been measured in accordance with IEC 79-1A; therefore, provisional assignment has been made to explosion group IIC which is considered safe.

6) The maximum experimental safe gap (MESG) is within the marginal range between explosion group IIA and IIB.

7) No maximum experimental safe gap (MESG) has been measured in accordance with IEC-79-1A; therefore, assignment has been made to the explosion group which is considered safe.

8) No maximum experimental safe gap (MESG) has been measured in accordance with IEC 79-1A; therefore, assignment has been made to the explosion group in compliance with EN 50014.

9) Assignment in accordance with IMO (International Code for the Construction and Equipment of Ships Carrying Dangerous Chemicals in Bulk) (IBC Code).

10) Relative density at 15 °C.

11) Relative density at 25 °C.

12) Relative density at 37 °C.

13) Indications related to the pure substance.

PART 4

Provisions concerning the use of packagings, tanks and bulk transport units

CHAPTER 4.1

GENERAL PROVISIONS

4.1.1   Packagings and tanks shall be used in accordance with the requirements of one of the international Regulations, bearing in mind the indications given in the list of substances of these international Regulations, namely:

- For packagings (including IBCs and large packagings): columns (9a) and (9b) of Chapter 3.2, Table A of RID or ADR, or the list of substances in Chapter 3.2 of the IMDG Code or the ICAO Technical Instructions;

- For portable tanks: columns (10) and (11) of Chapter 3.2, Table A of RID or ADR or the list of substances in the IMDG Code;

- For RID or ADR tanks: columns (12) and (13) of Chapter 3.2, Table A of RID or ADR.

4.1.2   The requirements to be implemented are as follows:

- For packagings (including IBCs and large packagings): Chapter 4.1 of RID, ADR, the IMDG Code or the ICAO Technical Instructions;

- For portable tanks: Chapter 4.2 of RID, ADR or the IMDG Code;

- For RID or ADR tanks: Chapter 4.3 of RID or ADR, and, where applicable, sections 4.2.5 or 4.2.6 of the IMDG Code;

- For fibre-reinforced plastics tanks: Chapter 4.4 of ADR;

- For vacuum-operated waste tanks: Chapter 4.5 of ADR.

4.1.3   For carriage in bulk of solids in vehicles, wagons or containers, the following requirements of the international Regulations shall be complied with:

- Chapter 4.3 of the IMDG Code; or

- Chapter 7.3 of ADR, taking account of indications in columns (10) or (17) of Table A of Chapter 3.2 of ADR, except that sheeted vehicles and containers are not allowed;

- Chapter 7.3 of RID, taking account of indications in columns (10) or (17) of Table A of Chapter 3.2 of RID, except that sheeted wagons and containers are not allowed.

4.1.4   Only packagings and tanks which meet the requirements of Part 6 may be used.

PART 5

Consignment procedures

CHAPTER 5.1

GENERAL PROVISIONS

5.1.1 **Application and general provisions**

This Part sets forth the provisions for dangerous goods consignments relative to marking, labelling, and documentation, and, where appropriate, authorisation of consignments and advance notifications.

5.1.2 **Use of overpacks**

5.1.2.1 (a) An overpack shall be marked with the word "OVERPACK" and the UN number preceded by the letters "UN", and shall be labelled as required for packages in 5.2.2, for each item of dangerous goods contained in the overpack, unless the markings and the labels representative of all dangerous goods contained in the overpack are visible. If the same marking or the same label is required for different packages, it only needs to be applied once.

 (b) Label conforming to model No. 11 illustrated in 5.2.2.2.2 shall be displayed on two opposite sides of the following overpacks:

 – overpacks containing packages which shall be labelled in accordance with 5.2.2.1.12, unless the labels remain visible; and

 – overpacks containing liquids in packages which need not be labelled in accordance with 5.2.2.1.12, unless the closures remain visible.

5.1.2.2 Each package of dangerous goods contained in an overpack shall comply with all applicable provisions of ADN. The "overpack" marking is an indication of compliance with this requirement. The intended function of each package shall not be impaired by the overpack.

5.1.2.3 The prohibitions on mixed loading also apply to these overpacks.

5.1.3 **Empty uncleaned packagings (including IBCs and large packagings), tanks, vehicles and containers for carriage in bulk**

5.1.3.1 Empty uncleaned packagings (including IBCs and large packagings), tanks (including tank-vehicles, battery-vehicles, demountable tanks, portable tanks, tank-containers, MEGCs), vehicles and containers for carriage in bulk having contained dangerous goods of the different classes other than Class 7, shall be marked and labelled as if they were full.

NOTE: For documentation, see Chapter 5.4.

5.1.3.2 Tanks and IBCs used for the carriage of radioactive material shall not be used for the storage or carriage of other goods unless decontaminated below the level of 0.4 Bq/cm^2 for beta and gamma emitters and low toxicity alpha emitters and 0.04 Bq/cm^2 for all other alpha emitters.

5.1.4 **Mixed packing**

When two or more dangerous goods are packed within the same outer packaging, the package shall be labelled and marked as required for each substance or article. If the same label is required for different goods, it only needs to be applied once.

5.1.5   **General provisions for Class 7**

5.1.5.1   *Requirements before shipments*

5.1.5.1.1   *Requirements before the first shipment of a package*

Before the first shipment of any package, the following requirements shall be fulfilled:

(a)   If the design pressure of the containment system exceeds 35 kPa (gauge), it shall be ensured that the containment system of each package conforms to the approved design requirements relating to the capability of that system to maintain its integrity under that pressure;

(b)   For each Type B(U), Type B(M) and Type C package and for each package containing fissile material, it shall be ensured that the effectiveness of its shielding and containment and, where necessary, the heat transfer characteristics and the effectiveness of the confinement system, are within the limits applicable to or specified for the approved design;

(c)   For packages containing fissile material, where, in order to comply with the requirements of 6.4.11.1 of ADR, neutron poisons are specifically included as components of the package, checks shall be performed to confirm the presence and distribution of those neutron poisons.

5.1.5.1.2   *Requirements before each shipment of a package*

Before each shipment of any package, the following requirements shall be fulfilled:

(a)   For any package it shall be ensured that all the requirements specified in the relevant provisions of ADN have been satisfied;

(b)   It shall be ensured that lifting attachments which do not meet the requirements of 6.4.2.2 of ADR have been removed or otherwise rendered incapable of being used for lifting the package, in accordance with 6.4.2.3 of ADR;

(c)   For each Type B(U), Type B(M) and Type C package and for each package containing fissile material, it shall be ensured that all the requirements specified in the approval certificates have been satisfied;

(d)   Each Type B(U), Type B(M) and Type C package shall be held until equilibrium conditions have been approached closely enough to demonstrate compliance with the requirements for temperature and pressure unless an exemption from these requirements has received unilateral approval;

(e)   For each Type B(U), Type B(M) and Type C package, it shall be ensured by inspection and/or appropriate tests that all closures, valves, and other openings of the containment system through which the radioactive contents might escape are properly closed and, where appropriate, sealed in the manner for which the demonstrations of compliance with the requirements of 6.4.8.7 of ADR were made;

(f)   For each special form radioactive material, it shall be ensured that all the requirements specified in the approval certificate and the relevant provisions of ADN have been satisfied;

(g) For packages containing fissile material the measurement specified in 6.4.11.4 (b) of ADR and the tests to demonstrate closure of each package as specified in 6.4.11.7 of ADR shall be performed where applicable;

(h) For each low dispersible radioactive material, it shall be ensured that all the requirements specified in the approval certificate and the relevant provisions of ADN have been satisfied.

5.1.5.2 *Approval of shipments and notification*

5.1.5.2.1 *General*

In addition to the approval for package designs described in Chapter 6.4 of ADR, multilateral shipment approval is also required in certain circumstances (5.1.5.2.2 and 5.1.5.2.3). In some circumstances it is also necessary to notify competent authorities of a shipment (5.1.5.2.4).

5.1.5.2.2 *Shipment approvals*

Multilateral approval shall be required for:

(a) the shipment of Type B(M) packages not conforming with the requirements of 6.4.7.5 of ADR or designed to allow controlled intermittent venting;

(b) the shipment of Type B(M) packages containing radioactive material with an activity greater than $3000 A_1$ or $3000 A_2$, as appropriate, or 1000 TBq, whichever is the lower;

(c) the shipment of packages containing fissile materials if the sum of the criticality safety indexes of the packages exceeds 50;

except that a competent authority may authorise carriage into or through its country without shipment approval, by a specific provision in its design approval (see 5.1.5.3.1).

5.1.5.2.3 *Shipment approval by special arrangement*

Provisions may be approved by a competent authority under which a consignment, which does not satisfy all of the applicable requirements of ADN may be carried under special arrangement (see 1.7.4).

5.1.5.2.4 *Notifications*

Notification to competent authorities is required as follows:

(a) Before the first shipment of any package requiring competent authority approval, the consignor shall ensure that copies of each applicable competent authority certificate applying to that package design have been submitted to the competent authority of each country through or into which the consignment is to be carried. The consignor is not required to await an acknowledgement from the competent authority, nor is the competent authority required to make such acknowledgement of receipt of the certificate;

(b) For each of the following types of shipments:

(i) Type C packages containing radioactive material with an activity greater than $3000 A_1$ or $3000 A_2$, as appropriate, or 1000 TBq, whichever is the lower;

(ii) Type B(U) packages containing radioactive material with an activity greater than 3000 A_1 or 3000 A_2, as appropriate, or 1000 TBq, whichever is the lower;

(iii) Type B(M) packages;

(iv) Shipment under special arrangement.

The consignor shall notify the competent authority of each country through or into which the consignment is to be carried. This notification shall be in the hands of each competent authority prior to the commencement of the shipment, and preferably at least 7 days in advance;

(c) The consignor is not required to send a separate notification if the required information has been included in the application for shipment approval;

(d) The consignment notification shall include:

(i) sufficient information to enable the identification of the package or packages including all applicable certificate numbers and identification marks;

(ii) information on the date of shipment, the expected date of arrival and proposed routeing;

(iii) the name(s) of the radioactive material(s) or nuclide(s);

(iv) descriptions of the physical and chemical forms of the radioactive material, or whether it is special form radioactive material or low dispersible radioactive material; and

(v) the maximum activity of the radioactive contents during carriage expressed in becquerels (Bq) with an appropriate SI prefix (see 1.2.2.1). For fissile material, the mass of fissile material in grams (g), or multiples thereof, may be used in place of activity.

5.1.5.3   *Certificates issued by the competent authority*

5.1.5.3.1   Certificates issued by the competent authority are required for the following:

(a) Designs for:

(i) special form radioactive material;

(ii) low dispersible radioactive material;

(iii) packages containing 0.1 kg or more of uranium hexafluoride;

(iv) all packages containing fissile material unless excepted by 6.4.11.2 of ADR;

(v) Type B(U) packages and Type B(M) packages;

(vi) Type C packages;

(b) Special arrangements;

(c) Certain shipments (see 5.1.5.2.2).

The certificates shall confirm that the applicable requirements are met, and for design approvals shall attribute to the design an identification mark.

The package design and shipment approval certificates may be combined into a single certificate.

Certificates and applications for these certificates shall be in accordance with the requirements in 6.4.23 of ADR.

5.1.5.3.2   The consignor shall be in possession of a copy of each applicable certificate. The consignor shall also have a copy of any instructions with regard to the proper closing of the package and any preparation for shipment before making any shipment under the terms of the certificates.

5.1.5.3.3   For package designs where a competent authority issued certificate is not required, the consignor shall, on request, make available for inspection by the competent authority, documentary evidence of the compliance of the package design with all the applicable requirements.

5.1.5.4   ***Summary of approval and prior notification requirements***

NOTE 1: *Before first shipment of any package requiring competent authority approval of the design, the consignor shall ensure that a copy of the approval certificate for that design has been submitted to the competent authority of each country en route (see 5.1.5.2.4 (a)).*

NOTE 2: *Notification required if contents exceed $3 \times 10^3 \, A_1$, or $3 \times 10^3 \, A_2$, or 1000 TBq (see 5.1.5.2.4 (b)).*

NOTE 3: *Multilateral approval of shipment required if contents exceed $3 \times 10^3 \, A_1$, or $3 \times 10^3 \, A_2$, or 1000 TBq, or if controlled intermittent venting is allowed (see 5.1.5.2).*

NOTE 4: *See approval and prior notification provisions for the applicable package for carrying this material.*

Subject	UN Number	Competent Authority approval required		Consignor required to notify the competent authorities of the country of origin and of the countries en route[a] before each shipment	Reference
		Country of origin	Countries en route[a]		
Calculation of unlisted A_1 and A_2 values	-	Yes	Yes	No	-
Excepted packages - package design - shipment	2908, 2909, 2910, 2911	 No No	 No No	 No No	-

Subject	UN Number	Competent Authority approval required		Consignor required to notify the competent authorities of the country of origin and of the countries en route[a] before each shipment	Reference
		Country of origin	Countries en route[a]		
LSA material[b] and SCO[b] Industrial packages types 1, 2 or 3, non fissile and fissile excepted - package design - shipment	2912, 2913, 3321, 3322	 No No	 No No	 No No	-
Type A packages,[b] non fissile and fissile excepted - package design - shipment	2915, 3332	 No No	 No No	 No No	-
Type B(U) packages,[b] non fissile and fissile excepted - package design - shipment	2916	 Yes No	 No No	 See Note 1 See Note 2	5.1.5.2.4 (b), 5.1.5.3.1 (a) 6.4.22.2
Type B(M) packages,[b] non fissile and fissile excepted - package design - shipment	2917	 Yes See Note 3	 Yes See Note 3	 No Yes	5.1.5.2.4 (b), 5.1.5.3.1 (a), 5.1.5.2.2. 6.4.22.3
Type C packages,[b] non fissile and fissile excepted - package design - shipment	3323	 Yes No	 No No	 See Note 1 See Note 2	5.1.5.2.4 (b), 5.1.5.3.1 (a) 6.4.22.2
Packages for fissile material - package design - shipment: - sum of criticality safety indexes not more than 50 - sum of criticality safety indexes greater than 50	2977, 3324, 3325, 3326, 3327, 3328, 3329, 3330, 3331, 3333	Yes[c] No[d] Yes	Yes[c] No[d] Yes	No See Note 2 See Note 2	5.1.5.3.1 (a), 5.1.5.2.2, 6.4.22.4
Special form radioactive material - design - shipment	- See Note 4	 Yes See Note 4	 No See Note 4	 No See Note 4	1.6.6.3, 5.1.5.3.1 (a) 6.4.22.5

Subject	UN Number	Competent Authority approval required		Consignor required to notify the competent authorities of the country of origin and of the countries en route[a] before each shipment	Reference
		Country of origin	Countries en route[a]		
Low dispersable radioactive material - design - shipment	- See Note 4	Yes See Note 4	No See Note 4	No See Note 4	5.1.5.3.1 (a), 6.4.22.5
Packages containing 0.1 kg or more of uranium hexafluoride - design - shipment	- See Note 4	Yes See Note 4	No See Note 4	No See Note 4	5.1.5.3.1 (a), 6.4.22.1
Special Arrangement - shipment	2919, 3331	Yes	Yes	Yes	1.7.4.2, 5.1.5.3.1 (b), 5.1.5.2.4 (b)
Approved packages designs subjected to transitional measures	-	See 1.6.6	See 1.6.6	See Note 1	1.6.6.1, 1.6.6.2, 5.1.5.2.4 (b), 5.1.5.3.1 (a), 5.1.5.2.2.

[a] *Countries from, through or into which the consignment is carried.*

[b] *If the radioactive contents are fissile material which is not excepted from the provisions for packages containing fissile material, then the provisions for fissile material packages apply (see 6.4.11 of ADR).*

[c] *Designs of packages for fissile material may also require approval in respect of one of the other items in the table.*

[d] *Shipments may, however, require approval in respect of one of the other items in the table.*

CHAPTER 5.2

MARKING AND LABELLING

5.2.1 **Marking of packages**

> ***NOTE***: *For markings related to the construction, testing and approval of packagings, large packagings, gas receptacles and IBCs, see Part 6 of ADR.*

5.2.1.1 Unless provided otherwise in ADN, the UN number corresponding to the dangerous goods contained, preceded by the letters "UN" shall be clearly and durably marked on each package. In the case of unpackaged articles the marking shall be displayed on the article, on its cradle or on its handling, storage or launching device.

5.2.1.2 All package markings required by this Chapter:

(a) shall be readily visible and legible;

(b) shall be able to withstand open weather exposure without a substantial reduction in effectiveness.

5.2.1.3 Salvage packagings shall additionally be marked with the word "**SALVAGE**".

5.2.1.4 Intermediate bulk containers of more than 450 litres capacity shall be marked on two opposite sides.

5.2.1.5 ***Additional provisions for goods of Class 1***

For goods of Class 1, packages shall, in addition, bear the proper shipping name as determined in accordance with 3.1.2. The marking, which shall be clearly legible and indelible, shall be in an official language of the country of origin and also, if that language is not English, French or German, in English, French or German unless any agreements concluded between the countries concerned in the transport operation provide otherwise.

5.2.1.6 ***Additional provisions for goods of Class 2***

Refillable receptacles shall bear the following particulars in clearly legible and durable characters:

(a) the UN number and the proper shipping name of the gas or mixture of gases, as determined in accordance with 3.1.2.

In the case of gases classified under an N.O.S. entry, only the technical name[1] of the gas has to be indicated in addition to the UN number.

---

[1] *Instead of the proper shipping name or , if applicable, of the proper shipping name of the n.o.s. entry followed by the technical name, the use of the following names is permitted:*
- *for UN No. 1078 refrigerant gas, n.o.s: mixture F1, mixture F2, mixture F3;*
- *for UN No. 1060 methylacetylene and propadiene mixtures, stabilized: mixture P1, mixture P2;*
- *for UN No. 1965 hydrocarbon gas mixture, liquefied, n.o.s: mixture A, mixture A01, mixture A02, mixture A0, mixture A1, mixture B1, mixture B2, mixture B, mixture C. The names customary in the trade and mentioned in 2.2.2.3, Classification code 2F, UN No. 1965, Note 1 may be used only as a complement;*
- *for UN No. 1010 Butadienes, stabilized: 1,2-Butadiene, stabilized, 1,3-Butadiene, stabilized .*

In the case of mixtures, not more than the two constituents which most predominantly contribute to the hazards have to be indicated;

(b)   for compressed gases filled by mass and for liquefied gases, either the maximum filling mass and the tare of the receptacle with fittings and accessories as fitted at the time of filling, or the gross mass;

(c)   the date (year) of the next periodic inspection.

These marks can either be engraved or indicated on a durable information disk or label attached on the receptacle or indicated by an adherent and clearly visible marking such as by printing or by any equivalent process.

NOTE 1: *See also 6.2.1.7 of ADR..*

NOTE 2: *For non refillable receptacles, see 6.2.1.8 of ADR..*

5.2.1.7   ***Special marking provisions for goods of Class 7***

5.2.1.7.1   Each package shall be legibly and durably marked on the outside of the packaging with an identification of either the consignor or consignee, or both.

5.2.1.7.2   For each package, other than excepted packages, the UN number preceded by the letters "UN" and the proper shipping name shall be legibly and durably marked on the outside of the packaging. In the case of excepted packages only the UN number, preceded by the letters "UN", is required.

5.2.1.7.3   Each package of gross mass exceeding 50 kg shall have its permissible gross mass legibly and durably marked on the outside of the packaging.

5.2.1.7.4   Each package which conforms to:

(a)   a Type IP-1 package, a Type IP-2 package or a Type IP-3 package design shall be legibly and durably marked on the outside of the packaging with "TYPE IP-1", "TYPE IP-2" or "TYPE IP-3" as appropriate;

(b)   a Type A package design shall be legibly and durably marked on the outside of the packaging with "TYPE A";

(c)   a Type IP-2 package, a Type IP-3 package or a Type A package design shall be legibly and durably marked on the outside of the packaging with the international vehicle registration code (VRI Code)[2] of the country of origin of design and the name of the manufacturers, or other identification of the packaging specified by the competent authority.

5.2.1.7.5   Each package which conforms to a design approved by the competent authority shall be legibly and durably marked on the outside of the packaging with:

(a)   the identification mark allocated to that design by the competent authority;

(b)   a serial number to uniquely identify each packaging which conforms to that design;

---

[2]   *Distinguishing sign for motor vehicles in international traffic prescribed in the Vienna Convention on Road Traffic (1968).*

(c)   in the case of a Type B(U) or Type B(M) package design, with "TYPE B(U)" or "TYPE B(M)"; and

(d)   in the case of a Type C package design, with "TYPE C".

5.2.1.7.6   Each package which conforms to a Type B(U), Type B(M) or Type C package design shall have the outside of the outermost receptacle which is resistant to the effects of fire and water plainly marked by embossing, stamping or other means resistant to the effects of fire and water with the trefoil symbol shown in the figure below.

Basic trefoil symbol with proportions based on a central circle
of radius X. The minimum allowable size of X shall be 4 mm.

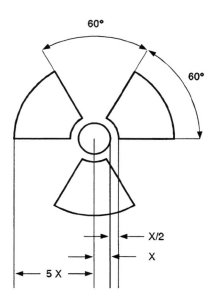

5.2.1.7.7   Where LSA-I or SCO-I material is contained in receptacles or wrapping materials and is carried under exclusive use as permitted by 4.1.9.2.3 of ADR, the outer surface of these receptacles or wrapping materials may bear the marking "RADIOACTIVE LSA-I" or "RADIOACTIVE SCO-I", as appropriate.

5.2.2   Labelling of packages

5.2.2.1   *Labelling provisions*

5.2.2.1.1   For each article or substance listed in Table A of Chapter 3.2, the labels shown in Column (5) shall be affixed unless otherwise provided for by a special provision in Column (6).

5.2.2.1.2   Indelible danger markings corresponding exactly to the prescribed models may be used instead of labels.

5.2.2.1.3-   *(Reserved)*
5.2.2.1.5

5.2.2.1.6   Except as provided in 5.2.2.2.1.2, each label shall:

(a)   be affixed to the same surface of the package, if the dimensions of the package allow; for packages of Class 1 and 7, near the mark indicating the proper shipping name;

(b)   be so placed on the package that it is not covered or obscured by any part or attachment to the packaging or any other label or marking; and

(c)   be displayed next to each other when more than one label is required.

Where a package is of such an irregular shape or small size that a label cannot be satisfactorily affixed, the label may be attached to the package by a securely affixed tag or other suitable means.

5.2.2.1.7   Intermediate bulk containers of more than 450 litres capacity shall be labelled on two opposite sides.

5.2.2.1.8   (*Reserved*)

5.2.2.1.9   *Special provisions for the labelling of self-reactive substances and organic peroxides*

(a)   the label conforming to model No. 4.1 also implies that the product may be flammable and hence no label conforming to model No. 3 is required. In addition, a label conforming to model No. 1 shall be applied for self-reactive substances Type B, unless the competent authority has permitted this label to be dispensed with for a specific packaging because test data have proven that the self-reactive substance in such a packaging does not exhibit explosive behaviour.

(b)   the label conforming to model No. 5.2 also implies that the product may be flammable and hence no label conforming to model No. 3 is required. In addition, the following labels shall be applied:

(i)   a label conforming to model No. 1 for organic peroxides type B, unless the competent authority has permitted this label to be dispensed with for a specific packaging because test data have proven that the organic peroxide in such a packaging does not exhibit explosive behaviour;

(ii)   a label conforming to model No. 8 is required when Packing Group I or II criteria of Class 8 are met.

For self-reactive substances and organic peroxides mentioned by name, the labels to be affixed are indicated in the list found in 2.2.41.4 and 2.2.52.4 respectively.

5.2.2.1.10   *Special provisions for the labelling of infectious substances packages*

In addition to the label conforming to model No. 6.2, infectious substances packages shall bear any other label required by the nature of the contents.

5.2.2.1.11   *Special provisions for the labelling of radioactive material*

5.2.2.1.11.1   Except as provided for large containers and tanks in accordance with 5.3.1.1.3, each package, overpack and container containing radioactive material shall bear at least two labels which conform to the models Nos. 7A, 7B, and 7C as appropriate according to the category (see 2.2.7.8.4) of that package, overpack or container. Labels shall be affixed to two opposite sides on the outside of the package or on the outside of all four sides of the container. Each overpack containing radioactive material shall bear at least two labels on opposite sides of the outside of the overpack. In addition, each package, overpack and container containing fissile material, other than fissile material excepted under 6.4.11.2 of ADR shall bear labels which conform to model No. 7E; such labels, where applicable shall be affixed adjacent to the labels for radioactive material. Labels shall not cover the markings specified in 5.2.1. Any labels which do not relate to the contents shall be removed or covered.

5.2.2.1.11.2 Each label conforming to models Nos. 7A, 7B, and 7C shall be completed with the following information:

(a) *Contents*:

(i) except for LSA-I material, the name(s) of the radionuclide(s) as taken from Table 2.2.7.7.2.1, using the symbols prescribed therein. For mixtures of radionuclides, the most restrictive nuclides shall be listed to the extent the space on the line permits. The group of LSA or SCO shall be shown following the name(s) of the radionuclide(s). The terms "LSA-II","LSA-III", "SCO-I" and "SCO-II" shall be used for this purpose;

(ii) for LSA-I material, only the term "LSA-I" is necessary; the name of the radionuclide is not necessary;

(b) *Activity*: The maximum activity of the radioactive contents during carriage expressed in becquerels (Bq) with the appropriate SI prefix (see 1.2.2.1). For fissile material, the mass of fissile material in grams (g), or multiples thereof, may be used in place of activity;

(c) For overpacks and containers the "contents" and "activity" entries on the label shall bear the information required in (a) and (b) above, respectively, totalled together for the entire contents of the overpack or container except that on labels for overpacks or containers containing mixed loads of packages containing different radionuclides, such entries may read "See Transport Documents";

(d) *Transport index (TI)*: see 2.2.7.6.1.1 and 2.2.7.6.1.2 (no transport index entry is required for category I-WHITE).

5.2.2.1.11.3 Each label conforming to the model No. 7E shall be completed with the criticality safety index (CSI) as stated in the certificate of approval for special arrangement or the certificate of approval for the package design issued by the competent authority.

5.2.2.1.11.4 For overpacks and containers, the criticality safety index (CSI) on the label shall bear the information required in 5.2.2.1.11.3 totalled together for the fissile contents of the overpack or container.

5.2.2.1.12 *Additional labelling*

With the exception of Classes 1 and 7, label conforming to model No. 11 illustrated in 5.2.2.2.2 shall be displayed on two opposite sides of a package on the following packages:

– packages containing liquids in receptacles, the closures of which are not visible from the outside;

– packages containing vented receptacles or vented receptacles without outer packaging; and

– packages containing refrigerated liquefied gases.

5.2.2.2 *Provisions for labels*

5.2.2.2.1 Labels shall satisfy the provisions below and conform, in terms of colour, symbols and general format, to the models shown in 5.2.2.2.2.

5.2.2.2.1.1 Labels, except labels conforming to model No. 11, shall be in the form of a square set at an angle of 45° (diamond-shaped) with minimum dimensions of 100 mm by 100 mm. They have a line of the same colour as the symbol, 5 mm inside the edge and running parallel with it. Labels conforming to model No. 11 shall be rectangular, of standard format A5 (148 × 210 mm). For receptacles intended for the carriage of refrigerated liquefied gases the standard format of A7 (74 x 105 mm) may also be used. If the size of the package so requires, the dimensions of the labels may be reduced, provided that they remain clearly visible.

5.2.2.2.1.2 Gas cylinders for Class 2 may, on account of their shape, orientation and securing mechanisms for carriage, bear labels representative of those specified in this section, which have been reduced in size, according to the dimensions outlined in ISO 7225:1994, *"Gas cylinders - Precautionary labels"*, for display on the non-cylindrical part (shoulder) of such cylinders.

Notwithstanding the provisions of 5.2.2.1.6, labels may overlap to the extent provided for by ISO 7225. However, in all cases, the primary risk label and the figures appearing on any label shall remain fully visible and the symbols recognizable.

5.2.2.2.1.3 Labels, except labels conforming to model No. 11, are divided into halves. With the exception of Divisions 1.4, 1.5 and 1.6, the upper half of the label is reserved for the pictorial symbol and the lower half for texts and the class number and the compatibility group letter as appropriate.

NOTE: For the labels of Classes 1, 2, 3, 5.1, 5.2, 7, 8 and 9, the respective class number shall be shown in the bottom corner. For the labels of Classes 4.1, 4.2 and 4.3 and of Classes 6.1 and 6.2 only figures 4 and 6 respectively shall be shown in the bottom corner (see 5.2.2.2.2).

5.2.2.2.1.4 Except for Divisions 1.4, 1.5 and 1.6, labels for Class 1 show in the lower half the division number and compatibility group letter for the substance or article. Labels for Divisions 1.4, 1.5 and 1.6 show in the upper half the division number and in the lower half the compatibility group letter.

5.2.2.2.1.5 On labels other than those for material of Class 7, the optional insertion of any text (other than the class number) in the space below the symbol shall be confined to particulars indicating the nature of the risk and precautions to be taken in handling.

5.2.2.2.1.6 The symbols, text and numbers shall be clearly legible and indelible and shall be shown in black on all labels except for:

(a)   the Class 8 label, where the text (if any) and class number shall appear in white;

(b)   labels with entirely green, red or blue backgrounds where they may be shown in white; and

(c)   labels conforming to model No. 2.1 displayed on cylinders and gas cartridges for gases of UN Nos. 1011, 1075, 1965 and 1978, where they may be shown in the background colour of the receptacle if adequate contrast is provided.

5.2.2.2.1.7 All labels shall be able to withstand open weather exposure without a substantial reduction in effectiveness.

5.2.2.2.2   *Specimen labels*

CLASS 1 HAZARD
Explosive substances or articles

(No.1)
Divisions 1.1, 1.2 and 1.3
Symbol (exploding bomb): black; Background: orange; Figure '1' in bottom corner

| (No 1.4) | (No 1.5) | (No 1.6) |
| Division 1.4 | Division 1.5 | Division 1.6 |

Background: orange; Figures: black; Numerals shall be about 30 mm in height
and be about 5 mm thick (for a label measuring 100 mm x 100 mm); Figure '1' in bottom corner

★★ Place for division - to be left blank if explosive is the subsidiary risk
★   Place for compatibility group - to be left blank if explosive is the subsidiary risk

CLASS 2 HAZARD
Gaz

(No.2.1)   (No.2.2)
Flammable gases   Non flammable, non-toxic gases
Symbol (flame): black or white;   Symbol (gas cylinder): black or white;
(except as provided for in 5.2.2.2.1.6 c)) Background: green; Figure '2' in bottom corner
Background: red; Figure '2' in bottom corner

(No 2.3)
Toxic gases
Symbol (skull and crossbones): black;
Background: white; Figure '2' in bottom corner

CLASS 3 HAZARD
Flammable liquids

(No 3)
Symbol (flame): black or white;
Background: red; Figure '3' in bottom corner

CLASS 4.1 HAZARD
Flammable solids, self-reactive substances and desensitized explosives

CLASS 4.2 HAZARD
Substances liable to spontaneous combustion

CLASS 4.3 HAZARD
Substances which, in contact with water, emit flammable gases

(No 4.1)
Symbol (flame): black;
Background: white with
seven vertical red stripes;
Figure '4' in bottom corner

(No 4.2)
Symbol (flame): black;
Background: upper half white,
lower half red;
Figure '4' in bottom corner

(No 4.3)
Symbol (flame): black or white;
Background: blue;
Figure '4' in bottom corner

CLASS 5.1 HAZARD
Oxidizing substances

CLASS 5.2 HAZARD
Organic peroxides

(No 5.1)   (No 5.2)
Symbol (flame over circle): black; Background: yellow;
Figures '5.1' in bottom corner   Figures '5.2' in bottom corner

CLASS 6.1 HAZARD
Toxic substances

(No 6.1)
Symbol (skull and crossbones): black;
Background: white; Figure '6' in bottom corner

CLASS 6.2 HAZARD
Infectious substances

(No 6.2)
The lower half of the label may bear the inscriptions: 'INFECTIOUS SUBSTANCE'
and 'In the case of damage or leakage immediately notify Public Health Authority';
Symbol (three crescents superimposed on a circle) and inscriptions: black;
Background: white; Figure '6' in bottom corner

CLASS 7 HAZARD
Radioactive material

(No. 7A)
Category I - White
Symbol (trefoil): black;
Background: white;
Text (mandatory): black in lower half of label:
'RADIOACTIVE'
'CONTENTS ....'
'ACTIVITY ......'
One red bar shall
follow the word 'RADIOACTIVE';
Figure '7' in bottom corner.

(No 7B)
Category II - Yellow

(No 7C)
Category III - Yellow

Symbol (trefoil): black;
Background: upper half yellow with white border, lower half white;
Text (mandatory): black in lower half of label:
'RADIOACTIVE'
'CONTENTS ....'
'ACTIVITY ......'
In a black outlined box: 'TRANSPORT INDEX;
Two red vertical bars shall   Three red vertical bars shall
follow the word 'RADIOACTIVE';   follow the word 'RADIOACTIVE';
Figure '7' in bottom corner.

(No. 7E)
Class 7 fissile material
Background: white;
Text (mandatory): black in upper half of label: 'FISSILE';
In a black outlined box in the lower half of the label:
'CRITICALITY SAFETY INDEX'
Figure '7' in bottom corner.

CLASS 8 HAZARD
Corrosive substances

CLASS 9 HAZARD
Miscellaneous dangerous substances and articles

(No. 8)
Symbol (liquids, spilling from two glass vessels
and attacking a hand and a metal): black;
Background: upper half white;
lower half black with white border;
Figure '8' in bottom corner

(No. 9)
Symbol (seven vertical stripes in upper half): black;
Background: white;
Figure '9' underlined in bottom corner

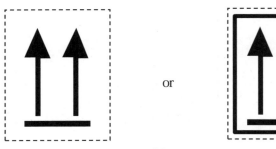

or

No11
Two black or red arrows on white
or suitable contrasting background

CHAPTER 5.3

PLACARDING AND MARKING OF CONTAINERS, MEGCs, TANK-CONTAINERS, PORTABLE TANKS, VEHICLES AND WAGONS

NOTE 1: *For marking and placarding of containers, MEGCs, tank-containers and portable tanks for carriage in a transport chain including a maritime journey, see also 1.1.4.2. If the provisions of 1.1.4.2 (c) are applied, only 5.3.1.3 and 5.3.2.1.1 of this Chapter are applicable.*

NOTE 2: *For the purposes of this subsection, "transport unit" means a motor vehicle without an attached trailer or a combination consisting of a motor vehicle and an attached trailer.*

5.3.1 **Placarding**

5.3.1.1 *General provisions*

5.3.1.1.1 As and when required in this section, placards shall be affixed to the exterior surface of containers, MEGCs, tank-containers, portable tanks, vehicles and wagons. Placards shall correspond to the labels required in Column (5) and, where appropriate, Column (6) of Table A of Chapter 3.2 for the dangerous goods contained in the container, MEGC, tank-container, portable tank, vehicle or wagon and shall conform to the specifications given in 5.3.1.7.

5.3.1.1.2 For Class 1, compatibility groups shall not be indicated on placards if the vehicle or wagon or container is carrying substances or articles belonging to two or more compatibility groups. Vehicles or wagons or containers carrying substances or articles of different divisions shall bear only placards conforming to the model of the most dangerous division in the order:

1.1 (most dangerous), 1.5, 1.2, 1.3, 1.6, 1.4 (least dangerous).

When 1.5D substances are carried with substances or articles of Division 1.2, the vehicle, wagon or container shall be placarded as Division 1.1.

5.3.1.1.3 For Class 7, the primary risk placard shall conform to model No. 7D as specified in 5.3.1.7.2. This placard is not required for vehicles, wagons or containers carrying excepted packages and for small containers.

Where both Class 7 labels and placards would be required to be affixed to vehicles, wagons, containers, MEGCs, tank-containers or portable tanks, an enlarged label corresponding to the label required may be displayed instead of placard No. 7D to serve both purposes.

5.3.1.1.4 Containers, MEGCs, tank-containers, portable tanks, vehicles or wagons containing goods of more than one class need not bear a subsidiary risk placard if the hazard represented by that placard is already indicated by a primary or subsidiary risk placard.

5.3.1.1.5 Placards which do not relate to the dangerous goods being carried, or residues thereof, shall be removed or covered.

5.3.1.2   *Placarding of containers, MEGCs, tank-containers and portable tanks*

NOTE: This subsection does not apply to swap-bodies, except tank swap bodies carried on vehicles bearing the orange markings stipulated in 5.3.2.

The placards shall be affixed to both sides and at each end of the container, MEGC, tank-container or portable tank.

When the tank-container or portable tank has multiple compartments and carries two or more dangerous goods, the appropriate placards shall be displayed along each side at the position of the relevant compartments and one placard of each model shown on each side at both ends.

5.3.1.3   *Placarding of vehicles carrying containers, MEGCs, tank-containers or portable tanks*

NOTE: This subsection does not apply to swap-bodies, except tank swap bodies carried on vehicles bearing the orange markings stipulated in 5.3.2.

If the placards affixed to the containers, MEGCs, tank-containers or portable tanks are not visible from outside the carrying vehicles, the same placards shall also be affixed to both sides and at the rear of the vehicle. Otherwise, no placard need be affixed on the carrying vehicle.

5.3.1.4   *Placarding of vehicles for carriage in bulk, wagons for carriage in bulk, tank-vehicles, tank-wagons, battery vehicles, battery-wagons, vehicles with demountable tanks and wagons with demountable tanks*

Placards shall be affixed to both sides and at the rear of the vehicle, or, for wagons, to both sides.

When the tank-vehicle, tank-wagon, the demountable tank carried on the vehicle or the demountable tank carried on the wagon has multiple compartments and carries two or more dangerous goods, the appropriate placards shall be displayed along each side at the position of the relevant compartments and (vehicles only) one placard of each model shown on each side at the rear of the vehicle. However, in such case, if all compartments have to bear the same placards, these placards need be displayed only once along each side and (vehicles only) at the rear of the vehicle.

Where more than one placard is required for the same compartment, these placards shall be displayed adjacent to each other.

NOTE: When, a tank semi-trailer is separated from its tractor to be loaded on board a ship or a vessel, placards shall also be displayed at the front of the semi-trailer.

5.3.1.5   *Placarding of vehicles carrying packages only*

NOTE: This sub-section applies also to vehicles or wagons carrying swap-bodies loaded with packages.

5.3.1.5.1   For vehicles carrying packages containing substances or articles of Class 1, placards shall be affixed to both sides and at the rear of the vehicle.

| 5.3.1.5.2 | For vehicles carrying radioactive material of Class 7 in packagings or IBCs (other than excepted packages), placards shall be affixed to both sides and at the rear of the vehicle. |

NOTE: If a vehicle carrying packages containing dangerous goods of classes other than Classes 1 and 7 is loaded on board a vessel for an ADN journey preceding a voyage by sea, placards shall be affixed to both sides and at the rear of the vehicle. Such placards may remain affixed to a vehicle for an ADN journey following a sea voyage.

| 5.3.1.5.3 | For wagons carrying packages, placards corresponding to the goods carried shall be affixed to both sides. |

5.3.1.6 ***Placarding of empty tank-vehicles, tank-wagons, vehicles with demountable tanks, wagons with demountable tanks, battery-vehicles, battery-wagons, MEGCs, tank-containers, portable tanks and empty vehicles, wagons and containers for carriage in bulk***

| 5.3.1.6.1 | Empty tank-vehicles, tank-wagons, vehicles with demountable tanks, wagons with demountable tanks, battery-vehicles, battery-wagons, MEGCs, tank-containers and portable tanks uncleaned and not degassed, and empty vehicles, wagons and containers for carriage in bulk, uncleaned, shall continue to display the placards required for the previous load. |

5.3.1.7 ***Specifications for placards***

| 5.3.1.7.1 | Except as provided in 5.3.1.7.2 for the Class 7 placard, a placard shall: |

(a) be not less than 250 mm by 250 mm, with a line of the same colour as the symbol running 12.5 mm inside the edge and parallel with it;

(b) correspond to the label required for the dangerous goods in question with respect to colour and symbol (see 5.2.2.2); and

(c) display the numbers (and for goods of Class 1, the compatibility group letter) prescribed for the dangerous goods in question in 5.2.2.2 for the corresponding label, in digits not less than 25 mm high.

| 5.3.1.7.2 | The Class 7 placard shall be not less than 250 mm by 250 mm with a black line running 5 mm inside the edge and parallel with it and is otherwise as shown below (Model No. 7D). The number "7" shall not be less than 25 mm high. The background colour of the upper half of the placard shall be yellow and of the lower half white, the colour of the trefoil and the printing shall be black. The use of the word "RADIOACTIVE" in the bottom half is optional to allow the use of this placard to display the appropriate UN number for the consignment. |

(No.7D)
Symbol (trefoil): black; Background: upper half yellow with white border, lower half white;
The lower half shall show the word "RADIOACTIVE" or alternatively, when required, the appropriate UN Number (see 5.3.2.1.2) and the figure "7" in the bottom corner.

5.3.1.7.3   For tanks with a capacity of not more than 3 m³ and for small containers, placards may be replaced by labels conforming to 5.2.2.2.

5.3.1.7.4   For Classes 1 and 7, if the size and construction of the vehicle are such that the available surface area is insufficient to affix the prescribed placards, their dimensions may be reduced to 100 mm on each side.

5.3.2   Orange-coloured plate marking

5.3.2.1   *General orange-coloured plate marking provisions*

5.3.2.1.1   Transport units carrying dangerous goods shall display two rectangular reflectorized orange-coloured plates conforming to 5.3.2.2.1, set in a vertical plane. They shall be affixed one at the front and the other at the rear of the transport unit, both perpendicular to the longitudinal axis of the transport unit. They shall be clearly visible.

5.3.2.1.2   When a hazard identification number is indicated in Column (20) of Table A of Chapter 3.2 of ADR, tank-vehicles, battery vehicles or transport units having one or more tanks carrying dangerous goods shall in addition display on the sides of each tank, each tank compartment or each element of battery vehicles, clearly visible and parallel to the longitudinal axis of the vehicle, orange-coloured plates identical with those prescribed in 5.3.2.1.1. These orange-coloured plates shall bear the hazard identification number and the UN number prescribed respectively in Columns (20) and (1) of Table A of Chapter 3.2 of ADR for each of the substances carried in the tank, in a compartment of the tank or in an element of a battery vehicle.

              The provisions of this paragraph are also applicable to tank-wagons, battery-wagons and wagons with movable tanks.

5.3.2.1.3   For tank-vehicles or transport units having one or more tanks carrying substances with UN Nos. 1202, 1203 or 1223, or aviation fuel classed under UN Nos. 1268 or 1863, but no other dangerous substance, the orange-coloured plates prescribed in 5.3.2.1.2 need not be affixed if the plates affixed to the front and rear in accordance with 5.3.2.1.1 bear the hazard identification number and the UN number prescribed for the most hazardous substance carried, i.e. the substance with the lowest flashpoint.

5.3.2.1.4   When a hazard identification number is indicated in Column (20) of Table A of Chapter 3.2 of ADR, transport units and containers carrying dangerous solid substances in bulk or packaged radioactive material with a single UN number under exclusive use and no other dangerous goods shall in addition display on the sides of each transport unit or container, clearly visible and parallel to the longitudinal axis of the vehicle, orange-coloured plates identical with those prescribed in 5.3.2.1.1. These orange-coloured plates shall bear the hazard identification number and the UN number prescribed respectively in Columns (20) and (1) of Table A of Chapter 3.2 of ADR for each of the substances carried in bulk in the transport unit or in the container or for the packaged radioactive material carried under exclusive use in the transport unit or in the container.

The provisions of this paragraph are also applicable to wagons for carriage in bulk and full wagon loads comprising packages containing only one substance. In the latter case the hazard identification number to be used is that indicated in Column (20) of Table A of Chapter 3.2 of RID.

5.3.2.1.5   For containers carrying dangerous solid substances in bulk and for tank-containers, MEGCs and portable tanks, the plates prescribed in 5.3.2.1.2 and 5.3.2.1.4 may be replaced by a self-adhesive sheet, by paint or by any other equivalent process, provided the material used for this purpose is weather-resistant and ensures durable marking. In this case, the provisions of the last sentence of 5.3.2.2.2, concerning resistance to fire, shall not apply.

5.3.2.1.6   For transport units carrying only one substance, the orange-coloured plates prescribed in 5.3.2.1.2 and 5.3.2.1.4 shall not be necessary provided that those displayed at the front and rear in accordance with 5.3.2.1.1 bear the hazard identification number and the UN number prescribed respectively in Columns (20) and (1) of Table A of Chapter 3.2 of ADR.

5.3.2.1.7   The above requirements are also applicable to empty fixed or demountable tanks, tank-containers, MEGCs, portable tanks and battery-vehicles, uncleaned and not degassed and empty vehicles and empty containers for carriage in bulk, uncleaned.

5.3.2.1.8   Orange-coloured plates which do not relate to dangerous goods carried, or residues thereof, shall be removed or covered. If plates are covered, the covering shall be total and remain effective after 15 minutes' engulfment in fire.

5.3.2.2   *Specifications for the orange-coloured plates*

5.3.2.2.1   The reflectorized orange-coloured plates shall be of 40 cm base and of 30 cm high; they shall have a black border of 15 mm wide. The orange-coloured plates may be separated in their middle with a black horizontal line of 15 mm thickness. If the size and construction of the vehicle are such that the available surface area is insufficient to affix these orange-coloured plates, their dimensions may be reduced to 300 mm for the base, 120 mm for the height and 10 mm for the black border.

A non-reflectorized colour is permitted for wagons.

NOTE: *The colour of the orange plates in conditions of normal use should have chromaticity coordinates lying within the area on the chromaticity diagram formed by joining the following coordinates:*

Chromaticity coordinates of points at the corners of the area on the chromaticity diagram				
x	0.52	0.52	0.578	0.618
y	0.38	0.40	0.422	0.38

Luminance factor of reflectorized colour: ß > 0.12.
Luminance factor of non-reflectorized colour (wagons): ß≥ 0.22
Reference centre E, standard illuminant C, normal incidence 45°, viewed at 0°.
Coefficient of reflex luminous intensity at an angle of illumination of 5°, viewed at 0.2°:
not less than 20 candelas per lux per m² (not required for wagons).

5.3.2.2.2   The hazard identification number and the UN number shall consist of black digits 100 mm high and of 15 mm stroke thickness. The hazard identification number shall be inscribed in the upper part of the plate and the UN number in the lower part; they shall be separated by a horizontal black line, 15 mm in stroke width, extending from side to side of the plate at mid-height (see 5.3.2.2.3). The hazard identification number and the UN number shall be indelible and shall remain legible after 15 minutes engulfment in fire.

5.3.2.2.3   *Example of orange-coloured plate with hazard identification number and UN number*

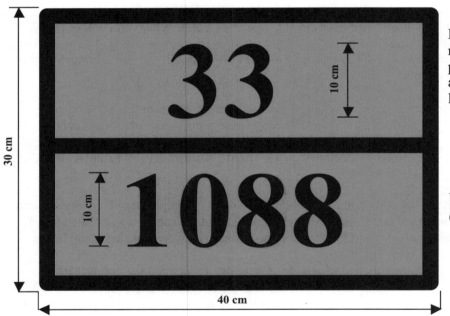

Hazard identification number (2 or 3 figures preceded where appropriate by the letter X, see 5.3.2.3)

UN number (4 figures)

Background orange.
Border, horizontal line and figures black, 15 mm thickness.

5.3.2.2.4   The permitted tolerances for dimensions specified in this sub-section are ± 10%.

5.3.2.3   *Meaning of hazard identification numbers*

5.3.2.3.1   The hazard identification number consists of two or three figures. In general, the figures indicate the following hazards:

2   Emission of gas due to pressure or to chemical reaction
3   Flammability of liquids (vapours) and gases or self-heating liquid
4   Flammability of solids or self-heating solid
5   Oxidizing (fire-intensifying) effect
6   Toxicity or risk of infection

7   Radioactivity

8   Corrosivity

9   Risk of spontaneous violent reaction

NOTE: *The risk of spontaneous violent reaction within the meaning of figure 9 includes the possibility following from the nature of a substance of a risk of explosion, disintegration and polymerization reaction following the release of considerable heat or flammable and/or toxic gases.*

Doubling of a figure indicates an intensification of that particular hazard.

Where the hazard associated with a substance can be adequately indicated by a single figure, this is followed by zero.

The following combinations of figures, however, have a special meaning: 22, 323, 333, 362, 382, 423, 44, 446, 462, 482, 539, 606, 623, 642, 823, 842, 90 and 99 (see 5.3.2.3.2 below).

If a hazard identification number is prefixed by the letter "X", this indicates that the substance will react dangerously with water. For such substances, water may only be used by approval of experts.

For substances of Class 1, the classification code in accordance with Column (3 b) of Table A of Chapter 3.2, shall be used as the hazard identification number. The classification code consists of:

-     the division number in accordance with 2.2.1.1.5; and

-     the compatibility group letter in accordance with 2.2.1.1.6.

5.3.2.3.2   The hazard identification numbers listed in Column (20) of Table A of Chapter 3.2 have the following meanings:

20   asphyxiant gas or gas with no subsidiary risk

22   refrigerated liquefied gas, asphyxiant

223   refrigerated liquefied gas, flammable

225   refrigerated liquefied gas, oxidizing (fire-intensifying)

23   flammable gas

238   flammable aerosols, corrosive

239   flammable gas, which can spontaneously lead to violent reaction

25   oxidizing (fire-intensifying) gas

26   toxic gas

263   toxic gas, flammable

265   toxic gas, oxidizing (fire-intensifying)

268   toxic gas, corrosive

28   aerosols, corrosive

285   aerosols, corrosive, oxidizing

30   flammable liquid (flashpoint between 23 °C and 61 °C, inclusive) or flammable liquid or solid in the molten state with a flashpoint above 61 °C, heated to a temperature equal to or above its flashpoint, or self-heating liquid

323   flammable liquid which reacts with water, emitting flammable gases

X323 flammable liquid which reacts dangerously with water, emitting flammable gases[1]

33   highly flammable liquid (flashpoint below 23 °C)

333   pyrophoric liquid

X333 pyrophoric liquid which reacts dangerously with water[1]
336 highly flammable liquid, toxic
338 highly flammable liquid, corrosive
X338 highly flammable liquid, corrosive, which reacts dangerously with water[1]
339 highly flammable liquid which can spontaneously lead to violent reaction
36 flammable liquid (flashpoint between 23 °C and 61 °C, inclusive), slightly toxic, or self-heating liquid, toxic
362 flammable liquid, toxic, which reacts with water, emitting flammable gases
X362 flammable liquid, toxic, which reacts dangerously with water, emitting flammable gases[1]
368 flammable liquid, toxic, corrosive
38 flammable liquid (flashpoint between 23 °C and 61 °C, inclusive), slightly corrosive or self-heating liquid, corrosive
382 flammable liquid, corrosive, which reacts with water, emitting flammable gases
X382 flammable liquid, corrosive, which reacts dangerously with water, emitting flammable gases[1]
39 flammable liquid, which can spontaneously lead to violent reaction

40 flammable solid, or self-reactive substance, or self-heating substance
423 solid which reacts with water, emitting flammable gases
X423 flammable solid which reacts dangerously with water, emitting flammable gases[1]
43 spontaneously flammable (pyrophoric) solid
44 flammable solid, in the molten state at an elevated temperature
446 flammable solid, toxic, in the molten state, at an elevated temperature
46 flammable or self-heating solid, toxic
462 toxic solid which reacts with water, emitting flammable gases
X462 solid which reacts dangerously with water, emitting toxic gases[1]
48 flammable or self-heating solid, corrosive
482 corrosive solid which reacts with water, emitting flammable gases
X482 solid which reacts dangerously with water, emitting corrosive gases[1]

50 oxidizing (fire-intensifying) substance
539 flammable organic peroxide
55 strongly oxidizing (fire-intensifying) substance
556 strongly oxidizing (fire-intensifying) substance, toxic
558 strongly oxidizing (fire-intensifying) substance, corrosive
559 strongly oxidizing (fire-intensifying) substance, which can spontaneously lead to violent reaction
56 oxidizing substance (fire-intensifying), toxic
568 oxidizing substance (fire-intensifying), toxic, corrosive
58 oxidizing substance (fire-intensifying), corrosive
59 oxidizing substance (fire-intensifying), which can spontaneously lead to violent reaction

60 toxic or slightly toxic substance
606 infectious substance
623 toxic liquid, which reacts with water, emitting flammable gases
63 toxic substance, flammable (flashpoint between 23 °C and 61 °C, inclusive)
638 toxic substance, flammable (flashpoint between 23 °C and 61 °C, inclusive), corrosive
639 toxic substance, flammable (flashpoint not above 61 °C) which can spontaneously lead to violent reaction
64 toxic solid, flammable or self-heating
642 toxic solid, which reacts with water, emitting flammable gases
65 toxic substance, oxidizing (fire-intensifying)

---

[1] *Water not to be used except by approval of experts.*

66	highly toxic substance
663	highly toxic substance, flammable (flashpoint not above 61 °C)
664	highly toxic solid, flammable or self-heating
665	highly toxic substance, oxidizing (fire-intensifying)
668	highly toxic substance, corrosive
669	highly toxic substance which can spontaneously lead to violent reaction
68	toxic substance, corrosive
69	toxic or slightly toxic substance, which can spontaneously lead to violent reaction

70   radioactive material
78   radioactive material, corrosive

80   corrosive or slightly corrosive substance
X80   corrosive or slightly corrosive substance, which reacts dangerously with water[1]
823   corrosive liquid which reacts with water, emitting flammable gases
83   corrosive or slightly corrosive substance, flammable (flashpoint between 23 °C and 61 °C, inclusive)
X83   corrosive or slightly corrosive substance, flammable, (flashpoint between 23 °C and 61 °C, inclusive), which reacts dangerously with water[1]
839   corrosive or slightly corrosive substance, flammable (flashpoint between 23 °C and 61 °C inclusive) which can spontaneously lead to violent reaction
X839   corrosive or slightly corrosive substance, flammable (flashpoint between 23 °C and 61 °C inclusive), which can spontaneously lead to violent reaction and which reacts dangerously with water[1]
84   corrosive solid, flammable or self-heating
842   corrosive solid which reacts with water, emitting flammable gases
85   corrosive or slightly corrosive substance, oxidizing (fire-intensifying)
856   corrosive or slightly corrosive substance, oxidizing (fire-intensifying) and toxic
86   corrosive or slightly corrosive substance, toxic
88   highly corrosive substance
X88   highly corrosive substance, which reacts dangerously with water[1]
883   highly corrosive substance, flammable (flashpoint between 23 °C and 61 °C inclusive)
884   highly corrosive solid, flammable or self-heating
885   highly corrosive substance, oxidizing (fire-intensifying)
886   highly corrosive substance, toxic
X886   highly corrosive substance, toxic, which reacts dangerously with water[1]
89   corrosive or slightly corrosive substance, which can spontaneously lead to violent reaction

90   environmentally hazardous substance; miscellaneous dangerous substances
99   miscellaneous dangerous substance carried at an elevated temperature.

5.3.3   Mark for elevated temperature substances

Tank-vehicles, tank-wagons, tank-containers, portable tanks, special vehicles special wagons or special containers or especially equipped vehicles, especially equipped wagons or especially equipped containers for which a mark for elevated temperature substances is required according to special provision 580 in Column (6) of Table A of Chapter 3.2 shall bear on both sides for wagons, on both sides and at the rear for vehicles, and on both sides and at each end for containers, tank-containers and portable tanks, a triangular shaped mark with sides of at least 250 mm, to be shown in red, as reproduced below.

---

[1]   *Water not to be used except by approval of experts.*

5.3.4   **Marking for carriage in a transport chain including maritime transport**

5.3.4.1   For carriage in a transport chain including maritime transport, containers, portable tanks and MEGCs are not required to carry the orange-coloured plate marking according to sections 5.3.2 and 5.3.3 if they carry the marking prescribed in section 5.3.2 of the IMDG Code, where:

(a)   The proper shipping name of the contents is durably marked on at least two sides:

–   of portable tanks and MEGCs;

–   of containers for carriage in bulk;

–   of containers containing dangerous goods in packages constituting only one substance for which the IMDG Code does not require a placard or the marine pollutant mark;

(b)   The UN number for the goods is displayed in black digits not less than 65 mm high:

–   either on a white background in the lower half of the placards affixed to the transport unit;

–   or on an orange rectangular panel not less than 120 mm high and 300 mm wide, with a 10 mm black border, to be placed immediately adjacent to the placard or the marine pollutant marks of the IMDG Code, or, if no placard or marine pollutant mark is prescribed, adjacent to the proper shipping name.

Example of marking for a tank-container carrying acetal, Class 3, UN No 1088, according to the IMDG Code

FIRST VARIANT

black flame on
red background

SECOND VARIANT

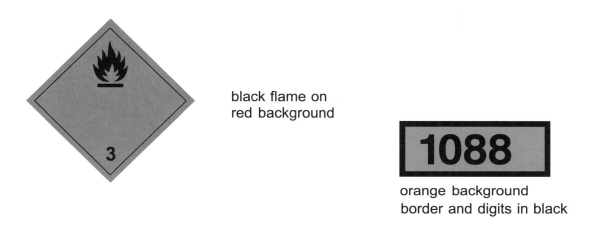

black flame on
red background

orange background
border and digits in black

5.3.4.2   If portable tanks, MEGCs or containers marked in accordance with 5.3.4.1 are carried on board a vessel loaded on vehicles, only paragraph 5.3.2.1.1 of section 5.3.2 applies to the carrying vehicle.

5.3.4.3   In addition to the placards, orange-coloured plate marking and marks prescribed or permitted by ADN, transport units may carry additional marks, placards and other markings prescribed where appropriate by the IMDG Code, for example, the marine pollutant mark or the "LIMITED QUANTITIES" mark.

CHAPTER 5.4

DOCUMENTATION

5.4.0   Any carriage of goods governed by ADN shall be accompanied by the documentation prescribed in this Chapter, as appropriate, unless exempted under 1.1.3.1 to 1.1.3.5.

NOTE 1: For the list of documentation to be carried on board vessels, see 8.1.2.

NOTE 2: The use of electronic data processing (EDP) or electronic data interchange (EDI) techniques as an aid to or instead of paper documentation is permitted, provided that the procedures used for the capture, storage and processing of electronics data meet the legal requirements as regards the evidential value and availability of data during transport in a manner at least equivalent to that of paper documentation.

5.4.1   Dangerous goods transport document and related information

5.4.1.1   *General information required in the transport document*

5.4.1.1.1   *General information required in the transport document for carriage in bulk or in packages*

The transport document(s) shall contain the following information for each dangerous substance, material or article offered for carriage:

(a)   the UN number, preceded by the letters "UN";

(b)   the proper shipping name supplemented, when applicable (see 3.1.2.8.1) with the technical name (see 3.1.2.8.1.1), as determined in accordance with 3.1.2.

(c)   –   For substances and articles of Class 1:   the classification code given in Column (3 b) of Table A of Chapter 3.2.

When, in Column (5) of Table A of Chapter 3.2, label model numbers are given other than 1, 1.4, 1.5 and 1.6, these label model numbers, in brackets, shall follow the classification code;

–   For radioactive material of Class 7: the Class number: "7";

–   For substances and articles of other classes: the label model numbers given in Column (5) of Table A of Chapter 3.2. When more than one label model number is given, the numbers following the first one shall be given in brackets. For substances and articles for which no label model is given in Column (5) of Table A in Chapter 3.2, their class according to Column (3a) shall be given instead;

(d)   where assigned, the packing group for the substance which may be preceded by the letters "PG" (e.g. "PG II"), or the initials corresponding to the words "Packing Group" in the languages used according to 5.4.1.4.1;

NOTE: For radioactive material of Class 7 with subsidiary risks, see special provision 172 (b) in Chapter 3.3.

(e)   the number and a description of the packages;

(f)   with the exception of empty means of containment, uncleaned, the total quantity of each item of dangerous goods bearing a different UN number, proper shipping name (as a volume or as a gross mass, or as a net mass as appropriate);

NOTE: *In the case of intended application of 1.1.3.6, the total quantity of dangerous goods for each transport category shall be indicated in the transport document in accordance with 1.1.3.6.3.*

(g)   the name and address of the consignor;

(h)   the name and address of the consignee(s);

(i)   a declaration as required by the terms of any special agreement.

The location and order in which the elements of information required appear in the transport document is left optional, except that (a), (b), (c) and (d) shall be shown either in sequence (a), (b), (c), (d) or in sequence (b), (c), (a), (d) with no information interspersed, except as provided in ADN.

Examples of such permitted dangerous goods descriptions are:

"UN 1098 ALLYL ALCOHOL, 6.1 (3), I" or
"ALLYL ALCOHOL, 6.1 (3) UN 1098, I"

The information required on a transport document shall be legible.

Although upper case is used in Chapter 3.1 and in Table A of Chapter 3.2 to indicate the elements which shall be part of the proper shipping name, and although upper and lower case are used in this Chapter to indicate the information required in the transport document, the use of upper or of lower case for entering the information in the transport document is left optional.

5.4.1.1.2   *General information required in the transport document for carriage in tank vessels*

The transport document(s) shall contain the following information for each dangerous substance or article offered for carriage:

(a)   the UN number preceded by the letters "UN" or the substance identification number;

(b)   the proper shipping name given in Column (2) of Table C of Chapter 3.2, supplemented, when applicable, by the technical name (see 3.1.2.8.1.1);

(c)   the class of the goods;

(d)   where assigned, the packing group for the substance, which may be preceded by the letters 'PG' (for example, 'PG II') or initials corresponding to the words 'Packing Group' in the languages used in accordance with 5.4.1.4.1;

(e)   *(Reserved)*;

(f)   the mass in tonnes;

(g)   the name and address of the consignor;

(h)   the name and address of the consignee(s).

The information required on a transport document shall be legible.

Although upper case is used in Chapter 3.1 and in Chapter 3.2 to indicate the elements which shall be part of the proper shipping name, and although upper and lower case are used in this Chapter to indicate the information required in the transport document, the use of upper or of lower case for entering the information in the transport document is left optional.

5.4.1.1.3   *Special provisions for wastes*

If waste containing dangerous goods (other than radioactive wastes) is being carried, the UN number and the proper shipping name shall be preceded by the word "**WASTE**", unless this term is part of the proper shipping name, e.g.:

"**WASTE, UN 1230 METHANOL, 3 (6.1), II**", or
"**WASTE, METHANOL, 3 (6.1), UN 1230, II**", or
"**WASTE, UN 1993 FLAMMABLE LIQUID, N.O.S., (toluene and ethyl alcohol), 3, II**"or
"**WASTE, FLAMMABLE LIQUID, N.O.S. (toluene and ethyl alcohol), 3, UN 1993, II**".

5.4.1.1.4   *Special provisions for dangerous goods packed in limited quantities*

No information is required in the transport document, if any, for carriage of dangerous goods packed in limited quantities according to Chapter 3.4.

5.4.1.1.5   *Special provisions for salvage packagings*

When dangerous goods are carried in a salvage packaging, the words "**SALVAGE PACKAGE**" shall be added after the description of the goods in the transport document.

5.4.1.1.6   *Special provision for empty means of containment*

5.4.1.1.6.1   For empty packagings, uncleaned, which contain the residue of dangerous goods of classes other than Class 7 including empty uncleaned receptacles for gases with a capacity of not more than 1000 litres, the description in the transport document shall be:

"EMPTY PACKAGING", "EMPTY RECEPTACLE", "EMPTY IBC", "EMPTY LARGE PACKAGING", as appropriate, followed by the information of the goods last loaded, as described in 5.4.1.1.1 (c).

See example as follows:

"**EMPTY PACKAGING, 6.1 (3)**".

5.4.1.1.6.2   For empty means of containment other than packagings, uncleaned, which contain the residue of dangerous goods of classes other than Class 7 and for empty uncleaned receptacles for gases with a capacity of more than 1000 litres, the description in the transport document shall be:

"EMPTY TANK VEHICLE", "EMPTY DEMOUNTABLE TANK", "EMPTY TANK CONTAINER", "EMPTY PORTABLE TANK", "EMPTY BATTERY-VEHICLE", "EMPTY MEGC", "EMPTY VEHICLE", "EMPTY CONTAINER", "EMPTY RECEPTACLE", followed by the words "last load" together with the information of the goods last loaded, as prescribed in 5.4.1.1.1 (a) to (d) in one of the sequences as prescribed.

See example as follows:

"EMPTY TANK-CONTAINER, LAST LOAD: UN 1098 ALLYLALCOHOL, 6.1(3), I" or
"EMPTY TANK-CONTAINER, LAST LOAD: ALLYLALCOHOL, 6.1(3), UN 1098, I"

5.4.1.1.6.3   If empty tanks, battery-vehicles and MEGCs, uncleaned, are carried to the nearest place where cleaning or repair can be carried out in accordance with the provisions of 4.3.2.4.3 of ADR or 7.5.8.1 of ADR, the following additional entry shall be made in the transport document: **"Carriage in accordance with 4.3.2.4.3 of ADR"** or **"Carriage in accordance with 7.5.8.1 of ADR"**.

5.4.1.1.6.4   For tank vessels with empty cargo tanks or cargo tanks that have been discharged, the master is deemed to be the consignor for the purpose of the transport documents required. In this case, the following particulars shall be entered on the transport document for each empty cargo tank or cargo tank that has been discharged:

   (a)   the number of the cargo tank;

   (b)   the UN number preceded by the letters "UN" or the substance identification number;

   (c)   the proper shipping name of the last substance carried, the class and, if applicable, the packing group in accordance with 5.4.1.1.2.

5.4.1.1.7   *Special provisions for carriage in a transport chain including maritime, road, rail or air carriage*

   For carriage in accordance with 1.1.4.2.1, a statement shall be included in the transport document, as follows: **"Carriage in accordance with 1.1.4.2.1"**.

5.4.1.1.8-   *(Reserved)*
5.4.1.1.9

5.4.1.1.10   *Special provisions for exemptions related to quantities carried per transport unit*

5.4.1.1.10.1   In the case of exemptions provided for in 1.1.3.6, the transport document shall bear the following inscription: **"Load not exceeding the exemption limits prescribed in 1.1.3.6."**

5.4.1.1.10.2   Where consignments from more than one consignor are carried in the same transport unit, the transport documents accompanying these consignments need not bear the inscription mentioned in 5.4.1.1.10.1.

5.4.1.1.11   *Special provisions for the carriage of IBCs after the date of expiry of the last periodic test inspection*

   For carriage in accordance with 4.1.2.2 of ADR or of RID, a statement to this effect shall be included in the transport document, as follows: **"Carriage in accordance with 4.1.2.2"**

5.4.1.1.12-   *(Reserved)*
5.4.1.1.13

5.4.1.1.14   *Special provisions for the carriage of substances carried under elevated temperature*

   If the proper shipping name of a substance which is carried or offered for carriage in a liquid state at a temperature equal to or exceeding 100 °C, or in a solid state at a temperature equal

- 202 -

to or exceeding 240° C, does not convey the elevated temperature condition (for example, by using the term **"MOLTEN"** or **"ELEVATED TEMPERATURE"** as part of the proper shipping name), the word **"HOT"** shall immediately precede the proper shipping name.

5.4.1.1.15   *Special provisions for the carriage of substances stabilized by temperature control*

If the word "STABILIZED" is part of the proper shipping name (see also 3.1.2.6), when stabilization is by means of temperature control, the control and emergency temperatures (see 2.2.41.1.17) shall be indicated in the transport document, as follows:

"Control temperature: ... °C   Emergency temperature: ... °C".

5.4.1.1.16   *Information required in accordance with special provision 640 in Chapter 3.3*

Where it is required by special provision 640 of Chapter 3.3, the transport document shall bear the inscription **"Special provision 640X"** where "X" is the capital letter appearing after the pertinent reference to special provision 640 in Column (6) of Table A of Chapter 3.2.

5.4.1.1.17   *Special provisions for the carriage of solids in bulk containers conforming to 6.11.4 of ADR*

When solid substances are carried in bulk containers conforming to 6.11.4 of ADR, the following statement shall be shown on the transport document (see NOTE at the beginning of 6.11.4 of ADR):

"Bulk container BK(x) approved by the competent authority of...".

5.4.1.1.18   *Special provisions for carriage in oil separator vessels and supply vessels*

5.4.1.1.2 and 5.4.1.1.6.3 are not applicable to oil separator vessels or supply vessels.

5.4.1.2   *Additional or special information required for certain classes*

5.4.1.2.1   *Special provisions for Class 1*

(a)   The transport document shall indicate, in addition to the requirements in 5.4.1.1.1 (f):

  –   the total net mass, in kg, of explosive contents[1] for each substance or article identified by its UN number;

  –   the total net mass, in kg, of explosive contents[1] for all substances and articles covered by the transport document.

(b)   For mixed packing of two different goods, the description of the goods in the transport document shall include the UN numbers and names printed in capitals in Columns (1) and (2) of Table A of Chapter 3.2 of both substances or articles. If more than two different goods are contained in the same package in conformity with the mixed packing provisions given in 4.1.10 of ADR special provisions MP1, MP2 and MP20 to MP24, the transport document shall indicate under the description of the goods the UN numbers of all the substances and articles contained in the package, in the form, **"Goods of UN Nos. ...".**

---

[1]   *For articles, "explosive contents" means the explosive substance contained in the article.*

(c) For the carriage of substances and articles assigned to an n.o.s. entry or the entry "0190 SAMPLES, EXPLOSIVE" or packed conforming to packing instruction P101 of 4.1.4.1 of ADR, a copy of the competent authority approval with the conditions of carriage shall be attached to the transport document. It shall be in an official language of the forwarding country and also, if that language is not English, French or German, in English, French or German unless agreements, if any, concluded between the countries concerned in the transport operation provide otherwise.

(d) If packages containing substances and articles of compatibility groups B and D are loaded together in the same vehicle or wagon in accordance with the requirements of 7.5.2.2 or ADR or RID, the approval certificate of the protective compartment or containment system in accordance with 7.5.2.2, note [a] under the table of ADR or RID, shall be attached to the transport document.

(e) When explosive substances or articles are carried in packagings conforming to packing instruction P101 of ADR, the transport document shall bear the inscription "**Packaging approved by the competent authority of ...**" (see 4.1.4.1, packing instruction P101).

NOTE: The commercial or technical name of the goods may be entered additionally to the proper shipping name in the transport document.

(f) *(Reserved)*

(g) When fireworks of UN Nos. 0333, 0334, 0335, 0336 and 0337 are carried, the transport document shall bear the inscription: "**Classification recognized by the competent authority of ...** (State referred to in special provision 645 of 3.3.1).

5.4.1.2.2 *Additional provisions for Class 2*

(a) For the carriage of mixtures (see 2.2.2.1.1) in tanks (demountable tanks, fixed tanks, portable tanks, tank-containers or elements of battery-vehicles or batteries-wagons or of MEGCs), the composition of the mixture as a percentage of the volume or as a percentage of the mass shall be given. Constituents below 1% need not be indicated (see also 3.1.2.8.1.2).

(b) For the carriage of cylinders, tubes, pressure drums, cryogenic receptacles and bundles of cylinders under the conditions of 4.1.6.10 of ADR, the following entry shall be included in the transport document: "**Carriage in accordance with 4.1.6.10 of ADR**".

5.4.1.2.3 *Additional provisions for self-reactive substances of Class 4.1 and organic peroxides of Class 5.2*

5.4.1.2.3.1 For self-reactive substances of Class 4.1 and for organic peroxides of Class 5.2 that require temperature control during carriage (for self-reactive substances see 2.2.41.1.17; for organic peroxides, see 2.2.52.1.15 to 2.2.52.1.17), the control and emergency temperatures shall be indicated in the transport document, as follows:

"Control temperature: ... °C   Emergency temperature: ... °C".

5.4.1.2.3.2 When for certain self-reactive substances of Class 4.1 and certain organic peroxides of Class 5.2 the competent authority has permitted the label conforming to model No. 1 to be dispensed with for a specific packaging (see 5.2.2.1.9), a statement to this effect shall be included in the transport document, as follows: "**The label conforming to model No. 1 is not required**".

5.4.1.2.3.3   When organic peroxides and self-reactive substances are carried under conditions where approval is required (for organic peroxides see 2.2.52.1.8, 4.1.7.2.2 and special provision TA2 of 6.8.4 of ADR; for self-reactive substances see 2.2.41.1.13 and 4.1.7.2.2, a statement to this effect shall be included in the transport document, e.g. **"Carriage in accordance with 2.2.52.1.8"**.

A copy of the approval of the competent authority with the conditions of carriage shall be attached to the transport document.

5.4.1.2.3.4   When a sample of an organic peroxide (see 2.2.52.1.9) or a self-reactive substance (see 2.2.41.1.15) is carried, a statement to this effect shall be included in the transport document, e.g. **"Carriage in accordance with 2.2.52.1.9"**.

5.4.1.2.3.5   When self-reactive substances type G (see Manual of Tests and Criteria, Part II, paragraph 20.4.2 (g)) are carried, the following statement may be given in the transport document: **"Not a self-reactive substance of Class 4.1"**.

When organic peroxides type G (see Manual of Tests and Criteria, Part II, paragraph 20.4.3 (g)) are carried, the following statement may be given in the transport document: **"Not a substance of Class 5.2"**.

5.4.1.2.4   *Additional provisions for Class 6.2*

In addition to the information concerning the consignee (see 5.4.1.1.1 (h)), the name and telephone number of a responsible person shall be indicated.

5.4.1.2.5   *Additional provisions for Class 7*

5.4.1.2.5.1   The following information shall be inserted in the transport document for each consignment of Class 7 material, as applicable, in the order given and immediately after the information required under 5.4.1.1.1 (a) to (c):

    (a)   The name or symbol of each radionuclide or, for mixtures of radionuclides, an appropriate general description or a list of the most restrictive nuclides;

    (b)   A description of the physical and chemical form of the material, or a notation that the material is special form radioactive material or low dispersible radioactive material. A generic chemical description is acceptable for chemical form. For radioactive material with a subsidiary risk, see last sentence of special provision 172 of Chapter 3.3;

    (c)   The maximum activity of the radioactive contents during carriage expressed in becquerels (Bq) with an appropriate SI prefix (see 1.2.2.1). For fissile material, the mass of fissile material in grams (g), or appropriate multiples thereof, may be used in place of activity;

    (d)   The category of the package, i.e. I-WHITE, II-YELLOW, III-YELLOW;

    (e)   The transport index (categories II-YELLOW and III-YELLOW only);

    (f)   For consignments including fissile material other than consignments excepted under 6.4.11.2 of ADR, the criticality safety index;

(g)   The identification mark for each competent authority approval certificate (special form radioactive material, low dispersible radioactive material, special arrangement, package design, or shipment) applicable to the consignment;

(h)   For consignments of more than one package, the information required in 5.4.1.1.1 and in (a) to (g) above shall be given for each package. For packages in an overpack, container, or conveyance, a detailed statement of the contents of each package within the overpack, container, or conveyance and, where appropriate, of each overpack, container, or conveyance shall be included. If packages are to be removed from the overpack, container, or conveyance at a point of intermediate unloading, appropriate transport documents shall be made available;

(i)   Where a consignment is required to be shipped under exclusive use, the statement **"EXCLUSIVE USE SHIPMENT"**; and

(j)   For LSA-II and LSA-III substances, SCO-I and SCO-II, the total activity of the consignment as a multiple of A_2.

5.4.1.2.5.2   The consignor shall provide in the transport documents a statement regarding actions, if any, that are required to be taken by the carrier. The statement shall be in the languages deemed necessary by the carrier or the authorities concerned, and shall include at least the following information:

(a)   Supplementary requirements for loading, stowage, carriage, handling and unloading of the package, overpack or container including any special stowage provisions for the safe dissipation of heat (see 7.1.4.14.7.3.2), or a statement that no such requirements are necessary;

(b)   Restrictions on the mode of carriage or vehicle and any necessary routeing instructions;

(c)   Emergency arrangements appropriate to the consignment.

5.4.1.2.5.3   The applicable competent authority certificates need not necessarily accompany the consignment. The consignor shall make them available to the carrier(s) before loading and unloading.

5.4.1.3   *(Reserved)*

5.4.1.4   *Format and language*

5.4.1.4.1   The document containing the information in 5.4.1.1 and 5.4.1.2 may be that already required by other regulations in force for carriage by another mode of carriage. In case of multiple consignees, the name and address of the consignees and the quantities delivered enabling the nature and quantities carried to be evaluated at any time, may be entered in other documents which are to be used or in any other documents made mandatory according to other specific regulations and which shall be on board the vehicle.

The particulars to be entered in the document shall be drafted in an official language of the forwarding country, and also, if that language is not English, French or German, in English, French or German, unless agreements concluded between the countries concerned in the transport operation, provide otherwise.

5.4.1.4.2   If by reason of the size of the load, a consignment cannot be loaded in its entirety on a single transport unit, at least as many separate documents, or copies of the single document, shall be made out as transport units loaded. Furthermore, in all cases, separate transport documents shall be made out for consignments or parts of consignments which may not be loaded together on the same vehicle by reason of the prohibitions set forth in 7.5.2 of ADR.

The information relative to the hazards of the goods to be carried (as indicated in 5.4.1.1) may be incorporated in, or combined with, an existing transport or cargo handling document. The layout of the information in the document (or the order of transmission of the corresponding data by electronic data processing (EDP) or electronic data interchange (EDI) techniques) shall be as provided in 5.4.1.1.1 or 5.4.1.1.2 as relevant.

When an existing transport document or cargo handling document cannot be used for the purposes of dangerous goods documentation for multimodal transport, the use of documents corresponding to the example shown in 5.4.4 is considered advisable.[2]

5.4.1.5   *Non-dangerous goods*

When goods mentioned by name in Table A of Chapter 3.2, are not subject to ADN because they are considered as non-dangerous according to Part 2, the consignor may enter in the transport document a statement to that effect, e.g.: "**Not goods of Class ...**"

NOTE: This provision may be used in particular when the consignor considers that, due to the chemical nature of the goods (e.g. solutions and mixtures) carried or to the fact that such goods are deemed dangerous for other regulatory purposes the consignment might be subject to control during the journey.

5.4.2   **Container packing certificate**

If the carriage of dangerous goods in a large container precedes a voyage by sea, a container packing certificate conforming to section 5.4.2 of the IMDG Code[3] shall be provided with the transport document.[4]

---

[2]   *If used, the relevant recommendations of the UN/ECE Working Party on Facilitation of International Trade Procedures may be consulted, in particular Recommendation No. 1 (United Nations Lay-out Key for Trade Documents) (ECE/TRADE/137, edition 96.1), Recommendation No. 11 (Documentary Aspects of the International Transport of Dangerous Goods) ECE/TRADE/204, edition 96.1) and Recommendation No. 22 (Lay-out Key for standard Consignment Instructions) (ECE/TRADE/168, edition 96.1). Refer to the Trade Data Elements Directory, Volume III, Trade Facilitation Recommendations (ECE/TRADE/200) (United Nations publication Sales No. E.96.II.E.13).*

[3]   *Guidelines for use in practice and in training for loading goods in transport units have also been drawn up by the International Maritime Organization (IMO), the International Labour Organization (ILO) and the United Nations Economic Commission for Europe (UN/ECE) and have been published by IMO ("IMO/ILO/UN-ECE Guidelines for Packing of Cargo Transport Units (CTUs)").*

[4]   *Section 5.4.2 of the IMDG Code requires the following:*

*"**5.4.2   Container/vehicle packing certificate***

5.4.2.1   When dangerous goods are packed or loaded into any container or vehicle, those responsible for packing the container or vehicle shall provide a "container/vehicle packing certificate" specifying the container/vehicle identification number(s) and certifying that the operation has been carried out in accordance with the following conditions:

.1   The container/vehicle was clean, dry and apparently fit to receive the goods;

.2   Packages, which need to be segregated in accordance with applicable segregation requirements, have not been packed together onto or in the container/vehicle

The functions of the transport document required under 5.4.1 and of the container packing certificate as provided above may be incorporated into a single document; if not, these documents shall be attached one to the other. If these functions are incorporated into a single document, the inclusion in the transport document of a statement that the loading of the container has been carried out in accordance with the applicable modal regulations together with the identification of the person responsible for the container packing certificate shall be sufficient.

NOTE: *The container packing certificate is not required for portable tanks, tank-containers and MEGCs.*

5.4.3 Instructions in writing

5.4.3.1 As a precaution against any accident or emergency that may occur or arise during carriage, the master shall be given instructions in writing, specifying concisely for each dangerous substance or article carried or for each group of goods presenting the same dangers to which the substance(s) or article(s) carried belong(s):

(unless approved by the competent authority concerned in accordance with 7.2.2.3 (of the IMDG Code));

.3 *All packages have been externally inspected for damage, and only sound packages have been loaded;*

.4 *Drums have been stowed in an upright position, unless otherwise authorised by the competent authority, and all goods have been properly loaded, and, where necessary, adequately braced with securing material to suit the mode(s) of transport for the intended journey;*

.5 *Goods loaded in bulk have been evenly distributed within the container/vehicle;*

.6 *For consignments including goods of class 1, other than division 1.4, the container/vehicle is structurally serviceable in conformity with 7.4.6 (of the IMDG Code);*

.7 *The container/vehicle and packages are properly marked, labelled, and placarded, as appropriate;*

.8 *When solid carbon dioxide (CO_2-dry ice) is used for cooling purposes, the container/vehicle is externally marked or labelled in a conspicuous place, such as, at the door end, with the words: "DANGEROUS CO_2 GAS (DRY ICE) INSIDE. VENTILATE THOROUGHLY BEFORE ENTERING"; and*

.9 *A dangerous goods transport document, as indicated in 5.4.1 (of the IMDG Code) has been received for each dangerous goods consignment loaded in the container/vehicle.*

NOTE: The container/vehicle packing certificate is not required for tanks.

5.4.2.2 The information required in the dangerous goods transport document and the container/vehicle packing certificate may be incorporated into a single document; if not, these documents shall be attached one to the other. If the information is incorporated into a single document, the document shall a signed declaration such as "It is declared that the packing of the goods into the container/vehicle has been carried out in accordance with the applicable provisions". This declaration shall be dated and the person signing this declaration shall be identified on the document.".

(a) - the name of the substance or article or group of goods;

- the Class; and

- the UN number, or for a group of goods, the UN numbers

(b) the nature of the danger inherent in these goods as well as the measures to be taken by the master and the personal protection equipment to be used by the master;

(c) the action to be taken and the treatment to be given in the event of any person coming into contact with the goods being carried or with any substances which might be expelled from them;

(d) the general actions to be taken, e.g. to warn other users of the waterway and passers-by and call the emergency services;

(e) the measures to be taken in case of breakage or other deterioration of the packagings or of the dangerous goods being carried, in particular where such dangerous goods have spilled;

(f) the special actions to be taken for certain goods, if applicable;

(g) the necessary equipment for additional and/or special actions, if applicable, if the equipment referred to in 8.1.5. is not sufficient.

5.4.3.2 These instructions shall be provided by the consignor and shall be handed out to the master at the latest when the dangerous goods are loaded on the vessel. Information on the content of the instructions shall be supplied to the carrier at the latest when the carriage order is given, so as to enable him to take the necessary steps to ensure that the employees concerned are aware of these instructions and are capable of carrying them out properly and to ensure that the necessary equipment is on board the vessel.

5.4.3.3 The consignor shall be responsible for the content of these instructions. They shall be provided in a language the master(s) taking over the dangerous goods is (are) able to read and to understand, and in all languages of the countries of origin, transit and destination. In the case of countries with more than one official language, the competent authority shall specify the official language or languages applicable throughout the territory or in each region or part of the territory.

5.4.3.4 These instructions shall be kept readily at hand in the wheelhouse. This requirement does not apply to oil separator vessels.

5.4.3.5 Instructions in writing according to 5.4.3 which are on board but which do not concern the goods on board shall be kept separate from the applicable instructions in such a way as to prevent confusion.

5.4.3.6 The master shall bring the instructions to the attention of the persons on board to enable them to understand them and carry them out properly.

5.4.3.7 In case of mixed loads of packaged goods including dangerous goods which belong to different groups of goods presenting the same dangers, the instructions in writing may be restricted to one instruction per class of dangerous goods carried on board of the vehicle. In such case no name of goods, or UN number has to be mentioned in the instructions.

5.4.3.8 These instructions shall be drafted according to the following format:

LOAD

- Mention of the following details concerning the goods for which these instructions are intended or applicable:

  - the name of the substance or article, or group of goods presenting the same dangers;

  - the Class; and

  - the UN number or, for a group of goods the, UN numbers.

- Description shall be restricted to e.g. the physical state with indication of any colour and mention of any odour, to aid identification of leakages or spillages.

NATURE OF DANGER

Short enumeration of dangers:

– Main danger;

– Additional dangers including possible delayed effects and dangers for the environment;

– Behaviour under fire or heating (decomposition, explosion, development of toxic fumes, etc.);

– If applicable, it shall be mentioned here that the goods carried react dangerously with water.

PERSONAL PROTECTION

Mention of the personal protection intended for the crew in accordance with the requirements of 8.1.5.

GENERAL ACTIONS TO BE TAKEN BY THE CREW

Mention of the following instructions:

– Inform the competent authority;

– No naked lights. No smoking;

– Remove people from the danger zone;

– Remain upwind;

– Notify the emergency services as soon as possible.

ADDITIONAL AND/OR SPECIAL ACTIONS TO BE TAKEN BY THE CREW

Appropriate instructions shall be included here as well as the list of equipment necessary for the crew to perform the additional and/or special actions according to the class(es) of the goods being carried.

It is considered that the crew should be instructed and trained to take additional actions with minor leakages or spillages to prevent their escalation, provided that this can be achieved without personal risk.

It is considered that any special action recommended by the consignor requires a special training of the crew. If applicable, appropriate instructions shall be included here as well as the list of equipment needed for these special actions.

FIRE

Information for the crew in case of fire:

Crew members should be instructed during training to deal with minor vessel fires. They shall not attempt to deal with any fire involving the load.

FIRST AID

Information for the crew in case of contact with the carried good(s).

ADDITIONAL INFORMATION

5.4.4. **Example of a multimodal dangerous goods form**

Example of a form which may be used as a combined dangerous goods declaration and container packing certificate for multimodal carriage of dangerous goods.

MULTIMODAL DANGEROUS GOODS FORM

1. Shipper/Consignor/Sender	2. Transport document number	
	3. Page 1 of Pages	4. Shipper's reference
		5. Freight Forwarder's reference

6. Consignee	7. Carrier (to be completed by the carrier)
	SHIPPER'S DECLARATION. I hereby declare that the contents of this consignment are fully and accurately described below by the proper shipping name, and are classified, packaged, marked and labelled/placarded and are in all respects in proper condition for transport according to the applicable international and national governmental regulations.

8. This shipment is within the limitations prescribed for: (Delete non-applicable)	9. Additional handling information
PASSENGER AND CARGO AIRCRAFT CARGO AIRCRAFT ONLY	

10. Vessel/ flight No. and date	11. Port/place of loading
12. Port/place of discharge	13. Destination

14. Shipping marks	* Number and kind of packages; description of goods	Gross mass (kg)	Net mass	Cube (m³)

15. Container identification No./ vehicle registration No.	16. Seal number (s)	17. Container/vehicle size & type	18. Tare (kg)	19. Total gross mass (including tare) (kg)

CONTAINER/VEHICLE PACKING CERTIFICATE I hereby declare that the goods described above have been packed/loaded into the container/vehicle identified above in accordance with the applicable provisions ** **MUST BE COMPLETED AND SIGNED FOR ALL CONTAINER/VEHICLE LOADS BY PERSON RESPONSIBLE FOR PACKING/LOADING**	21.RECEIVING ORGANIZATION RECEIPT Received the above number of packages/containers/trailers in apparent good order and condition unless stated hereon: RECEIVING ORGANIZATION REMARKS:	
20. Name of company	Haulier's name	22. Name of company (OF SHIPPER PREPARING THIS NOTE)
Name/Status of declarant	Vehicle reg. No.	Name/Status of declarant
Place and date	Signature and date	Place and date
Signature of declarant	DRIVER'S SIGNATURE	Signature of declarant

** See 5.4.2.

* FOR DANGEROUS GOODS: you must specify: proper shipping name, hazard class, UN no., packing group (where assigned) and any other element of information required under applicable national and international regulations

MULTIMODAL DANGEROUS GOODS FORM

Continuation Sheet

1. Shipper/Consignor/Sender	2. Transport document number	
	3. Page 1 of pages	4. Shipper's reference
		5. Freight Forwarder's reference

14. Shipping marks	* Number and kind of packages; description of goods	Gross mass (kg)	Net mass	Cube (m³)

* FOR DANGEROUS GOODS: you must specify: proper shipping name, hazard class, UN no., packing group (where assigned) and any other element of information required under applicable national and international regulations

- 213 -

CHAPTER 5.5

SPECIAL PROVISIONS

5.5.1   **Special provisions for the consignment of infectious substances**

5.5.1.1   Unless an infectious substance cannot be consigned by any other means, live vertebrate or invertebrate animals shall not be used to consign such a substance. Such animals shall be packed, marked, indicated, and carried in accordance with the relevant regulations governing the carriage of animals.[1]

5.5.1.2   *(Reserved)*

5.5.1.3   Dead animals which are known or reasonably believed to contain an infectious substance shall be packed, marked, labelled and carried in accordance with the conditions[2] specified by the competent authority of the country of origin.[3]

5.5.2   **Special provisions for fumigated vehicles, wagons, containers and tanks**

5.5.2.1   For the carriage of UN No. 3359 FUMIGATED UNIT (vehicle, wagon, container or tank) the transport document shall show the information required in 5.4.1.1.1, the date of fumigation and the type of the fumigant used. These particulars shall be drafted in an official language of the forwarding country and also, if the language is not English, French or German, in English, French or German, unless agreements, if any, concluded between the countries concerned in the transport operation provide otherwise. In addition, instructions for disposal of any residual fumigant including fumigation devices (if used) shall be provided.

5.5.2.2   A warning sign as specified in 5.5.2.3 shall be placed on each fumigated vehicle, wagon, container or tank in a location where it will be easily seen by persons attempting to enter the interior of the container or vehicle. The particulars concerning the warning sign shall be drafted in a language considered appropriate by the consignor.

5.5.2.3   The fumigation warning sign shall be rectangular and shall not be less than 300 mm wide and not less than 250 mm high. The markings shall be black print on a white background with lettering not less than 25 mm high. An illustration of this sign is given in the figure below.

---

[1]   *Regulations governing the carriage of live animals are contained in, e.g. Directive 91/628/EEC of 19 November 1991 on the protection of animals during transport (Official Journal of the European Communities No. L 340 of 11.12.1991, p. 17) and in the Recommendations of the Council of Europe (Ministerial Committee) on the carriage of certain animal species.*

[2]   *Such regulations are contained e.g. in the Council of the European Communities Directive 90/667/EEC of 27.11.1990, laying down the veterinary rules for the disposal and processing of animal waste, for its placing on the market and for the prevention of pathogens in feedstuffs of animal or fish origin and amending Directive 90/425/EEC (Official Journal of the European Communities, No. L 363 of 27.12.1990, pp. 0051-0060).*

[3]   *If the country of origin is not a contracting party to ADN, the competent authority of the first country contracting party to ADN reached by the consignment.*

Fumigation warning sign

DANGER

THIS UNIT IS UNDER FUMIGATION
WITH [fumigant name *] APPLIED ON
[the date *]
[the time *]

DO NOT ENTER

Not less than 250 mm

* Insert details as appropriate

◄———— Not less than 300 mm ————►

PART 6

Requirements for the construction and testing of packagings (including IBCs and large packagings), tanks and bulk transport units

CHAPTER 6.1

GENERAL REQUIREMENTS

6.1.1   Packagings (including IBCs and large packagings) and tanks shall meet the following requirements of ADR in respect of construction and testing:

Chapter 6.1:	Requirements for the construction and testing of packagings;
Chapter 6.2:	Requirements for the construction and testing of pressure receptacles, aerosol dispensers and small receptacles containing gas (gas cartridges);
Chapter 6.3:	Requirements for the construction and testing of packagings for Class 6.2 substances;
Chapter 6.4:	Requirements for the construction, testing and approval of packages and material of Class 7;
Chapter 6.5	Requirements for the construction and testing of intermediate bulk containers (IBCs);
Chapter 6.6	Requirements for the construction and testing of large packagings;
Chapter 6.7	Requirements for the design, construction, inspection and testing of portable tanks and UN multiple-element gas containers (MEGCs);
Chapter 6.8	Requirements for the construction, equipment, type approval, inspections and tests, and marking of fixed tanks (tank-vehicles), demountable tanks and tank-containers and tank swap bodies, with shell made of metallic materials and battery-vehicles and multiple element gas containers (MEGCs);
Chapter 6.9	Requirements for the design, construction, equipment, type approval, testing and marking of fibre-reinforced plastics (FRP) fixed tanks (tank-vehicles), demountable tanks, tank-containers and tank swap bodies;
Chapter 6.10	Requirements for the construction, equipment, type approval, inspection and marking of vacuum-operated waste tanks.
Chapter 6.11	Requirements for the design, construction, inspection and testing of bulk containers

6.1.2   Portable tanks may also meet the requirements of Chapter 6.7 or, if appropriate, Chapter 6.9 of the IMDG Code.

6.1.3   Tank-vehicles may also meet the requirements of Chapter 6.8 of the IMDG Code.

6.1.4   Tank wagons, with fixed or removable tanks and battery-wagons shall meet the requirements of Chapter 6.8 of the IMDG Code.

6.1.5   Bodies of vehicles for bulk carriage shall, if necessary, meet the requirements of Chapter 6.11 or of Chapter 9.5 of ADR.

6.1.6   When the provisions of 7.3.1.1 (a) of RID or ADR are applied, the bulk containers shall meet the requirements of Chapter 6.11 of RID or ADR.

PART 7

Requirements concerning loading, carriage, unloading and handling of cargo

CHAPTER 7.1

DRY CARGO VESSELS

7.1.0   **General requirements**

7.1.0.1   The provisions of 7.1.0 to 7.1.6 are applicable to dry cargo vessels.

7.1.0.2-   *(Reserved)*
7.1.0.99

7.1.1   **Mode of carriage of goods**

7.1.1.1-   *(Reserved)*
7.1.1.9

7.1.1.10   *Carriage of packages*

Unless otherwise specified, the masses given for packages shall be the gross masses. When packages are carried in containers or vehicles, the mass of the container or vehicle shall not be included in the gross mass of such packages.

7.1.1.11   *Carriage in bulk*

Carriage of dangerous goods in bulk shall be prohibited except where this mode of carriage is explicitly authorized in column (8) of Table A of Chapter 3.2. The code "B" shall then appear in this column.

7.1.1.12   *Ventilation*

The ventilation of holds is required only if it is prescribed in 7.1.4.12 or by an additional requirement "VE ..." in column (10) of Table A of Chapter 3.2.

7.1.1.13   *Measures to be taken prior to loading*

Additional measures to be taken prior to loading are required only if prescribed in 7.1.4.13 or by an additional requirement "LO ..." in column (11) of Table A of Chapter 3.2 (see also 7.1.6.13).

7.1.1.14   *Handling and stowage of cargo*

During the handling and stowage of cargo additional measures are required only if prescribed in 7.1.4.14 or by an additional requirement "HA ..." in column (11) of Table A of Chapter 3.2.

7.1.1.15   *(Reserved)*

7.1.1.16   *Measures to be taken during loading, carriage, unloading and handling of cargo*

The additional measures to be taken prior to loading are required only if prescribed in 7.1.4.16 or by an additional requirement "IN ..." in column (11) of Table A of Chapter 3.2.

7.1.1.17   *(Reserved)*

7.1.1.18   *Carriage in containers, in intermediate bulk containers (IBCs) and in large packagings, in MEGCs, in portable tanks and in tank-containers*

The carriage of containers, IBCs, large packagings, MEGCs portable tanks and tank-containers shall be in accordance with the provisions applicable to the carriage of packages.

7.1.1.19   *Vehicles and wagons*

The carriage of vehicles and wagons shall be in accordance with the provisions applicable to the carriage of packages.

7.1.1.20   *(Reserved)*

7.1.1.21   *Carriage in cargo tanks*

The carriage of dangerous goods in cargo tanks in dry-cargo vessels is prohibited.

7.1.1.22-
7.1.1.99   *(Reserved)*

7.1.2   **Requirements applicable to vessels**

7.1.2.0   *Permitted vessels*

7.1.2.0.1   Dangerous goods may be carried in quantities not exceeding those indicated in 7.1.4.1.1, or, if applicable, in 7.1.4.1.2:

–   In dry cargo vessels conforming to the applicable construction requirements of 9.1.0.0 to 9.1.0.79; or

–   In seagoing vessels conforming to the applicable construction requirements of 9.1.0.0 to 9.1.0.79, or otherwise to the requirements of 9.2.0 to 9.2.0.79.

7.1.2.0.2   Dangerous goods of classes 2, 3, 4.1, 4.2, 4.3, 5.1, 5.2, 6.1, 7, 8 or 9, with the exception of those for which a No. 1 model label is required in column (5) of table A of Chapter 3.2, may be carried in quantities greater than those indicated in 7.1.4.1.1 and 7.1.4.1.2:

–   In double-hull dry cargo vessels conforming to the applicable construction requirements of 9.1.0.80 to 9.1.0.95; or

–   In double-hull seagoing vessels conforming to the applicable construction requirements of 9.1.0.80 to 9.1.0.95, or otherwise to the requirements of 9.2.0 to 9.2.0.95.

7.1.2.1-
7.1.2.4   *(Reserved)*

7.1.2.5   *Instructions for the use of devices and installations*

Where specific safety rules have to be complied with when using any device or installation, instructions for the use of the particular device or installation shall be readily available for consultation at appropriate places on board in the language normally spoken on board and also if that language is not English, French or German, in English, French or German unless agreements concluded between the countries concerned in the transport operation provide otherwise.

7.1.2.6- 7.1.2.18	*(Reserved)*

7.1.2.19 ***Pushed convoys and side-by-side formations***

7.1.2.19.1 Where at least one vessel of a convoy or side-by-side formation is required to be in possession of a certificate of approval, all vessels of such convoy or side-by-side formation shall be provided with an appropriate certificate of approval.

Vessels not carrying dangerous goods shall comply with the requirements of the following paragraphs:

7.1.2.5, 8.1.5, 8.1.6.1, 8.1.6.3, 8.1.7, 8.1.8, 8.1.9, 9.1.0.0, 9.1.0.12.3, 9.1.0.17.2, 9.1.0.17.3, 9.1.0.31, 9.1.0.32, 9.1.0.34, 9.1.0.41, 9.1.0.52.2, 9.1.0.52.3, 9.1.0.56, 9.1.0.71 and 9.1.0.74.

7.1.2.19.2 For the purposes of the application of the provisions of this Part with the exception of 7.1.4.1.1 and 7.1.4.1.2, the entire pushed convoy or the side-by-side formation shall be deemed to be a single vessel.

7.1.2.20- 7.1.2.99	*(Reserved)*

7.1.3 **General service requirements**

7.1.3.1 ***Access to holds, double-hull spaces and double bottoms; inspections***

7.1.3.1.1 Access to the holds is not permitted except for the purpose of loading or unloading and carrying out inspections or cleaning work.

7.1.3.1.2 Access to the double-hull spaces and the double bottoms is not permitted while the vessel is under way.

7.1.3.1.3 If the concentration of gases or the oxygen content of the air in holds, double-wall spaces or double bottoms has to be measured before entry the results of these measurements shall be recorded in writing. The measurement may only be effected by persons equipped with suitable breathing apparatus for the substance carried.

Entry into the spaces is not permitted for the purpose of measuring.

7.1.3.1.4 In case of suspected damage to packages, the gas concentration in holds containing dangerous goods of Classes 2, 3, 5.2, 6.1 and 8 for which EX and/or TOX appears in column (9) of Table A of Chapter 3.2, shall be measured before any person enters these holds.

7.1.3.1.5 The gas concentration in holds and in adjacent holds containing dangerous goods carried in bulk or without packaging for which EX and/or TOX appears in column (9) of Table A of Chapter 3.2, shall be measured before any person enters these holds.

7.1.3.1.6 Entry into holds where damage is suspected to packages in which dangerous goods of Classes 2, 3, 5.2, 6.1 and 8 are carried as well as entry into double-hull spaces and double bottoms is not permitted except where:

    – there is no lack of oxygen and no measurable amount of dangerous substances in a dangerous concentration; or

–   the person entering the space wears a self-contained breathing apparatus and other necessary protective and rescue equipment and is secured by a line. Entry into these spaces is only permitted if this operation is supervised by a second person for whom the same equipment is readily at hand. Another two persons capable of giving assistance in an emergency shall be on the vessel within calling distance.

7.1.3.1.7   Entry into holds where dangerous goods are carried in bulk or without packaging as well as entry into double-hull space and double bottoms is not permitted except where:

–   there is no lack of oxygen and no measurable amount of dangerous substances in a dangerous concentration; or

–   the person entering the space wears a self-contained breathing apparatus and other necessary protective and rescue equipment and is secured by a line. Entry into these spaces is only permitted if this operation is supervised by a second person for whom the same equipment is readily at hand. Another two persons capable of giving assistance in an emergency shall be on the vessel within calling distance.

7.1.3.2-
7.1.3.7   *(Reserved)*

7.1.3.8   *Repair and maintenance work*

No repair or maintenance work liable to cause sparks, or requiring the use of an open flame or electric current, shall be undertaken in the protected area or on deck within 3 metres fore and aft of it, unless permission has been given by the competent authority, or a gas-free certificate has been issued for the protected area.

The use of chromium vanadium steel screwdrivers and wrenches or screwdrivers and wrenches of equivalent material from the point of view of spark-formation is permitted.

7.1.3.9-
7.1.3.14   *(Reserved)*

7.1.3.15   *Dangerous goods training*

When dangerous goods are carried an expert shall be on board the vessel.

7.1.3.16-
7.1.3.19   *(Reserved)*

7.1.3.20   *Water ballast*

Double-hull spaces and double bottoms may be used for water ballast.

7.1.3.21   *(Reserved)*

7.1.3.22   *Opening of holds*

7.1.3.22.1   Dangerous goods shall be protected against the influences of weather and against spray water except during loading and unloading or during inspection.

This provision does not apply when dangerous goods are loaded in sprayproof containers, IBCs, or large packagings, or in MEGCs, portable tanks, tank-containers, vehicles or wagons which are covered or sheeted.

7.1.3.22.2	Where dangerous goods are carried in bulk, the holds shall be covered with hatch covers.
7.1.3.23-7.1.3.30	*(Reserved)*

7.1.3.31 *Engines*

The use of engines running on fuels having a flashpoint below 55° C (e.g. petrol engines) is prohibited.

This requirement does not apply to the petrol-operated outboard motors of lifeboats.

7.1.3.32 *Oil fuel tanks*

Double bottoms with a height of at least 0.6 m may be used as oil fuel tanks provided that they have been constructed in accordance with Chapters 9.1 or 9.2.

7.1.3.33-7.4.3.40	*(Reserved)*

7.1.3.41 *Fire and naked light*

7.1.3.41.1	The use of fire or naked light is prohibited.

This provision does not apply to the accommodation and the wheelhouse.

7.1.3.41.2	Heating, cooking and refrigerating appliances shall not be fuelled with liquid fuels, liquid gas or solid fuels.

Cooking and refrigerating appliances may only be used in the accommodation and in the wheelhouse.

7.1.3.41.3	Heating appliances or boilers fuelled with liquid fuels having a flashpoint above 55° C which are installed in the engine room or in another suitable space may, however, be used.

7.1.3.42 *Heating of holds*

The heating of holds or the operation of a heating system in the holds is prohibited.

7.1.3.43	*(Reserved)*

7.1.3.44 *Cleaning operations*

The use of liquids having a flashpoint below 55° C for cleaning purposes is prohibited.

7.1.3.45-7.1.3.50	*(Reserved)*

7.1.3.51 *Electrical installations*

7.1.3.51.1	The electrical installations shall be properly maintained.
7.1.3.51.2	The use of movable electric cables is prohibited in the protected area. This provision does not apply to:

– intrinsically safe electric circuits;

–   electric cables for connecting signal lights or gangway lighting, provided the socket is permanently fitted to the vessel close to the signal mast or gangway;

–   electric cables for connecting containers;

–   electric cables for electrically operated hatch cover gantries;

–   electric cables for connecting submerged pumps;

–   electric cables for connecting hold ventilators.

7.1.3.51.3   The sockets for connecting the signal lights and gangway lighting and for connecting containers, submerged pumps, hatch cover gantries, or hold fans shall not be live except when the signal lights or the gangway lighting are switched on or when the containers or the submerged pumps or the hatch cover gantries or hold fans are in operation. In the protected area, connecting or disconnecting shall not be possible except when the sockets are not live.

7.1.3.51.4   The electrical installations in the holds shall be kept switched off and protected against unintentional connection.

This provision does not apply to permanently installed cables passing through the holds, to movable cables connecting containers, or to electrical apparatus of a "certified safe type".

7.1.3.52-
7.1.3.69   *(Reserved)*

7.1.3.70   *Aerials, lightning conductors, wire cables and masts*

7.1.3.70.1   No part of an aerial for electronic apparatus, no lightning conductor and no wire cable shall be situated above the holds.

7.1.3.70.2   No part of aerials for radiotelephones shall be located within 2.00 m from substances or articles of Class 1.

7.1.3.71-
7.1.3.99   *(Reserved)*

7.1.4   **Additional requirements concerning loading, carriage, unloading and other handling of the cargo**

7.1.4.1   *Limitation of the quantities carried*

7.1.4.1.1   Subject to 7.1.4.1.3, the following gross masses shall not be exceeded on any vessel. For pushed convoys and side-by-side formations this gross mass applies to each unit of the convoy or formation.

Class 1

All substances and articles of Division 1.1 of compatibility group A	90 kg[1]
All substances and articles of Division 1.1 of compatibility groups B, C, D. E, F, G, J or L	15,000 kg[2]
All substances and articles of Division 1.2 of compatibility groups B, C, D, E, F, G, H, J or L	50,000 kg
All substances and articles of Division 1.3 of compatibility groups C, G, H, J or L	300,000 kg[3]
All substances and articles of Division 1.4 of compatibility groups B, C, D, E, F, G or S	1,100,000 kg
All substances of Division 1.5 of compatibility group D	15,000 kg[2]
All articles of Division 1.6 of compatibility group N	300,000 kg[3]
Empty packagings, uncleaned	1,100,000 kg

Note:

[1]   *In not less than three batches of a maximum of 30 kg each, distance between batches not less than 10.00 m.*

[2]   *In not less than three batches of a maximum of 5 000 kg each, distance between batches not less than 10.00 m.*

[3]   *A wooden partition is permitted for subdividing a hold.*

Class 2

All goods for which label No. 2.3 is required in column (5) of Table A of Chapter 3.2: total	120 000 kg
All goods for which label No. 2.1 is required in column (5) of Table A of Chapter 3.2: total	300 000 kg
Other goods	No limitation

Class 3

All goods for which label No. 6.1 is required in column (5) of Table A of Chapter 3.2: total	120 000 kg
Other goods	300 000 kg

Class 4.1

UN Nos. 3221, 3222, 3231 and 3232, total	15 000 kg
All goods of packing group I; all goods of packing group II for which label No. 6.1 is required in column (5) of Table A of Chapter 3.2; self-reactive substances of types C, D, E and F (UN Nos. 3223 to 3230 and 3233 to 3240); other substances of classification code SR1 or SR2 (UN Nos. 2956, 3241, 3242 and 3251); and desensitized explosive substances of packing group II (UN Nos. 2907, 3319 and 3344): total	120 000 kg
Other goods	No limitation

Class 4.2

All goods of packing groups I or II for which label No. 6.1 is required in column (5) of Table A of Chapter 3.2: total	300 000 kg
Other goods	No limitation

Class 4.3

All goods of packing groups I or II for which label No. 3, 4.1 or 6.1 is required in column (5) of Table A of Chapter 3.2: total	300 000 kg
Other goods	No limitation

Class 5.1

All goods of packing groups I or II for which label No. 6.1 is required in column (5) of Table A of Chapter 3.2: total	300 000 kg
Other goods	No limitation

Class 5.2

UN Nos. 3101, 3102, 3111 and 3112: total	15 000 kg
All other goods: total	120 000 kg

Class 6.1

All goods of packing group I	120 000 kg
All goods of packing group II	300 000 kg
Other goods	No limitation

Class 7

UN Nos. 2912, 2913, 2915, 2917, 2919, 2977, 2978 and 3321 to 3333	0 kg
Other goods	No limitation

Class 8

All goods of packing group I; goods of packing group II for which label No. 3 or 6.1 is required in column (5) of the table in Chapter 3.2: total	300 000 kg
Other goods	No limitation

Class 9

All goods of packing group II	300 000 kg
Other goods	No limitation

7.1.4.1.2   Subject to 7.1.4.1.3, the maximum quantity of dangerous goods permitted on board a vessel or on board each unit of a pushed convoy or side-by-side formation is 1,100,000 kg.

7.1.4.1.3   The limitations of 7.1.4.1.1 and 7.1.4.1.2 shall not apply in the case of transport of dangerous goods of classes 2, 3, 4.1, 4.2, 4.3, 5.1, 5.2, 6.1, 7, 8 and 9, except of those for which a label of Model No 1 is required in column (5) of Table A of Chapter 3.2, on board double-hull vessels complying with the additional requirements of 9.1.0.88 to 9.1.0.95 or 9.2.0.88 to 9.2.0.95.

7.1.4.1.4   Where substances and articles of different divisions of Class 1 are loaded in a single vessel in conformity with the provisions for prohibition of mixed loading of 7.1.4.3.3 or 7.1.4.3.4, the entire load shall not exceed the smallest maximum net mass given in 7.1.4.1.1 above for the goods of the most dangerous division loaded, the order of precedence being 1.1, 1.5, 1.2, 1.3, 1.6, 1.4.

7.1.4.1.5   Where the total net mass of the explosive substances contained in the explosive substances and articles carried is not known, the table in 7.1.4.1.1 above shall apply to the gross mass of the cargo.

7.1.4.1.6   For activity limits, transport index (TI) limits and criticality safety indices (CSI) in the case of the carriage of radioactive material, see 7.1.4.14.7.

7.1.4.2   *Prohibition of mixed loading (bulk)*

Vessels carrying substances of Class 5.1 in bulk shall not carry any other goods.

7.1.4.3   *Prohibition of mixed loading (packages in holds)*

7.1.4.3.1   Goods of different classes shall be separated by a minimum horizontal distance of 3.00 m. They shall not be stowed one on top of the other.

7.1.4.3.2   Irrespective of the quantity, dangerous goods for which marking with three blue cones or three blue lights is prescribed in column (12) of Table A of Chapter 3.2 shall not be stowed in the same hold together with flammable goods for which marking with one blue cone or one blue light is prescribed in column (12) of Table A of Chapter 3.2.

7.1.4.3.3   Packages containing substances or articles of Class 1 and packages containing substances of Classes 4.1 or 5.2 for which marking with three blue cones or three blue lights is prescribed in column (12) of Table A of Chapter 3.2 shall be separated by a distance of not less than 12 m from goods of all other classes.

7.1.4.3.4   Substances and articles of Class 1 shall not be stowed in the same hold, except as indicated in the following table:

Compatibility group	A	B	C	D	E	F	G	H	J	L	N	S
A	X	-	-	-	-	-	-	-	-	-	-	-
B	-	X	-	1	-	-	-	-	-	-	-	X
C	-	-	X	X	X	-	X	-	-	-	2,3	X
D	-	1	X	X	X	-	X	-	-	-	2,3	X
E	-	-	X	X	X	-	X	-	-	-	2,3	X
F	-	-	-	-	-	X	-	-	-	-	-	X
G	-	-	X	X	X	-	X	-	-	-	-	X
H	-	-	-	-	-	-	-	X	-	-	-	X
J	-	-	-	-	-	-	-	-	X	-	-	X
L	-	-	-	-	-	-	-	-	-	4	-	-
N	-	-	2,3	2,3	2,3	-	-	-	-	-	2	X
S	-	X	X	X	X	X	X	X	X	-	X	X

"X" indicates that explosive substances of corresponding compatibility groups in accordance with Part 2 of these Regulations may be stowed in the same hold.

[1]   *Packages containing substances or articles assigned to compatibility groups B and D may be loaded together in the same hold provided that they are carried in containers or vehicles or wagons with complete metal walls.*

[2]   *Different categories of articles of Division 1.6, compatibility group N, may be carried together as articles of Division 1.6, compatibility group N, only when it is proven by testing or analogy that there is no additional risk of sympathetic detonation between the articles. Otherwise they should be treated as hazard Division 1.1.*

[3]   *When articles of compatibility group N are carried with substances or articles of compatibility groups C, D or E, the articles of compatibility group N should be considered as having the characteristics of compatibility group D.*

4/ *Packages with substances or articles of compatibility group L may be stowed in the same hold with packages containing the same type of substances or articles of the same compatibility group.*

7.1.4.3.5 For the carriage of material Class 7 (UN Nos. 2916, 2917, 3323, 3328, 3329 and 3330) in Type B(U) or Type B(M) or Type C packages, the controls, restrictions or provisions specified in the competent authority approval certificate shall be complied with.

7.1.4.3.6 For the carriage of material of Class 7 (UN Nos. 2919 and 3331) under special arrangement, the special provisions specified by the competent authority shall be met. In particular, mixed loading shall not be permitted unless specifically authorized by the competent authority.

7.1.4.4 *Prohibition of mixed loading (containers, vehicles, wagons)*

7.1.4.4.1 7.1.4.3 shall not apply to packages stowed in containers, vehicles or wagons in accordance with international regulations.

7.1.4.4.2 7.1.4.3 shall not apply to:

- closed containers with complete metal walls;

- vehicles and wagons with closed body having complete metal walls;

- tank-containers, portable tanks and MEGCs;

- tank-vehicles and tank-wagons.

7.1.4.4.3 For containers other than those referred to in paragraph 7.1.4.4.1 and 7.1.4.4.2 above the separation distance required by 7.1.4.3.1 may be reduced to 2.4 m (width of container).

7.1.4.5 *Prohibition of mixed loading (seagoing vessels)*

For seagoing vessels and inland waterway vessels, where the latter only carry containers, the prohibition of mixed loading shall be deemed to have been met if the stowage and segregation requirements of the IMDG Code have been complied with.

7.1.4.6 *(Reserved)*

7.1.4.7 *Places of loading and unloading*

7.1.4.7.1 The dangerous goods shall be loaded or unloaded only at the places designated or approved for this purpose by the competent authority.

7.1.4.7.2 When substances or articles of Class 1 and substances of Classes 4.1 or 5.2 for which marking with three blue cones or three blue lights is prescribed in column (12) of Table A of Chapter 3.2 are on board, no goods of any kind may be loaded or unloaded except at the places designated or permitted for this purpose by the competent local authority.

7.1.4.8 *Time and duration of loading and unloading operations*

7.1.4.8.1 Loading and unloading operations of substances or articles of Class 1 and substances of Classes 4.1 or 5.2 for which marking with three blue cones or three blue lights is prescribed in column (12) of Table A of Chapter 3.2 shall not start without permission in writing from the competent authority. This provision also applies to loading or unloading of other goods when substances or articles of Class 1 or substances of Classes 4.1 or 5.2 for which marking with three blue cones or three blue lights is prescribed in column (12) of Table A of Chapter 3.2 are on board.

7.1.4.8.2	Loading and unloading operations of substances or articles of Class 1 and substances of Classes 4.1 or 5.2 shall be suspended in the event of a storm.

7.1.4.9 *Cargo transfer operations*

Partial or complete cargo transfer into another vessel without permission from the competent authority is prohibited outside a cargo transfer place approved for this purpose.

7.1.4.10 *Precautions with respect to foodstuffs, other articles of consumption and animal feeds*

7.1.4.10.1 When special provision 802 is indicated for a dangerous good in column (6) of Table A of Chapter 3.2, precautions shall be taken as follows with respect to foodstuffs, other articles of consumption and animal feeds:

Packages, including intermediate bulk containers (IBCs), and uncleaned empty packagings, including uncleaned empty intermediate bulk containers (IBCs), bearing labels conforming to models Nos. 6.1 or 6.2, and those bearing labels of Class 9, containing substances of Class 9, UN Nos. 2212, 2315, 2590, 3151, 3152 or 3245, shall not be stacked on or loaded in immediate proximity to packages known to contain foodstuffs, other articles of consumption or animal feeds in the same hold and at places of loading and unloading or trans-shipment.

When these packages, bearing the said labels, are loaded in immediate proximity of packages known to contain foodstuffs, other articles of consumption or animal feeds, they shall be kept apart from the latter:

(a) by complete partitions which should be as high as the packages bearing the said labels, or

(b) by packages not bearing labels conforming to models Nos. 6.1, 6.2 or 9 or packages bearing labels of Class 9 but not containing substances of that class, UN Nos. 2212, 2315, 2590, 3151, 3152 or 3245, or

(c) by a space of at least 0.8 m,

unless the packages bearing said labels are provided with an additional packaging or are completely covered (e.g. by a sheeting, a fibreboard cover or other measures).

7.1.4.11 *Stowage plan*

7.1.4.11.1 The master shall enter on a stowage plan the dangerous goods stowed in the individual holds or on deck. The goods shall be described as in the transport document in accordance with 5.4.1.1.1 (a), (b), (c) and (d).

7.1.4.11.2 Where the dangerous goods are transported in containers, the number of the container shall suffice. In this case, the stowage plan shall contain as an annex a list of all containers with their numbers and the description of the goods contained therein in accordance with 5.4.1.1.1 (a), (b), (c) and (d).

7.1.4.12 *Ventilation*

7.1.4.12.1 During loading or unloading of road vehicles into or from the holds of ro-ro-vessels, there shall be not less than five changes of air per hour based upon the total volume of the empty hold.

7.1.4.12.2 On board vessels carrying dangerous goods only in containers placed in open holds, ventilators do not require to be incorporated but must be on board. Where damage is suspected, the holds shall be ventilated so as to reduce the concentration of gases given off by the cargo to less than 10% of the lower explosive limit or in the case of toxic gases to below any significant concentration.

7.1.4.12.3 If tank-containers, portable tanks, MEGCs, road tank vehicles or tank wagons are carried in closed holds, such holds shall be permanently ventilated for ensuring five air changes per hour.

7.1.4.13 *Measures to be taken before loading*

The holds and cargo decks shall be cleaned prior to loading. The holds shall be ventilated.

7.1.4.14 *Handling and stowage of the cargo*

7.1.4.14.1 The various components of the cargo shall be stowed such as to prevent them from shifting in relation to one another or to the vessel and such that no damage can be caused by other cargo.

7.1.4.14.2 Dangerous goods shall be stowed at a distance of not less than 1 m from the accommodation, the engine rooms, the wheelhouse and any sources of heat.

When the accommodation or wheelhouse is situated above a hold, dangerous goods shall in no case be stowed beneath such accommodation or wheelhouse.

7.1.4.14.3 Packages shall be protected against heat, sunlight and the effects of the weather. This provision does not apply to vehicles, wagons, tank-containers, portable tanks, MEGCs and containers.

Where packages are not enclosed in vehicles, wagons or containers but loaded on deck, they shall be covered with tarpaulins that are not readily flammable.

The ventilation shall not be obstructed.

7.1.4.14.4 The dangerous goods shall be stowed in the holds. However, dangerous goods packed or loaded in:

– containers having complete sprayproof walls;

– MEGCs;

– vehicles having complete sprayproof walls;

– tank-containers or portable tanks;

– tank vehicles or tank wagons;

may be carried on deck in the protected area.

7.1.4.14.5 Packages containing dangerous goods of Classes 3, 4.1, 4.2, 5.1 or 8 may be stowed on deck provided that drums are used or that they are contained in containers with complete walls or vehicles or wagons with complete walls. Substances of Class 2 may be stowed on deck in the protected area, provided they are contained in cylinders.

7.1.4.14.6   For seagoing vessels, the stowage requirements set out in 7.1.4.14.1 to 7.1.4.14.5 above and 7.1.4.14.7 below shall be deemed to have been met, if the relevant stowage provisions of the IMDG Code and, in the case of carriage in bulk, those set out in subsection 9.3 of the BC Code have been complied with.

7.1.4.14.7   *Handling and stowage of radioactive material*

NOTE 1: *"Critical group" means a group of members of the public which is reasonably homogeneous with respect to its exposure for a given radiation source and given exposure pathway and is typical of individuals receiving the highest effective dose by the given exposure pathway from the given source.*

NOTE 2: *"Members of the public" means in a general sense, any individuals in the population except when subject to occupational or medical exposure.*

NOTE 3: *"Workers" are any persons who work, whether full time, part-time or temporarily, for an employer and who have recognized rights and duties in relation to occupational radiation protection.*

7.1.4.14.7.1   *Segregation*

7.1.4.14.7.1.1   Packages, overpacks, containers MEGCs, tanks, vehicles, and wagons shall be segregated during carriage:

(a)   From areas where persons other than those referred to in paragraph (c) have regular access:

  (i)   in accordance with Table A below; or

  (ii)   by a distance calculated to ensure members of the critical group in that area receive less than 1mSv per year, taking account of the exposures expected to be delivered by all other relevant sources and practices under control;

and

(b)   From undeveloped photographic film and mailbags, in accordance with Table B below;

  NOTE: *Mailbags shall be assumed to contain undeveloped film and plates and therefore be separated from radioactive material in the same way.*

and

(c)   from workers in regularly occupied working areas either:

  (i)   in accordance with Table A below; or

  (ii)   by a distance calculated to ensure that workers in that area receive less than 5mSv per year;

  NOTE: *Workers subject to individual monitoring for the purpose of radiation protection shall not be considered for the purpose of segregation;*

and

(d)   from other dangerous goods in accordance with 7.1.4.3.

NOTE: *Except in the case of shipment under special arrangement, mixing of packages containing different types of radioactive material including fissile material, and mixing of different kinds of packages with different transport indexes is permitted without specific competent authority approval provided that transport index limits are not exceeded. In the case of shipment under special arrangement, mixing is not permitted except as specifically authorized by the special arrangement.*

Table A: Minimum distances between packages of category II-YELLOW or of category III-YELLOW and persons

Sum of transport indexes not more than	Exposure time per year (hours)			
	Areas where members of the public have regular access		Regularly occupied working areas	
	50	250	50	250
	Segregation distance in metres, no shielding material intervening, from:			
2	1	3	0.5	1
4	1.5	4	0.5	1.5
8	2.5	6	1.0	2.5
12	3	7.5	1.0	3
20	4	9.5	1.5	4
30	5	12	2	5
40	5.5	13.5	2.5	5.6
50	6.5	15.5	3	6.5

7.1.4.14.7.1.2 Category II-YELLOW or III-YELLOW packages or overpacks shall not be carried in compartments occupied by passengers, except those exclusively reserved for couriers specially authorized to accompany such packages or overpacks.

7.1.4.14.7.1.3 No persons other than the master of the vessel or the vehicle embarked and the other members of the crew shall be permitted in vessels carrying packages, overpacks or containers bearing category II-YELLOW or III-YELLOW labels.

7.1.4.14.7.1.4 Radioactive material shall be sufficiently segregated from undeveloped photographic film. The basis for determining segregation distances for this purpose shall be that the radiation exposure of undeveloped photographic film due to the carriage of radioactive material be limited to 0.1 mSv per consignment of such film (see Table B below).

Table B: Minimum distances between packages of category II-YELLOW or of category III-YELLOW and packages bearing the word "FOTO", or mailbags

Total number of packages not more than		Sum of transport indexes not more than	Journey or storage duration, in hours							
Category			1	2	4	10	24	48	120	240
III-yellow	II-yellow		Minimum distances in metres							
		0.2	0.5	0.5	0.5	0.5	1	1	2	3
		0.5	0.5	0.5	0.5	1	1	2	3	5
	1	1	0.5	0.5	1	1	2	3	5	7
	2	2	0.5	1	1	1.5	3	4	7	9
	4	4	1	1	1.5	3	4	6	9	13
	8	8	1	1.5	2	4	6	8	13	18
1	10	10	1	2	3	4	7	9	14	20
2	20	20	1.5	3	4	6	9	13	20	30
3	30	30	2	3	5	7	11	16	25	35
4	40	40	3	4	5	8	13	18	30	40
5	50	50	3	4	6	9	14	20	32	45

7.1.4.14.7.2   *Activity limits*

The total activity in a single hold or compartment of vessel, or in another conveyance, for carriage of LSA material or SCO articles in Type IP-1, Type IP-2, Type IP-3 or unpackaged, shall not exceed the limits shown in Table C below:

Table C: Conveyance activity limits for LSA material and SCO in industrial packages or unpackaged

Nature of material or articles	Activity limit for conveyances other than by vessel	Activity limit for a hold or compartment of vessel
LSA-I	No limit	No limit
LSA-II and LSA-III non-combustible solids	No limit	$100A_2$
LSA-II and LSA-III combustible solids, and all liquids and gases	$100A_2$	$10A_2$
SCO	$100A_2$	$10A_2$

7.1.4.14.7.3   *Stowage during carriage and storage in transit*

7.1.4.14.7.3.1   Consignments shall be securely stowed

7.1.4.14.7.3.2   Provided that its average surface heat flux does not exceed $15W/M^2$ and that the immediately surrounding cargo is not in bags, a package or overpack may be carried or stored among packaged general cargo without any special stowage provisions except as may be specifically required by the competent authority in an applicable approval certificate.

7.1.4.14.7.3.3   Loading of containers and accumulation of packages, overpacks and containers shall be controlled as follows:

(a) Except under the conditions of exclusive use, the total number of packages, overpacks and containers aboard a single conveyance shall be so limited that the total sum of the transport indexes aboard the conveyance does not exceed the values shown in Table D below. For consignments of LSA-I material there shall be no limit on the sum of the transport indexes;

(b) Where a consignment is carried under exclusive use, there shall be no limit on the sum of the transport indexes aboard a single conveyance;

(c) The radiation level under routine conditions of carriage shall not exceed 2 mSv/h at any point on, and 0.1 mSv/h at 2 m from, the external surface of the conveyance, except for consignments carried under exclusive use, for which the radiation limits around the conveyance are set forth in 7.1.4.14.7.3.5 (b) and (c);

(d) The total sum of the criticality safety indexes in a container and aboard a conveyance shall not exceed the values shown in Table E below.

Table D: Transport Index limits for containers and conveyances not under exclusive use

Type of container or conveyance	Limit on total sum of transport indexes in a container or aboard a conveyance
Small container	50
Large container	50
Vehicle or wagon	50
Vessel	50

Table E: Criticality Safety Index for containers and vehicles containing fissile material

Type of container or conveyance	Limit on total sum of criticality safety indexes	
	Not under exclusive use	Under exclusive use
Small container	50	n.a.
Large container	50	100
Vehicle or wagon	50	100
Vessel	50	100

7.1.4.14.7.3.4 Any package or overpack having either a transport index greater than 10, or any consignment having a criticality safety index greater than 50, shall be carried only under exclusive use.

7.1.4.14.7.3.5 For consignments under exclusive use in vehicles or wagons, the radiation level shall not exceed:

(a) 10 mSV/h at any point on the external surface of any package or overpack, and may only exceed 2 mSv/h provided that:

(i) the vehicle or wagon is equipped with an enclosure which, during routine conditions of carriage, prevents the access of unauthorized persons to the interior of the enclosure;

(ii) provisions are made to secure the package or overpack so that its position within the vehicle or wagon enclosure remains fixed during routine conditions of carriage; and

(iii) there is no loading or unloading during the shipment;

(b)   2 mSv/h at any point on the outer services of the vehicle or wagon, including the upper and lower surfaces, or, in the case of an open vehicle or wagon, at any point on the vertical planes projected from the outer edges of the vehicle or wagon, on the upper surface of the load, and on the lower external surface of the vehicle or wagon; and

(c)   0.1 mSv/h at any point 2 m from the vertical planes represented by the outer lateral surfaces of the vehicle or wagon, or, if the load is carried in an open vehicle or wagon, at any point 2 m from the vertical planes projected from the outer edges of the vehicle or wagon.

7.1.4.14.7.3.6   Packages or overpacks having a surface radiation area greater than 2 mSv/h, unless being carried in or on a vehicle or wagon under exclusive use and unless they are removed from the vehicle or wagon when on board the vessel shall not be transported by vessel except under special arrangement.

7.4.1.14.7.3.7   The transport of consignments by means of a special use vessel which, by virtue of its design, or by reason of its being chartered, is dedicated to the purpose of carrying radioactive material, shall be excepted from the requirements specified in 7.1.4.14.7.3.3 provided that the following conditions are met:

(a)   A radiation protection programme for the shipment shall be approved by the competent authority of the flag state of the vessel and, when requested, by the competent authority at each port of call of the transit countries;

(b)   Stowage arrangements shall be predetermined for the whole voyage including any consignments to be loaded at ports of call en route; and

(c)   The loading, carriage and unloading of the consignments shall be supervised by persons qualified in the transport of radioactive material.

7.1.4.14.7.4   *Segregation of packages containing fissile material during carriage and storage in transit*

7.1.4.14.7.4.1   Any group of packages, overpacks, and containers containing fissile material stored in transit in any one storage area shall be so limited that the total sum of the criticality safety indexes in the group does not exceed 50. Each group shall be stored so as to maintain a spacing of at least 6 m from other such groups.

7.1.4.14.7.4.2   Where the total sum of the criticality safety indexes on board a vehicle or in a container exceeds 50, as permitted in Table E above, storage shall be such as to maintain a spacing of at least 6 m from other groups of packages, overpacks or containers containing fissile material or other vehicles carrying radioactive material. The space between such groups may be used for other dangerous goods of ADN. The carriage of other goods with consignments under exclusive use is permitted provided that the pertinent provisions have been taken by the consignor and that carriage is not prohibited under other requirements.

7.1.4.14.7.5   *Damaged or leaking packages, contaminated packagings*

7.1.4.14.7.5.1   If it is evident that a package is damaged or leaking, or if it is suspected that the package may have leaked or been damaged, access to the package shall be restricted and a qualified person shall, as soon as possible, assess the extent of contamination and the resultant radiation level of the package. The scope of the assessment shall include the package, the vehicle, the wagon, the adjacent loading and unloading areas, and, if necessary, all other material which has been carried in the vessel. When necessary, additional steps for the protection of persons property and the environment, in accordance with provisions established by the competent authority, shall be taken to overcome and minimize the consequences of such leakage or damage.

7.1.4.14.7.5.2   Packages damaged or leaking radioactive contents in excess of allowable limits for normal conditions of carriage may be removed to an acceptable interim location under supervision, but shall not be forwarded until repaired or reconditioned and decontaminated.

7.1.4.14.7.5.3   Vehicles, wagons, vessels and equipment used regularly for the carriage of radioactive material shall be periodically checked to determine the level of contamination. The frequency of such checks shall be related to the likelihood of contamination and the extent to which radioactive material is carried.

7.1.4.14.7.5.4   Except as provided in paragraph 7.1.4.14.7.5.6, any vessel, or equipment or part thereof which has become contaminated above the limits specified in 7.1.4.14.7.5.5 in the course of carriage of radioactive material, or which shows a radiation level in excess of 5 µSv/h at the surface, shall be decontaminated as soon as possible by a qualified person and shall not be re-used unless the non-fixed contamination does not exceed the limits specified in 7.1.4.14.7.5.5, and the radiation level resulting from the fixed contamination on surfaces after decontamination is less than 5 µSv/h at the surface.

7.1.4.14.7.5.5   For the purposes of 7.1.4.14.7.5.4, non-fixed contamination shall not exceed:

–   4 Bq/cm^2 for beta and gamma emitters and low toxicity alpha emitters;

–   0.4 Bq/cm^2 for all other alpha emitters.

These are average limits applicable to any area of 300 cm^2 on any part of the surface.

7.1.4.14.7.5.6   Vessels dedicated to the carriage of radioactive material under exclusive use shall be excepted from the requirements of the previous paragraph 7.1.4.14.7.5.4 solely with regard to its internal surfaces and only for as long as it remains under that specific exclusive use.

7.1.4.14.7.6   *Limitation of the effect of temperature*

7.1.4.14.7.6.1   If the temperature of the accessible outer surfaces of a Type B (U) or Type B (M) package could exceed 50° C in the shade, carriage is permitted only under exclusive use. As far as practicable, the surface temperature shall be limited to 85° C. Account may be taken of barriers or screens intended to give protection to transport workers without the barriers or screens being subject to any test.

7.1.4.14.7.6.2   If the average heat flux from the external surfaces of a Type B (U) or B (M) package could exceed 15 W/m^2, the special stowage requirements specified in the competent authority package design approval certificate shall be met.

7.1.4.14.7.7   *Other provisions*

If neither the consignor nor the consignee can be identified or if the consignment cannot be delivered to the consignee and the carrier has no instructions from the consignor the consignment shall be placed in a safe location and the competent authority shall be informed as soon as possible and a request made for instructions on further action.

7.1.4.15   *Measures to be taken after unloading*

7.1.4.15.1   After unloading the holds shall be inspected and cleaned if necessary. In the case of carriage in bulk, this requirement does not apply if the new cargo comprises the same goods as the previous cargo.

7.1.4.15.2   For material of Class 7 see also 7.1.4.14.7.5.

7.1.4.15.3   A transport unit or hold space which has been used to carry infectious substances shall be inspected for release of the substance before re-use. If the infectious substances were released during carriage, the transport unit or hold space shall be decontaminated before it is re-used. Decontamination may be achieved by any means which effectively inactivates the released infectious substance.

7.1.4.16   *Measures to be taken during loading, carriage, unloading and handling of the cargo*

The filling or emptying of receptacles, road tank vehicles tank wagons, intermediate bulk containers (IBCs), large packagings, MEGCs, portable tanks or tank-containers on board the vessel is prohibited without special permission from the competent local authority.

7.1.4.17-   *(Reserved)*
7.1.4.40-

7.1.4.41   *Fire and naked light*

The use of fire or naked light is prohibited while substances or articles of Divisions 1.1, 1.2, 1.3, 1.5 or 1.6 are on board and the holds are open or the goods to be loaded are located at a distance of less than 50 m from the vessel.

7.1.4.42-   *(Reserved)*
7.1.4.50

7.1.4.51   *Electrical equipment*

The use of radiotelephone or radar transmitters is not permitted, while substances or articles of Divisions 1.1, 1.2, 1.3, 1.5 or 1.6 are being loaded or unloaded.

This shall not apply to VHF-transmitters of the vessel, in cranes or in the vicinity of the vessel, provided the power of the VHF-transmitter does not exceed 25 W and no part of its aerial is located at a distance less than 2.00 m from the substances or articles mentioned above.

7.1.4.52   *(Reserved)*

7.1.4.53   *Lighting*

If loading, or unloading is performed at night or in conditions of poor visibility, effective lighting shall be provided.

If provided from the deck, it shall be effected by properly secured electric lamps which shall be positioned in such a way that they cannot be damaged.

Where these lamps are positioned on deck in the protected area, they shall be of limited explosion risk type.

7.1.4.54-   *(Reserved)*
7.1.4.74

7.1.4.75   *Risk of sparking*

All electrically continuous connections between the vessel and the shore as well as appliances used in the protected area shall be so designed that they do not present a source of ignition.

7.1.4.76   *Synthetic ropes*

During loading or unloading operations, the vessel may be moored by means of synthetic ropes only when steel cables are used to prevent the vessel from going adrift.

Steel cables sheathed in synthetic material or natural fibres are considered as equivalent when the minimum tensile strength required in accordance with the Regulations referred to in 1.1.4.6 is obtained from the steel strands.

However, during loading or unloading of containers, vessels may be moored by means of synthetic ropes.

7.1.4.77-   *(Reserved)*
7.1.4.99

7.1.5   **Additional requirements concerning the operation of vessels**

7.1.5.0   *Marking*

7.1.5.0.1   Vessels carrying dangerous goods listed in Table A of Chapter 3.2 shall, in accordance with Chapter 3 of the European Code for Inland Waterways (CEVNI), display the markings prescribed in this table.

7.1.5.0.2   Vessels carrying the dangerous goods listed in Table A of Chapter 3.2 in packages placed exclusively in containers shall display the number of blue cones or blue lights indicated in column (12) of Table A of Chapter 3.2 where:

–   three blue cones or three blue lights are required, or

–   two blue cones or two blue lights are required, a substance of Class 2 is involved or packing group I is indicated in column (4) of Table A of Chapter 3.2 and the total gross mass of these dangerous goods exceeds 30,000 kg, or

–   one blue cone or one blue light is required, a substance of Class 2 is involved or packing group I is indicated in column (4) of Chapter 3.2 and the total gross mass of these dangerous goods exceeds 130,000 kg.

7.1.5.0.3   Vessels carrying empty, uncleaned tanks, battery vehicles, battery wagons or MEGCs shall display the marking referred to in column (12) of Table A of Chapter 3.2 if these units have contained dangerous goods for which this table prescribes marking.

7.1.5.0.4   Where more than one marking could apply to a vessel, only the marking which includes the greatest number of blue cones or blue lights shall apply, i.e. in the following order of precedence:

–   three blue cones or three blue lights; or

–   two blue cones or two blue lights; or

        –   one blue cone or one blue light.

7.1.5.0.5   By derogation from paragraph 7.1.5.0.1, and in accordance with the footnotes to article 3.14 of the European Code for Inland Waterways (CEVNI), the competent authority of a Contracting Party may authorize seagoing vessels temporarily operating in an inland navigation area on the territory of this Contracting Party, the use of the day and night signals prescribed in the Recommendations on the Safe Transport of Dangerous Cargoes and Related Activities in Port Areas adopted by the Maritime Safety Committee of the International Maritime Organization (by night an all-round fixed red light and by day flag "B" of the International Code of Signals), instead of the signals prescribed in 7.1.5.0.1. Contracting Parties which have taken the initiative with respect to the derogation granted shall notify the Executive Secretary of the United Nations Economic commission for Europe, who shall bring this derogation to the attention of the Administrative Committee.

7.1.5.1   *Mode of navigation*

7.1.5.1.1   The competent authorities may impose restrictions on the inclusion of tank vessels in pushed conveys of large dimension.

7.1.5.1.2   When vessels carry substances or articles of Class 1, or substances of Classes 4.1 or 5.2 for which marking with three blue cones or three blue lights is prescribed in column (12) of Table A of Chapter 3.2, or material of Class 7 of UN Nos. 2912, 2913, 2915, 2916, 2917, 2919, 2977, 2978 or 3321 to 3333, the competent authority may impose restrictions on the dimensions of convoys or side-by-side formations. Nevertheless, the use of a motorized vessel giving temporary towing assistance is permitted.

7.1.5.2   *Vessels under way*

Vessels carrying substances or articles of Class 1, or substances of Classes 4.1 or 5.2 for which marking with three blue cones or three blue lights is prescribed in column (12) of Table A of Chapter 3.2, when under way shall keep not less than 50 m away from any other vessel, if possible.

7.1.5.3   *Mooring*

Vessels shall be moored securely, but in such a way that they can be released quickly in an emergency.

7.1.5.4   *Berthing*

7.1.5.4.1   The distances to be kept by vessels carrying dangerous goods at berth from other vessels shall not be less than the distance prescribed by the European Code for Inland Waterways.

7.1.5.4.2   An expert in accordance with 7.1.3.15 shall be permanently on board berthed vessels carrying dangerous goods for which marking is prescribed in column (12) of Table A of Chapter 3.2.

The competent authority may, however, exempt from this obligation those vessels which are berthed in a harbour basin or in an accepted berthing position.

7.1.5.4.3   Outside the berthing areas specifically designated by the competent authority, the distances to be kept by berthed vessels shall not be less than:

        –   100 m   from residential areas, civil engineering structures or storage tanks, if the vessel is required to be marked with one blue cone or one blue light in accordance with the requirements of column (12) of Table A of Chapter 3.2;

| | – | 100 m | from civil engineering structures and storage tanks and 300 m from residential areas if the vessel is required to be marked with two blue cones or two blue lights in accordance with the requirements of column (12) of Table A of Chapter 3.2; |

– 100 m from civil engineering structures and storage tanks and 300 m from residential areas if the vessel is required to be marked with two blue cones or two blue lights in accordance with the requirements of column (12) of Table A of Chapter 3.2;

– 500 m from residential areas, civil engineering structures and storage tanks if the vessel is required to be marked with three blue cones or three blue lights in accordance with the requirements of column (12) of Table A of Chapter 3.2.

While waiting in front of locks or bridges, vessels are allowed to keep distances different from and lower than those given above. In no case shall the distance be less than 100 m.

7.1.5.4.4   The competent authority may prescribe distances lower than those given in 7.1.5.4.3 above, especially taking local conditions into account.

7.1.5.5   *Stopping of vessels*

If navigation of a vessel carrying substances and articles of Class 1 or substances of Class 4.1 or 5.2 for which marking with three blue cones or three blue lights is prescribed in column (12) of Table A of Chapter 3.2 threatens to become dangerous owing either to:

– external factors (bad weather, unfavourable conditions of the waterway, etc.), or

– the condition of the vessel itself (accident or incident),

the vessel shall be stopped at a suitable berthing area as far away as possible from residential areas, harbours, civil engineering structures or storage tanks for gas or flammable liquids, regardless of the provisions set out in 7.1.5.4.

The competent authority shall be notified without delay.

7.1.5.6-   *(Reserved)*
7.1.5.7

7.1.5.8   **Reporting duty**

7.1.5.8.1   In the States where the reporting duty is in force, the master of a vessel for which marking in accordance with 7.1.5.0 is required shall, prior to the start of any voyage, report the following particulars to the competent authority of the State in which the voyage has started:

– name of the vessel;

– official number;

– dead-weight tonnage;

– description of the dangerous goods carried as given in the transport document (UN number or identification number, proper shipping name, class and, where applicable, packing group and/or classification code) together with the quantity in each case;

> **NOTE**: *The gross mass of the packages containing substances or articles of Class 1 shall be declared in addition to the net mass of explosive substances and of explosive substances contained in the articles.*

- number of persons on board;

- port of destination; and

- planned shipping route.

This reporting duty shall apply in each State territory once to both passages upstream and downstream so far as the competent authorities so require. The information may be given orally (e.g. by radio-telephone, where appropriate by automatic wireless message service) or in writing.

7.1.5.8.2   When passing the other traffic control stations designated by the competent authority, the following particulars shall be reported:

- name of the vessel;

- official number;

- dead-weight tonnage.

7.1.5.8.3   Changes to any of the particulars referred to in 7.1.5.8.1 shall be reported to the competent authority without delay.

7.1.5.8.4   The information is confidential and shall not be passed on to third parties by the competent authority.

The competent authority may, however, in the event of an accident, inform the emergency services of the relevant particulars required for organizing emergency action.

7.1.5.9-   *(Reserved)*
7.1.5.99

7.1.6   Additional requirements

7.1.6.1-   *(Reserved)*
7.1.6.10

7.1.6.11   *Carriage in bulk*

The following additional requirements shall be met when they are indicated in column (11) of Table A of Chapter 3.2:

CO01:   The surfaces of holds shall be coated or lined such that they are not readily flammable and not liable to impregnation by the cargo.

CO02:   Any part of the holds and of the hatchway covers which may come into contact with this substance shall consist of metal or of wood having a specific density of not less than 0.75 kg/dm^3 (seasoned wood).

CO03:   The inner surfaces of holds shall be lined or coated so as to prevent corrosion.

ST01:   The substances shall have been stabilized in accordance with the requirements applicable to ammonium nitrate fertilizers set out in the BC Code. Stabilizing shall be certified by the consignor in the transport document.

In those States where this is required, these substances may be carried in bulk only with the approval of the competent national authority.

ST02: These substances may be carried in bulk if the results of the trough test according to Appendix D.4 of the BC Code show that the self-sustaining decomposition rate is not greater than 25 cm/h.

RA01: The materials may be carried in bulk provided that:

(a) for materials other than natural ores, carriage is under exclusive use and there is no escape of contents out of the vessel and no loss of shielding under normal conditions of transport; or

(b) for natural ores, carriage is under exclusive use.

RA02: The materials may be carried in bulk provided that:

(a) they are carried in a vessel so that, under normal conditions of transport, there is no escape of contents or loss of shielding;

(b) they are carried under exclusive use if the contamination on the accessible and inaccessible surfaces is greater than 4 Bq/cm^2 (10^{-4} Ci/cm^2) for beta and gamma emitters and low toxicity alpha emitters or 0.4 Bq/cm^2 (10^{-5} µCi/cm^2) for all other alpha emitters;

(c) measures are taken to ensure that radioactive material is not released into the vessel, if it is suspected that non-fixed contamination exists on inaccessible surfaces of more than 4 Bq/cm^2 (10^{-4} µCi/cm^2) for beta and gamma emitters and low toxicity alpha emitters or 0.4 Bq/cm2 (10-5 µCi/cm2) for all other alpha emitters.

RA03: Surface Contaminated Objects (SCO-II) shall not be carried in bulk.

7.1.6.12   *Ventilation*

The following additional requirements shall be met when they are indicated in column (10) of Table A of Chapter 3.2:

VE01: Holds containing these substances shall be ventilated with the ventilators operating at full power, where after measurement it has been established that the concentration of gases given off by the cargo exceeds 10% of the lower explosive limit. The measurement shall be carried out immediately after loading. The measurement shall be repeated after one hour for monitoring purposes. The results of the measurement shall be recorded in writing.

VE02: Holds containing these substances shall be ventilated with the ventilators operating at full power, where after measurement it has been established that the holds are not free from gases given off by the cargo. The measurement shall be carried out immediately after loading. The measurement shall be repeated after one hour for monitoring purposes. The results of the measurement shall be recorded in writing.

VE03: Spaces such as holds, accommodation and engine rooms, adjacent to holds containing these goods shall be ventilated.

After unloading holds shall undergo forced ventilation.

After ventilation, the concentration of gases in the holds shall be measured.

The results of the measurement shall be recorded in writing.

7.1.6.13   *Measures to be taken before loading*

The following additional requirements shall be met when they are indicated in column (11) of Table A of Chapter 3.2:

LO01:   Before these substances or articles are loaded, it shall be ensured that there are no metal objects in the hold which are not an integral part of the vessel.

LO02:   These substances may be loaded in bulk only if their temperature is not above 55° C.

LO03:   Before loading these substances in bulk or unpackaged, holds should be made as dry as possible.

LO04:   Any loose organic material shall be removed from holds before loading these substances in bulk.

LO05:   Prior to carriage of pressure receptacles it shall be ensured that the pressure has not risen due to potential hydrogen generation.

7.1.6.14   *Handling and stowage of cargo*

The following additional requirements shall be met when they are indicated in column (11) of Table A of Chapter 3.2:

HA01:   These substances shall be stowed at a distance of not less than 3.00 m from the accommodation, engine rooms, the wheelhouse and from any sources of heat.

HA02:   These substances or articles shall be stowed at a distance of not less than 2.00 m from the sides of the vessel.

HA03:   Any friction, impact, jolting, overturning or dropping shall be prevented during handling of these substances or articles.

All packages loaded in the same hold shall be stowed and wedged as to prevent any jolting or friction during transport.

HA04:   Stacking of non-dangerous goods on top of packages containing these substances or articles is prohibited.

HA05:   Where these substances or articles are loaded together with other goods in the same hold, these substances or articles shall be loaded after, and unloaded before, all the other goods.

This provision does not apply if the substances or articles of Class 1 are contained in containers.

HA06:   While these substances or articles are being loaded or unloaded, no loading or unloading operations shall take place in the other holds and no filling or emptying of fuel tanks shall be allowed. The competent authority may, however, permit exemptions from this provision.

HA07: It is prohibited to load or unload these substances in bulk or unpackaged if there is a danger that they may get wet because of the prevailing weather conditions.

HA08: If the packages with these substances are not contained in a container, they shall be placed on gratings and covered with waterproof tarpaulins arranged in such a way that the water drains off to the outside and the air circulation is not hindered.

HA09: If these substances are carried in bulk they shall not be loaded in the same hold together with flammable substances.

HA10: These substances shall be stowed on deck in the protected area. For seagoing vessels, the stowage requirements are deemed to be met if the provisions of the IMDG Code are complied with.

7.1.6.15   *(Reserved)*

7.1.6.16   ***Measures to be taken during loading, carriage, unloading and handling***

The following additional requirements shall be met when they are indicated in column (11) of Table A of Chapter 3.2:

IN01: After loading and unloading of these substances in bulk or unpackaged and before leaving the cargo transfer site, the concentration of gases in the accommodation, engine rooms and adjacent holds shall be measured by the consignor or consignee using a flammable gas detector.

Before any person enters a hold and prior to unloading, the concentration of gases shall be measured by the consignee of the cargo.

The hold shall not be entered or unloading started until the concentration of gases in the airspace above the cargo is below 50% of the lower explosive limit.

If significant concentrations of gases are found in these spaces, the necessary safety measures shall be taken immediately by the consignor or the consignee.

IN02: If a hold contains these substances in bulk or unpackaged, the gas concentration shall be measured in all other spaces of the vessel which are used by the crew at least once every eight hours with a toximeter. The results of the measurements shall be recorded in writing.

IN03: If a hold contains these substances in bulk or unpackaged, the master shall make sure every day by checking the bilge wells or pump ducts that no water has entered the bilges.

Water which has entered the bilges shall be removed immediately.

7.1.6.17-   *(Reserved)*
7.1.9.99

CHAPTER 7.2

TANK VESSELS

7.2.0   **General requirements**

7.2.0.1   The provisions of 7.2.0 to 7.2.5 are applicable to tank vessels.

7.2.0.2-   *(Reserved)*
7.2.0.99

7.2.1   **Mode of carriage of goods**

7.2.1.1-   *(Reserved)*
7.2.1.20

7.2.1.21   *Carriage in cargo tanks*

7.2.1.21.1   Substances, their assignment to the various types of tank vessels and the special conditions for their carriage in these tank vessels, are listed in Table C of Chapter 3.2.

7.2.1.21.2   Substances, which according to column (6) of Table C of Chapter 3.2, have to be carried in a tank vessel of type N, open, may also be carried in a tank vessel of type N, open, with flame-arresters; type N, closed; types C or G provided that all conditions of carriage prescribed for tank vessels of type N, open, as well as all other conditions of carriage prescribed in the list of substances of Table C are met.

7.2.1.21.3   Substances which, according to column (6) of Table C of Chapter 3.2 have to be carried in a tank vessel of type N, open, with flame-arresters, may also be carried in tank vessels of type N, closed, and types C or G provided that all conditions of carriage prescribed for tank vessels of type N, open, with flame arresters, as well as all other conditions of carriage prescribed in the list of substances of Table C are met.

7.2.1.21.4   Substances which, according to column (6) of Table C of Chapter 3.2 have to be carried in a tank vessel of type N, closed, may also be carried in tank vessels of type C or G provided that all conditions of carriage prescribed for tank vessels of type N, closed, as well as all other conditions of carriage prescribed in the list of substances of Table C are met.

7.2.1.21.5   Substances which, according to column (6) of Table C of Chapter 3.2 have to be carried in tank vessels of type C may also be carried in tank vessels of type G provided that all conditions of carriage prescribed for tank vessels of type C as well as all other conditions of carriage prescribed in the list of substances of Table C are met.

7.2.1.21.6   Oily and greasy wastes resulting from the operation of the vessel may only be carried in fire-resistant receptacles, fitted with a lid, or in cargo tanks.

7.2.1.22-   *(Reserved)*
7.2.1.99

7.2.2   **Requirements applicable to vessels**

7.2.2.0   *Permitted vessels*

NOTE 1: The relief pressure of the safety valves or of the high-velocity vent valves shall be indicated in the certificate of approval (see 8.6.1.3).

NOTE 2: The design pressure and the test pressure of cargo tanks shall be indicated in the certificate of the classification society prescribed in 9.3.1.8.1 or 9.3.2.8.1 or 9.3.3.8.1.

NOTE 3: Where a vessel carries cargo tanks with different valve-relief pressures, the relief pressure of each tank shall be indicated in the certificate of approval and the design and test pressures of each tank shall be indicated in the certificate of the classification society.

7.2.2.0.1   Dangerous substances may be carried in tank vessels of Types N, C or G in accordance with the requirements of Chapters 9.2, 9.3 or 9.4 respectively. The type of tank vessel to be used is specified in column (6) of Table C of Chapter 3.2 and in 7.2.1.21.

NOTE: The substances accepted for carriage in the vessel are indicated in the certificate to be drawn up by the classification society (se 1.16.1.2.5).

7.2.2.1-   *(Reserved)*
7.2.2.4

7.2.2.5   *Instructions for the use of devices and installations*

Where specific safety rules have to be complied with when using any device or installation, instructions for the use of the particular device or installation shall be readily available for consultation at appropriate places on board in the language normally spoken on board, and also, if that language is not English, French or German, in English, French or German unless agreements concluded between the countries concerned in the transport operation provide otherwise.

7.2.2.6   *Gas detection system*

The sensors of the gas detection system shall be set at not more than 20% of the lower explosive limit of the substances allowed for carriage in the vessel.

The system shall have been approved by the competent authority or a recognized classification society.

7.2.2.7   *(Reserved)*
7.2.2.18

7.2.2.19   *Pushed convoys and side-by-side formations*

7.2.2.19.1   Where at least one vessel of a convoy or side-by-side formation is required to be in possession of a certificate of approval, all vessels of such convoy or side-by-side formation shall be provided with an appropriate certificate of approval.

Vessels not carrying dangerous goods shall comply with the provisions of 7.1.2.19.

7.2.2.19.2   For the purposes of the application of this Part, the entire pushed convoy or side-by-side formation shall be deemed to be a single vessel.

7.2.2.19.3   When a pushed convoy or a side-by-side formation comprises a tank vessel carrying dangerous substances, vessels used for propulsion shall meet the requirements of the following paragraphs:

7.2.2.5, 8.1.4, 8.1.5, 8.1.6.1, 8.1.6.3, 8.1.7, 8.1.8, 8.1.9, 9.3.3.0.1, 9.3.3.0.3 (d), 9.3.3.0.5, 9.3.3.10.1, 9.3.3.10.2, 9.3.3.12.4, 9.3.3.12.6, 9.3.3.16, 9.3.3.17.1 to 9.3.3.17.4, 9.3.3.31.1 to 9.3.3.31.5, 9.3.3.32.2, 9.3.3.34.1, 9.3.3.34.2, 9.3.3.40.1 (however, one single fire or ballast pump shall be sufficient), 9.3.3.40.2, 9.3.3.41, 9.3.3.50.1 (c), 9.3.3.50.2, 9.3.3.51, 9.3.3.52.3, 9.3.3.52.4 to 9.3.3.52.6, 9.3.3.56.5, 9.3.3.71 and 9.3.3.74.

7.2.2.20   *(Reserved)*

7.2.2.21   **Safety and control equipment**

It shall be possible to interrupt loading or unloading of substances of Class 2 and substances assigned to UN Nos. 1280 and 2983 of Class 3 by means of switches installed at two locations on the vessel (fore and aft) and at two locations ashore (directly at the access to the vessel and at an appropriate distance on the quay). Interruption of loading and unloading shall be effected by the means of a quick action stop valve which shall be directly fitted to the flexible connecting hose between the vessel and the shore facility.

The system of disconnection shall be designed in accordance with the closed circuit principle.

7.2.2.22   **Cargo tank openings**

When substances for which a type C vessel is required in column (6) of Table C of Chapter 3.2 are carried, the high-velocity vent valves shall be set so that blowing-off does not normally occur while the vessel is under way.

7.2.2.23-   *(Reserved)*
7.2.2.99

7.2.3   **General service requirements**

7.2.3.1   **Access to cargo tanks, residual cargo tanks, cargo pump-rooms below deck, cofferdams, double-hull spaces, double bottoms and hold spaces; inspections**

7.2.3.1.1   The cofferdams shall be empty. They shall be inspected once a day in order to ascertain that they are dry (except for condensation water).

7.2.3.1.2   Access to the cargo tanks, residual cargo tanks, cofferdams, double-hull spaces, double bottoms and hold spaces is not permitted except for carrying out inspections or cleaning operations.

7.2.3.1.3   Access to the double-hull spaces and the double bottoms is not permitted while the vessel is under way.

7.2.3.1.4   When the gas concentration or oxygen content has to be measured before entry into cargo tanks, residual cargo tanks, cargo pump-rooms below deck, cofferdams, double-hull spaces, double bottoms or hold spaces, the results of these measurements shall be recorded in writing.

The measurement may only be effected by persons equipped with breathing apparatus suited to the substance carried.

Entry into these spaces is not permitted for the purpose of measuring.

7.2.3.1.5   Before any person enters cargo tanks, the cargo pump-rooms below deck, cofferdams, double-hull spaces, double bottoms or hold spaces:

(a)   When dangerous substances of Classes 2, 3, 4.1, 6.1, 8 or 9 for which a flammable gas detector is required in column (18) of Table C of Chapter 3.2 are carried on board the vessel, it shall be established, by means of this device that the gas concentration in these cargo tanks, cargo pump-rooms below deck, cofferdams, double-hull spaces, double bottoms or hold spaces is not more than 50% of the lower explosive limit of the cargo. For the cargo pump-rooms below deck this may be determined by means of the permanent gas detection system;

(b)   When dangerous substances of Classes 2, 3, 4.1, 6.1, 8 or 9 for which a toximeter is required in column (18) of Table C of Chapter 3.2 are carried on board the vessel, it shall be established, by means of this device that the cargo tanks, cargo pump-rooms below deck, cofferdams, double-hull spaces, double bottoms or hold spaces do not contain any significant concentration of toxic gases.

7.2.3.1.6   Entry into empty cargo tanks, the cargo pump-rooms below deck, cofferdams, double-hull spaces, double bottoms and hold spaces is not permitted, except where:

–   there is no lack of oxygen and no measurable amount of dangerous substances in dangerous concentrations; or

–   the person entering the spaces wears a self-contained breathing apparatus and other necessary protective and rescue equipment, and is secured by a line. Entry into these spaces is only permitted if this operation is supervised by a second person for whom the same equipment is readily at hand. Another two persons capable of giving assistance in an emergency shall be on the vessel within calling distance. If a rescue winch has been installed, only one other person is sufficient.

7.2.3.2   *Cargo pump-rooms below deck*

7.2.3.2.1   When carrying dangerous substances of classes 3, 4.1, 6.1, 8 or 9, the cargo pump-rooms below deck shall be inspected daily so as to ascertain that there are no leaks. The bilges and the drip pans shall be kept clean and free from products.

7.2.3.2.2   When the gas detection system is activated, the loading and unloading operations shall be stopped immediately. All shut-off devices shall be closed and the cargo pump-rooms shall be evacuated immediately. All entrances shall be closed. The loading or unloading operations shall not be continued except when the damage has been repaired or the fault eliminated.

7.2.3.3-   *(Reserved)*
7.2.3.5

7.2.3.6   *Gas detection system*

The gas detection system shall be maintained and calibrated in accordance with the instructions of the manufacturer.

7.2.3.7   *Gas-freeing of empty cargo tanks*

7.2.3.7.1   Empty or unloaded cargo tanks having previously contained dangerous substances of Class 2, Class 3, with classification code "T" in column (3b) of Table C of Chapter 3.2, Class 6.1 or packing group I of Class 8, may only be gas-freed at the locations designated or approved for such purpose by the competent authority. Gas-freeing may be carried out only by competent persons or companies approved for that purpose.

7.2.3.7.2   Gas-freeing of empty or unloaded cargo tanks having contained dangerous goods other than those referred to under 7.2.3.7.1 above, may be carried out while the vessel is under way by means of suitable venting equipment with the tank lids closed and by leading the gas/air mixtures through flame-arresters capable of withstanding steady burning. In normal conditions of operation, the gas concentration in the vented mixture at the outlet shall be less than 50% of the lower explosive limit. The suitable venting equipment may be used for gas-freeing by extraction only when a flame-arrester is fitted immediately before the ventilation fan on the extraction side. The gas concentration shall be measured once each hour during the two first hours after the beginning of the gas-freeing operation by forced ventilation or by extraction, by an expert referred to in 7.2.3.15. The results of these measurements shall be recorded in writing.

Gas-freeing is, however, prohibited within the area of locks including their lay-bys.

7.2.3.7.3   Where gas-freeing of cargo tanks having previously contained the dangerous goods referred to in 7.2.3.7.1 above is not practicable at the locations designated or approved for this purpose by the competent authority, gas-freeing may be carried out while the vessel is under way, provided that:

–   the requirements of 7.2.3.7.2 are complied with; the concentration of dangerous substances in the vented mixture at the outlet shall, however, be not more than 10% of the lower explosive limit;

–   there is no risk involved for the crew;

–   any entrances or openings of spaces connected to the outside are closed; this provision does not apply to the air supply openings of the engine room;

–   any member of the crew working on deck is wearing suitable protective equipment;

–   it is not carried out within the area of locks including their lay-bys, under bridges or within densely populated areas.

7.2.3.7.4   Gas-freeing operations shall be interrupted when, due to unfavourable wind conditions, dangerous concentrations of gases are to be expected outside the cargo area in front of accommodation, the wheelhouse and service spaces. The critical state is reached as soon as concentrations of more than 20% of the lower explosive limit have been detected in those areas by measurements by means of portable equipment.

7.2.3.7.5   The marking prescribed in column (19) of Table C of Chapter 3.2 may be withdrawn when, after gas-freeing of the cargo tanks, it has been ascertained, using the equipment described in column (18) of Table C of Chapter 3.2, that the cargo tanks no longer contain flammable gases in concentrations of more than 10% of the lower explosive limit or do not contain any significant concentration of toxic gases.

7.2.3.8   *Repair and maintenance work*

No repair or maintenance work liable to cause sparks or requiring the use of an open flame or electric current shall be undertaken unless permission has been given by the competent authority or a certificate attesting gas-free condition has been issued for the vessel.

In the service spaces outside the cargo area repair and maintenance work may be undertaken, provided the doors and openings are closed and the vessel is not being loaded, unloaded or gas-freed.

The use of chromium vanadium steel screwdrivers and wrenches or screwdrivers and wrenches of equivalent material from the point of view of spark formation is permitted.

7.2.3.9-   *(Reserved)*
7.2.3.11

7.2.3.12 Ventilation

7.2.3.12.1 While the machinery in the service spaces is operating, the extension ducts connected to the air inlets, if any, shall be in the upright position; otherwise the inlets shall be closed. This provision does not apply to air inlets of service spaces outside the cargo area, provided the inlets without extension duct are located not less than 0.50 m above the deck.

7.2.3.12.2 The ventilation of pump rooms shall be in operation:

– at least 30 minutes before entry and during occupation;

– during loading, unloading and gas-freeing; and

– after the gas detection system has been activated.

7.2.3.13-
7.2.3.14 *(Reserved)*

7.2.3.15 Expert on board the vessel

When dangerous substances are carried, an expert, referred to in 8.2.1 shall be on board the vessel. In addition,

– when dangerous substances are carried, for which a type G tank vessel is prescribed in column (6) of Table C of Chapter 3.2, this expert shall be the expert referred to in 8.2.1.5; and

– when dangerous substances are carried, for which a type C tank vessel is prescribed in column (6) of Table C of Chapter 3.2, this expert shall be the expert referred to in 8.2.1.7.

7.2.3.16-
7.2.3.19 *(Reserved)*

7.2.3.20 Water ballast

7.2.3.20.1 Cofferdams and hold spaces containing insulated cargo tanks shall not be filled with water. Double-hull spaces, double bottoms and hold spaces may be filled with ballast water provided the cargo tanks have been discharged.

If the cargo tanks are not empty, double-hull spaces and double bottoms may be filled with ballast water provided this has been taken into account in the damage-control plan and the ballast tanks are not filled to more than 90% of their capacity and provided this is not prohibited in column (20) of Table C of Chapter 3.2.

7.2.3.20.2 Where ballast water is discharged from cargo tanks, an appropriate entry shall be made in the loading journal.

7.2.3.21 *(Reserved)*

7.2.3.22 Entrances to hold spaces, cargo pump-rooms below deck, cofferdams, opening of cargo tanks and residual cargo tanks; closing devices

The cargo tanks, residual cargo tanks and entrances to cargo pump-rooms below deck, cofferdams and hold spaces shall remain closed. This requirement shall not apply to cargo pump-rooms on board oil separator and supply vessels or to the other exceptions set out in this Part.

7.2.3.23- 7.2.3.24	*(Reserved)*

7.2.3.25   **Connections between pipes**

7.2.3.25.1   Connecting two or more of the following groups of pipes is prohibited:

(a)   pipes for loading and unloading;

(b)   pipes for ballasting and draining cargo tanks, cofferdams, hold spaces, double-hull spaces and double bottoms;

(c)   pipes located outside the cargo area.

7.2.3.25.2   The provision of 7.2.3.25.1 above does not apply to removable pipe connections between cofferdam pipes and

–   pipes for loading and unloading;

–   pipes located outside the cargo area while the cofferdams have to be filled with water .

In these cases the connections shall be designed so as to prevent water from being drawn from the cargo tanks. The cofferdams shall be emptied only by means of educators or an independent system within the cargo area.

7.2.3.25.3   The provisions of 7.2.3.25.1 (b) and (c) above do not apply to:

–   pipes intended for ballasting and draining double-hull spaces and double bottoms which have not common boundary with the cargo tanks;

–   pipes intended for ballasting hold spaces where the pipes of the fire-fighting system within the cargo area are used for this purpose. Hold spaces shall be stripped only by means of educators or an independent system within the cargo area.

7.2.3.26- 7.2.3.28	*(Reserved)*

7.2.3.29   **Lifeboats**

7.2.3.29.1   The lifeboat required in accordance with the Regulations referred to in 1.1.4.6 shall be stowed outside the cargo area. The lifeboat may, however, be stowed in the cargo area provided an easily accessible collective life-saving appliance conforming to the Regulations referred to in 1.1.4.6 is available within the accommodation area.

7.2.3.29.2   7.2.3.29.1 above does not apply to oil separator or supply vessels.

7.2.3.30   *(Reserved)*

7.2.3.31   **Engines**

7.2.3.31.1   The use of engines running on fuels having a flashpoint below 55° C (e.g. petrol engines) is prohibited. This requirement does not apply to the outboard motors of lifeboats.

7.2.3.31.2	The carriage of power-driven conveyances such as passenger cars and motor boats in the cargo area is prohibited.

7.2.3.32   *Oil fuel tanks*

Double bottoms with a height of at least 0.6 m may be used as oil fuel tanks, provided they have been constructed in accordance with Part 9.

7.2.3.33- 7.2.3.40	*(Reserved)*

7.2.3.41   *Fire and naked light*

7.2.3.41.1	The use of fire or naked light is prohibited.

This provision does not apply to the accommodation and the wheelhouse.

7.2.3.41.2	Heating, cooking and refrigerating appliances shall not be fuelled with liquid fuels, liquid gas or solid fuels.

Cooking and refrigerating appliances may only be used in the accommodation and in the wheelhouse.

7.2.3.41.3	Heating appliances or boilers fuelled with liquid fuels having a flashpoint above 55° C which are installed in the engine room or in another suitable space may, however, be used.

7.2.3.42   *Cargo heating system*

7.2.3.42.1	Heating of the cargo is not permitted except where there is risk of solidification of the cargo or where the cargo, because of its viscosity, cannot be unloaded in the usual manner.

In general, a liquid shall not be heated up to a temperature above its flashpoint.

Special provisions are included in column 20 of Table C of Chapter 3.2.

7.2.3.42.2	Cargo tanks containing substances which are heated during transport shall be equipped with devices for measuring the temperature of the cargo.
7.2.3.42.3	During unloading, the cargo heating system may be used provided that the space where it has been installed meets in all respects the provisions of 9.3.2.52.3 (b) or 9.3.3.52.3 (b).
7.2.3.42.4	The provisions of 7.2.3.42.3 above do not apply when the cargo heating system is supplied with steam from shore and only the circulation pump is in operation, as well as when the flashpoint of the cargo being unloaded is not less than 61° C.
7.2.3.43	*(Reserved)*

7.2.3.44   *Cleaning operations*

The use of liquids having a flashpoint below 55° C for cleaning purposes is permitted only in the cargo area.

7.2.3.45- 7.2.3.50	*(Reserved)*

7.2.3.51   *Electrical installations*

7.2.3.51.1   The electrical installations shall be properly maintained in a faultless condition.

7.2.3.51.2   The use of movable electric cables is prohibited in the cargo area.

This provision does not apply to:

–   intrinsically safe electric circuits;

–   electric cables for connecting signal lights or gangway lighting, provided the socket is permanently fitted to the vessel close to the signal mast or gangway;

–   electric cables for connecting submerged pumps on board oil separator vessels.

7.2.3.51.3   The sockets for connecting the signal lights and gangway lighting or for submerged pumps on board oil separator vessels shall not be live except when the signal lights or the gangway lighting or the submerged pumps on board oil separator vessels are switched on.

Connecting or disconnecting shall not be possible except when the sockets are not live.

7.2.3.52-   *(Reserved)*
7.2.3.70

7.2.3.71   *Admittance on board*

When the vessel is required to be marked with two blue cones or two blue lights in accordance with column (19) of Table C of Chapter 3.2, no persons under 14 years of age shall be permitted on board.

7.2.3.72-   *(Reserved)*
7.2.3.99

7.2.4   **Additional requirements concerning loading, carriage, unloading and other handling of cargo**

7.2.4.1   *Limitation of the quantities carried*

7.2.4.1.1   The carriage of packages in the cargo area is prohibited. This prohibition does not apply to:

–   residual cargo, cargo residues and slops in approved intermediate bulk containers (IBCs), tank-containers or portable tanks having a maximum individual capacity of not more than $2.00\ m^3$; not more than six such intermediate bulk containers, tank-containers or portable tanks, however, shall be carried. These intermediate bulk containers, tank-containers or portable tanks shall meet the requirements of international regulations applicable to the substance concerned and shall comply with the provisions of 9.3.2.26.4 or 9.3.3.26.4 for the reception of residual cargo, cargo residues or slops;

–   to cargo samples, up to a maximum of 30, of substances accepted for carriage in the tank vessel, where the maximum contents are 500 ml per receptacle. Receptacles shall meet the packing requirements referred to in Part 4 and shall be placed on board, at a specific point in the cargo area, such that under normal conditions of carriage they cannot break or be punctured and their contents cannot spill in the hold space. Fragile receptacles shall be suitably padded.

7.2.4.1.2 On board oil separator vessel receptacles with a maximum capacity of 2.00 m^3 oily and greasy wastes resulting from the operation of vessels may be placed in the cargo area provided that these receptacles are properly secured.

7.2.4.1.3 On board supply vessel packages of dangerous goods may be carried in the cargo area up to a gross quantity of 5,000 kg provided that this possibility is mentioned in the certificate of approval. The packages shall be properly secured and shall be protected against heat, sun and bad weather.

7.2.4.1.4 On board supply vessels or other vessels delivering products for the operation of vessels, the number of cargo samples referred to in 7.2.4.1.1 may be increased from 30 to a maximum of 500.

7.2.4.2 ***Reception of oily and greasy wastes resulting from the operation of vessels and delivery of products for the operation of vessels***

7.2.4.2.1 The reception of unpackaged liquid oily and greasy wastes resulting from the operation of vessels may only be effected by suction.

7.2.4.2.2 The landing and reception of oily and greasy wastes may not take place during the loading and unloading of substances for which protection against explosion is required column (16) of Table C of Chapter 3.2 nor during the gas-freeing of tank vessels. This requirement does not apply to oil separator vessels provided that the provisions for protection against explosion applicable to the dangerous substance are complied with.

7.2.4.2.3 Berthing and handing over of products for the operation of vessels shall not take place during the loading or unloading of substances for which protection against explosions is required column (16) of Table C of Chapter 3.2 nor during the gas-freeing of tank vessels. This requirement does not apply to supply vessels provided that the provisions for protection against explosion applicable to the dangerous substance are complied with.

7.2.4.2.4 The competent authority may issue derogations to the requirements of 7.2.4.2.1 and 7.2.4.2.2 above. During unloading it may also issue derogations to 7.2.4.2.3 above.

7.2.4.3-
7.2.4.6 *(Reserved)*

7.2.4.7 ***Places of loading and unloading***

7.2.4.7.1 Tank vessels shall be loaded, unloaded or gas-freed only at the places designated or approved for this purpose by the competent authority.

7.2.4.7.2 The reception of unpackaged oily and greasy liquid wastes resulting from the operation of vessels and the handing over of products for the operation of vessels shall not be taken to be loading or unloading within the meaning of 7.2.4.7.1 above.

7.2.4.8 *(Reserved)*

7.2.4.9 ***Cargo transfer operations***

Partial or complete cargo transfer without permission from the competent authority is prohibited outside a cargo transfer place approved for this purpose.

7.2.4.10 *Checklist*

7.2.4.10.1 Loading or unloading shall not be started before a check list for the cargo in question has been completed and questions 1 to 18 of the list have been checked off with an "X". Irrelevant questions should be deleted. The list shall be completed in duplicate and signed by the master or a person mandated by himself and the person responsible for the handling at the shore facilities. If a positive response to all the questions is not possible loading or unloading is only permitted with the consent of the competent authority.

7.2.4.10.2 The list shall conform to the model in 8.6.3.

7.2.4.10.3 The checklist shall be printed at least in languages understood by the master and the person responsible for the handling at the shore facilities.

7.2.4.10.4 The provisions of 7.2.4.10.1 to 7.2.4.10.3 above shall not apply to the reception of oily and greasy wastes by oil separator vessels nor to the handing over of products for the operation of vessels by supply vessels.

7.2.4.11 *Loading journal; loading plan*

[7.2.4.11.1 The master shall record without delay in a loading journal all activities relating to loading, unloading, cleaning, gas-freeing, discharge of washing water and reception or discharge of ballast water (in cargo tanks). The goods shall be described as in the transport document (UN number or substance identification number, proper shipping name, class, and, where applicable classification code and/or packing group).][1]

7.2.4.11.2 The master shall enter on a cargo stowage plan the goods carried in the individual cargo tanks. The goods shall be described as in the transport document (UN number or substance identification number, proper shipping name, class and, where applicable, packing group).

7.2.4.12 *(Reserved)*

7.2.4.13 Measures to be taken before loading

7.2.4.13.1 When residues of the previous cargo may cause dangerous reactions with the next cargo, any such residues shall be properly removed.

Substances which react dangerously with other dangerous goods shall be separated by a cofferdam, an empty space, a pump-room, an empty cargo tank or a cargo tank loaded with a substance which does not react with the cargo.

Where an empty, uncleaned cargo tank, or a cargo tank containing cargo residues of a substance liable to react dangerously with other dangerous goods, this separation is not required if the master has taken appropriate measures to avoid a dangerous reaction.

7.2.4.13.2 Before the start of loading operations, any prescribed safety and control devices and any items of equipment shall, if possible, be checked and controlled for the proper functioning.

7.2.4.13.3 Before the start of loading operations the overflow control device switch shall be connected to the shore installation.

---

[1] *It is not necessary to apply this paragraph from the 1ˢᵗ January 2003. The date of application will be defined later.*

7.2.4.14   *Cargo handling and stowage*

Dangerous goods shall be loaded in the cargo area in cargo tanks, in cargo residue tanks or in packages permitted under 7.2.4.1.1.

7.2.4.15   *Measures to be taken after unloading*

7.2.4.15.1   After each unloading operating the cargo tanks and the cargo piping shall be emptied by means of the stripping system in accordance with the conditions laid down in the testing procedure. This provision need not be complied with if the new cargo is the same as the previous cargo.

Residual cargo shall be discharged ashore by means of the equipment provided to that effect or shall be stored in the vessel's own residual cargo tank or stored in intermediate bulk containers (IBCs) or tank-containers or portable tanks permitted according to 7.2.4.1.1, 9.3.2.26.3 or 9.3.3.26.3.

7.2.4.15.2   During the filling of permitted residual cargo tanks, intermediate bulk containers (IBCs), tank-containers or portable tanks, gases shall be safely evacuated.

7.2.4.15.3   After additional stripping, cargo tanks and pipes for loading and unloading shall, if necessary, be cleaned and gas-freed by persons or companies approved for this purpose by the competent authority in places approved for this purpose.

7.2.4.16   *Measures to be taken during loading, carriage, unloading and handling*

7.2.4.16.1   The loading rate and the maximum operational pressure of the cargo pumps shall be determined in agreement with the personnel at the shore installation.

7.2.4.16.2   All safety or control devices required in the cargo tanks shall remain switched on. During carriage this provision is only applicable for the installations mentioned in 9.3.1.21.1 (e) and (f), 9.3.2.21.1 (e) and (f) or 9.3.3.21.1 (e) and (f).

In the event of a failure of a safety or control device, loading or unloading shall be suspended immediately.

When a cargo pump-room is located below deck, the prescribed safety and control devices in the cargo pump-room shall remain permanently switched on.

Any failure of the gas detection system shall be immediately signalled in the wheelhouse and on deck by a visual and audible warning.

7.2.4.16.3   The shut-off devices of the cargo piping as well as of the pipes of the stripping systems shall remain closed except during loading, unloading, stripping, cleaning or gas-freeing operations.

7.2.4.16.4   If the vessel is fitted with a transverse bulkhead according to 9.3.1.25.3, 9.3.2.25.3 or 9.3.3.25.3, the doors in this bulkhead shall be closed during loading and unloading.

7.2.4.16.5   Receptacles intended for recovering possible liquid spillage shall be placed under connections to shore installations used for loading and unloading. This requirement shall not apply to the carriage of substances of Class 2.

7.2.4.16.6   In case of recovery of the gas-air mixture from shore into the vessel, the pressure at the connection point shall not be more than the operating pressure of the high velocity vent valve.

7.2.4.16.7	When a tank vessel conforms to 9.3.2.25.5 (d) or 9.3.3.22.5 (d), the individual cargo tanks shall be closed off during transport and opened during loading, unloading and gas-freeing.
7.2.4.16.8	Persons entering the premises located in the below deck cargo area during loading or unloading shall wear the equipment referred to in 8.1.5 if this equipment is prescribed in column (18) of Table C of Chapter 3.2.
	Persons connecting or disconnecting the loading and unloading pipes or the vapour pipes or gas discharge pipes, or taking samples, carrying out measurements, replacing the flame arrester plate stack or relieving pressure in cargo tanks shall wear the equipment referred to in 8.1.5. If this equipment is prescribed in column (18) of Table C of Chapter 3.2.
7.2.4.16.9	During loading or unloading in a closed tank vessel of substances for which an open type N vessel or an open type N vessel with a flame arrester is sufficient according to columns (6) and (7) of Table C of Chapter 3.2, the cargo tanks may be opened using the safe pressure-relief device referred to in 9.3.2.22.4 (a) or 9.3.3.22.4 (a).
7.2.4.16.10	7.2.4.16.9 shall not apply when the cargo tanks contain gases or vapour from substances for the carriage of which a closed-type tank vessel is required in columns (6) and (7) of Table C of Chapter 3.2.
7.2.4.16.11	The nozzle closure referred to in 9.3.1.21.1 (g), 9.3.2.21.1 (g) or 9.3.3.21.1 (g) can be opened only after a gastight connection has been made to the closed or partly closed sampling device.
7.2.4.16.12	For substances requiring protection against explosions according to column (17) of Table C of Chapter 3.2, the connection of the vapour pipe or the gas discharge piping to the shore installation shall be such that the vessel is protected against detonations and the passage of flames from the shore. The protection of the vessel against detonations and the passage of flames from the shore is not required when the cargo tanks are inerted in accordance with 7.2.4.19.
7.2.4.16.13	The bulwark ports, openings in the foot rail, etc., shall not be capable of being closed off.
7.2.4.16.14	If supervision is required in column (20) of Table C of Chapter 3.2 for substances of Classes 2 or 6.1, loading and unloading shall be carried out under the supervision of a person who is not a member of the crew and has been mandated for the task by the consignor or the consignee.
7.2.4.16.15	The initial cargo throughput established in the loading instructions shall be such as to ensure that no electrostatic charge exists at the start of loading.

7.2.4.17   *Closing of windows and doors*

7.2.4.17.1	During loading, unloading and gas-freeing operations, all entrances or openings of spaces which are accessible from the deck and all openings of spaces facing the outside shall remain closed.

This provision does not apply to:

–   air intakes of running engines;

–   ventilation inlets of engine rooms while the engines are running;

–   air intakes of the overpressure ventilation system referred to in 9.3.1.52.3 (b), 9.3.2.52.3 (b) or 9.3.3.52.3 (b);

–   air intakes of air conditioning in installations if these openings are fitted with a gas detection system referred to in 9.3.1.52.3. (b), 9.3.2.52.3 (b) or 9.3.3.52.3 (b).

These entrances and openings may only be opened when necessary and for a short time, after the master has given his permission.

7.2.4.17.2   After the loading, unloading and gas-freeing operations, the spaces which are accessible from the deck shall be ventilated.

7.2.4.17.3   The provisions of 7.2.4.17.1 and 7.2.4.17.2 above shall not apply to the reception of oily and greasy wastes resulting from the operation of vessels nor to the handing over of products for the operation of vessels.

7.2.4.18   ***Monitoring of gaseous phases in cargo tanks and adjacent empty spaces***

7.2.4.18.1   For the gaseous phases of tanks, inerting or blanketing may be necessary. These are defined as follows:

–   inerting: cargo tanks and their piping and other spaces for which this process is prescribed are filled with gases or vapours which prevent combustion, do not react with the cargo and maintain this state;

–   blanketing: cargo tanks and their piping are filled with a liquid, gas or vapour which separates the cargo from the air and maintains this situation.

7.2.4.18.2   When inerting or blanketing of the cargo is prescribed, the following requirements shall apply:

(a)   A sufficient quantity of inert gas for loading or unloading shall be on board or shall be capable of being produced if it is not possible to obtain it on shore. A sufficient quantity of inert gas to offset normal losses occurring during carriage shall be on board;

(b)   The inerting facility on board the vessel shall be capable of maintaining a permanent minimum pressure of 7 kPa (0.07 bar) in the spaces to be inerted. In addition, the inerting facility shall not increase the pressure in the cargo tank to a pressure greater than that at which the pressure valve is regulated;

(c)   For the blanketing of the cargo the requirements referred to in (a) and (b) for inerting shall apply as regards the quantity of gas required for blanketing;

(d)   The parts above the surface of the liquid covered by a layer of gas shall be fitted with monitoring devices so as to ensure the correct atmosphere on a permanent basis;

(e)   Inerting or blanketing of flammable cargoes shall be carried out in such a way as to reduce the electrostatic charge as far as possible when the inerting agent is added.

7.2.4.18.3   For certain substances the requirements for the monitoring of the gaseous phases in cargo tanks and in adjacent empty spaces are given in column (20) of Table C of Chapter 3.2.

7.2.4.18.4   *Inerting of tanks*

When anti-explosion protection is required in column (17) of Table C of Chapter 3.2, cargo tanks and their piping shall be purged in an appropriate form of any air that may be present using inert gas and maintained in an air-free state.

7.2.4.19   *Inerting of tank vessels*

The cargo tanks of a closed tank vessel, loaded or empty, which have not been cleaned of substances for which the use of a closed tank vessel of type C or type N with anti-explosion protection is prescribed in columns (6) and (7) of Table C of Chapter 3.2 shall be inerted in accordance with 7.2.4.18. The inerting shall be performed so as to ensure that the oxygen content is less than 8% in volume.

Inerting is not prescribed when the tank vessel is in conformity with 9.3.2.22.5 or 9.3.3.22.5.

7.2.4.20   *(Reserved)*

7.2.4.21   *Filling of cargo tanks*

7.2.4.21.1   The degree of filling given in column (11) of Table C of Chapter 3.2 or calculated in accordance with 7.2.4.21.3 below shall not be exceeded.

7.2.4.21.2   The provisions of 7.2.4.21.1 above do not apply to cargo tanks the contents of which are maintained at the filling temperature during carriage by means of heating equipment. In this case calculation of the degree of filling at the beginning of carriage and control of the temperature shall be such that, during carriage, the maximum allowable degree of filling is not exceeded.

7.2.4.21.3   For carriage of substances having a relative density higher than that stated in the certificate of approval, the degree of filling shall be calculated in accordance with the following formula.

Permitted degree of filling (%) = $\dfrac{a}{b} \times 100$

a = relative density stated in the certificate of approval
b = relative density of the substance.

The degree of filling given in column (11) of Table C of Chapter 3.2 shall, however, not be exceeded.

7.2.4.21.4   If the degree of filling of 97.5% is exceeded a technical installation shall be authorized to pump off the overflow. During such an operation an automatic visual alarm shall be activated on deck.

7.2.4.22   *Opening of openings of cargo tanks*

7.2.4.22.1   Opening of cargo tanks apertures shall be permitted only after the tanks have been relived of pressure.

7.2.4.22.2   Opening of sampling outlets and ullage openings and opening of the housing of the flame arrester shall not be permitted except for the purpose of inspecting or cleaning empty cargo tanks.

When in column (17) of Table C of Chapter 3.2 anti-explosion protection is required, the opening of cargo tank covers or of the housing of the flame arrester for the purpose of mounting or removing the flame arrester plate stack in unloaded cargo tanks shall be permitted only if the cargo tanks in question have been gas-freed and the concentration of flammable gases in the tanks is less than 10% of the lower explosive limit.

7.2.4.22.3   Sampling shall be permitted only if a device prescribed in column (13) of Table C of Chapter 3.2 or a device ensuring a higher level of safety is used.

Opening of sampling outlets and ullage openings of cargo tanks loaded with substances for which marking with two blue cones or blue lights is prescribed in column (19) of Table C of Chapter 3.2 shall be permitted only when loading has been interrupted for not less than 10 minutes.

7.2.4.22.4   The sampling receptacles including all accessories such as ropes, etc., shall consist of electrostatically conductive material and shall, during sampling, be electrically connected to the vessel's hull.

7.2.4.22.5   The duration of opening shall be limited to the time necessary for control, cleaning, gauging or sampling.

7.2.4.22.6   Pressure relief of cargo tanks is permitted only when carried out by means of the device for safe pressure relief prescribed in 9.3.2.22.4 (a) or 9.3.3.22.4 (a).

7.2.4.22.7   The provisions of 7.2.4.22.1 to 7.2.4.22.6 above shall not apply to oil separator or supply vessels.

7.2.4.23   *(Reserved)*

7.2.4.24   Simultaneous loading and unloading

During loading or unloading of cargo tanks, no other cargo shall be loaded or unloaded. The competent authority may grant exceptions during unloading.

7.2.4.25   Cargo piping

7.2.4.25.1   Loading and unloading as well as stripping of cargo tanks shall be carried out by means of the fixed cargo piping of the vessel.

The metal fittings of the connections to the shore piping shall be electrically earthed so as to prevent the accumulation of electrostatic charges.

7.2.4.25.2   The cargo piping shall not be extended by rigid or flexible pipes fore or aft beyond the cofferdams.

This requirement shall not apply to hoses used for the reception of oily and greasy wastes resulting from the operation of vessels and the delivery of products for the operation of vessels.

7.2.4.25.3   The shut-off devices of the cargo piping shall not be open except as necessary during loading, unloading or gas-freeing operations.

7.2.4.25.4   The liquid remaining in the piping shall be completely drained into the cargo tanks, if possible, or safely removed. This requirement shall not apply to supply vessels.

7.2.4.25.5   The gas/air mixtures shall be returned ashore through a gas recovery or compensation pipe during loading operations when a closed type vessel is required in column (7) of Table C of Chapter 3.2.

7.2.4.25.6	When substances of Class 2 are carried the requirements of 7.2.4.25.4 shall be deemed to have been satisfied if the pipes for loading and unloading have been purged with the cargo gas or with nitrogen.
7.2.4.26- 7.2.4.27	*(Reserved)*

7.2.4.28   *Water-spray system*

7.2.4.28.1	If a water-spray system is required in column (9) of Table C of Chapter 3.2, it shall be kept ready for operation during loading or unloading operations and during the voyage.
7.2.4.28.2	When water-spraying is required in column (9) of Table C of Chapter 3.2 and the pressure of the gaseous phase in the cargo tanks may reach 80% of the relief pressure of the high velocity vent valves, the master shall take all measures compatible with safety to prevent the pressure from reaching that value. He shall in particular activate the water-spray system.
7.2.4.28.3	If a water-spray system is required in column (9) of Table C of Chapter 3.2 and remark 23 is indicated in column (20) of Table C of Chapter 3.2, the instrument measuring the internal pressure shall activate an alarm when the internal pressure reaches 40 kPa. The water-spray system shall immediately be activated and remain in operation until the internal pressure drops to 30 kPa.
7.2.4.29- 7.2.4.39	*(Reserved)*

7.2.4.40   *Fire-extinguishing arrangements*

During loading and unloading, the fire extinguishing systems, the hoses and spray nozzles shall be kept ready for operation in the cargo area on deck.

7.2.4.41   *Fire or naked light*

During loading, unloading or gas-freeing operations fires and naked lights are prohibited on board the vessel.

However, the provisions of 7.2.3.42.3 and 7.2.3.42.4 are applicable.

7.2.4.42   *Cargo heating system*

The maximum allowable temperature for carriage indicated in column (20) of Table C of Chapter 3.2 shall not be exceeded.

7.2.4.43- 7.2.4.50	*(Reserved)*

7.2.4.51   *Electrical installations*

7.2.4.51.1	During loading, unloading or gas-freeing operations, only electrical equipment conforming to the rules for construction in Part 9 or which are installed in spaces complying with the conditions of 9.3.1.52.3, 9.3.2.52.3 or 9.3.3.52.3, may be used.
7.2.4.51.2	Electrical equipment which has been switched off by the device referred to in 9.3.1.52.3 (b), 9.3.2.52.3 (b) or 9.3.3.52.3 (b) shall only be switched on after the gas-free condition has been established in these spaces.

| 7.2.4.52 | (Reserved) |

7.2.4.53 *Lighting*

If loading or unloading is performed at night or in conditions of poor visibility, effective lighting shall be provided. If provided from the deck, it shall be effected by properly secured electric lamps which shall be positioned in such a way that they cannot be damaged. Where these lamps are positioned in the cargo area, they shall be of the "certified safe" type.

| 7.2.4.54-
7.2.4.59 | (Reserved) |

7.2.4.60 *Special equipment*

The shower and the eye and face bath prescribed in the rules for construction shall be kept ready in all weather conditions for use during loading and unloading operations and cargo transfer operations by pumping.

| 7.2.4.61-
7.2.4.73 | (Reserved) |

7.2.4.74 *Prohibition of smoking, fire and naked light*

The prohibition of smoking does not apply in accommodation or wheelhouses conforming to the provisions of 9.3.1.52.3 (b), 9.3.2.52.3 (b) or 9.3.3.52.3 (b).

7.2.4.75 *Risk of sparking*

All electrical connections between the vessel and the shore shall be so designed that they do not present a source of ignition.

7.2.4.76 *Synthetic ropes*

During loading and unloading operations, the vessel may be moored by means of synthetic ropes only when steel cables are used to prevent the vessel from going adrift.

Steel cables sheathed in synthetic material or natural fibres are considered as equivalent when the minimum tensile strength required in accordance with the Regulations referred to in 1.1.4.6 is obtained from the steel strands.

Oil separator vessels may, however, be moored by means of synthetic ropes during the reception of oily and greasy wastes resulting from the operation of vessels, as may supply vessels during the delivery of products for the operation of vessels.

| 7.2.4.77-
7.2.4.99 | (Reserved) |

7.2.5 **Additional requirements concerning the operation of vessels**

7.2.5.0 *Marking*

7.2.5.0.1 Vessels carrying dangerous goods listed in Table C of Chapter 3.2 shall display the number of blue cones or blue lights indicated in column (19) and in accordance with CEVNI.

7.2.5.0.2　Where more than one marking could apply to a vessel, only the marking which includes the greatest number of blue cones or blue lights shall apply, i.e. in the following order of precedence:

- two blue cones or two blue lights; or

- one blue cone or one blue light.

7.2.5.0.3　By derogation from 7.2.5.0.1 above, and in accordance with the footnotes to article 3.14 of the CEVNI, the competent authority of a Contracting Party may authorize seagoing vessels temporarily operating in an inland navigation area on the territory of this Contracting Party, the use of the day and night signals prescribed in the Recommendations on the Safe Transport of Dangerous Cargoes and Related Activities in Port Areas adopted by the Maritime Safety Committee of the International Maritime Organization (by night an all-round fixed red light and by day flag "B" of the International Code of Signals), instead of the signals prescribed in 7.2.5.0.1. The competent authority which has taken the initiative with respect to the derogation granted shall notify the Executive Secretary of the United Nations Economic Commission for Europe, who shall bring this derogation to the attention of the Administrative Committee.

7.2.5.1　*Mode of navigation*

The competent authorities may impose restrictions on the inclusion of tank vessels in pushed convoys of large dimension.

7.2.5.2　*(Reserved)*

7.2.5.3　*Mooring*

Vessels shall be moored securely, but in such as way that electrical power cables and flexible hoses are not subject to tensile strain and the vessels can be released quickly in an emergency.

7.2.5.4　*Berthing*

7.2.5.4.1　The distances from other vessels to be kept by vessels carrying dangerous goods shall be not less than those prescribed by the Regulations referred to in 1.1.4.6.

7.2.5.4.2　An expert, as required by 7.2.3.15 shall be permanently on board berthed vessels carrying dangerous substances. The competent authority may, however, exempt from this obligation those vessels which are berthed in the harbour basin or in a permitted berthing position.

7.2.5.4.3　Outside the berthing areas specifically designated by the local competent authority, the distances to be kept by berthed vessels shall not be less than:

- 100 m　from residential areas, civil engineering structures or storage tanks, if the vessel is required to be marked with one blue cone or blue light in accordance with column (19) of Table C of Chapter 3.2;

- 100 m　from civil engineering structures and storage tanks; and 300 m from residential areas if the vessel is required to be marked with two blue cones or two blue lights in accordance with column (19) of Table C of Chapter 3.2.

While waiting in front of locks or bridges, vessels are allowed to keep distances less than those given above. In no case shall the distance be less than 100 m.

7.2.5.4.4   The local competent authority may prescribe distances less than those given in 7.1.5.4.3 above.

7.2.5.5-   *(Reserved)*
7.2.5.7

7.2.5.8   *Reporting duty*

7.2.5.8.1   In the States where the reporting duty is in force, the master of a vessel for which marking in accordance with 7.2.5.0 is required shall, prior to the start of any voyage, report the following particulars to the competent authority of the State in which the voyage has started:

–   name of the vessel;

–   official number;

–   dead-weight tonnage;

–   description of the dangerous substances carried as given in the transport document (UN number or identification number, proper shipping name, class and, where applicable, packing group and/or classification code) together with the quantity in each case;

–   number of persons on board;

–   port of destination; and

–   planned shipping route.

This reporting duty shall apply in each State territory once to both passages upstream and downstream so far as the competent authorities so require. The information may be given orally (e.g. by radio-telephone, where appropriate by automatic wireless message service) or in writing.

7.2.5.8.2   When passing the other traffic control stations designated by the competent authority, the following particulars shall be reported:

–   name of the vessel;

–   official number;

–   dead-weight tonnage.

7.2.5.8.3   Changes to any of the particulars referred to in 7.2.5.8.1 shall be reported to the competent authority without delay.

7.2.5.8.4   The information is confidential and shall not be passed on to third parties by the competent authority.

The competent authority may, however, in the event of an accident, inform the emergency services of the relevant particulars required for organizing emergency action.

7.2.5.9-   *(Reserved)*
7.2.9.99

PART 8

Provisions for vessel crews, equipment, operation and documentation

CHAPTER 8.1

GENERAL REQUIREMENTS APPLICABLE TO VESSELS AND EQUIPMENT

8.1.1   *(Reserved)*

8.1.2   Documents

8.1.2.1   In addition to the documents required by other regulations, the following documents shall be kept on board:

    (a)   The vessel's certificate of approval referred to in 8.1.8;

    (b)   Transport documents referred to in 5.4.1 for all dangerous goods on board and, where necessary the container packing certificate (see 5.4.2);

    (c)   The instructions in writing prescribed in 5.4.3 for all dangerous goods on board;

    (d)   A copy of the ADN with its annexed Regulations which may be a copy which can be consulted by electronic means at any time;

    (e)   The inspection certificate of the insulation resistance of the electrical installations prescribed in 8.1.7;

    (f)   The inspection certificate of the fire-extinguishing equipment and fire-hoses prescribed in 8.1.6.1;

    (g)   A book in which all required measurement results are recorded;

    (h)   A copy of the relevant text of the special authorizations referred to in 1.5 if the transport operation is performed under this/these special authorization(s);

    (i)   Means of identification, which include a photograph, for each crew member, in accordance with 1.10.1.4.

8.1.2.2   In addition to the documents prescribed in 8.1.2.1, the following documents shall be carried on board dry cargo vessels:

    (a)   The loading plan prescribed in 7.1.4.11;

    (b)   The ADN specialized knowledge certificate prescribed in 8.2.12;

    (c)   For vessels which have to conform to the conditions of damage-control (see 9.1.0.95)

        –   a damage-control plan;

        –   the documents concerning intact stability as well as all conditions of intact stability taken into account for the damaged stability calculation in a form the master understands;

        –   the certificate of the classification society (see 9.1.0.88 or 9.2.0.88).

8.1.2.3   In addition to the documents prescribed in 8.1.2.1, the following documents should be carried on board tank vessels:

[(a)   The loading journal prescribed in 7.2.4.11;][1]

(b)   The ADN specialized knowledge certificate prescribed in 8.2.1.2, and, for the carriage of gases for which type G is prescribed in Chapter 3.2, Table C, column (6), the specialized knowledge certificate for the carriage of gases in tank vessels (see 8.2.1.3) and, for the carriage of chemicals for which type C is prescribed in Chapter 3.2, Table C, column (6), the specialized knowledge certificate for the carriage of chemicals in tank vessels (see 8.2.1.4);

(c)   For vessels which have to conform to the conditions of damage-control (see 9.3.1.15 or 9.3.2.15)

    –   a damage-control plan;

    –   the documents concerning intact stability as well as all conditions of intact stability taken into account for the damaged stability calculation in a form the master understands;

(d)   The documents concerning the electrical installations prescribed in 9.3.1.50, 9.3.2.50 or 9.3.3.50;

(e)   The classification certificate prescribed in 9.3.1.8, 9.3.2.8 or 9.3.3.8;

(f)   The flammable gas detector certificate prescribed in 9.3.1.8.3, 9.3.2.8.2 or 9.3.3.8.3;

(g)   The certificate listing all dangerous goods accepted for carriage in the vessel, referred to in 1.11.1.2.5;

(h)   The inspection certificate for the pipes for loading and unloading prescribed in 8.1.6.2;

(i)   The instructions relating to the loading and unloading flows prescribed in 9.3.2.25.9 or 9.3.3.25.9.

[(j)   The inspection certificate for the stripping installation prescribed in 8.6.4.2;][1]

(k)   In the event of the carriage of goods having a melting point $\geq$ 0° C, heating instructions;

(l)   The inspection certificate for the pressure relief and vacuum relief valves prescribed in 8.1.6.5.

8.1.2.4   The instructions in writing referred to in 5.4.3 shall be handed to the master before loading. They shall be kept readily at hand in the wheelhouse.

    On board dry cargo vessels, the transport documents shall be handed to the master before loading and on board tank vessels they shall be handed to him after loading.

8.1.2.5   The instructions in writing which are not applicable to the dangerous goods on board the vessel shall be kept separate from those which are applicable so as to avoid any confusion.

---

[1]   *It is not necessary to apply this subparagraph from the 1ˢᵗ January 2003. The date of application will be defined later.*

8.1.2.6   The presence on board of the certificate of approval is not required in the case of pusher barges which are not carrying dangerous goods, provided that the following additional particulars are indicated, in identical lettering, on the metal plate furnished by CEVNI:

Number of the certificate of approval: ...
issued by: ...
valid until: ...

The barge-owner shall thereafter keep the certificate of approval in his possession.

The similarity of the particulars on the plate and those contained in the certificate of approval shall be certified by a competent authority which shall affix its stamp to the plate.

8.1.2.7   The presence on board of the certificate of approval is not required in the case of dry cargo barges or tank barges carrying dangerous goods provided that the metal plate furnished by CEVNI is supplemented by a second metal plate reproducing by photo-optical means a copy of the entire certificate of approval.

The barge-owner shall thereafter keep the certificate of approval in his possession.

The similarity of the particulars on the metal plate and the certificate of approval shall be certified by an inspection commission which shall affix its stamp to the plate.

8.1.2.8   All documents shall be drawn up in a language the master is able to read and understand and if that language is not English, French or German, in English, French or German unless agreements concluded between the countries concerned in the transport operation provide otherwise. They shall also be drawn up in one of these languages.

8.1.2.9   8.1.2.1 (b), 8.1.2.1 (g), 8.1.2.4 and 8.1.2.5 do not apply to oil separator vessels or supply vessels. 8.1.2.1 (c) does not apply to oil separator vessels.

8.1.3   (*Reserved*)

8.1.4   Fire-extinguishing arrangements

In addition to the fire-extinguishing appliances prescribed in the Regulations referred to in 1.1.4.6, each vessel shall be equipped with at least two additional hand fire-extinguishers having the same capacity. The fire-extinguishing agent contained in these additional hand fire-extinguishers shall be suitable and sufficient in quantity for fighting fires involving the dangerous goods carried.

8.1.5   Special equipment

8.1.5.1   Insofar as the provisions of Chapter 3.2, Tables A or C require, the following equipment shall be available on board:

PP: for each member of the crew, a pair of protective goggles, a pair of protective gloves, a protective suit and a suitable pair of protective shoes (or protective boots, if necessary). On board tank vessels, protective boots are required in all cases;

EP: a suitable escape device for each person on board;

EX: a flammable gas detector with the instructions for its use;

TOX: a toximeter with the instructions for its use;

A: a breathing apparatus ambient air-dependent;

8.1.5.2 Materials and additional protective equipment specified by the consignor in the instructions shall be provided by the consignor and shall be available on board.

8.1.5.3 For pushed convoys or side-by-side formations under way, it shall be sufficient, however, if the pusher tug or the vessel propelling the formation is equipped with the special equipment referred to in 8.1.5.1 above, when this is required in Chapter 3.2, Tables A or C.

8.1.6 Checking and inspection of equipment

8.1.6.1 The fire-extinguishing appliances and hoses shall be inspected at least once every two years by persons authorized for this purpose by the competent authority. Proof of inspection shall be affixed to the fire-extinguishing appliances. A certificate concerning this inspection shall be carried on board.

8.1.6.2 The hoses for loading and unloading shall be inspected once a year by persons authorized for this purpose by the competent authority. A certificate concerning this inspection shall be carried on board.

8.1.6.3 The special equipment referred to in 8.1.5.1 and the gas detection system shall be checked and inspected in accordance with the instructions of the manufacturer concerned by persons authorized for this purpose or by the competent authority. A certificate concerning this inspection shall be carried on board.

8.1.6.4 The measuring instruments prescribed in 8.1.5.1 shall be checked each time before use by the user in accordance with the instructions for use.

8.1.6.5 The pressure relief and vacuum relief valves prescribed in 9.3.1.22, 9.3.2.22 and 9.3.3.22 shall be inspected on each renewal of the certificate of approval by the manufacturer or by a firm approved by the manufacturer. A certificate concerning this inspection shall be carried on board.

8.1.6.6 The stripping system referred to in 9.3.2.25.10 or 9.3.3.25.10 shall be subjected to a water test before its first use or after a modification. The test and the establishment of the residual quantities shall be carried out in accordance with the provisions of 8.6.4.2. The certificate concerning the test referred to in 8.6.4.3 shall be carried on board.

8.1.7 Electrical installations

The insulation resistance of the electrical installations, the earthing and the certified safe type electrical equipment shall be inspected whenever the certificate of approval is renewed and, in addition, within the third year from the date of issue of the certificate of approval by a person authorized for this purpose by the competent authority. An appropriate inspection certificate shall be kept on board.

8.1.8 Certificate of approval

8.1.8.1 Dry cargo vessels carrying dangerous goods in quantities greater than exempted quantities, the vessels referred to in 7.1.2.19.1, tank vessels carrying dangerous goods and the vessels referred to in 7.2.2.19.3 shall be provided with an appropriate certificate of approval.

8.1.8.2 The certificate of approval shall attest that the vessel has been inspected and that its construction and equipment comply with the requirements of these Regulations.

8.1.8.3   The certificate of approval shall be issued in accordance with the requirements and procedures set out in Chapter 1.16.

It shall conform to the model in 8.6.1.1 or 8.6.1.3.

For tank vessels, the relief pressure of the safety valves or of the high-velocity vent valves shall be entered in the certificate of approval.

If a vessel has cargo tanks with different valve opening pressures, the opening pressure of each tank shall be entered in the certificate of approval.

NOTE: *For procedures concerning:*

–   *the issue of certificates: see 1.16.2;*

–   *the application for issue of certificates: see 1.16.5;*

–   *the amendments to be made to the certificate of approval: see 1.16.6;*

–   *the presentation of the vessel for inspection: see 1.16.7;*

–   *the first inspection (if the vessel does not yet have the certificate of approval or if the validity of the certificate of approval expired more than six months ago): see 1.16.8;*

–   *the special inspection (if the vessel's hull or equipment has undergone alterations liable to diminish safety in respect of the carriage of dangerous goods or has sustained damage affecting such safety): see 1.16.9;*

–   *the periodic inspection for the renewal of the certificate of approval: see 1.16.10;*

–   *the extension of the certificate of approval without an inspection: see 1.16.11;*

–   *the right of official inspection by the competent authority of a Contracting Party: see 1.16.12;*

–   *the withholding and return of the certificate of approval: see 1.16.13;*

–   *the issue of a duplicate copy: see 1.16.14;*

8.1.8.4   The certificate of approval shall be valid for not more than five years. The date on which the period of validity expires shall be shown on the certificate. The competent authority which issued the certificate may, without inspection of the vessel, extend the validity of the certificate by not more than one year. Such extension may be granted only once within two periods of validity (see 1.16.11).

8.1.8.5   If the vessel's hull or equipment has undergone alterations liable to reduce the safety as regards the carriage of dangerous goods or has sustained damage affecting such safety, the vessel shall undergo a further inspection in (see 1.16.9).

8.1.8.6   The certificate of approval may be withdrawn if the vessel is not properly maintained or if the vessel's construction or equipment no longer complies with the applicable provisions of these Regulations (see 1.16.13).

8.1.8.7   The certificate of approval may only be withdrawn by the authority by which it has been issued.

Nevertheless, in the cases referred to in 8.1.8.5 and 8.1.8.6 above, the competent authority of the State in which the vessel is staying may prohibit its use for the carriage of those dangerous goods for which the certificate is required. For this purpose it may withdraw the certificate until such time as the vessel again complies with the applicable provisions of these Regulations. In that case it shall notify the competent authority which issued the certificate.

8.1.8.8 Notwithstanding 8.1.8.7 above, any competent authority may amend or withdraw the certificate of approval at the request of the vessel's owner, provided that it so notifies the competent authority which issued the certificate.

8.1.9 Provisional certificate of approval

NOTE: *For procedures concerning the issue of certificates, see Chapter 1.16.*

8.1.9.1 For a vessel which is not provided with a certificate of approval, a provisional certificate of approval of limited duration may be issued in the following cases, subject to the following conditions:

(a) The vessel complies with the applicable provisions of these Regulations, but the normal certificate of approval could not be issued in time. The provisional certificate of approval shall be valid for an appropriate period but not exceeding three months;

(b) The vessel does not comply with every applicable provisions of these Regulations after sustaining damage. In this case the provisional certificate of approval shall be valid only for a single specified voyage and for a specified cargo. The competent authority may impose additional conditions.

8.1.9.2 The provisional certificate of approval shall conform to the model in 8.6.1.2 or 8.6.1.4 of these Regulations or a single model certificate combining a provisional certificate of inspection and the provisional certificate of approval provided that the single model certificate contains the same information as 8.6.1.2 or 8.6.1.4 and is approved by the competent authority.

[8.1.10 Loading journal

All tank vessels shall be provided with a loading journal in accordance with the provisions of the CEVNI. The original of the loading journal shall be kept on board for not less than 12 months after the last entry is made.

The first loading journal shall be issued by the authority which issued the certificate of approval. Subsequent journals may be issued by authorities competent to do so.][1]

---

[1] *It is not necessary to apply this subparagraph from the 1st January 2003. The date of application will be defined later.*

CHAPTER 8.2

REQUIREMENTS CONCERNING TRAINING

8.2.1   **General requirements concerning training of experts**

8.2.1.1   An expert shall not be less than 18 years of age.

8.2.1.2   An expert is a person who has a special knowledge of the ADN. Proof of this knowledge shall be furnished by means of a certificate from a competent authority or from an agency recognized by the competent authority.

     This certificate shall be issued to persons who, after training, have passed a qualifying ADN examination.

8.2.1.3   The experts referred to in 8.2.1.2 shall take part in a basic training course. Training shall take place in the context of classes approved by the competent authority. The primordial objective of the training is to make the experts aware of the hazards of the carriage of dangerous goods and provide them with the necessary basic knowledge to reduce the dangers of an incident to a minimum, to enable them to take the necessary measures to ensure their own safety, general safety and the protection of the environment and to limit the consequences of the incident. This training, which shall include individual practical exercises, takes the form of a basic course; it shall cover at least the objectives referred to in 8.2.2.3.1.1 and in 8.2.2.3.1.2 or 8.2.2.3.1.3.

8.2.1.4   Experts for the carriage of gases shall take part in an advanced course covering at least the objectives referred to in 8.2.2.3.3.1. Training shall take place in the context of classes approved by the competent authority. An expert certificate shall be issued to persons who, after training, have successfully passed an examination concerning the carriage of gases and have produced evidence of not less than one year's work on board a type G vessel during a period of two years prior to or following the examination.

8.2.1.5   Experts for the carriage of chemicals shall take part in an advanced course covering at least the objectives referred to in 8.2.2.3.3.2. Training shall take place in the context of classes approved by the competent authority. An expert certificate shall be issued to persons who, after training, have successfully passed an examination concerning the carriage of chemicals and have produced evidence of not less than one year's work on board a type C vessel during a period of two years prior to or following the examination.

8.2.1.6   After five years the expert shall furnish proof, in the form of relevant particulars entered in the certificate by the competent authority or by a body recognized by it, of participation in a refresher or advanced course taken in the last year prior to the expiry of the certificate, covering at least the objectives referred to in 8.2.2.3.1.1 and in 8.2.2.3.1.2 or 8.2.2.3.1.3 and comprising current new developments in particular. The new period of invalidity shall begin on the expiry date of the certificate; in other cases it shall begin on the date of the certificate of participation in the course.

8.2.1.7   After five years, the expert for the carriage of gases shall furnish proof, in the form of relevant particulars entered in the certificate by the competent authority or by a body recognized by it,

     —   that during the year preceding the expiry of the certificate, he has participated in a refresher or advanced course covering at least the objectives referred to in 8.2.2.3.3.1 and comprising current new developments in particular, or

– that during the previous two years he has performed a period of work of not less than one year on board a type G tank vessel.

When the refresher or advanced training course is taken in the year preceding the date of expiry of the certificate, the new period of validity shall begin on the expiry date of the preceding certificate, but in other cases it shall begin on the date of certification of participation in the course.

8.2.1.8   After five years, the expert for the carriage of chemicals shall furnish proof, in the form of relevant particulars entered in the certificate by the competent authority or by a body recognized by it,

– that during the year preceding the expiry of the certificate, he has participated in a refresher or advanced course covering at least the objectives referred to in 8.2.2.3.3.2 and comprising current new developments in particular, or

– that during the previous two years he had performed a period of work of not less than one year on board a type C tank vessel.

When the refresher or advanced training course is taken in the year preceding the date of expiry of the certificate, the new period of validity shall begin on the expiry date of the preceding certificate, but in other cases it shall begin on the date of certification of participation in the course.

8.2.1.9   The document attesting training and experience in accordance with the requirements of Chapter V of the STCW Code on Training and Qualifications of Masters, Officers and Ratings of Tankers carrying LPG/LNG shall be equivalent to the certificate referred to in 8.2.1.4, provided it has been recognized by a competent authority. No more than five years shall have passed since the date of issue or renewal of such a document.

8.2.1.10   The document attesting training and experience in accordance with Chapter V of the STCW Code for officers concerning personnel in charge of cargo on tank vessels carrying chemicals in bulk shall be equivalent to the certificate referred to in 8.2.1.5, provided it has been recognized by a competent authority. No more than five years shall have passed since the date of issue or renewal of such a document.

8.2.1.11   The certificate shall conform to the model in 8.6.2.

8.2.2   Special requirements for the training of experts

8.2.2.1   Theoretical knowledge and practical abilities shall be acquired as a result of training in theory and practical exercises. The theoretical knowledge shall be tested by an examination. During the refresher and advanced courses exercises and tests shall ensure that the participant takes an active role in the training.

8.2.2.2   The training organizer shall ensure that participants have a good knowledge of the subject and shall take into account the latest developments concerning the Regulations and the requirements for training in the transport of dangerous goods. Teaching shall relate closely to practice. In accordance with the approval, the teaching syllabus shall be drawn up on the basis of the objectives referred to in 8.2.2.3.1.1 to 8.2.2.3.1.3 and in 8.2.2.3.3.1 or 8.2.2.3.3.2. Basic training and the refresher and advanced courses shall comprise individual practical exercises (see 8.2.2.3.1.1).

8.2.2.3   *Organization of training*

Basic training and the refresher and advanced courses shall be organized in the context of basic courses (see 8.2.2.3.1) and if necessary specialization courses (see 8.2.2.3.3). The courses referred to in 8.2.2.3.1 may comprise three variants: transport of dry cargo, transport in tank vessels and combined transport of dry cargo and transport in tank vessels.

8.2.2.3.1   *Basic course*

Basic course on the transport of dry cargo

Prior training:	none
Knowledge:	ADN in general, except Chapter 3.2, Table C, Chapters 7.2 and 9.3
Authorized for:	vessels carrying dry cargo only
Training:	general 8.2.2.3.1.1 and dry cargo vessels 8.2.2.3.1.2

Basic course on transport by tank vessels

Prior training:	none
Knowledge:	ADN in general, except Chapter 3.2, Tables A and B, Chapters 7.1, 9.1, 9.2 and sections 9.3.1 and 9.3.2
Authorized for:	type N tank vessels only
Training:	general 8.2.2.3.1.1 and tank vessels 8.2.2.3.1.3

Combined basic course on dry cargo and tank vessels

Prior training:	none
Knowledge:	ADN in general, except sections 9.3.1 and 9.3.2
Authorized for:	dry cargo vessels and type N tank vessels
Training:	general 8.2.2.3.1.1, dry cargo vessels 8.2.2.3.1.2 and tank vessels 8.2.2.3.1.3

8.2.2.3.1.1   The general part of the basic training course shall comprise at least the following objectives:

General:

-        Objectives and structure of ADN.

Construction and equipment:

-        Construction and equipment of vessels subject to ADN.

Measurement techniques:

-        Measurements of toxicity, oxygen content, explosivity.

Knowledge of products:

-        Classification and hazard characteristics of the dangerous goods.

Loading, unloading and transport:

-        Loading, unloading, general service requirements and requirements relating to transport.

Documents:

-       Documents which must be on board during transport.

Hazards and measures of prevention:

-       General safety measures.

Practical exercises:

-       Practical exercises, in particular with respect to entry into spaces, use of fire-extinguishers, fire-fighting equipment and personal protective equipment as well as flammable gas detectors, oxygen meters and toximeters.

8.2.2.3.1.2   The "dry cargo vessels" part of the basic training course shall comprise at least the following objectives:

Construction and equipment:

-       Construction and equipment of dry cargo vessels.

Treatment of holds and adjacent spaces:

-       degassing, cleaning, maintenance,
-       ventilation of holds and spaces outside the cargo area.

Loading, unloading and transport:

-       loading, unloading, general service and transport requirements,
-       labelling of packages.

Documents:

-       documents which must be on board during transport.

Hazards and measures of prevention:

-       general safety measures,
-       personal protective and safety equipment.

8.2.2.3.1.3   The "tank vessel" part of the basic training course shall comprise at least the following objectives:

Construction and equipment:

-       construction and equipment of tank vessels,
-       ventilation,
-       loading and unloading systems.

Treatment of cargo tanks and adjacent spaces:

-       degassing, cleaning, maintenance,
-       heating and cooling of cargo,
-       handling of residual cargo tanks.

Measurement and sampling techniques:

- measurements of toxicity, oxygen content and explosivity,
- sampling.

Loading, unloading and transport:

- loading, unloading, general service and transport requirements.

Documents:

- documents which must be on board during transport.

Hazards and measures of prevention:

- prevention and general safety measures,
- spark formation,
- personal protective and safety equipment,
- fires and fire-fighting.

8.2.2.3.2 *Refresher and advanced training courses*

Refresher and advanced training course on transport of dry cargo

Prior training:	valid ADN "dry cargo vessels" or combined "dry cargo vessels/tank vessels" certificate
Knowledge:	ADN in general, except Chapter 3.2, Table C, Chapters 7.2 and 9.3
Authorized for:	dry cargo vessels only
Training:	general 8.2.2.3.1.1 and dry cargo vessels 8.2.2.3.1.2

Refresher and advanced training course on transport in tank vessels

Prior training:	valid ADN "tank vessels" or combined "dry cargo vessels/tank vessels" certificate
Knowledge:	ADN in general, except Chapter 3.2, Tables A and B, Chapters 7.1, 9.1 and 9.2 and sections 9.3.1 and 9.3.2
Authorized for:	type N vessels only
Training:	general 8.2.2.3.1.1 and tank vessels 8.2.2.3.1.3

Refresher and advanced training course on combined transport in "dry cargo vessels/tank vessels"

Prior training:	valid ADN combined "dry cargo vessels and tank vessels"certificate
Knowledge:	ADN in general, including sections 9.3.1 and 9.3.2
Authorized for:	dry cargo vessels and type N tank vessels
Training:	general 8.2.2.3.1.1, dry cargo vessels 8.2.2.3.1.2 and tank vessels 8.2.2.3.1.3

8.2.2.3.3 Specialization courses

Specialization course on gases

Prior training:	valid ADN "tank vessels" or combined "dry cargo vessels/tank vessels" certificate
Knowledge:	ADN, in particular knowledge relating to loading, transport, unloading and handling of gases
Authorized for:	types N and G vessels
Training:	gases 8.2.2.3.3.1

Specialization course on chemicals

Prior training:	valid ADN "tank vessels" or combined "dry cargo vessels/tank vessels" certificate
Knowledge:	ADN, in particular knowledge relating to loading, transport, unloading and handling of chemicals
Authorized for:	types N and C tank vessels
Training:	chemicals 8.2.2.3.3.2

8.2.2.3.3.1   The specialization course on gases shall comprise at least the following objectives:

Knowledge of physics and chemistry:

- laws of gases, e.g. Boyle, Gay-Lussac and fundamental law
- partial pressures and mixtures, e.g. definitions and simple calculations, pressure increase and gas release from cargo tanks
- Avogadro's number and calculation of masses of ideal gas and application of the mass formula
- density and volume of liquids, e.g. density, volume in terms of temperature increase and maximum degree of filling
- critical pressure and temperature
- polymerization, e.g. theoretical and practical questions, conditions of carriage
- vaporization, condensation, e.g. definition, liquid volume and vapour volume ratio
- mixtures, e.g. vapour pressure, composition and hazard characteristics
- chemical bonds and formulae.

Practice:

- flushing of cargo tanks, e.g. flushing in the event of a change of cargo, addition of air to the cargo, methods of flushing (degassing) before entering cargo tanks
- sampling
- danger of explosion
- health risks
- gas concentration measures, e.g. which apparatus to use and how to use it
- monitoring of closed spaces and entry to these spaces
- certificates for degassing and permitted work
- degree of filling and over-filling
- safety installations
- pumps and compressors.

Emergency measures:

- physical injury, e.g. liquefied gases on the skin, breathing in gas, assistance
- irregularities relating to the cargo, e.g. leak in a connection, over-filling, polymerization and hazards in the vicinity of the vessel.

8.2.2.3.3.2   The specialization course on chemicals shall comprise at least the following objectives:

Knowledge of physics and chemistry:

- chemical products, e.g. molecules, atoms, physical state, acids, bases, oxidation
- density, pressure and volume of liquids, e.g. density, volume and pressure in terms of temperature increase, maximum degree of filling
- critical temperature
- polymerization, e.g. theoretical and practical questions, conditions of carriage

- mixtures, e.g. vapour pressure, composition and hazard characteristics
- chemical bonds and formulae.

Practice:

- cleaning of cargo tanks, e.g. degassing, washing, residues, cargo residues
- loading and unloading, e.g. vapour pipes systems, rapid closing devices, effects of temperature
- sampling
- danger of explosion
- health risks
- gas concentration measures, e.g. which apparatus to use and how to use it
- monitoring of closed spaces and entry to these spaces
- certificates for degassing and permitted work
- degree of filling and over-filling
- safety installations
- pumps and compressors.

Emergency measures:

- physical injury, e.g. liquefied gases on the skin, breathing in gas, assistance
- irregularities relating to the cargo, e.g. leak in a connection, over-filling, polymerization and hazards in the vicinity of the vessel.

8.2.2.3.4   *Refresher and advanced training courses*

Refresher and advanced training course on gases

Prior training:	valid ADN "gases" certificate
Knowledge:	ADN, in particular, loading, transport, unloading and handling of gases
Authorization for:	types N and G tank vessels
Training:	gases 8.2.2.3.3.1

Refresher and advanced training course on chemicals

Prior training:	valid ADN "chemicals" certificate
Knowledge:	ADN, in particular, loading, transport, unloading and handling of chemicals
Authorization for:	types N and C tank vessels
Training:	chemicals 8.2.2.3.3.2

8.2.2.4   *Planning of refresher and specialization courses*

The following minimum periods of training shall be observed:

Basic "dry cargo vessels course"	24 lessons of 45 minutes each
Basic "tank vessels" course	24 lessons of 45 minutes each
Basic combined course	32 lessons of 45 minutes each
Specialization course on gases	16 lessons of 45 minutes each
Specialization course on chemicals	16 lessons of 45 minutes each

Each day of training may comprise not more than eight lessons.

If the theoretical training is by correspondence, equivalences to the above-mentioned lessons shall be determined. Training by correspondence shall be completed within a period of nine months.

Approximately 30% of basic training shall be devoted to practical exercises. Practical exercises shall, where possible, be undertaken during the period of theoretical training; in any event, they shall be completed not later than three months following the completion of theoretical training.

8.2.2.5   *Planning of refresher and advanced training courses*

The refresher and advanced training courses shall take place before the expiry of the deadline referred to in 8.2.1.4, 8.2.1.6 or 8.2.1.8.

The following minimum periods of training shall be observed:

Basic refresher course:

-	dry cargo vessels	16 lessons of 45 minutes each
-	tank vessels	16 lessons of 45 minutes each
-	combined dry cargo vessels and tank vessels	16 lessons of 45 minutes each

Specialization refresher course on gases   8 lessons of 45 minutes each

Specialization refresher course on chemicals   8 lessons of 45 minutes each

Each day of training may comprise not more than eight lessons.

If the theoretical training is by correspondence, equivalences to the above-mentioned lessons shall be determined. Training by correspondence shall be completed within a period of nine months.

Approximately 50% of basic training shall be devoted to practical exercises. Practical exercises shall, where possible, be undertaken during the period of theoretical training; in any event, they shall be completed not later than three months following the completion of theoretical training.

8.2.2.6   *Approval of training courses*

8.2.2.6.1   Training courses shall be approved by the competent authority.

8.2.2.6.2   Approval shall be granted only on written application.

8.2.2.6.3   Applications for approval shall be accompanied by:

(a)   the detailed course curriculum showing the course topics and the length of time to be devoted to them, as well as the teaching methods envisaged;

(b)   the roster of teaching staff, listing their qualifications and the subjects to be taught by each one;

(c)   information on classrooms and teaching materials, as well as on the facilities available for practical exercises;

(d)   enrolment requirements, e.g. the number of participants.

8.2.2.6.4　　　The competent authority shall be responsible for monitoring training courses and examinations.

8.2.2.6.5　　　The approval comprises the following conditions, <u>inter alia</u>:

(a)　　　training courses shall conform to the information accompanying the application for approval;

(b)　　　the competent authority may send inspectors to attend training courses and examinations;

(c)　　　the timetables for the various training courses shall be notified in advance to the competent authority.

Approval shall be granted in writing. It may be withdrawn in the event of failure to comply with the conditions of approval.

8.2.2.6.6　　　The approval document shall indicate whether the course in question is a basic training course, a specialization course or a refresher and advanced training course.

8.2.2.6.7　　　If, after approval is granted, the organizer of the training course wishes to change conditions affecting the approval, he shall seek the prior agreement of the competent authority. This provision shall apply in particular to amendments to syllabuses.

8.2.2.6.8　　　Training courses shall take account of the current developments in the various subjects taught. The course organizer shall be responsible for ensuring that recent developments are brought to the attention of, and properly understood by, teachers.

8.2.2.7　　　*Examinations*

8.2.2.7.1　　　*Basic training courses*

8.2.2.7.1.1　　　After initial training, including practical exercises, and ADN basic training examination shall be taken. This examination shall be held either immediately after the training courses or within six months following the completion of such courses.

8.2.2.7.1.2　　　In the examination the candidate shall furnish evidence that, in accordance with the basic training course, he has the knowledge, understanding and capabilities required of an expert on board a vessel.

8.2.2.7.1.3　　　The Administrative Committee shall establish a list of questions comprising the objectives set out in 8.2.2.3.1.1 to 8.2.2.3.1.3. The examination questions shall be selected from this list. The candidate shall not have advance knowledge of the questions selected.

8.2.2.7.1.4　　　The model attached to the list of questions is to be used to compile the examination questions.

8.2.2.7.1.5　　　The examination shall be written. Candidates shall be asked 30 questions. The examination shall last 60 minutes. It is deemed to have been passed if at least 25 of the 30 questions have been answered correctly. During the examination, candidates may consult the texts of regulations on dangerous goods and CEVNI.

8.2.2.7.2　　　*Specialization course on gases and chemicals*

8.2.2.7.2.1　　　Candidates who are successful in the ADN basic training examination may apply for enrolment in a "gases" and/or "chemicals" specialization course, to be followed by an examination. The examination shall be based on the Administrative Committee[1]'s list of questions.

8.2.2.7.2.2   During the examination the candidate shall furnish proof that, in accordance with the "gases" and/or "chemicals" specialization course, he has the knowledge, understanding and capabilities required of the expert on board vessels carrying gases or chemicals, respectively.

8.2.2.7.2.3   The Administrative Committee shall prepare a list of questions for the examination, comprising the objectives set out in 8.2.2.3.3.1 or 8.2.2.3.3.2. The examination questions shall be selected from the list. The candidate shall not have advance knowledge of the questions selected.

8.2.2.7.2.4   In the event of multiple training courses a single examination may be organized.

8.2.2.7.2.5   The examination shall be written.

The candidate is to be asked 30 multiple-choice questions and one substantive question. The examination shall last a total of 120 minutes, of which 60 minutes for the multiple-choice questions and 60 minutes for the substantive question.

The examination shall be marked out of a total of 60, of which 30 marks will go to the multiple-choice questions (one mark per question) and 30 to the substantive question (the distribution of marks is left to the appreciation of the Administrative Committee). A total of 44 marks must be achieved to pass. However, not less than 20 marks must be obtained in each subject. If the candidate obtains 44 but does not achieve 20 in one subject, the subject in question may be set in a resit.

The texts of regulations and technical literature are permitted during the examination.

8.2.2.8   *ADN specialized knowledge certificate*

The issue and renewal of the ADN specialized knowledge certificate conforming to 8.6.2, shall be the responsibility of the competent authority.

Certificates shall be issued to:

–   candidates who have attended a basic training course and have passed the ADN examination;

–   candidates who have taken part in a refresher or advanced training course.

The validity of the basic training certificate shall be five years as from the date of the examination.

The validity of the 'gases' and/or 'chemicals' specialized training certificate shall be brought into line with the validity of the basic training certificate.

If the refresher and advanced training course was not fully completed before the expiry of the period of validity of the certificate, a new certificate shall not be issued until the candidate has completed a further initial basic training course and passed an examination referred to in 8.2.2.7 above.

---

[1] *Before the entry into force of the Agreement, or until the Administrative Committee adopts the list of questions, this list of questions shall be drafted by the competent authority. It is recommended that the competent authority should use the lists of questions drawn up by the Central Commission for the Navigation of the Rhine or the Danube Commission.*

8.2.3   **Training**

8.2.3.1   *Training syllabus and subjects*

8.2.3.1.1   *Basic course*

Basic course on the transport of dry cargo

Prior training:	none
Knowledge:	ADN in general, except Chapter 3.2, Table C, Chapters 7.2 and 9.3
Authorized for:	vessels carrying dry cargo only

Basic course on transport by tank vessels

Prior training:	none
Knowledge:	ADN in general, except Chapter 3.2, Tables A and B, Chapters 7.1, 9.1 and 9.2, 9.3.1 and 9.3.2
Authorized for:	type N tank vessels only

Combined basic course dry cargo and transport in tank vessels

Prior training:	none
Knowledge:	ADN in general, including 9.3.1 and 9.3.2
Authorized for:	dry cargo vessels and type N tank vessels

8.2.3.1.2   *Refresher and advanced training courses based on the certified basic courses referred to in 8.2.3.1.1*

Prior training:	Valid ADN certificate referred to in 8.2.3.1.1
Authorized for:	depending on the refresher and advanced course taken: only dry cargo vessels, only type N tank vessels or dry cargo vessels and type N tank vessels

Specialization course in gases

Prior training:	basic tank vessel or combined training
Knowledge:	ADN, in particular, knowledge of loading, carriage, unloading and handling of gases
Authorized for:	tank vessels of types N and G

Specialization course in chemicals

Prior training:	basic tank vessel or combined training
Knowledge:	ADN, in particular, knowledge of loading, carriage, unloading and handling of chemicals
Authorized for:	tank vessels of types N and C

8.2.3.2   *Purpose and content of training course*

8.2.3.2.1   The following provisions are applicable to the approval of the expert training courses in accordance with 8.2.1.2, 8.2.1.4 and 8.2.1.5.

8.2.3.2.2   The purpose of the training courses is to provide the theoretical and practical knowledge referred to in 8.2.2.3.2, 8.2.2.3.4 or 8.2.2.3.5.

8.2.3.2.3   *Planning of initial training*

The following periods of training are to be completed:

basic training course on dry cargo vessels:	24 lessons of 45 minutes
each basic training course on tank vessels:	24 lessons of 45 minutes
each combined basic training course:	32 lessons of 45 minutes
each specialization course on gases:	16 lessons of 45 minutes
each specialization course on chemicals:	16 lessons of 45 minutes

One day's training may comprise a maximum of eight lessons.

If theoretical training is by correspondence, equivalences with the above-mentioned lessons shall be determined. Training by correspondence must be completed within nine months.

Approximately 30% of basic training shall be devoted to practical exercises. These practical exercises shall if possible be completed during the theoretical training period; in any event, they shall take place not more than three months following the completion of theoretical training.

8.2.3.2.4   *Planning of refresher and advanced training courses*

Additional training courses are intended to refresh existing knowledge and provide information on new developments in the technical and legal fields and in relation to subject matter.

These courses shall take place before the expiry of the period referred to in 8.2.1.6, 8.2.1.7 or 8.2.1.8.

The duration of training courses shall be as follows:

Basic refresher course:

dry cargo vessels	16 lessons of 45 minutes each
tank vessels	16 lessons of 45 minutes each
combined dry cargo vessels and tank vessels	16 lessons of 45 minutes each

Specialization refresher course on gases:	8 lessons of 45 minutes each
Specialization refresher course on chemicals:	8 lessons of 45 minutes each

Each day of training may comprise not more than eight lessons.

If the theoretical training is by correspondence, equivalences to the above-mentioned lessons shall be determined. Training by correspondence shall be completed within a period of nine months.

Approximately 50% of basic training shall be devoted to practical exercises. Practical exercises shall, where possible, be undertaken during the period of theoretical training; in any event, they shall be completed not later than three months following the completion of theoretical training.

8.2.3.3   *Approval of training courses*

8.2.3.3.1   Training courses shall be approved by the competent authority.

8.2.3.3.2   Approval shall be granted only on written application.

8.2.3.3.3   Applications for approval shall be accompanied by:

    (a)   the detailed course curriculum showing the course topics and the length of time to be devoted to them, as well as the teaching method envisaged;

    (b)   the roster of teaching staff, listing their qualifications and the subjects to be taught by each one;

    (c)   information on classrooms and teaching materials, as well as on the facilities available for practical exercises;

    (d)   enrolment requirements.

8.2.3.3.4   The competent authority shall be responsible for monitoring training courses and examinations.

8.2.3.3.5   The competent authority shall grant approval in writing. Such approval shall be subject to the following conditions, <u>inter alia</u>:

    (a)   training courses shall conform to the information accompanying the application for approval;

    (b)   the competent authority may send inspectors to attend training courses;

    (c)   the timetables for the various training courses shall be notified in advance to the competent authority;

    (d)   approval may be withdrawn in the event of failure to abide by the approval conditions.

8.2.3.3.6   The approval document shall indicate whether the course in question is a basic training course, a specialization course or a refresher and advanced training course.

8.2.3.3.7   If, after approval is granted, the organizer of the training course wishes to change conditions affecting the approval, he shall seek the prior agreement of the competent authority. This provision shall apply in particular to the replacement of serving teachers and amendments to syllabuses.

8.2.3.4   *Conduct of training courses*

Training courses shall take account of the current developments in the various subjects taught. The course organizer shall be responsible for ensuring that recent developments are brought to the attention of, and properly understood by, teachers.

CHAPTER 8.3

MISCELLANEOUS REQUIREMENTS TO BE COMPLIED WITH BY THE CREW OF THE VESSEL

8.3.1 **Persons authorized on board**

8.3.1.1 Only the following persons are authorized to be on board:

(a) members of the crew;

(b) persons who, although not being members of the crew, normally live on board; and

(c) persons who are on board for official reasons.

8.3.1.2 The persons referred to in 8.3.1 (b) are not authorized to remain in the protected area of dry cargo vessels or in the cargo area of tank vessels except for short periods.

8.3.2 **Portable lamps**

On board dry cargo vessels, the only portable lamps permitted in the protected area are lamps having their own source of power.

On board tank vessels, the only portable lamps permitted in the cargo area are lamps having their own source of power.

They shall be of the certified safe type.

8.3.3 **Admittance on board**

No unauthorized person shall be permitted on board. This prohibition shall be displayed on notice boards at appropriate places.

8.3.4 **Prohibition on smoking, fire and naked light**

Smoking on board the vessel is prohibited. This prohibition shall be displayed on notice boards at appropriate places.

This prohibition does not apply to the accommodation or the wheelhouse provided their windows, doors, skylights and hatches are closed.

8.3.5 **Risk of sparking**

Work liable to cause sparking is prohibited in the cargo area of tank vessels. This provision does not apply to mooring work.

CHAPTER 8.4

(Reserved)

CHAPTER 8.5

(Reserved)

CHAPTER 8.6

DOCUMENTS

8.6.1   **Certificate of approval**

8.6.1.1   *Model for a certificate of approval for dry cargo vessels*

1

Competent authority: ....

Space reserved for the emblem and name of the State

Certificate of approval No.:

1.   Name of vessel ....

2.   Official number ....

3.   Type of vessel ....

4.   Additional requirements: vessel referred to in 7.1.2.19.1[1]
     vessel referred to in 7.2.2.19.3[1]
     The vessel complies with the additional rules of
     construction referred to in 9.1.0.80 to 9.1.0.95/ 9.2.0.80 to
     9.2.0.95 for double hull vessels[1]

5.   Permitted derogations: ....
....
....
....
....

6.   The validity of this certificate of approval expires on .... (date)

7.   The previous certificate of approval No. ....was issued on ....
by .... (competent authority)

8.   The vessel is approved for the carriage of dangerous goods following:
- inspection on[1] .... (date)
- certification by a recognized classification society[1]
Name of the classification society[1] .... (date) ....

9.   Subject to permitted equivalences:[1] ....
....
....
....

10.   Subject to special authorizations:[1] ....
....
....
....

11.   Issued at: .... on ....
             (place)   (date)

12.   (Stamp)   ....
                                            (competent authority)

                                            ....
                                            (signature)

---

[1] Delete as appropriate

Extension of the validity of the certificate of approval

13.   The validity of this certificate is extended under Chapter 1.16 of ADN

        until ....
               (date)

14.   .... on ....
        (place)   (date)

                                                            ....
15.   (Stamp)   (competent authority)

                                                            ....
                                                              (signature)

8.6.1.2   *Model for a provisional certificate of approval for dry cargo vessels*

1

Competent authority: ....
Space reserved for the emblem and name of the State

Provisional certificate of approval No: ....

1.   Name of vessel ....
2.   Official number ....
3.   Type of vessel ....
4.   Additional requirements:

                         vessel subject to 7.1.2.19.1[1]
                         vessel subject to 7.2.2.19.3[1]
                         The vessel complies with the additional requirements of
                         9.1.0.80 to 9.1.0.95/9.2.0.80. to 9.2.0.95 for double hull
                         vessels[1]

5.   Permitted derogations: ....
       ....
       ....

6.   The provisional certificate of approval is valid[1] ....
       6.1   until ....

       6.2   for a single journey from .... to ....

7.   Issued at .... on ....
       (place)   (date)

8.   (Stamp)   ....
                                      (competent authority)

                                      ....
                                      (signature)

....

---

[1] Delete as appropriate.

NOTE: *This model provisional certificate of approval may be replaced by a single certificate model combining a provisional certificate of inspection and the provisional certificate of approval, provided that this single certificate model contains the same particulars as the model above and is approved by the competent authorities.*

8.6.1.3   *Model for a certificate of approval for tank vessels*

Competent authority: ....
Space reserved for the emblem and name of the State

Certificate of approval No.:

1.   Name of vessel ....
2.   Official number ....
3.   Type of vessel ....
4.   Type of tank vessel ....
5.   Types of cargo tanks   1.   Pressure cargo tanks[1][2]
                                                     2.   Closed cargo tanks[1][2]
                                                     3.   Open cargo tanks with flame arresters[1][2]
                                                     4.   Open cargo tanks[1][2]

6.   Types of cargo tanks   1.   Independent cargo tanks[1][2]
                                                     2.   Integral cargo tanks[1][2]
                                                     3.   Cargo tank wall distinct from the hull[1][2]

7.   Opening pressure of high-velocity vent valves/safety valves .... k/Pa[1][2]

8.   Additional equipment:

     •   Sampling device
           closed ....yes/no[1][2]
           partly closed .... yes/no[1][2]
           sampling opening .... yes/no[1][2]
     •   Water-spray system .... yes/no[1][2]
     •   Cargo heating system:
           possibility of cargo heating from shore ..... yes/no[1][2]
           cargo heating installation on board .... yes/no[1][2]
     •   Cargo refrigeration system .... yes/no[1][2]
     •   Cargo pump-room below deck .... yes/no[1][2]
     •   Pressure relief device .... yes/no[1][2] in ....
     •   Gas supply/return line according to ....
           piping and installation heated .... yes/no[1][2]

9.   Electrical equipment:
     •   Temperature class: ....
     •   Explosion group: ....

10.   Loading rate: .... m³/h
       (see loading instructions)

_____

[1]   Delete as appropriate.

[2]   If the tanks are not all of the same condition, see page 3.

11. Permitted relative density: ....

12. Additional observations ....
....

13. The validity of this certificate of approval expires on .... (date)

14. The previous certificate of approval No. .... was issued on ....
by .... (competent authority)

15. The vessel is approved for the carriage of dangerous goods listed in the attestation
attached to this certificate following:
-       inspection on[1] (date)..
-       certification by a recognized classification society[1]
-       Name of the classification society[1].. (date) ....

16. Subjected to permitted equivalences:[1]
....
....

17. Subject to special authorizations:[1]
....
....

18. Issued at: ....   on ....
                     (place)   (date)

19. (Stamp)   ....
                                                                               (competent authority)

                                                                       ....
                                                                               (signature)

_____
[1] Delete as appropriate

Extension of the validity of the certificate of approval

20. The validity of this certificate is extended under Chapter 1.16 of ADN

    Until ....
    (date)

21. ....   on ....
    (place)   (date)

22. (Stamp)   ....
                                                                               (competent authority)

                                                                       ....
                                                                               (signature)

If the cargo tanks of the vessel are not all of the same condition or the equipment is not the same, their condition and their equipment should be indicated below:

Cargo tank number	1	2	3	4	5	6	7	8	9	10	11	12
pressure cargo tank												
closed cargo tank												
open cargo tank with flame arrester												
open cargo tank												
independent cargo tank												
integral cargo tank												
cargo tank wall distinct from the hull												
opening pressure of the high-velocity vent valve												
closed sampling device												
partly closed sampling device												
sampling opening												
water-spray system												
internal pressure alarm 40 kPa												
possibility of cargo heating from shore												
cargo heating installation												
cargo refrigeration installation												
gas supply/return line according to 9.3.2.22.5 or 9.3.3.22.5												
gas supply line and heated installation												

8.6.1.4   *Model for a certificate of approval for tank vessels*

Competent authority: ....
Space reserved for the emblem and name of the State

Provisional certificate of approval No: ....
1.   Name of vessel ....
2.   Official number ....
3.   Type of vessel ....
4.   Type of tank vessel ....

5.   Types of cargo tanks   1.   Independent cargo tanks   1 2
                                   2.   Integral cargo tanks   1 2
                                   3.   Cargo tank wall distinct from the hull   1 2

6.   Types of cargo tanks   1.   Pressure cargo tanks   1 2
                                   2.   Closed cargo tanks   1 2
                                   3.   Open cargo tanks with flame arresters   1 2
                                   4.   Open cargo tanks   1 2

7.   Opening pressure of high-velocity vent valves/safety valves .... kPa   1 2

8.   Additional equipment:
      • Sampling device
            closed .... yes/no[1][2]
            partly closed .... yes/no[1][2]
            sampling opening .... yes/no[1][2]
      • Water-spray system .... yes/no[1][2]
      • Cargo heating system:
            possibility of cargo heating from shore .... yes/no[1][2]
            cargo heating installation on board .... yes/no[1][2]
      • cargo refrigeration system .... yes/no[1][2]
      • cargo pump-room below deck .... yes/no[1][2]

9.   Electrical equipment:
      • Temperature class: ....
      • Explosion group: ....

10.   Loading rate ....   m³/h

11.   Permitted relative density: ....

12.   Additionnal observations: ....

....
_____
[1] Delete as appropriate.

[2] If the tanks are not all of the same type, see page 3

13. The provisional certificate of approval is valid[1] ....
    13.1   until ....

    13.2   for a single journey from .... to ....

14. Issued at .... on ....
    (place)   (date)

15. (Stamp)   ....
                                    (competent authority)

                                    ....
                                    (signature)

----

[1] Delete as appropriate.

NOTE: *This model provisional certificate of approval may be replaced by a single certificate model combining a provisional certificate of inspection and the provisional certificate of approval, provided that this single certificate model contains the same particulars as the model above and is approved by the competent authorities.*

If the cargo tanks of the vessel are not all of the same condition or the equipment is not the same, their condition and their equipment should be indicated below:

Cargo tank number	1	2	3	4	5	6	7	8	9	10	11	12
pressure cargo tank												
closed cargo tank												
open cargo tank with flame arrester												
open cargo tank												
independent cargo tank												
integral cargo tank												
cargo tank wall distinct from the hull												
opening pressure of the high-velocity vent valve												
closed sampling device												
partly closed sampling device												
sampling opening												
water-spray system												
internal pressure alarm 40 kPa ……..												
possibility of cargo heating from shore												
cargo heating installation												
cargo refrigeration installation												
gas supply/return line according to 9.3.2.22.5 or 9.3.3.22.5												
gas supply line and heated installation												

8.6.2   **Certificate of special knowledge of ADN according to 8.2.1.2, 8.2.1.4 or 8.2.1.5**

(Format: A6, Colour: orange)

(Space reserved for the emblem of State, competent authority)

ADN certificate

of special knowledge of ADN

No. of certificate: ....

Name
First name(s): ....

Born on: ....

Nationality: ....

Signature of holder: ....

The holder of this certificate has special knowledge of ADN

The certificate is valid for special knowledge of ADN according to
8.2.1.2 (dry cargo vessels)*
8.2.1.2 (tanks vessels)*
8.2.1.4*
8.2.1.5*

until: ....

Issued by: ....

Date: ....

(Stamp)

Signature: ....

_____
* Delete as appropriate.

(Recto)   *(Verso)*

8.6.3   **Checklist ADN**

1

Checklist ADN

concerning the observance of safety provisions and the implementation of the necessary measures for loading/unloading

- **Particulars of vessel**

....   No. ....
(name of vessel)   (official number)

....
(vessel type)

- **Particulars of loading or unloading operations**

....
(shore loading or unloading installation)   (place)

....
(date)   (time)

- **Particulars of the cargo**

Quantity m^3	Name of product	Identification number	Class
....	....	....	....
....	....	....	....
....	....	....	....

- **Particulars of last cargo***

Name of product	Identification number	Class
....	....	....
....	....	....
....	....	....

---

* *To be filled in only if vessel is to be loaded.*

Loading rate (not to be filled in if vessel is to be loaded with gas)

Name of substance	Cargo tank number	agreed rate of loading/unloading					
		start		half way		end	
		rate m³/h	quantity m³	rate m³/h	quantity m³	rate m³/h	quantity m³
....	....	....	....	....	....	......	....
....	....	....	....	....	....	......	....
....	....	....	....	....	....	......	....

Will the cargo piping be drained after loading or unloading by stripping or by blowing residual quantities to the shore installation/to the vessel?*

by blowing*
by stripping*

If drained by blowing, how?

....
(e.g. air, inert gas, sleeve)

.... kPa
(permissible maximum pressure in the cargo tank)

....litres
(estimated residual quantity)

Questions to the master or the person mandated by him and the person in charge at the loading/unloading place

Loading/unloading may only be started after all questions on the checklist have been checked off by "X", i.e. answered with YES and the list has been signed by both persons.

Non-applicable questions have to be deleted.

If not all questions can be answered with YES, loading/unloading is only allowed with consent of the competent authority.

---

* *Delete as appropriate.*

			vessel	**3** loading/ unloading place
1.	Is the vessel permitted to carry this cargo?		O*	O*
2.	Did the master or the person mandated by him receive the instructions in writing referred to in 5.4.3 from the consignor?		O*	O*
3.	Is the vessel well moored in view of local circumstances?		O	–
4.	Have suitable means been provided at the fore and at the aft of the vessel, for boarding or leaving, including in cases of emergency?		O	O
5.	Are the escape routes and the loading/unloading place adequately lighted?		O	O
6.	Vessel/shore connection			
	6.1	Are the cargo hoses between vessel and shore in satisfactory condition?	–	O
		Are these hoses correctly connected?	–	O
	6.2	Are all the connecting flanges fitted with suitable gaskets?	–	O
	6.3	Are all the connecting bolts fitted and tightened?	O	O
	6.4	Are the shoreside loading arms free to move in all directions and do the hoses have enough room for easy movement?	–	O
7.	Are all flanges of the connections of the pipes for loading and unloading and of the vapour pipe not in use, correctly blanked off?		O	O
8.	Are suitable means of collecting leakages placed under the pipe connections which are in use?		O	O
9.	Are the movable connecting pieces between the ballast and bilge piping on the one hand and the pipes for loading and unloading on the other hand disconnected?		O	-
10.	Is continuous and suitable supervision of loading/unloading ensured for the whole period of the operation?		O	O
11.	Is communication between vessel and shore ensured?		O	O

----

* *To be filled in only if vessel is to be loaded.*

		vessel	loading/ unloading place **4**
12.1	For the loading of the vessel, is the vapour pipe, where required, or if it exists, connected with the shore gas return line?	O	O
12.2	Is it ensured that the shore installation is such that the pressure at the connecting point cannot exceed the opening pressure of the high-velocity vent valves?	–	O*
12.3	When anti-explosion protection is required in Chapter 3.2,Table C, column (17) does the shore installation ensure that its venting pipe or pressure compensation pipe is such that the vessel is protected against detonations and flame fronts from the shore.	–	O
13.	Is it know what actions are to be taken in the event of an "Emergency-stop" and an "Alarm"?	O	O
14.	Check on the most important operational requirements:		
	– Are the required fire extinguishing systems and appliances operational?	O	O
	– Have all valves and other closing devices been checked for correct open - or closed position?	O	O
	– Has smoking been generally prohibited?	O	O
	– Are the flame-operated heating, cooking and cooling applications on board turned off?	O	–
	– Are the liquefied gas installations shut off at the main check valve?	O	–
	– Is the voltage cut off from the radar installations?	O	–
	– Is all electrical equipment marked red switched off?	O	–
	– Are all windows and doors closed?	O	–
15.1	Has the starting working pressure of the vessels cargo discharge pump been adjusted to the permissible working pressure of the shore installation?	O	–
15.2	Has the starting working pressure of the shore pump been adjusted to the permissible working pressure of the on board installation?	–	O
16.	Is the liquid level alarm-installation operational?	O	–
17.	Is the level control device activating the overflow prevention system plugged in, in working order and tested?	O	O

			vessel	**5** loading/ unloading place
18.	To be filled in only in the case of loading or unloading of substances for the carriage of which a vessel of the closed type or a vessel of the open type with flame arrester is required. Are the cargo tank hatches and cargo tank inspection, gauging and sampling openings closed or protected by flame arresters in good condition?		O	–

Checked, filled in and signed

for the vessel: for the installation of loading and unloading

....
          name (in capital letters)   name (in capital letters)

....
                  (signature)   (signature)

Explanation

Question 3

"Well moored" means that the vessel is fastened to the pier or the cargo transfer station in such a way that, without intervention of a third person, movements of the vessel in any direction that could hamper the operation of the cargo transfer gear will be prevented. Established or predictable variations of the water-level at that location and special factors have to be taken into account.

Question 4

It must be possible to board or escape from the vessel at any time. If there is none or only one protected escape route available at the shoreside for a quick escape from the vessel in case of emergency, a suitable means of escape has to be provided on the vessel side (e.g. a lowered dinghy).

Question 6

A valid inspection certificate for the loading/unloading hoses must be available on board. The material of the hoses must be able to withstand the expected loads and be suitable for cargo transfer of the respective substances. The term cargo hoses includes hoses as well as the shoreside loading/discharging arms. The cargo transfer hoses between vessel and shore must be placed so that they cannot be damaged by variations of the water-level, passing vessels and/or loading/unloading operations. All flange connections are to be fitted with appropriate gaskets and sufficient bolt connections in order to exclude the possibility of leakage.

Question 10

Loading/unloading must be supervised on board and ashore so that dangers which may occur in the vicinity of cargo hoses can be recognized immediately. When supervision is effected by additional technical means it must be agreed between the shore installation and the vessel how it is to be ensured.

Question 11

For a safe loading/unloading operation good communications between vessel and shore are required. For this purpose telephone and radio equipment may be used only if of an explosion protected type and located within reach of the supervisor.

Question 13

Before the start of the loading/unloading operation the representative of the shore installation and the master or the person mandated by him must agree on the applicable procedure. The specific properties of the substances to be loaded/unloaded have to be taken into account.

8.6.4   **Discharge of residual quantities and stripping systems**

8.6.4.1   *Device for the discharge of residual quantities*

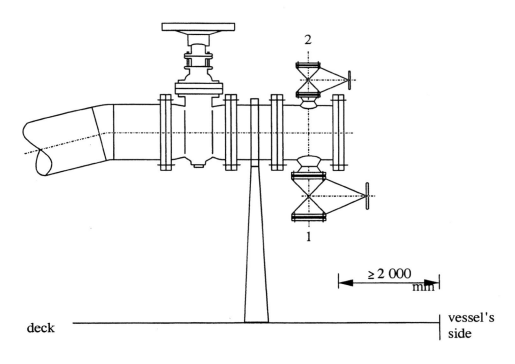

1.   Connection for the discharge of residual quantities

2.   Connection of the shore installation intended for blowing residual quantities to the short installation by means of a gas

8.6.4.2   *Test of the stripping system*

8.6.4.2.1   Before the start of the test, the cargo tanks and their piping shall be clean. The cargo tanks shall be safe for entry.

8.6.4.2.2   During the test, the trim and list of the vessel shall not exceed normal operating values.

8.6.4.2.3   During the test, a back pressure of not less than 300 kPa (3 bar) shall be maintained at the device for discharge of residual quantities fitted on the pipe for unloading.

8.6.4.2.4   The test shall comprise :

(a)   The filling of the cargo tank with water until the suction intake inside the tank is submerged;

(b)   The pumping out of the water and the emptying of the cargo tank and the corresponding piping by means of the tank's stripping system;

(c)   The collection of the remaining water at the following points:

–   The cargo tank suction intake;

–   The bottom of the cargo tank where water has collected;

–   The lowest point drain of the cargo pump;

–   At all the lowest points of the piping associated with the cargo tank up to the device for the discharge of residual quantities.

8.6.4.2.5   The quantity of water collected as described in 8.6.4.2.4 (c) shall be measured precisely and noted in the test certificate referred to in 8.6.4.3.

8.6.4.2.6   The competent authority or the recognized classification society shall set out all the operations required for the test in the test certificate.

This certificate shall include at least the following data:

–   trim of the vessel during the test;

–   list of the vessel during the test;

–   tank unloading order;

–   back pressure at the device for the discharge of residual quantities;

–   residual quantity per tank;

–   residual quantity per piping system;

–   duration of the stripping operation;

–   cargo tank plan, duly completed.

8.6.4.3   *Certificate for the test of the stripping system*

Certificate for the test of the stripping system

1.   Name of vessel: ....

2.   Official number: ....

3.   Type of tank vessel: ....

4.   Number of certificate of approval: ....

5.   Date of test: ....

6.   Place of test: ....

7.   Number of cargo tanks: ....

8.   The following residual quantities were measured during the test

    Tank 1: ....litres   Tank 2: ....litres
    Tank 3: ....litres   Tank 4: ....litres
    Tank 5: ....litres   Tank 6: ....litres
    Tank 7: ....litres   Tank 8: ....litres
    Tank 9: ....litres   Tank 10: ....litres
    Tank 11: ....litres   Tank 12: ....litres
    Slop tank 1: ....litres   Slop tank 2 : ... .litres
    Slop tank 3: ... . litres
    Piping system 1: ....litres
    Piping system 2: ....litres

9.   During the test, the back pressure at the device for the discharge of residual quantities
    was ....kPa.

10.   The tanks were discharged in the following order:

    tank...,   tank...,   tank...,   tank...,   tank...,
    tank....,   tank...,   tank...,   tank...,   tank...,

11.   During the test, the trim of the vessel was ....
    and the list of the vessel was ....

12.   The total duration of the stripping operation was... h.

    ....
         (date)   (signature)

PART 9

Rules for construction

CHAPTER 9.1

RULES FOR CONSTRUCTION OF DRY CARGO VESSELS

9.1.0   **Rules for construction applicable to dry cargo vessels**

Provisions of 9.1.0.0 to 9.1.0.79 apply to dry cargo vessels.

9.1.0.0   *Materials of construction*

The vessel's hull shall be constructed of shipbuilding steel or other metal, provided that this metal has at least equivalent mechanical properties and resistance to the effects of temperature and fire.

9.1.0.1-   (*Reserved*)
9.1.0.10

9.1.0.11   **Holds**

9.1.0.11.1   (a)   Each hold shall be bounded fore and aft by watertight metal bulkheads.

            (b)   The holds shall have no common bulkhead with the oil fuel tanks.

9.1.0.11.2   The bottom of the holds shall be such as to permit them to be cleaned and dried.

9.1.0.11.3   The hatchway covers shall be spraytight and weathertight or be covered by waterproof tarpaulins.

Tarpaulins used to cover the holds shall not readily ignite.

9.1.0.11.4   No heating appliances shall be installed in the holds.

9.1.0.12   *Ventilation*

9.1.0.12.1   Ventilation of each hold shall be provided by means of two mutually independent extraction ventilators having a capacity of not less than five changes of air per hour based on the volume of the empty hold. The ventilator fan shall be designed so that no sparks may be emitted on contact of the impeller blades with the housing and no static electricity may be generated. The extraction ducts shall be positioned at the extreme ends of the hold and extend down to not more than 50 mm above the bottom. The extraction of gases and vapours through the duct shall also be ensured for carriage in bulk.

Ventilators are not required on vessels only carrying dangerous goods packed in containers. If the extraction ducts are movable they shall be suitable for the ventilator assembly and capable of being firmly fixed. Protection shall be ensured against bad weather and spray. The air intake shall be ensured during ventilation.

9.1.0.12.2   The ventilation system of a hold shall be arranged so that dangerous gases cannot penetrate into the accommodation, wheelhouse or engine rooms.

9.1.0.12.3   Ventilation shall be provided for the accommodation and for service spaces.

9.1.0.13-   (*Reserved*)
9.1.0.16

9.1.0.17 *Accommodation and service spaces*

9.1.0.17.1   The accommodation shall be separated from the holds by metal bulkheads having no openings.

9.1.0.17.2   Gastight closing appliances shall be provided for openings in the accommodation and wheelhouse facing the holds.

9.1.0.17.3   No entrances or openings of the engine rooms and service spaces shall face the protected area.

9.1.0.18-   (*Reserved*)
9.1.0.19

9.1.0.20   *Water ballast*

The double-hull spaces and double bottoms may be arranged for being filled with water ballast.

9.1.0.21-   (*Reserved*)
9.1.0.30

9.1.0.31   *Engines*

9.1.0.31.1   Only internal combustion engines running on fuel having a flashpoint above 55 °C are allowed.

9.1.0.31.2   The air vents in the engine rooms and the air intakes of the engines which do not take air in directly from the engine room shall be located not less than 2.00 m from the protected area.

9.1.0.31.3   Sparking shall not be possible in the protected area.

9.1.0.32   *Oil fuel tanks*

9.1.0.32.1   Double bottoms within the hold area may be arranged as oil fuel tanks provided their depth is not less than 0.6 m. Oil fuel pipes and openings to such tanks are not permitted in the holds.

9.1.0.32.2   The air pipes of all oil fuel tanks shall be led to 0.50 m above the open deck. Their open ends and the open ends of the overflow pipes leaking to the deck shall be fitted with a protective device consisting of a gauze grid or by a perforated plate.

9.1.0.33   (*Reserved*)

9.1.0.34   *Exhaust pipes*

9.1.0.34.1   Exhausts shall be evacuated from the vessel into the open air either upwards through an exhaust pipe .or through the shell plating. The exhaust outlet shall be located not less than 2.00 m from the hatchway openings. The exhaust pipes of engines shall be arranged so that the exhausts are led away from the vessel. The exhaust pipes shall not be located within the protected area.

9.1.0.34.2   Exhaust pipes shall be provided with a device preventing the escape of sparks, e.g. spark arresters.

9.1.0.35 *Stripping installation*

The stripping pumps intended for the holds shall be located in the protected area. This requirement shall not apply when stripping is effected by eductors.

9.1.0.36- *(Reserved)*
9.1.0.39

9.1.0.40 *Fire-extinguishing arrangements*

9.1.0.40.1 A fire-extinguishing system shall be installed on the vessel. This system shall comply with the following requirements:

- It shall be supplied by two independent fire or ballast pumps one of which shall be ready for use at any time. These pumps shall not be installed in the same space;

- It shall be provided with a water main fitted with at least three hydrants in the protected area above deck. Three suitable and sufficiently long hoses with spray nozzles having a diameter of not less than 12 mm shall be provided. It shall be possible to reach any point of the deck in the protected area simultaneously with at least two jets of water which do not emanate from the same hydrant. A spring-loaded non-return valve shall be fitted to ensure that no gases can escape through the fire-extinguishing system into the accommodation or service spaces outside the protected area;

- The capacity of the system shall be at least sufficient for a jet of water to reach a distance of not less than the vessel's breadth from any location on board with two spray nozzles being used at the same time.

A single fire or ballast pump shall suffice on board pushed barges without their own means of propulsion.

9.1.0.40.2 In addition, the engine rooms shall be provided with a permanently fixed fire-extinguishing system meeting the following requirements:

9.1.0.40.2.1 *Extinguishing agents*

For the protection of spaces in engine rooms, boiler rooms and pump rooms, only permanently fixed fire-extinguishing systems using the following extinguishing agents are permitted:

(a) CO_2 (carbon dioxide);

(b)   HFC 227 ea (heptafluoropropane);

(c)   IG-541 (52% nitrogen, 40% argon, 8% carbon dioxide).

Other extinguishing agents are permitted only on the basis of recommendations by the Administrative Committee.

9.1.0.40.2.2 *Ventilation, air extraction*

(a)   The combustion air required by the combustion engines which ensure propulsion should not come from spaces protected by permanently fixed fire-extinguishing systems. This requirement is not mandatory if the vessel has two independent main engine rooms with a gastight separation or if, in addition to the main engine room, there is a separate engine room installed with a bow thruster that can independently ensure propulsion in the event of a fire in the main engine room.

(b) All forced ventilation systems in the space to be protected shall be shut down automatically as soon as the fire-extinguishing system is activated.

(c) All openings in the space to be protected which permit air to enter or gas to escape shall be fitted with devices enabling them to be closed rapidly. It shall be clear whether they are open or closed.

(d) · Air escaping from the pressure-relief valves of the pressurised air tanks installed in the engine rooms shall be evacuated to the open air.

(e) Overpressure or negative pressure caused by the diffusion of the extinguishing agent shall not destroy the constituent elements of the space to be protected. It shall be possible to ensure the safe equalisation of pressure.

(f) Protected spaces shall be provided with a means of extracting the extinguishing agent. If extraction devices are installed, it shall not be possible to start them up during extinguishing.

9.1.0.40.2.3   *Fire alarm system*

The space to be protected shall be monitored by an appropriate fire alarm system. The alarm signal shall be audible in the wheelhouse, the accommodation and the space to be protected.

9.1.0.40.2.4   *Piping system*

(a) The extinguishing agent shall be routed to and distributed in the space to be protected by means of a permanent piping system. Piping installed in the space to be protected and the reinforcements it incorporates shall be made of steel. This shall not apply to the connecting nozzles of tanks and compensators provided that the materials used have equivalent fire-retardant properties. Piping shall be protected against corrosion both internally and externally.

(b) The discharge nozzles shall be so arranged as to ensure the regular diffusion of the extinguishing agent.

9.1.0.40.2.5   *Triggering device*

(a) Automatically activated fire-extinguishing systems are not permitted.

(b) It shall be possible to activate the fire-extinguishing system from a suitable point located outside the space to be protected.

(c) Triggering devices shall be so installed that they can be activated in the event of a fire and so that the risk of their breakdown in the event of a fire or an explosion in the space to be protected is reduced as far as possible.

Systems which are not mechanically activated shall be supplied from two energy sources independent of each other. These energy sources shall be located outside the space to be protected. The control lines located in the space to be protected shall be so designed as to remain capable of operating in the event of a fire for a minimum of 30 minutes. The electrical installations are deemed to meet this requirement if they conform to the IEC 60331-21:1999 standard.

When the triggering devices are so placed as not to be visible, the component concealing them shall carry the "Fire-fighting system" symbol, each side being not less than 10 cm in length, with the following text in red letters on a white ground:

Fire-extinguishing system

(d)   If the fire-extinguishing system is intended to protect several spaces, it shall comprise a separate and clearly-marked triggering device for each space;

(e)   The instructions shall be posted alongside all triggering devices and shall be clearly visible and indelible. The instructions shall be in a language the master can read and understand and if this language is not English, French or German, they shall be in English, French or German. They shall include information concerning:

   (i)   the activation of the fire-extinguishing system;

   (ii)   the need to ensure that all persons have left the space to be protected;

   (iii)   the correct behaviour of the crew in the event of activation;

   (iv)   the correct behaviour of the crew in the event of the failure of the fire-extinguishing system to function properly.

(f)   The instructions shall mention that prior to the activation of the fire-extinguishing system, combustion engines installed in the space and aspirating air from the space to be protected, shall be shut down.

9.1.0.40.2.6   *Alarm device*

(a)   Permanently fixed fire-extinguishing systems shall be fitted with an audible and visual alarm device;

(b)   The alarm device shall be set off automatically as soon as the fire-extinguishing system is first activated. The alarm device shall function for an appropriate period of time before the extinguishing agent is released; it shall not be possible to turn it off;

(c)   Alarm signals shall be clearly visible in the spaces to be protected and their access points and be clearly audible under operating conditions corresponding to the highest possible sound level. It shall be possible to distinguish them clearly from all other sound and visual signals in the space to be protected;

(d)   Sound alarms shall also be clearly audible in adjoining spaces, with the communicating doors shut, and under operating conditions corresponding to the highest possible sound level;

(e)   If the alarm device is not intrinsically protected against short circuits, broken wires and drops in voltage, it shall be possible to monitor its operation;

(f)   A sign with the following text in red letters on a white ground shall be clearly posted at the entrance to any space the extinguishing agent may reach:

WARNING, FIRE-EXTINGUISHING SYSTEM!
LEAVE THIS SPACE IMMEDIATELY WHEN THE ... (DESCRIPTION)
ALARM IS ACTIVATED!

9.1.0.40.2.7   *Pressurised tanks, fittings and piping*

(a)   Pressurised tanks, fittings and piping shall conform to the requirements of the competent authority.

(b)   Pressurised tanks shall be installed in accordance with the manufacturer's instructions.

(c)   Pressurised tanks, fittings and piping shall not be installed in the accommodation.

(d)   The temperature of cabinets and storage spaces for pressurised tanks shall not exceed 50 °C.

(e)   Cabinets or storage spaces on deck shall be securely stowed and shall have vents so placed that in the event of a pressurised tank not being gastight, the escaping gas cannot penetrate into the vessel. Direct connections with other spaces are not permitted.

9.1.0.40.2.8   *Quantity of extinguishing agent*

If the quantity of extinguishing agent is intended for more than one space, the quantity of extinguishing agent available does not need to be greater than the quantity required for the largest of the spaces thus protected.

9.1.0.40.2.9   *Installation, maintenance, monitoring and documents*

(a)   The mounting or modification of the system shall only be performed by a company specialised in fire-extinguishing systems. The instructions (product data sheet, safety data sheet) provided by the manufacturer of the extinguishing agent or the system shall be followed.

(b)   The system shall be inspected by an expert:

(i)   before being brought into service;

(ii)   each time it is put back into service after activation;

(iii)   after every modification or repair;

(iv)   regularly, not less than every two years.

(c)   During the inspection, the expert is required to check that the system conforms to the requirements of 9.1.0.40.2.

(d)   The inspection shall include, as a minimum:

(i)   an external inspection of the entire system;

(ii)   an inspection to ensure that the piping is leakproof;

(iii)   an inspection to ensure that the control and activation systems are in good working order;

(iv)   an inspection of the pressure and contents of tanks;

(v)   an inspection to ensure that the means of closing the space to be protected are leakproof;

(vi)   an inspection of the fire alarm system;

(vii)   an inspection of the alarm device.

(e)   The person performing the inspection shall establish, sign and date a certificate of inspection.

(f)   The number of permanently fixed fire-extinguishing systems shall be mentioned in the inspection certificate.

9.1.0.40.2.10   *Fire-extinguishing system operating with CO_2*

In addition to the requirements contained in 9.1.0.40.2.1 to 9.1.0.40.2.9, fire-extinguishing systems using CO_2 as an extinguishing agent shall conform to the following provisions:

(a)   Tanks of CO_2 shall be placed in a gastight space or cabinet separated from other spaces. The doors of such storage spaces and cabinets shall open outwards; they shall be capable of being locked and shall carry on the outside the symbol "Warning: danger," not less than 5 cm high and "CO_2" in the same colours and the same size;

(b)   Storage cabinets or spaces for CO_2 tanks located below deck shall only be accessible from the outside. These spaces shall have an artificial ventilation system with extractor hoods and shall be completely independent of the other ventilation systems on board;

(c)   The level of filling of CO_2 tanks shall not exceed 0.75 kg/l. The volume of depressurised CO_2 shall be taken to be 0.56 m^3/kg;

(d)   The concentration of CO_2 in the space to be protected shall be not less than 40% of the gross volume of the space. This quantity shall be released within 120 seconds. It shall be possible to monitor whether diffusion is proceeding correctly;

(e)   The opening of the tank valves and the control of the diffusing valve shall correspond to two different operations;

(f)   The appropriate period of time mentioned in 9.1.0.40.2.6 (b) shall be not less than 20 seconds. A reliable installation shall ensure the timing of the diffusion of CO_2.

9.1.0.40.2.11   *Fire-extinguishing system operating with HFC-227 ea (heptafluoropropane)*

In addition to the requirements of 9.1.0.40.2.1 to 9.1.0.40.2.9, fire-extinguishing systems using HFC-227 ea as an extinguishing agent shall conform to the following provisions:

(a)   Where there are several spaces with different gross volumes, each space shall be equipped with its own fire-extinguishing system;

(b)   Every tank containing HFC-227 ea placed in the space to be protected shall be fitted with a device to prevent overpressure. This device shall ensure that the contents of the tank are safely diffused in the space to be protected if the tank is subjected to fire, when the fire-extinguishing system has not been brought into service;

(c)   Every tank shall be fitted with a device permitting control of the gas pressure;

(d)   The level of filling of tanks shall not exceed 1.15 kg/l. The specific volume of depressurised HFC-227 ea shall be taken to be 0.1374 m^3/kg;

(e)   The concentration of HFC-227 ea in the space to be protected shall be not less than 8% of the gross volume of the space. This quantity shall be released within 10 seconds;

(f)   Tanks of HFC-227 ea shall be fitted with a pressure monitoring device which triggers an audible and visual alarm in the wheelhouse in the event of an unscheduled loss of propellant gas. Where there is no wheelhouse, the alarm shall be triggered outside the space to be protected;

(g)   After discharge, the concentration in the space to be protected shall not exceed 10.5% (volume);

(h)   The fire-extinguishing system shall not comprise aluminium parts.

9.1.0.40.2.12   *Fire-extinguishing system operating with IG-541*

In addition to the requirements of 9.1.0.40.2.1 to 9.1.0.40.2.9, fire-extinguishing systems using IG-541 as an extinguishing agent shall conform to the following provisions:

(a)   Where there are several spaces with different gross volumes, every space shall be equipped with its own fire-extinguishing system;

(b)   Every tank containing IG-541 placed in the space to be protected shall be fitted with a device to prevent overpressure. This device shall ensure that the contents of the tank are safely diffused in the space to be protected if the tank is subjected to fire, when the fire-extinguishing system has not been brought into service;

(c)   Each tank shall be fitted with a device for checking the contents;

(d)   The filling pressure of the tanks shall not exceed 200 bar at a temperature of +15 °C;

(e)   The concentration of IG-541 in the space to be protected shall be not less than 44% and not more than 50% of the gross volume of the space. This quantity shall be released within 120 seconds.

9.1.0.40.2.13   *Fire-extinguishing system for physical protection*

In order to ensure physical protection in the engine rooms, boiler rooms and pump rooms, fire-extinguishing systems are accepted solely on the basis of recommendations by the Administrative Committee.

9.1.0.40.3   The two hand fire-extinguishers referred to in 8.1.4 shall be located in the protected area.

9.1.0.40.4   The fire-extinguishing agent in the permanently fixed fire-extinguishing system shall be suitable and sufficient for fighting fires.

9.1.0.41   *Fire and naked light*

9.1.0.41.1   The outlets of funnels shall be located not less than 2 m from the hatchway openings. Arrangements shall be provided to prevent the escape of sparks and the entry of water.

9.1.0.41.2   Heating, cooking and refrigerating appliances shall not be fuelled with liquid fuels, liquid gas or solid fuels. The installation in the engine room or other separate space of heating appliances fuelled with liquid fuel having a flashpoint above 55 °C is, however, permitted.

Cooking and refrigerating appliances are permitted only in wheelhouses with metal floor and in the accommodation.

9.1.0.41.3 Electric lighting appliances only are permitted outside the accommodation and the wheelhouse.

9.1.0.42-
9.1.0.51 *(Reserved)*

9.1.0.52 *Type and location of electrical equipment*

9.1.0.52.1 It shall be possible to isolate the electrical equipment in the protected area by means of centrally located switches except where:

- it is of a certified safe type corresponding at least to temperature class T4 and explosion group II B; and

- in the protected area it is of the limited explosion risk type.

The corresponding electrical circuits shall have control lamps to indicate whether or not the circuits are live.

The switches shall be protected against unintended unauthorized operation. The sockets used in this area shall be so designed as to prevent connections being made except when they are not live. Submerged pumps installed or used in the holds shall be of the certified safe type at least for temperature class T4 and explosion group II B.

9.1.0.52.2 Electric motors for hold ventilators which are arranged in the air flow shall be of the certified safe type.

9.1.0.52.3 Sockets for the connection of signal lights, gangway lighting and containers shall be fitted to the vessel close to the signal mast or the gangway or the containers. Sockets intended to supply the submerged pumps and hold ventilators shall be permanently fitted to the vessel in the vicinity of the hatches.

9.1.0.53-
9.1.0.55 *(Reserved)*

9.1.0.56 *Electric cables*

9.1.0.56.1 Cables and sockets in the protected area shall be protected against mechanical damage.

9.1.0.56.2 Movable cables are prohibited in the protected area, except for intrinsically safe electric circuits or for the supply of signal lights and gangway lighting, for containers, for submerged pumps, hold ventilators and for electrically operated cover gantries.

9.1.0.56.3 For movable cables permitted in accordance with 9.1.0.56.2 above, only rubber-sheathed cables of type H07 RN-F in accordance with 245 IEC 66 or cables of at least equivalent design having conductors with a cross-section of not less than 1.5 mm^2, shall be used. These cables shall be as short as possible and installed so that accidental damage is not likely to occur.

9.1.0.57-
9.1.0.69 *(Reserved)*

9.1.0.70   *Metal wires, masts*

All metal wires passing over the holds and all masts shall be earthed, unless they are electrically bonded to the metal hull of the vessel through their installation.

9.1.0.71   *Admittance on board*

The notice boards displaying the prohibition of admittance in accordance with 7.1.3.71 shall be clearly legible from either side of the vessel.

9.1.0.72-   *(Reserved)*
9.1.0.73

9.1.0.74   *Prohibition of smoking, fire and naked light*

9.1.0.74.1   The notice boards displaying the prohibition of smoking in accordance with 7.1.3.74 shall be clearly legible from either side of the vessel.

9.1.0.74.2   Notice boards indicating the circumstances under which the prohibition applies shall be fitted near the entrances to the spaces where smoking or the use of fire or naked light is not always prohibited.

9.1.0.74.3   Ashtrays shall be provided close to each exit of the accommodation and the wheelhouse.

9.1.0.75-   *(Reserved)*
9.1.0.79

9.1.0.80   *Additional rules applicable to double-hull vessels*

The rules of 9.1.0.88 to 9.1.0.99 are applicable to double-hull vessels intended to carry dangerous goods of Classes 2, 3, 4.1, 4.2, 4.3, 5.1, 5.2, 6.1, 7, 8 or 9, except those for which label No. 1 is prescribed in column (5) of Table A of Chapter 3.2, in quantities exceeding those of 7.1.4.1.1.

9.1.0.81-   *(Reserved)*
9.1.0.87

9.1.0.88   *Classification*

9.1.0.88.1   Double-hull vessels intended to carry dangerous goods of Classes 2, 3, 4.1, 4.2, 4.3, 5.1, 5.2, 6.1, 7, 8 or 9 except those for which label No. 1 is prescribed in column (5) of Table A of Chapter 3.2, in quantities exceeding those referred to in 7.1.4.1.1 shall be built or transformed under survey of a recognised classification society in accordance with the rules established by this classification society to its highest class. This shall be confirmed by the classification society by the issue of an appropriate certificate.

9.1.0.88.2   Continuation of class is not required.

9.1.0.88.3   Future conversions and major repairs to the hull shall be carried out under survey of this classification society.

9.1.0.89-   *(Reserved)*
9.1.0.90

9.1.0.91 *Holds*

9.1.0.91.1 The vessel shall be built as a double-hull vessel with double-hull spaces and double bottom within the protected area.

9.1.0.91.2 The distance between the sides of the vessel and the longitudinal bulkheads of the hold shall be not less than 0.80 m. Regardless of the requirements relating to the width of walkways on deck, a reduction of this distance to 0.60 m is permitted, provided that, compared with the scantlings specified in the rules for construction published by a recognised classification society, the following reinforcements have been made:

(a) Where the vessel's sides are constructed according to the longitudinal framing system, the frame spacing shall not exceed 0.60 m.

The longitudinals shall be supported by web frames with lightening holes similar to the floors in the double bottom and spaced not more than 1.80 m apart;

(b) Where the vessel's sides are constructed according to the transverse framing system, either:

– two longitudinal side shell stringers shall be fitted. The distance between the two stringers and between the uppermost stringer and the gangboard shall not exceed 0.80 m. The depth of the stringers shall be at least equal to that of the transverse frames and the cross-section of the face plate shall be not less than 15 cm^2.

The longitudinal stringers shall be supported by web frames with lightening holes similar to plate floors in the double bottom and spaced not more than 3.60 m apart. The transverse shell frames and the hold bulkhead vertical stiffeners shall be connected at the bilge by a bracket plate with a height of not less than 0.90 m and thickness equal to the thickness of the floors; or

– web frames with lightening holes similar to the double bottom plate floors shall be arranged on each transverse frame;

(c) The gangboards shall be supported by transverse bulkheads or cross-ties spaced not more than 32 m apart.

As an alternative to compliance with the requirements of (c) above, a proof by calculation, issued by a recognised classification society confirming that additional reinforcements have been fitted in the double-hull spaces and that the vessel's transverse strength may be regarded as satisfactory.

9.1.0.91.3 The depth of the double bottom shall be not less than 0.50 m. The depth below a suction well may however be locally reduced to 0.40 m, provided that the suction well has a capacity of not more than 0.03 m^3.

9.1.0.92 *Emergency exit*

Spaces the entrances or exits of which are partly or fully immersed in damaged condition shall be provided with an emergency exit not less than 0.10 m above the waterline. This does not apply to forepeak and afterpeak.

9.1.0.93 *Stability (general)*

9.1.0.93.1 Proof of sufficient stability shall be furnished including stability in the damaged condition.

9.1.0.93.2   The basic values for the stability calculation - the vessel's lightweight and the location of the centre of gravity - shall be determined either by means of an inclining experiment or by detailed mass and moment calculation. In the latter case the lightweight shall be checked by means of a lightweight test with a resulting difference of not more than ± 5% between the mass determined by the calculation and the displacement determined by the draught readings.

9.1.0.93.3   Proof of sufficient intact stability shall be furnished for all stages of loading and unloading and for the final loading condition.

          Floatability after damage shall be proved for the most unfavourable loading condition. For this purpose calculated proof of sufficient stability shall be established for critical intermediate stages of flooding and for the final stage of flooding. Negative values of stability in intermediate stages of flooding may be accepted only if the continued range of curve of righting lever in damaged condition indicates adequate positive values of stability.

9.1.0.94   *Stability (intact)*

9.1.0.94.1   The requirements for intact stability resulting from the damaged stability calculation shall be fully complied with.

9.1.0.94.2   For the carriage of containers, proof of sufficient stability shall also be furnished in accordance with the provisions of the Regulations referred to in 1.1.4.6.

9.1.0.94.3   The most stringent of the requirements of 9.1.0.94.1 and 9.1.0.94.2 above shall prevail for the vessel.

9.1.0.95   *Stability (damaged condition)*

9.1.0.95.1   The following assumptions shall be taken into consideration for the damaged condition:

      (a)   The extent of side damage is as follows:

longitudinal extent:	at least 0.10 L, but not less than 5.00 m;
transverse extent:	0.59 m;
vertical extent:	from the baseline upwards without limit;

      (b)   The extent of bottom damage is as follows:

longitudinal extent:	at least 0.10 L, but not less than 5.00 m;
transverse extent:	3.00 m;
vertical extent:	from the base 0.49 m upwards, the sump excepted;

      (c)   Any bulkheads within the damaged area shall be assumed damaged, which means that the location of bulkheads shall be chosen so as to ensure that the vessel remains afloat after the flooding of two or more adjacent compartments in the longitudinal direction.

          The following provisions are applicable:

          –   For bottom damage also two adjacent athwartships compartments shall be assumed as flooded;

          –   The lower edge of any openings that cannot be closed watertight (e.g. doors, windows, access hatchways) shall, at the final stage of flooding, be not less than 0.10 m above the damage waterline;

–   In general, permeability shall be assumed to be 95%. Where an average permeability of less than 95% is calculated for any compartment, this calculated value may be used.

However, the following minimum values shall be used:

– engine rooms:	85%
– accommodation:	95%
– double bottoms, oil fuel tanks, ballast tanks, etc., depending on whether, according to their function, they have to be assumed as full or empty for the vessel floating at the maximum permissible draught:	0% or 95%

For the main engine room only the one-compartment standard needs to be taken into account, i.e. the end bulkheads of the engine room shall be assumed as not damaged.

9.1.0.95.2   At the stage of equilibrium (final stage of flooding) the angle of heel shall not exceed 12°. Non-watertight openings shall not be immersed before reaching the stage of equilibrium. If such openings are immersed before that stage, the corresponding spaces shall be considered as flooded for the purpose of stability calculation.

The positive range of the righting lever curve beyond the position of equilibrium shall have a righting lever of ≥0.05 m in association with an area under the curve of ≥0.0065 m.rad. The minimum values of stability shall be satisfied up to immersion of the first non-weathertight opening and in any event up to an angle of heel ≤27°. If non-weathertight openings are immersed before that stage, the corresponding spaces shall be considered as flooded for the purposes of stability calculation.

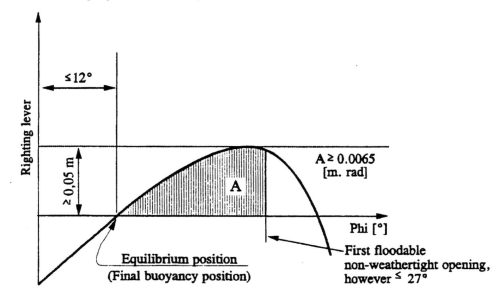

9.1.0.95.3   Inland navigation vessels carrying containers which have not been secured shall satisfy the following damage stability criteria:

At the stage of equilibrium (final stage of flooding) the angle of heel shall not exceed 5°. Non-watertight openings shall not be immersed before reaching the stage of equilibrium. If such openings are immersed before that stage, the corresponding spaces shall be considered as flooded for the purpose of stability calculation;

The positive range of the righting lever curve beyond the position of equilibrium shall have an area under the curve of ≥0.0065 m.rad. The minimum values of stability shall be satisfied up to immersion of the first non-weathertight opening and in any event up to an angle of heel ≤10°. If non-weathertight openings are immersed before that stage, the corresponding spaces shall be considered as flooded for the purposes of stability calculation.

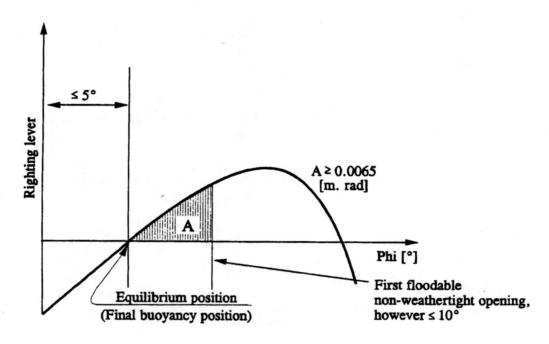

9.1.0.95.4   If openings through which undamaged compartments may become additionally flooded are capable of being closed watertight, the closing devices shall be appropriately marked.

9.1.0.95.5   Where cross- or down-flooding openings are provided for reduction of unsymmetrical flooding, the time for equalisation shall not exceed 15 minutes if during the intermediate stages of flooding sufficient stability has been proved.

9.1.0.96-   (Reserved)
9.1.0.99

CHAPTER 9.2

RULES FOR CONSTRUCTION APPLICABLE TO SEAGOING VESSELS WHICH COMPLY WITH THE REQUIREMENTS OF THE SOLAS 74 CONVENTION, CHAPTER II-2, REGULATION 19 OR SOLAS 74, CHAPTER II-2, REGULATION 54

9.2.0   The requirements of 9.2.0.0 to 9.2.0.79 are applicable to seagoing vessels which comply with the following requirements:

- SOLAS 74, Chapter II-2, Regulation 19 in its amended version; or

- SOLAS 74, Chapter II-2, Regulation 54 in its amended version in accordance with the resolutions mentioned in Chapter II-2, Regulation 1, paragraph 2.1, provided that the vessel was constructed before 1 July 2002.

Seagoing vessels which do not comply with the above-mentioned requirements of the SOLAS 74 Convention shall meet the requirements of 9.1.0.0 to 9.1.0.79.

9.2.0.0   *Materials of construction*

The vessels hull shall be constructed of shipbuilding steel or other metal, provided that this metal has at least equivalent mechanical properties and resistance to the effects of temperature and fire.

9.2.0.1-
9.2.0.19   *(Reserved)*

9.2.0.20   *Water ballast*

The double-hull spaces and double bottoms may be arranged for being filled with water ballast.

9.2.0.21-
9.2.0.30   *(Reserved)*

9.2.0.31   *Engines*

9.2.0.31.1   Only internal combustion engines running on a fuel having a flashpoint above 60 °C, are allowed.

9.2.0.31.2   Air intakes of the engines shall be located not less than 2.00 m from the protected area.

9.2.0.31.3   Sparking shall not be possible in the protected area.

9.2.0.32-
9.2.0.33   *(Reserved)*

9.2.0.34   *Exhaust pipes*

9.2.0.34.1   Exhausts shall be evacuated from the vessel into the open-air either upwards through an exhaust pipe or through the shell plating. The exhaust outlet shall be located not less than 2.00 m from the hatchway openings. The exhaust pipes of engines shall be arranged so that the exhausts are led away from the vessel. The exhaust pipes shall not be located within the protected area.

9.2.0.34.2	Exhaust pipes shall be provided with a device preventing the escape of sparks, e.g. spark arresters.
9.2.0.35- 9.2.0.40	*(Reserved)*

9.2.0.41 *Fire and naked light*

9.2.0.41.1	The outlets of funnels shall be located not less than 2.00 m from the hatchway openings. Arrangements shall be provided to prevent the escape of sparks and the entry of water.
9.2.0.41.2	Heating, cooking and refrigerating appliances shall not be fuelled with liquid fuels, liquid gas or solid fuels. The installation in the engine room or other separate space of heating appliances fuelled with liquid fuel having a flashpoint above 55 °C shall, however, be permitted. Cooking and refrigerating appliances are permitted only in wheelhouses with metal floor and in the accommodation.
9.2.0.41.3	Electric lighting appliances only are permitted outside the accommodation and the wheelhouse.
9.2.0.42- 9.2.0.70	*(Reserved)*

9.2.0.71 *Admittance on board*

The notice boards displaying the prohibition of admittance in accordance with 8.3.3 shall be clearly legible from either side of the vessel.

9.2.0.72- 9.2.0.73	*(Reserved)*

9.2.0.74 *Prohibition of smoking, fire and naked light*

9.2.0.74.1	The notice boards displaying the prohibition of smoking in accordance with 8.3.4 shall be clearly legible from either side of the vessel.
9.2.0.74.2	Notice boards indicating the circumstances under which the prohibition applies shall be fitted near the entrances to the spaces where smoking or the use of fire or naked light is not always prohibited.
9.2.0.74.3	Ashtrays shall be provided close to each exit of the wheelhouse.
9.2.0.75- 9.2.0.79	*(Reserved)*

9.2.0.80 *Additional rules applicable to double-hull vessels*

The rules of 9.2.0.88 to 9.2.0.99 are applicable to double-hull vessels intended to carry dangerous goods of Classes 2, 3, 4.1, 4.2, 4.3, 5.1, 5.2, 6.1, 7, 8 or 9, except those for which label No. 1 is prescribed in column (5) of Table A of Chapter 3.2, in quantities exceeding those of 7.1.4.1.1.

9.2.0.81- 9.2.0.87	*(Reserved)*

9.2.0.88   *Classification*

9.2.0.88.1   Double-hull vessels intended to carry dangerous goods of Classes 2, 3, 4.1, 4.2, 4.3, 5.1, 5.2, 6.1, 7, 8 or 9 except those for which label No. 1 is prescribed in column (5) of Table A of Chapter 3.2, in quantities exceeding those referred to in 7.1.4.1, shall be built under survey of a recognised classification society in accordance with the rules established by that classification society to its highest class. This shall be confirmed by the classification society by the issue of an appropriate certificate.

9.2.0.88.2   The vessel's class shall be continued.

9.2.0.89-
9.2.0.90   (*Reserved*)

9.2.0.91   **Holds**

9.2.0.91.1   The vessel shall be built as a double-hull vessel with double-wall spaces and double bottom within the protected area.

9.2.0.91.2   The distance between the sides of the vessel and the longitudinal bulkheads of the hold shall be not less than 0.80 m. A locally reduced distance at the vessel's ends shall be permitted, provided the smallest distance between vessel's side and the longitudinal bulkhead (measured perpendicular to the side) is not less than 0.60 m. The sufficient structural strength of the vessel (longitudinal, transverse and local strength) shall be confirmed by the class certificate.

9.2.0.91.3   The depth of the double bottom shall be not less than 0.50 m.

The depth below the suction wells may however be locally reduced to 0.40 m, provided the suction well has a capacity of not more than 0.03 m³.

9.2.0.92   (*Reserved*)

9.2.0.93   **Stability (general)**

9.2.0.93.1   Proof of sufficient stability shall be furnished including stability in the damaged condition.

9.2.0.93.2   The basic values for the stability calculation - the vessel's lightweight and the location of the centre of gravity - shall be determined either by means of an inclining experiment or by detailed mass and moment calculation. In the latter case the lightweight shall be checked by means of a lightweight test with a resulting difference of not more than ± 5% between the mass determined by the calculation and the displacement determined by the draught readings.

9.2.0.93.3   Proof of sufficient intact stability shall be furnished for all stages of loading and unloading and for the final loading condition.

Floatability after damage shall be proved for the most unfavourable loading condition. For this purpose calculated proof of sufficient stability shall be established for critical intermediate stages of flooding and for the final stage of flooding. Negative values of stability in intermediate stages of flooding may be accepted only if the continued range of curve of righting lever in damaged condition indicates adequate positive values of stability.

9.2.0.94   *Stability (intact)*

9.2.0.94.1   The requirements for intact stability resulting from the damaged stability calculation shall be fully complied with.

9.2.0.94.2   For the carriage of containers, additional proof of sufficient stability shall be furnished in accordance with the requirements of the Regulations referred to in 1.1.4.6.

9.2.0.94.3   The most stringent of the requirements of 9.2.0.94.1 and 9.2.0.94.2 shall prevail for the vessel.

9.2.0.94.4   For seagoing vessels the provisions of 9.2.0.94.2 above may be regarded as having been complied with if the stability conforms to Resolution A.749 (18) from the International Maritime Organization and the stability documents have been checked by the competent authority. This applies only when all containers are secured as usual on seagoing vessels and a relevant stability document has been approved by the competent authority.

9.2.0.95   *Stability (damaged condition)*

9.2.0.95.1   The following assumptions shall be taken into consideration for the damaged condition:

(a)   The extent of side damage is as follows:

longitudinal extent:	at least 0.10 L, but not less than 5.00 m;
transverse extent:	0.59 m;
vertical extent:	from the baseline upwards without limit;

(b)   The extent of bottom damage is as follows:

longitudinal extent:	at least 0.10 L, but not less than 5.00 m;
transverse extent:	3.00 m;
vertical extent:	from the base 0.49 m upwards, the sump excepted;

(c)   Any bulkheads within the damaged area shall be assumed damaged, which means that the location of bulkheads shall be chosen so that the vessel will remain afloat after flooding of two or more adjacent compartments in the longitudinal direction.

The following provisions are applicable:

–   For bottom damage, adjacent athwartship compartments shall also be assumed as flooded;

–   The lower edge of any openings that cannot be closed watertight (e.g. doors, windows, access hatchways) shall, at the final stage of flooding, be not less than 0.10 m above the damage waterline;

–   In general, permeability shall be assumed to be 95%. Where an average permeability of less than 95% is calculated for any compartment, this calculated value may be used.

However, the following minimum values shall be used:

–   engine rooms   85%

–   accommodation   95%

| – | double bottoms, oil fuel tanks, ballast tanks, etc., depending on whether according to their function, they have to be assumed as full or empty for the vessel floating at the maximum permissible draught | 0% or 95% |

For the main engine room only the one-compartment standard needs to be taken into account. (Consequently, the end bulkheads of the engine room shall be assumed as not damaged.)

9.2.0.95.2   At the stage of equilibrium (final stage of flooding) the angle of heel shall not exceed 12°. Non-watertight openings shall not be immersed before reaching the stage of equilibrium. If such openings are immersed before that stage, the corresponding spaces shall be considered as flooded for the purpose of stability calculation.

The positive range of the righting lever curve beyond the position of equilibrium shall have a righting lever of ≥0.05 m in association with an area under the curve of ≥0.0065 m.rad. The minimum values of stability shall be satisfied up to immersion of the first non-weathertight opening and in any event up to an angle of heel ≤27°. If non-weathertight openings are immersed before that stage, the corresponding spaces shall be considered as flooded for the purposes of stability calculation.

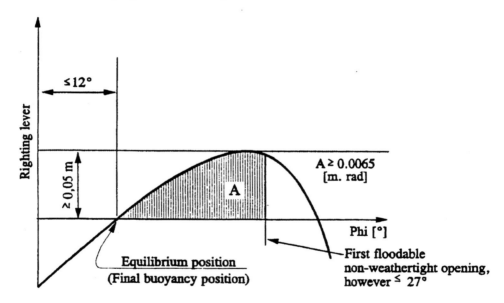

9.2.0.95.3   If openings through which undamaged compartments may become additionally flooded are capable of being closed watertight, the closing devices shall be appropriately marked.

9.2.0.95.4   Where cross- or down-flooding openings are provided for reduction of unsymmetrical flooding, the time for equalisation shall not exceed 15 minutes if during the intermediate stages of flooding sufficient stability has been proved.

9.2.0.96-
9.2.0.99   (*Reserved*)

CHAPTER 9.3

RULES FOR CONSTRUCTION OF TANK VESSELS

9.3.1   **Rules for construction of type G tank vessels**

The provisions of 9.3.1.0 to 9.3.1.99 apply to type G tank vessels.

9.3.1.0   *Materials of construction*

9.3.1.0.1   (a)   The vessel's hull and the cargo tanks shall be constructed of shipbuilding steel or other at least equivalent metal.

               The independent cargo tanks may also be constructed of other materials, provided these have at least equivalent mechanical properties and resistance against the effects of temperature and fire.

           (b)   Every part of the vessel including any installation and equipment which may come into contact with the cargo shall consist of materials which can neither be dangerously affected by the cargo nor cause decomposition of the cargo or react with it so as to form harmful or hazardous products.

9.3.1.0.2   Except where explicitly permitted in 9.3.1.0.3 below or in the certificate of approval, the use of wood, aluminium alloys or plastic materials within the cargo area is prohibited.

9.3.1.0.3   (a)   The use of wood, aluminium alloys or plastic materials within the cargo area is only permitted for:

               –   gangways and external ladders;

               –   movable items of equipment;

               –   chocking of cargo tanks which are independent of the vessel's hull and chocking of installations and equipment;

               –   masts and similar round timber;

               –   engine parts;

               –   parts of the electrical installation;

               –   lids of boxes which are placed on the deck.

           (b)   The use of wood or plastic materials within the cargo area is only permitted for:

               –   supports and stops of any kind.

           (c)   The use of plastic materials or rubber within the cargo area is only permitted for:

               –   all kinds of gaskets (e.g. for dome or hatch covers);

               –   electric cables;

               –   hoses for loading and unloading;

               –   insulation of cargo tanks and of hoses for loading and unloading.

(d)   All permanently fitted materials in the accommodation or wheelhouse, with the exception of furniture, shall not readily ignite. They shall not evolve fumes or toxic gases in dangerous quantities, if involved in a fire.

9.3.1.0.4   The paint used in the cargo area shall not be liable to produce sparks in case of impact.

9.3.1.0.5   The use of plastic material for vessel's boats is permitted only if the material does not readily ignite.

9.3.1.1-   (*Reserved*)
9.3.1.7

9.3.1.8   *Classification*

9.3.1.8.1   The tank vessel shall be built under survey of a recognised classification society in accordance with the rules established by that classification society for its highest class, and the tank vessel shall be classed accordingly.

The vessel's class shall be continued.

The classification society shall issue a certificate certifying that the vessel is in conformity with the rules of this section.

The design pressure and the test pressure of cargo tanks shall be entered in the certificate.

If a vessel has cargo tanks with different valve opening pressures, the design and test pressures of each tank shall be entered in the certificate.

The classification society shall draw up a certificate mentioning all the dangerous goods accepted for carriage by the vessel (see also 1.16.1.2.5).

9.3.1.8.2   The cargo pump-rooms shall be inspected by a recognised classification society whenever the certificate of approval has to be renewed as well as during the third year of validity of the certificate of approval. The inspection shall comprise at least:

–   an inspection of the whole system for its condition, for corrosion, leakage or conversion works which have not been approved;

–   a checking of the condition of the gas detection system in the cargo pump-rooms.

Inspection certificates signed by the recognised classification society with respect to the inspection of the cargo pump-rooms shall be kept on board. The inspection certificates shall at least include particulars of the above inspection and the results obtained as well as the date of the inspection.

9.3.1.8.3   The condition of the gas detection system referred to in 9.3.1.52.3 (b) shall be checked by a recognised classification society whenever the certificate of approval has to be renewed and during the third year of validity of the certificate of approval. A certificate signed by the recognised classification society shall be kept on board.

9.3.1.9   (*Reserved*)

9.3.1.10   *Protection against the penetration of gases*

9.3.1.10.1   The vessel shall be designed so as to prevent gases from penetrating into the accommodation and the service spaces.

9.3.1.10.2   The lower edges of door-openings in the sidewalls of superstructures and the coamings of access hatches to under-deck spaces shall have a height of not less than 0.50 m above the deck

This requirement need not be complied with if the wall of the superstructures facing the cargo area extends from one side of the ship to the other and has doors the sills of which have a height of not less than 0.50 m. The height of this wall shall not be less than 2.00 m. In this case, the lower edges of door-openings in the sidewalls of superstructures and the coamings of access hatches behind this wall shall have a height of not less than 0.10 m. The sills of engine room doors and the coamings of its access hatches shall, however, always have a height of not less than 0.50 m.

9.3.1.10.3   The bulwarks, foot-rails, etc shall be provided with sufficiently large openings which are located directly above the deck.

9.3.1.11   *Hold spaces and cargo tanks*

9.3.1.11.1   (a)   The maximum permissible capacity of a cargo tank shall be determined in accordance with the following table:

$L \times B \times H$ (m^3)	Maximum permissible capacity of a cargo tank (m^3)
up to 600	$L \times B \times H \times 0.3$
600 to 3 750	$180 + (L \times B \times H - 600) \times 0.0635$
> 3 750	380

In the table above $L \times B \times H$ is the product of the main dimensions of the tank vessel in metres (according to the measurement certificate), where:

L   =   overall length of the hull;
B   =   extreme breadth of the hull;
H   =   shortest vertical distance between the top of the keel and the lowest point of the deck at the side of the vessel (moulded depth) within the cargo area;

For trunk vessels, H shall be replaced by H', where H' shall be obtained from the following formula:

$$H' = H + \left(ht \times \frac{bt}{B} \times \frac{lt}{L} \right)$$

where:

ht   =   trunk height (distance between trunk deck and main deck measured on trunk side at L/2);
bt   =   trunk breadth;
lt   =   trunk length;

(b)   Pressure cargo tanks whose ratio of length to diameter exceeds 7 are prohibited.

(c)   The pressure cargo tanks shall be designed for a cargo temperature of + 40 °C.

9.3.1.11.2   (a)   In the cargo area, the hull shall be designed as follows:[1]

– as a double-hull and double bottom vessel. The internal distance between the sideplatings of the vessel and the longitudinal bulkheads shall not be less than 0.80 m, the height of the double bottom shall be not less than 0.60 m, the cargo tanks shall be supported by saddles extending between the tanks to not less than 20° below the horizontal centreline of the cargo tanks.

Refrigerated cargo tanks shall be installed only in hold spaces bounded by double-hull spaces and double-bottom. Cargo tank fastenings shall meet the requirements of a recognised classification society; or

– as a single-hull vessel with the sideplatings of the vessel between gangboard and top of floor plates provided with side stringers at regular intervals of not more than 0.60 m which are supported by web frames spaced at intervals of not more than 2.00 m. The side stringers and the web frames shall have a height of not less than 10% of the depth, however, not less than 0.30 m. The side stringers and web frames shall be fitted with a face plate made of flat steel and having a cross-section of not less that 7.5 cm^2 and 15 cm^2, respectively.

The distance between the sideplating of the vessel and the cargo tanks shall be not less than 0.80 m and between the bottom and the cargo tanks not less than 0.60 m. The depth below the suction wells may be reduced to 0.50 m.

The lateral distance between the suction well of the cargo tanks and the bottom structure shall be not less than 0.10 m.

The cargo tank supports and fastenings shall be as follows:

– the cargo tanks shall be supported by saddles extending between the tanks to not less than 10° below the horizontal centreline of the tanks; and

– for adjacent cylindrical cargo tanks, a spacer of 500 mm × 450 mm shall be provided at the saddles, and a spacer of 2,000 mm × 450 mm shall be provided midway between the saddles.

The spacers shall fit the adjacent cargo tanks closely.

The spacers shall consist of an energy-absorbing material.

(b)   The cargo tanks shall be fixed so that they cannot float.

(c)   The capacity of a suction well shall be limited to not more than 0.10 m^3. For pressure cargo tanks, however, the capacity of a suction well may be of 0.20 m^3.

(d)   Side-stringers linking or supporting the load-bearing components of the sides of the vessel with the load-bearing components of the longitudinal walls of cargo tanks and side-stringers linking the load-bearing components of the vessel's bottom with the tank-bottom are prohibited.

---

[1]   *For a different design of the hull in the cargo area, proof shall be furnished by way of calculation that in the event of a lateral collision with another vessel having a straight bow, an energy of 22 MJ can be absorbed without any rupture of the cargo tanks and the piping leading to the cargo tanks.*

9.3.1.11.3   (a)   The hold spaces shall be separated from the accommodation and service spaces outside the cargo area below deck by bulkheads provided with a Class A-60 fire protection insulation according to SOLAS 74, Chapter II-2, Regulation 3. A space of not less than 0.20 m shall be provided between the cargo tanks and the end bulkheads of the hold spaces. Where the cargo tanks have plane end bulkheads this space shall be not less than 0.50 m.

(b)   The hold spaces and cargo tanks shall be capable of being inspected.

(c)   All spaces in the cargo area shall be capable of being ventilated. Means for checking their gas-free condition shall be provided.

9.3.1.11.4   The bulkheads bounding the hold spaces shall be watertight. The cargo tanks and the end bulkheads of the hold spaces as well as the bulkheads bounding the cargo area shall have no openings or penetrations below deck. Penetrations through bulkheads between two hold spaces are, however, permitted. The bulkhead between the engine room and the service spaces within the cargo area or between the engine room and a hold space may be fitted with penetrations provided that they conform to the requirements of 9.3.1.17.5.

9.3.1.11.5   Double-hull spaces and double bottoms in the cargo area shall be arranged for being filled with ballast water only. Double bottoms may, however, be used as oil fuel tanks, provided they comply with the requirements of 9.3.1.32.

9.3.1.11.6   (a)   A space in the cargo area below deck may be arranged as a service space, provided that the bulkhead bounding the service space extends vertically to the bottom and the bulkhead not facing the cargo area extends from one side of the vessel to the other in one frame plane. This service space shall only be accessible from the deck.

(b)   The service space shall be watertight with the exception of its access hatches and ventilation inlets.

(c)   No pipes for loading or unloading shall be fitted within the service space referred to under (a) above.

Pipes for loading and unloading may be fitted in the cargo pump-rooms below deck only when they conform to the provisions of 9.3.1.17.6.

9.3.1.11.7   Where service spaces are located in the cargo area under deck, they shall be arranged so as to be easily accessible and to permit persons wearing protective clothing and breathing apparatus to safely operate the service equipment contained therein. They shall be designed so as to allow injured or unconscious personnel to be removed from such spaces without difficulty, if necessary by means of fixed equipment.

9.3.1.11.8   Hold spaces and other accessible spaces within the cargo area shall be arranged so as to ensure that they may be completely inspected and cleaned in an appropriate manner. The dimensions of openings, except for those of double-hull spaces and double bottoms which do not have a wall adjoining the cargo tanks, shall be sufficient to allow a person wearing breathing apparatus to enter or leave the space without difficulty. These openings shall have a minimum cross-sectional area of 0.36 m^2 and a minimum side length of 0.50 m. They shall be designed so as to allow injured or unconscious personnel to be removed from the bottom of such spaces without difficulties, if necessary by means of fixed equipment. In these spaces the distance between the reinforcements shall not be less than 0.50 m. In double bottoms this distance may be reduced to 0.45 m.

Cargo tanks may have circular openings with a diameter of not less than 0.68 m.

9.3.1.12   *Ventilation*

9.3.1.12.1   Each hold space shall have two openings the dimensions and location of which shall be such as to permit effective ventilation of any part of the hold space. If there are no such openings, it shall be possible to fill the hold spaces with inert gas or dry air.

9.3.1.12.2   Double-hull spaces and double bottoms within the cargo area which are not arranged for being filled with ballast water and cofferdams between engine rooms and pump-rooms, if they exist, shall be provided with ventilation systems.

9.3.1.12.3   Any service spaces located in the cargo area below deck shall be provided with a system of forced ventilation with sufficient power for ensuring at least 20 changes of air per hour based on the volume of the space. The ventilator fan shall be designed so as that no spark may be emitted on contact of the impeller blades with the housing and no static electricity may be generated.

The ventilation exhaust ducts shall extend down to 50 mm above the bottom of the service space. The air shall be supplied through a duct at the top of the service space. The air inlets shall be located not less than 2.00 m above the deck, at a distance of not less than 2.00 m from tank openings and 6.00 m from the outlets of safety valves.

The extension pipes, which may be necessary, may be of the hinged type.

9.3.1.12.4   Ventilation of accommodation and service spaces shall be possible.

9.3.1.12.5   Ventilators used for gas-freeing of cargo tanks shall be designed so that no sparks may be emitted on contact of the impeller blades with the housing and no static electricity may be generated.

9.3.1.12.6   Notice boards shall be fitted at the ventilation inlets indicating the conditions when they shall be closed. All ventilation inlets of accommodation and service spaces leading outside shall be fitted with fire flaps. Such ventilation inlets shall be located not less than 2.00 m from the cargo area.

Ventilation inlets of service spaces in the cargo area below deck may be located within such area.

9.3.1.13   *Stability (general)*

9.3.1.13.1   Proof of sufficient stability shall be furnished including for stability in damaged condition.

9.3.1.13.2   The basic values for the stability calculation - the vessel's lightweight and location of the centre of gravity - shall be determined either by means of an inclining experiment or by detailed mass and moment calculation. In the latter case the lightweight of the vessel shall be checked by means of a lightweight test with a tolerance limit of ± 5% between the mass determined by calculation and the displacement determined by the draught readings.

9.3.1.13.3   Proof of sufficient intact stability shall be furnished for all stages of loading and unloading and for the final loading condition.

Floatability after damage shall be proved for the most unfavourable loading condition. For this purpose, calculated proof of sufficient stability shall be established for critical intermediate stages of flooding and for the final stage of flooding. Negative values of stability in intermediate stages of flooding may be accepted only if the continued range of curve of righting lever in damaged condition indicates adequate positive values of stability.

9.3.1.14   *Stability (intact)*

The requirements for intact stability resulting from the damaged stability calculation shall be fully complied with.

9.3.1.15   *Stability (damaged condition)*

9.3.1.15.1   The following assumptions shall be taken into consideration for the damaged condition:

(a)   The extent of side damage is as follows:

longitudinal extent:	at least 0.10 L, but not less than 5.00 m;
transverse extent:	0.79 m;
vertical extent:	from the base line upwards without limit;

(b)   The extent of bottom damage is as follows:

longitudinal extent:	at least 0.10 L, but not less than 5.00 m;
transverse extent:	3.00 m;
vertical extent:	from the base 0.59 m upwards, the well excepted;

(c)   Any bulkheads within the damaged area shall be assumed damaged, which means that the location of bulkheads shall be chosen so as to ensure that the vessel remains afloat after the flooding of two or more adjacent compartments in the longitudinal direction.

The following provisions are applicable:

–   For bottom damage, adjacent athwartship compartments shall also be assumed as flooded;

–   The lower edge of any non-watertight openings (e.g. doors, windows, access hatchways) shall, at the final stage of flooding, be not less than 0.10 m above the damage waterline;

–   In general, permeability shall be assumed to be 95%. Where an average permeability of less than 95% is calculated for any compartment, this calculated value obtained may be used.

However, the following minimum values shall be used:

– engine rooms:	85%;
– accommodation:	95%;
– double bottoms, oil fuel tanks, ballast tanks, etc., depending on whether, according to their function, they have to be assumed as full or empty for the vessel floating at the maximum permissible draught:	0% or 95%.

For the main engine room only the one-compartment standard need be taken into account, i.e. the end bulkheads of the engine room shall be assumed as not damaged.

9.3.1.15.2   At the stage of equilibrium (final stage of flooding), the angle of heel shall not exceed 12°. Non-watertight openings shall not be flooded before reaching the stage of equilibrium. If such openings are immersed before that stage, the corresponding spaces shall be considered as flooded for the purpose of stability calculation.

The positive range of the righting lever curve beyond the stage of equilibrium shall have a righting level of ≥0.05 m in association with an area under the curve of ≥0.0065 m.rad. The minimum values of stability shall be satisfied up to immersion of the first non-weathertight opening and in any event up to an angle of heel ≤27°. If non-watertight openings are immersed before that stage, the corresponding spaces shall be considered as flooded for the purpose of stability calculation.

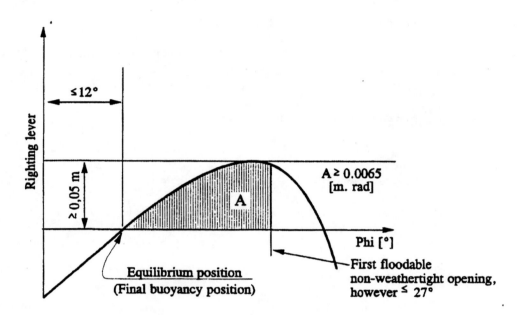

9.3.1.15.3   If openings through which undamaged compartments may additionally become flooded are capable of being closed watertight, the closing appliances shall be marked accordingly.

9.3.1.15.4   When cross- or down-flooding openings are provided for reduction of unsymmetrical flooding, the time for equalisation shall not exceed 15 minutes, if during the intermediate stages of flooding sufficient stability has been proved.

9.3.1.16   *Engine rooms*

9.3.1.16.1   Internal combustion engines for the vessel's propulsion as well as internal combustion engines for auxiliary machinery shall be located outside the cargo area. Entrances and other openings of engine rooms shall be at a distance of not less than 2.00 m from the cargo area.

9.3.1.16.2   The engine room shall be accessible from the deck; the entrances shall not face the cargo area. When the doors are not located in a recess whose depth is at least equal to the door width, the hinges shall face the cargo area.

9.3.1.17   *Accommodation and service spaces*

9.3.1.17.1   Accommodation spaces and the wheelhouse shall be located outside the cargo area forward of the fore vertical plane or abaft the aft vertical plane bounding the part of cargo area below deck. Windows of the wheelhouse which are located not less than 1.00 m above the bottom of the wheelhouse may tilt forward.

9.3.1.17.2 Entrances to spaces and openings of superstructures shall not face the cargo area. Doors opening outward and not located in a recess the depth of which is at least equal to the width of the doors shall have their hinges facing the cargo area.

9.3.1.17.3 Entrances from the deck and openings of spaces facing the weather shall be capable of being closed. The following instruction shall be displayed at the entrance of such spaces:

**DO NOT OPEN DURING LOADING, UNLOADING OR GAS-FREEING
WITHOUT PERMISSION FROM THE MASTER.
CLOSE IMMEDIATELY.**

9.3.1.17.4 Entrances and windows of superstructures and accommodation spaces which can be opened as well as other openings of these spaces shall be located not less than 2.00 m from the cargo area. No wheelhouse doors and windows shall be located within 2.00 m from the cargo area, except where there is no direct connection between the wheelhouse and the accommodation.

9.3.1.17.5 (a) Driving shafts of the bilge or ballast pumps may penetrate through the bulkhead between the service space and the engine room, provided the arrangement of the service space is in compliance with 9.3.1.11.6.

(b) The penetration of the shaft through the bulkhead shall be gastight and shall have been approved by a recognised classification society.

(c) The necessary operating instructions shall be displayed.

(d) Penetrations through the bulkhead between the engine room and the service space in the cargo area, and the bulkhead between the engine room and the hold spaces may be provided for electrical cables, hydraulic lines and piping for measuring, control and alarm systems, provided that the penetrations have been approved by a recognised classification society. The penetrations shall be gastight. Penetrations through a bulkhead with an "A-60" fire protection insulation according to SOLAS 74, Chapter II-2, Regulation 3, shall have an equivalent fire protection.

(e) Pipes may pass through the bulkhead between the engine room and the service space in the cargo area provided that these are pipes between the mechanical equipment in the engine room and the service space which do not have any openings within the service space and which are provided with shut-off devices at the bulkhead in the engine room.

(f) Pipes from the engine room may pass through the service space in the cargo area or a hold space to the outside provided that within the service space or hold space they are of the thick-walled type and have no flanges or openings.

(g) Where a driving shaft of auxiliary machinery penetrates through a wall located above the deck the penetration shall be gastight.

9.3.1.17.6 A service space located within the cargo area below deck shall not be used as a cargo pump-room for the vessel's own gas discharging system, e.g. compressors or the compressor/heat exchanger/pump combination, except where:

– the pump-room is separated from the engine room or from service spaces outside the cargo area by a cofferdam or a bulkhead with an "A-60" fire protection insulation according to SOLAS 74, Chapter II-2, Regulation 3, or by a service space or a hold space;

–   the "A-60" bulkhead required above does not include penetrations referred to in 9.3.1.17.5 (a);

–   ventilation exhaust outlets are located not less than 6.00 m from entrances and openings of the accommodation and service spaces;

–   the access hatches and ventilation inlets can be closed from the outside;

–   all pipes for loading and unloading (at the suction side and delivery side) are led through the deck above the pump-room. The necessary operation of the control devices in the pump-room, starting of pumps or compressors and control of the liquid flow rate shall be effected from the deck;

–   the system is fully integrated in the gas and liquid piping system;

–   the cargo pump-room is provided with a permanent gas detection system which automatically indicates the presence of explosive gases or lack of oxygen by means of direct-measuring sensors and which actuates a visual and audible alarm when the gas concentration has reached 20% of the lower explosive limit. The sensors of this system shall be placed at suitable positions at the bottom and directly below the deck.

Measurement shall be continuous.

The audible and visual alarms are installed in the wheelhouse and in the cargo pump-room and, when the alarm is actuated, the loading and unloading system is shut down. Failure of the gas detection system shall be immediately signalled in the wheelhouse and on deck by means of audible and visual alarms;

–   the ventilation system prescribed in 9.3.1.12.3 has a capacity of not less than 30 changes of air per hour based on the total volume of the service space.

9.3.1.17.7   The following instruction shall be displayed at the entrance of the cargo pump-room:

**BEFORE ENTERING THE CARGO PUMP-ROOM CHECK WHETHER
IT IS FREE FROM GASES AND CONTAINS SUFFICIENT OXYGEN
DO NOT OPEN DOORS AND ENTRANCE OPENINGS WITHOUT
THE PERMISSION OF THE MASTER.
LEAVE IMMEDIATELY IN THE EVENT OF ALARM.**

9.3.1.18-
9.3.1.20   *(Reserved)*

9.3.1.21   *Safety and control installations*

9.3.1.21.1   Cargo tanks shall be provided with the following equipment:

(a)   *(Reserved)*;

(b)   a level gauge;

(c)   a level alarm device which is activated at the latest when a degree of filling of 86% is reached;

(d)   a high level sensor for actuating the facility against overflowing at the latest when a degree of filling of 97.5% is reached;

(e)   an instrument for measuring the pressure;

(f)   an instrument for measuring the temperature of the cargo;

(g)   a nozzle with a closure connected to a sampling device of the closed type;

(h)   (*Reserved*)

9.3.1.21.2   When the degree of filling in per cent is determined, an error of not more than 0.5% is permitted. It shall be calculated on the basis of the total cargo tank capacity including the expansion trunk.

9.3.1.21.3   The level gauge shall allow readings from the control position of the shut-off devices of the particular cargo tank.

9.3.1.21.4   The level alarm device shall give a visual and audible warning on board when actuated. The level alarm device shall be independent of the level gauge.

9.3.1.21.5   The high level sensor referred to in 9.3.1.21.1 (d) shall give a visual and audible alarm on board and at the same time actuate an electrical contact which in the form of a binary signal interrupts the electric current loop provided and fed by the shore facility, thus initiating measures at the shore facility against overflowing during loading operations.

The signal shall be transmitted to the shore facility via a watertight two-pin plug of a connector device in accordance with IEC Publication No. 309 (1992) for direct current of 40 to 50 volts, identification colour white, position of the nose 10 h.

The plug shall be permanently fitted to the vessel close to the shore connections of the loading and unloading pipes.

The high level sensor shall also be capable of switching off the vessel's own discharging pump.

The high level sensor shall be independent of the level alarm device, but it may be connected to the level gauge.

9.3.1.21.6   The visual and audible signals given by the level alarm device shall be clearly distinguishable from those of the high level sensor.

The visual alarm shall be visible at each control position on deck of the cargo tank stop valves. It shall be possible to easily check the functioning of the sensors and electric circuits or these shall be of the "failsafe" design.

9.3.1.21.7   When the pressure or the temperature exceeds a set value, the instruments for measuring the pressure and the temperature of the cargo shall activate a visual and an audible alarm in the wheelhouse. When the wheelhouse is unoccupied the alarm shall also be perceptible in a location occupied by a crew member.

When the pressure exceeds a set value during loading or unloading, the instrument for measuring the pressure shall simultaneously initiate an electrical contact which, by means of the plug referred to in 9.3.1.21.5 above, enables measures to be taken to interrupt the loading operation. When the vessel's own discharge pump is used, it shall be switched off automatically. The sensor for the alarms referred to above may be connected to the alarm installation.

If the overpressure or the vacuum measurement is effected using a manometer, its indicator scale shall not be less than 0.14 m in diameter. The maximum permissible overpressure or vacuum values shall be indicated by a red mark.

The manometers shall be capable of being read at any time from the location where it is possible to interrupt loading or unloading.

9.3.1.21.8 Where the control elements of the shut-off devices of the cargo tanks are located in a control room, reading of the level gauges shall be possible in the control room and the visual and audible warning given by the level alarm device, the high level sensor referred to in 9.3.2.21.1 (d) and the instruments for measuring the pressure and temperature of the cargo shall be noticeable in the control room and on deck.

Satisfactory monitoring of the cargo area shall be ensured from the control room.

9.3.1.21.9 The closed sampling device penetrating through the boundary of the cargo tank but constituting a part of a closed system shall be designed so that during sampling no gas or liquid may escape from the cargo tank. The device shall be of a type approved by the competent authority for this purpose.

9.3.1.21.10 The vessel shall be so equipped that loading or unloading operations can be interrupted by means of switches, i.e. the quick-action stop valve located on the flexible vessel-to-shore connecting line must be capable of being closed. The switches shall be placed at the two points on the vessel (fore and aft).

The interruption systems shall be designed according to the quiescent current principle.

9.3.1.22 *Cargo tank openings*

9.3.1.22.1 Cargo tank openings shall be located on deck in the cargo area.

9.3.1.22.2 Cargo tank openings shall be fitted with gastight closures capable of withstanding the test pressure in accordance with 9.3.1.23.1.

9.3.1.22.3 The exhaust outlets of the pressure relief valves shall be located not less than 2.00 m above the deck at a distance of not less than 6.00 m from the accommodation and from the service spaces located outside the cargo area. This height may be reduced when within a radius of 1.00 m round the pressure relief valve outlet there is no equipment, no work is being carried out and signs indicate the area.

9.3.1.22.4 The closing devices normally used in loading and unloading operations shall not be capable of producing sparks when operated.

9.3.1.23 *Pressure test*

9.3.1.23.1 Cargo tanks and pipes for loading and unloading shall comply with the provisions concerning pressure vessels which have been established by the competent authority or a recognised classification society for the substances carried.

The test pressure of refrigerated cargo tanks shall be not less than 25 kPa (0.25 bar) gauge pressure.

9.3.1.23.2 Any cofferdams shall be subjected to initial tests before being put into service and thereafter at the prescribed intervals.

The test pressure shall be not less than 10 kPa (0.10 bar) gauge pressure.

9.3.1.23.3 The maximum intervals for the periodic tests referred to in 9.3.1.23.2 above shall be 11 years.

9.3.1.24 *(Reserved)*

9.3.1.25 *Pumps and piping*

9.3.1.25.1 Pumps, compressors and accessory loading and unloading piping shall be placed in the cargo area. Cargo pumps and compressors shall be capable of being shut down from the cargo area and, in addition, from a position outside the cargo area. Cargo pumps and compressors situated on deck shall be located not less than 6.00 m from entrances to, or openings of, the accommodation and service spaces outside the cargo area.

9.3.1.25.2 (a) Pipes for loading and unloading shall be independent of any other piping of the vessel. No cargo piping shall be located below deck, except those inside the cargo tanks and in the service spaces intended for the installation of the vessel's own gas discharging system.

(b) *(Reserved)*

(c) Pipes for loading and unloading shall be clearly distinguishable from other piping, e.g. by means of colour marking.

(d) The pipes for loading and unloading on deck, the vapour pipes with the exception of the shore connections but including the safety valves, and the valves shall be located within the longitudinal line formed by the outer boundaries of the domes and not less than one quarter of the vessel's breadth from the outer shell. This requirement does not apply to the relief pipes situated behind the safety valves. If there is, however, only one dome athwartships, these pipes and their valves shall be located at a distance not less than 2.70 m from the shell.

Where cargo tanks are placed side by side, all the connections to the domes shall be located on the inner side of the domes. The external connections may be located on the fore and aft centre line of the dome. The shut-off devices shall be located directly at the dome or as close as possible to it. The shut-off devices of the loading and unloading piping shall be duplicated, one of the devices being constituted by a remote-controlled quick-action stop device. When the inside diameter of a shut-off device is less than 50 mm this device may be regarded as a safety device against bursts in the piping.

(e) The shore connections shall be located not less than 6.00 m from the entrances to or openings of, the accommodation and service spaces outside the cargo area.

(f) Each shore connection of the vapour pipe and shore connections of the pipes for loading and unloading, through which the loading or unloading operation is carried out, shall be fitted with a shut-off device and a quick-action stop valve. However, each shore connection shall be fitted with a blind flange when it is not in operation.

9.3.1.25.3 The distance referred to in 9.3.1.25.1 and 9.3.1.25.2 (e) may be reduced to 3.00 m if a transverse bulkhead complying with 9.3.1.10.2 is situated at the end of the cargo area. The openings shall be provided with doors.

The following notice shall be displayed on the doors:

DO NOT OPEN DURING LOADING AND UNLOADING WITHOUT

9.3.1.25.4   Every component of the pipes for loading and unloading shall be electrically connected to the hull.

9.3.1.25.5   The stop valves or other shut-off devices of the pipes for loading and unloading shall indicate whether they are open or shut.

9.3.1.25.6   The pipes for loading and unloading shall have, at the test pressure, the required elasticity, leakproofness and resistance to pressure.

9.3.1.25.7   The pipes for loading and unloading shall be fitted with pressure gauges at the inlet and outlet of the vessel's own gas discharging system.

Where these pressure gauges are manometers, the indicator scale shall have a diameter of not less than 0.14 m.

Reading of the pressure gauges shall be possible from the control position of the vessel's own gas discharging system. The maximum permissible overpressure or vacuum shall be indicated by a red mark.

9.3.1.25.8   Use of the cargo piping for ballasting purposes shall not be possible.

9.3.1.26   *(Reserved)*

9.3.1.27   *Cargo refrigeration systems*

9.3.1.27.1   When refrigeration is required in column (9) of Table C of Chapter 3.2, the vessel shall be provided with two independent refrigeration systems:

(a)   The capacity of the cargo refrigeration systems shall be such that, in the event of the failure of one system, the remaining system may maintain the temperature of the cargo at such a value that gas cannot escape through safety devices;

(b)   If the systems are operated electrically, they shall be connected to two electric circuits which are independent of each other and which are supplied by at least two different sources of electrical power. In addition, there shall be a possibility for connection to a power source on shore; the necessary connecting cable shall be available on board;

(c)   Cargo tanks, piping and accessories shall be insulated so that, in the event of a failure of all cargo refrigeration systems, the entire cargo remains for at least 52 hours in a condition not causing the safety valves to open.

This provision shall be satisfied in the following ambience temperature conditions:

air temperature: +30 °C;
water temperature: +20 °C;

(d)   The cargo refrigeration systems shall be arranged so that their function can be taken over by a third system independent of the vessel.

9.3.1.27.2   The safety devices and the connecting lines from the refrigeration system shall be connected to the cargo tanks above the liquid phase of the cargo when the tanks are filled to their maximum permissible degree of filling. They shall remain within the gaseous phase, even if the vessel has a list up to 12 degrees.

9.3.1.27.3   The cargo refrigeration system shall be installed in a separate service space provided with forced mechanical ventilation.

9.3.1.27.4   For all cargo systems, the heat transmission coefficient shall be determined by calculation. The correctness of the calculation shall be checked by means of a refrigeration test (heat balance test).

This test shall be performed in accordance with the rules set up by a recognised classification society.

9.3.1.27.5   A certificate from a recognised classification society stating that 9.3.1.27.1 and 9.3.1.27.4 above have been complied with shall be submitted together with the application for issue or renewal of the certificate of approval.

9.3.1.28   *Water-spray system*

When water-spraying is required in column (9) of Table C of Chapter 3.2 a water-spray system shall be installed in the cargo area on deck for the purpose of reducing gases given off by the cargo by spraying water over the whole surface.

The system shall be fitted with a connection device for supply from the shore. The spray nozzles shall be so installed that released gases are precipitated safely. The system shall be capable of being put into operation from the wheelhouse and from the deck. The capacity of the water-spray system shall be such that when all the spray nozzles are in operation, the outflow is of 50 litres per square metre of cargo deck area and per hour.

9.3.1.29-   (*Reserved*)
9.3.1.30

9.3.1.31   *Engines*

9.3.1.31.1   Only internal combustion engines running on fuel with a flashpoint of more than 55 °C are allowed.

9.3.1.31.2   Ventilation inlets of the engine room and, when the engines do not take in air directly from the engine room, the air intakes of the engines shall be located not less than 2.00 m from the cargo area.

9.3.1.31.3   Sparking shall not be possible within the cargo area.

9.3.1.31.4   The surface temperature of the outer parts of engines used during loading or unloading operations, as well as that of their air inlets and exhaust ducts shall not exceed the allowable temperature according to the temperature class. This provision does not apply to engines installed in service spaces provided the provisions of 9.3.1.52.3 (b) are fully complied with.

9.3.1.31.5   The ventilation in the closed engine room shall be designed so that, at an ambient temperature of 20 °C, the average temperature in the engine room does not exceed 40 °C.

9.3.1.32   *Oil fuel tanks*

9.3.1.32.1   When the vessel is fitted with hold spaces and double bottoms, double bottoms within the cargo area may be arranged as a liquid oil fuel tanks, provided their depth is not less than 0.60 m.

Liquid oil fuel pipes and openings of such tanks are not permitted in the hold space.

9.3.1.32.2	Open ends of air pipes of all liquid oil fuel tanks shall extend to not less than 0.5 m above the open deck. The open ends and the open ends of overflow pipes leading on the deck shall be fitted with a protective device consisting of a gauze diaphragm or a perforated plate.
9.3.1.33	(*Reserved*)

9.3.1.34 *Exhaust pipes*

9.3.1.34.1	Exhausts shall be evacuated from the vessel into the open air either upwards through an exhaust pipe or through the shell plating. The exhaust outlet shall be located not less than 2 m from the cargo area. The exhaust pipes of engines shall be arranged so that the exhausts are led away from the vessel. The exhaust pipes shall not be located within the cargo area.
9.3.1.34.2	Exhaust pipes shall be provided with a device preventing the escape of sparks, e.g. spark arresters.

9.3.1.35 *Bilge pumping and ballasting arrangements*

9.3.1.35.1	Bilge and ballast pumps for spaces within the cargo area shall be installed within such area.

This provision does not apply to:

–　　double-hull spaces and double bottoms which do not have a common boundary wall with the cargo tanks;

–　　cofferdams and hold spaces where ballasting is carried out using the piping of the fire-fighting system in the cargo area and bilge-pumping is performed using educators.

9.3.1.35.2	Where the double bottom is used as a liquid oil fuel tank, it shall not be connected to the bilge piping system.
9.3.1.35.3	Where the ballast pump is installed in the cargo area, the standpipe and its outboard connection for suction of ballast water shall be located within the cargo area.
9.3.1.35.4	It shall be possible for an under-deck pump-room to be stripped in an emergency using a system located in the cargo area and independent of any other system. This stripping system shall be located outside the pump-room.
9.3.1.36- 9.3.1.39	(*Reserved*)

9.3.1.40 *Fire-extinguishing arrangements*

9.3.1.40.1	A fire-extinguishing system shall be installed on the vessel.

This system shall comply with the following requirements:

–　　It shall be supplied by two independent fire or ballast pumps, one of which shall be ready for use at any time. These pumps shall not be installed in the same space;

–　　It shall be provided with a water main fitted with at least three hydrants in the cargo area above deck. Three suitable and sufficiently long hoses with spray nozzles having a diameter of not less than 12 mm shall be provided. It shall be possible to reach any point of the deck in the cargo area simultaneously with at least two jets of water which do not emanate from the same hydrant.

A spring-loaded non-return valve shall be fitted to ensure that no gases can escape through the fire-extinguishing system into the accommodation or service spaces outside the cargo area;

– The capacity of the system shall be at least sufficient for a jet of water to have a minimum reach of not less than the vessel's breadth from any location on board with two spray nozzles being used at the same time.

9.3.1.40.2   In addition the engine rooms, the cargo pump-room and all spaces containing special equipment (switchboards, compressors, etc.) for the refrigerant equipment if any, shall be provided with a permanently fixed fire-extinguishing system meeting the following requirements:

9.3.1.40.2.1   *Extinguishing agents*

For the protection of spaces in engine rooms, boiler rooms and pump rooms, only permanently fixed fire-extinguishing systems using the following extinguishing agents are permitted:

(a) CO_2 (carbon dioxide);

(b)   HFC 227 ea (heptafluoropropane);

(c)   IG-541 (52% nitrogen, 40% argon, 8% carbon dioxide).

Other extinguishing agents are permitted only on the basis of recommendations by the Administrative Committee.

9.3.1.40.2.2   *Ventilation, air extraction*

(a)   The combustion air required by the combustion engines which ensure propulsion should not come from spaces protected by permanently fixed fire-extinguishing systems. This requirement is not mandatory if the vessel has two independent main engine rooms with a gastight separation or if, in addition to the main engine room, there is a separate engine room installed with a bow thruster that can independently ensure propulsion in the event of a fire in the main engine room.

(b)   All forced ventilation systems in the space to be protected shall be shut down automatically as soon as the fire-extinguishing system is activated.

(c)   All openings in the space to be protected which permit air to enter or gas to escape shall be fitted with devices enabling them to be closed rapidly. It shall be clear whether they are open or closed.

(d)   Air escaping from the pressure-relief valves of the pressurised air tanks installed in the engine rooms shall be evacuated to the open air.

(e)   Overpressure or negative pressure caused by the diffusion of the extinguishing agent shall not destroy the constituent elements of the space to be protected. It shall be possible to ensure the safe equalisation of pressure.

(f)   Protected spaces shall be provided with a means of extracting the extinguishing agent. If extraction devices are installed, it shall not be possible to start them up during extinguishing.

9.3.1.40.2.3   *Fire alarm system*

The space to be protected shall be monitored by an appropriate fire alarm system. The alarm signal shall be audible in the wheelhouse, the accommodation and the space to be protected.

9.3.1.40.2.4   *Piping system*

(a)   The extinguishing agent shall be routed to and distributed in the space to be protected by means of a permanent piping system. Piping installed in the space to be protected and the reinforcements it incorporates shall be made of steel. This shall not apply to the connecting nozzles of tanks and compensators provided that the materials used have equivalent fire-retardant properties. Piping shall be protected against corrosion both internally and externally.

(b)   The discharge nozzles shall be so arranged as to ensure the regular diffusion of the extinguishing agent.

9.3.1.40.2.5   *Triggering device*

(a)   Automatically activated fire-extinguishing systems are not permitted.

(b)   It shall be possible to activate the fire-extinguishing system from a suitable point located outside the space to be protected.

(c)   Triggering devices shall be so installed that they can be activated in the event of a fire and so that the risk of their breakdown in the event of a fire or an explosion in the space to be protected is reduced as far as possible.

Systems which are not mechanically activated shall be supplied from two energy sources independent of each other. These energy sources shall be located outside the space to be protected. The control lines located in the space to be protected shall be so designed as to remain capable of operating in the event of a fire for a minimum of 30 minutes. The electrical installations are deemed to meet this requirement if they conform to the IEC 60331-21:1999 standard.

When the triggering devices are so placed as not to be visible, the component concealing them shall carry the "Fire-fighting system" symbol, each side being not less than 10 cm in length, with the following text in red letters on a white ground:

Fire-extinguishing system

(d)   If the fire-extinguishing system is intended to protect several spaces, it shall comprise a separate and clearly-marked triggering device for each space.

(e)   The instructions shall be posted alongside all triggering devices and shall be clearly visible and indelible. The instructions shall be in a language the master can read and understand and if this language is not English, French or German, they shall be in English, French or German. They shall include information concerning:

    (i)   the activation of the fire-extinguishing system;

    (ii)   the need to ensure that all persons have left the space to be protected;

        (iii)   the correct behaviour of the crew in the event of activation;

        (iv)   the correct behaviour of the crew in the event of the failure of the fire-extinguishing system to function properly.

(f)   The instructions shall mention that prior to the activation of the fire-extinguishing system, combustion engines installed in the space and aspirating air from the space to be protected, shall be shut down.

9.3.1.40.2.6   *Alarm device*

(a)   Permanently fixed fire-extinguishing systems shall be fitted with an audible and visual alarm device.

(b)   The alarm device shall be set off automatically as soon as the fire-extinguishing system is first activated. The alarm device shall function for an appropriate period of time before the extinguishing agent is released; it shall not be possible to turn it off.

(c)   Alarm signals shall be clearly visible in the spaces to be protected and their access points and be clearly audible under operating conditions corresponding to the highest possible sound level. It shall be possible to distinguish them clearly from all other sound and visual signals in the space to be protected.

(d)   Sound alarms shall also be clearly audible in adjoining spaces, with the communicating doors shut, and under operating conditions corresponding to the highest possible sound level.

(e)   If the alarm device is not intrinsically protected against short circuits, broken wires and drops in voltage, it shall be possible to monitor its operation.

(f)   A sign with the following text in red letters on a white ground shall be clearly posted at the entrance to any space the extinguishing agent may reach:

WARNING, FIRE-EXTINGUISHING SYSTEM!
LEAVE THIS SPACE IMMEDIATELY WHEN THE ... (DESCRIPTION)
ALARM IS ACTIVATED!

9.3.1.40.2.7   *Pressurised tanks, fittings and piping*

(a)   Pressurised tanks, fittings and piping shall conform to the requirements of the competent authority.

(b)   Pressurised tanks shall be installed in accordance with the manufacturer's instructions.

(c)   Pressurised tanks, fittings and piping shall not be installed in the accommodation.

(d)   The temperature of cabinets and storage spaces for pressurised tanks shall not exceed 50 °C.

(e)   Cabinets or storage spaces on deck shall be securely stowed and shall have vents so placed that in the event of a pressurised tank not being gastight, the escaping gas cannot penetrate into the vessel. Direct connections with other spaces are not permitted.

9.3.1.40.2.8   *Quantity of extinguishing agent*

If the quantity of extinguishing agent is intended for more than one space, the quantity of extinguishing agent available does not need to be greater than the quantity required for the largest of the spaces thus protected.

9.3.1.40.2.9   *Installation, maintenance, monitoring and documents*

(a)   The mounting or modification of the system shall only be performed by a company specialised in fire-extinguishing systems. The instructions (product data sheet, safety data sheet) provided by the manufacturer of the extinguishing agent or the system shall be followed.

(b)   The system shall be inspected by an expert:

   (i)   before being brought into service;

   (ii)   each time it is put back into service after activation;

   (iii)   after every modification or repair;

   (iv)   regularly, not less than every two years.

(c)   During the inspection, the expert is required to check that the system conforms to the requirements of 9.3.1.40.2.

(d)   The inspection shall include, as a minimum:

   (i)   an external inspection of the entire system;

   (ii)   an inspection to ensure that the piping is leakproof;

   (iii)   an inspection to ensure that the control and activation systems are in good working order;

   (iv)   an inspection of the pressure and contents of tanks;

   (v)   an inspection to ensure that the means of closing the space to be protected are leakproof;

   (vi)   an inspection of the fire alarm system;

   (vii)   an inspection of the alarm device.

(e)   The person performing the inspection shall establish, sign and date a certificate of inspection.

(f)   The number of permanently fixed fire-extinguishing systems shall be mentioned in the inspection certificate.

9.3.1.40.2.10   *Fire-extinguishing system operating with CO_2*

In addition to the requirements contained in 9.3.1.40.2.1 to 9.3.1.40.2.9, fire-extinguishing systems using CO_2 as an extinguishing agent shall conform to the following provisions:

(a) Tanks of CO_2 shall be placed in a gastight space or cabinet separated from other spaces. The doors of such storage spaces and cabinets shall open outwards; they shall be capable of being locked and shall carry on the outside the symbol "Warning: danger", not less than 5 cm high and "CO_2" in the same colours and the same size;

(b) Storage cabinets or spaces for CO_2 tanks located below deck shall only be accessible from the outside. These spaces shall have an artificial ventilation system with extractor hoods and shall be completely independent of the other ventilation systems on board;

(c) The level of filling of CO_2 tanks shall not exceed 0.75 kg/l. The volume of depressurised CO_2 shall be taken to be 0.56 m^3/kg;

(d) The concentration of CO_2 in the space to be protected shall be not less than 40% of the gross volume of the space. This quantity shall be released within 120 seconds. It shall be possible to monitor whether diffusion is proceeding correctly;

(e) The opening of the tank valves and the control of the diffusing valve shall correspond to two different operations;

(f) The appropriate period of time mentioned in 9.3.1.40.2.6 (b) shall be not less than 20 seconds. A reliable installation shall ensure the timing of the diffusion of CO_2.

9.3.1.40.2.11   *Fire-extinguishing system operating with HFC-227 ea (heptafluoropropane)*

In addition to the requirements of 9.1.0.40.2.1 to 9.1.0.40.2.9, fire-extinguishing systems using HFC-227 ea as an extinguishing agent shall conform to the following provisions:

(a) Where there are several spaces with different gross volumes, each space shall be equipped with its own fire-extinguishing system;

(b) Every tank containing HFC-227 ea placed in the space to be protected shall be fitted with a device to prevent overpressure. This device shall ensure that the contents of the tank are safely diffused in the space to be protected if the tank is subjected to fire, when the fire-extinguishing system has not been brought into service;

(c) Every tank shall be fitted with a device permitting control of the gas pressure;

(d) The level of filling of tanks shall not exceed 1.15 kg/l. The specific volume of depressurised HFC-227 ea shall be taken to be 0.1374 m^3/kg;

(e) The concentration of HFC-227 ea in the space to be protected shall be not less than 8% of the gross volume of the space. This quantity shall be released within 10 seconds;

(f) Tanks of HFC-227 ea shall be fitted with a pressure monitoring device which triggers an audible and visual alarm in the wheelhouse in the event of an unscheduled loss of propellant gas. Where there is no wheelhouse, the alarm shall be triggered outside the space to be protected;

(g) After discharge, the concentration in the space to be protected shall not exceed 10.5% (volume);

(h) The fire-extinguishing system shall not comprise aluminium parts.

9.3.1.40.2.12   *Fire-extinguishing system operating with IG-541*

In addition to the requirements of 9.3.1.40.2.1 to 9.3.1.40.2.9, fire-extinguishing systems using IG-541 as an extinguishing agent shall conform to the following provisions:

(a)   Where there are several spaces with different gross volumes, every space shall be equipped with its own fire-extinguishing system;

(b)   Every tank containing IG-541 placed in the space to be protected shall be fitted with a device to prevent overpressure. This device shall ensure that the contents of the tank are safely diffused in the space to be protected if the tank is subjected to fire, when the fire-extinguishing system has not been brought into service;

(c)   Each tank shall be fitted with a device for checking the contents;

(d)   The filling pressure of the tanks shall not exceed 200 bar at a temperature of +15 °C;

(e)   The concentration of IG-541 in the space to be protected shall be not less than 44% and not more than 50% of the gross volume of the space. This quantity shall be released within 120 seconds.

9.3.1.40.2.13   *Fire-extinguishing system for physical protection*

In order to ensure physical protection in the engine rooms, boiler rooms and pump rooms, fire-extinguishing systems are accepted solely on the basis of recommendations by the Administrative Committee.

9.3.1.40.3   The two hand fire-extinguishers referred to in 8.1.4 shall be located in the cargo area.

9.3.1.40.4   The fire-extinguishing agent and the quantity contained in the permanently fixed fire-extinguishing system shall be suitable and sufficient for fighting fires.

9.3.1.41   *Fire and naked light*

9.3.1.41.1   The outlets of funnels shall be located not less than 2.00 m from the cargo area. Arrangements shall be provided to prevent the escape of sparks and the entry of water.

9.3.1.41.2   Heating, cooking and refrigerating appliances shall not be fuelled with liquid fuels, liquid gas or solid fuels.

The installation in the engine room or in another separate space of heating appliances fuelled with liquid fuel having a flash-point above 55 °C is, however, permitted.

Cooking and refrigerating appliances are permitted only in the accommodation.

9.3.1.41.3   Only electrical lighting appliances are permitted.

9.3.1.42-
9.3.1.49   *(Reserved)*

9.3.1.50   *Documents concerning electrical installations*

9.3.1.50.1   In addition to the documents required by the Regulations referred to in 1.1.4.6, the following documents shall be on board:

(a) a drawing indicating the boundaries of the cargo area and the location of the electrical equipment installed in this area;

(b) a list of the electrical equipment referred to in (a) above including the following particulars:

machine or appliance, location, type of protection, type of protection against explosion, testing body and approval number;

(c) a list of or general plan indicating the electrical equipment outside the cargo area which may be operated during loading, unloading or gas-freeing. All other electrical equipment shall be marked in red. See 9.3.1.52.3 and 9.3.1.52.4.

9.3.1.50.2 The documents listed above shall bear the stamp of the competent authority issuing the certificate of approval.

9.3.1.51 *Electrical installations*

9.3.1.51.1 Only distribution systems without return connection to the hull are permitted.

This provision does not apply to:

– local installations outside the cargo area (e.g. connections of starters of diesel engines);

– the device for checking the insulation level referred to in 9.3.1.51.2 below.

9.3.1.51.2 Every insulated distribution network shall be fitted with an automatic device with a visual and audible alarm for checking the insulation level.

9.3.1.51.3 For the selection of electrical equipment to be used in zones presenting an explosion risk, the explosion groups and temperature classes assigned to the substances carried in the list of substances shall be taken into consideration (See columns (15) and (16) of Table C of Chapter 3.2).

9.3.1.52 *Type and location of electrical equipment*

9.3.1.52.1 (a) Only the following equipment may be installed in cargo tanks and pipes for loading and unloading (comparable to zone 0):

– measuring, regulation and alarm devices of the EEx (ia) type of protection.

(b) Only the following equipment may be installed in the cofferdams, double-hull spaces, double bottoms and hold spaces (comparable to zone 1):

– measuring, regulation and alarm devices of the certified safe type;

– lighting appliances of the "flame-proof enclosure" or "apparatus protected by pressurization" type of protection;

– hermetically sealed echo sounding devices the cables of which are led through thick-walled steel tubes with gastight connections up to the main deck;

– cables for the active cathodic protection of the shell plating in protective steel tubes such as those provided for echo sounding devices.

(c)   Only the following equipment may be installed in the service spaces in the cargo area below deck (comparable to zone 1):

–   measuring, regulation and alarm devices of the certified safe type;

–   lighting appliances of the "flame-proof enclosure" or "apparatus protected by pressurization" type of protection;

–   motors driving essential equipment such as ballast pumps; they shall be of the certified safe type.

(d)   The control and protective equipment of the electrical equipment referred to in (a), (b) and (c) above shall be located outside the cargo area if they are not intrinsically safe.

(e)   The electrical equipment in the cargo area on deck (comparable to zone 1) shall be of the certified safe type.

9.3.1.52.2   Accumulators shall be located outside the cargo area.

9.3.1.52.3   (a)   Electrical equipment used during loading, unloading and gas-freeing during berthing and which are located outside the cargo area (comparable to zone 2) shall be at least of the "limited explosion risk" type.

(b)   This provision does not apply to:

(i)   lighting installations in the accommodation, except for switches near entrances to accommodation;

(ii)   radiotelephone installations in the accommodation or the wheelhouse;

(iii)   electrical installations in the accommodation, the wheelhouse or the service spaces outside the cargo areas if:

1.   These spaces are fitted with a ventilation system ensuring an overpressure of 0.1 kPa (0.001 bar) and none of the windows is capable of being opened; the air intakes of the ventilation system located as far away as possible, however, not less than 6.00 m from the cargo area and not less than 2.00 m above the deck;

2.   The spaces are fitted with a gas detection system with sensors:

–   at the suction inlets of the ventilation system;

–   directly at the top edge of the sill of the entrance doors of the accommodation and service spaces;

3.   The gas concentration measurement is continuous;

4.   When the gas concentration reaches 20% of the lower explosive limit, the ventilators shall be switched off. In such a case and when the overpressure is not maintained or in the event of failure of the gas detection system, the electrical installations which do not comply with (a) above, shall be switched off. These operations shall be performed immediately and automatically and activate the emergency lighting in the accommodation, the wheelhouse and the service spaces, which shall comply at least with the "limited explosion risk" type. The switching-off

shall be indicated in the accommodation and wheelhouse by visual and audible signals;

5.   The ventilation system, the gas detection system and the alarm of the switch-off device fully comply with the requirements of (a) above;

6.   The automatic switch-off device is set so that no automatic switching-off may occur while the vessel is under way.

9.3.1.52.4   The electrical equipment which does not meet the requirements set out in 9.3.1.52.3 above together with its switches shall be marked in red. The disconnection of such equipment shall be operated from a centralised location on board.

9.3.1.52.5   An electric generator which is permanently driven by an engine and which does not meet the requirements of 9.3.1.52.3 above, shall be fitted with a switch capable of shutting down the excitation of the generator. A notice board with the operating instructions shall be displayed near the switch.

9.3.1.52.6   Sockets for the connection of signal lights and gangway lighting shall be permanently fitted to the vessel close to the signal mast or the gangway. Connecting and disconnecting shall not be possible except when the sockets are not live.

9.3.1.52.7   The failure of the power supply for the safety and control equipment shall be immediately indicated by visual and audible signals at the locations where the alarms are usually actuated.

9.3.1.53   *Earthing*

9.3.1.53.1   The metal parts of electrical appliances in the cargo area which are not live as well as protective metal tubes or metal sheaths of cables in normal service shall be earthed, unless they are so arranged that they are automatically earthed by bonding to the metal structure of the vessel.

9.3.1.53.2   The provisions of 9.3.1.53.1 above apply also to equipment having service voltages of less than 50 V.

9.3.1.53.3   Independent cargo tanks shall be earthed.

9.3.1.53.4   Metal intermediate bulk containers (IBCs) and tank-containers, used as residual cargo tanks or slop tanks, shall be capable of being earthed.

9.3.1.54-
9.3.1.55   *(Reserved)*

9.3.1.56   *Electrical cables*

9.3.1.56.1   All cables in the cargo area shall have a metallic sheath.

9.3.1.56.2   Cables and sockets in the cargo area shall be protected against mechanical damage.

9.3.1.56.3   Movable cables are prohibited in the cargo area, except for intrinsically safe electric circuits or for the supply of signal lights and gangway lighting.

9.3.1.56.4   Cables of intrinsically safe circuits shall only be used for such circuits and shall be separated from other cables not intended for being used in such circuits (e.g. they shall not be installed together in the same string of cables and they shall not be fixed by the same cable clamps).

9.3.1.56.5 For movable cables intended for signal lights and gangway lighting, only sheathed cables of type H 07 RN-F in accordance with 245 IEC 66 or cables of at least equivalent design having conductors with a cross-section of not less than 1.5 mm^2 shall be used.

These cables shall be as short as possible and installed so that damage is not likely to occur.

9.3.1.57-
9.3.1.59 *(Reserved)*

9.3.1.60 *Special equipment*

A shower and an eye and face bath shall be provided on the vessel at a location which is directly accessible from the cargo area.

9.3.1.61-
9.3.1.70 *(Reserved)*

9.3.1.71 *Admittance on board*

The notice boards displaying the prohibition of admittance in accordance with 8.3.3 shall be clearly legible from either side of the vessel.

9.3.1.72-
9.3.1.73 *(Reserved)*

9.3.1.74 *Prohibition of smoking, fire or naked light*

9.3.1.74.1 The notice boards displaying the prohibition of smoking in accordance with 8.3.4 shall be clearly legible from either side of the vessel.

9.3.1.74.2 Notice boards indicating the circumstances under which the prohibition is applicable shall be fitted near the entrances to the spaces where smoking or the use of fire or naked light is not always prohibited.

9.3.1.74.3 Ashtrays shall be provided close to each exit of the accommodation and the wheelhouse.

9.3.1.75-
9.3.1.91 *(Reserved)*

9.3.1.92 *Emergency exit*

Spaces the entrances or exits of which are likely to become partly or completely immersed in the damaged condition shall have an emergency exit which is situated not less than 0.10 m above the damage waterline. This does not apply to forepeak and afterpeak.

9.3.1.93-
9.3.1.99 *(Reserved)*

9.3.2 *Rules for construction of type C tank vessels*

The rules for construction of 9.3.2.0 to 9.3.2.99 apply to type C tank vessels.

9.3.2.0 *Materials of construction*

9.3.2.0.1 (a) The vessel's hull and the cargo tanks shall be constructed of shipbuilding steel or other at least equivalent metal.

The independent cargo tanks may also be constructed of other materials, provided these have at least equivalent mechanical properties and resistance against the effects of temperature and fire.

(b)   Every part of the vessel including any installation and equipment which may come into contact with the cargo shall consist of materials which can neither be dangerously affected by the cargo nor cause decomposition of the cargo or react with it so as to form harmful or hazardous products.

(c)   Inside vapour pipes and gas discharge pipes shall be protected against corrosion.

9.3.2.0.2   Except where explicitly permitted in 9.3.2.0.3 below or in the certificate of approval, the use of wood, aluminium alloys or plastic materials within the cargo area is prohibited.

9.3.2.0.3   (a)   The use of wood, aluminium alloys or plastic materials within the cargo area is only permitted for:

- gangways and external ladders;

- movable items of equipment (aluminium gauging rods are, however permitted, provided that they are fitted with brass feet or protected in another way to avoid sparking);

- chocking of cargo tanks which are independent of the vessel's hull and chocking of installations and equipment;

- masts and similar round timber;

- engine parts;

- parts of the electrical installation;

- loading and unloading appliances;

- lids of boxes which are placed on the deck.

(b)   The use of wood or plastic materials within the cargo area is only permitted for:

- supports and stops of any kind.

(c)   The use of plastic materials or rubber within the cargo area is only permitted for:

- coating of cargo tanks and of pipes for loading and unloading;

- all kinds of gaskets (e.g. for dome or hatch covers);

- electric cables;

- hoses for loading and unloading;

- insulation of cargo tanks and of hoses for loading and unloading.

(d)   All permanently fitted materials in the accommodation or wheelhouse, with the exception of furniture, shall not readily ignite. They shall not evolve fumes or toxic gases in dangerous quantities, if involved in a fire.

9.3.2.0.4 The paint used in the cargo area shall not be liable to produce sparks in case of impact.

9.3.2.0.5 The use of plastic material for vessel's boats is permitted only if the material does not readily ignite.

9.3.2.1- (*Reserved*)
9.3.2.7

9.3.2.8 *Classification*

9.3.2.8.1 The tank vessel shall be built under survey of a recognised classification society in accordance with the rules established by that classification society for its highest class, and the tank vessel shall be classed accordingly.

The vessel's class shall be continued.

The classification society shall issue a certificate certifying that the vessel is in conformity with the rules of this section.

The design pressure and the test pressure of cargo tanks shall be entered in the certificate.

If a vessel has cargo tanks with different valve opening pressures, the design and test pressures of each tank shall be entered in the certificate.

The classification society shall draw up a certificate mentioning all the dangerous goods accepted for carriage by the vessel (see also 1.16.1.2.5).

9.3.2.8.2 The cargo pump-rooms shall be inspected by a recognised classification society whenever the certificate of approval has to be renewed as well as during the third year of validity of the certificate of approval. The inspection shall comprise at least:

–   an inspection of the whole system for its condition, for corrosion, leakage or conversion works which have not been approved;

–   a checking of the condition of the gas detection system in the cargo pump-rooms.

Inspection certificates signed by the recognised classification society with respect to the inspection of the cargo pump-rooms shall be kept on board. The inspection certificates shall at least include particulars of the above inspection and the results obtained as well as the date of the inspection.

9.3.2.8.3 The condition of the gas detection system referred to in 9.3.2.52.3 (b) shall be checked by a recognised classification society whenever the certificate of approval has to be renewed and during the third year of validity of the certificate of approval. A certificate signed by the recognised classification society shall be kept on board.

9.3.2.9 (*Reserved*)

9.3.2.10 *Protection against the penetration of gases*

9.3.2.10.1 The vessel shall be designed so as to prevent gases from penetrating into the accommodation and the service spaces.

9.3.2.10.2   The lower edges of door-openings in the sidewalls of superstructures and the coamings of access hatches to under-deck spaces shall have a height of not less than 0.50 m above the deck.

This requirement need not be complied with if the wall of the superstructures facing the cargo area extends from one side of the ship to the other and has doors the sills of which have a height of not less than 0.50 m. The height of this wall shall be not less than 2.00 m. In this case, the lower edges of door-openings in the sidewalls of superstructures and of coamings of access hatches behind this wall shall have a height of not less than 0.10 m. The sills of engine-room doors and the coamings of its access hatches shall, however, always have a height of not less than 0.50 m.

9.3.2.10.3   The bulwarks, foot-rails, etc. shall be provided with sufficiently large openings which are located directly above the deck.

9.3.2.11   *Hold spaces and cargo tanks*

9.3.2.11.1   (a)   The maximum permissible capacity of a cargo tank shall be determined in accordance with the following table:

$L \times B \times H$ (m³)	Maximum permissible capacity of a cargo tank (m³)
up to 600	$L \times B \times H \times 0.3$
600 to 3 750	$180 + (L \times B \times H - 600) \times 0.0635$
> 3 750	380

In the table above $L \times B \times H$ is the product of the main dimensions of the tank vessel in metres (according to the measurement certificate), where:

L = overall length of the hull;
B = extreme breadth of the hull;
H = shortest vertical distance between the top of the keel and the lowest point of the deck at the side of the vessel (moulded depth) within the cargo area.

(b)   The relative density of the substances to be carried shall be taken into consideration in the design of the cargo tanks. The maximum relative density shall be indicated in the certificate of approval.

(c)   When the vessel is provided with pressure cargo tanks, these tanks shall be designed for a working pressure of 400 kPa (4 bar).

(d)   For vessels with a length of not more than 50.00 m, the length of a cargo tank shall not exceed 10.00 m; and

For vessels with a length of more than 50.00 m, the length of a cargo tank shall not exceed 0.20 L.

This provision does not apply to vessels with independent built-in cylindrical tanks having a length to diameter ratio ≤ 7.

9.3.2.11.2   (a)   In the cargo area (except cofferdams) the vessel shall be designed as a flush-deck double-hull vessel, with double-hull spaces and double bottoms, but without a trunk.

Cargo tanks independent of the vessels' hull and refrigerated cargo tanks may only be installed in a hold space which is bounded by double-hull spaces and double bottoms in accordance with 9.3.2.11.7 below. The cargo tanks shall not extend beyond the deck.

(b)   The cargo tanks independent of the vessel's hull shall be fixed so that they cannot float.

(c)   The capacity of a suction well shall be limited to not more than 0.10 m³.

(d)   Side-stringers linking or supporting the load-bearing components of the sides of the vessel with the load-bearing components of the longitudinal walls of cargo tanks and side-stringers linking the load-bearing components of the vessel's bottom with the tank-bottom are prohibited.

9.3.2.11.3   (a)   The cargo tanks shall be separated by cofferdams of at least 0.60 m in width from the accommodation, engine room and service spaces outside the cargo area below deck or, if there are no such accommodation, engine room and service spaces, from the vessel's ends. Where the cargo tanks are installed in a hold space, a space of not less than 0.50 m shall be provided between such tanks and the end bulkheads of the hold space. In this case an insulated end bulkhead meeting at least the definition for Class "A-60" according to SOLAS 74, Chapter II-2, Regulation 3, shall be deemed equivalent to a cofferdam. For pressure cargo tanks, the 0.50 m distance may be reduced to 0.20 m.

(b)   Hold spaces, cofferdams and cargo tanks shall be capable of being inspected.

(c)   All spaces in the cargo area shall be capable of being ventilated. Means for checking their gas-free condition shall be provided.

9.3.2.11.4   The bulkheads bounding the cargo tanks, cofferdams and hold spaces shall be watertight. The cargo tanks, cofferdams and the end bulkheads of the hold spaces, as well as the bulkheads bounding the cargo area shall have no openings or penetrations below deck. Penetrations through bulkheads between two hold spaces are, however, permitted.

The bulkhead between the engine room and the cofferdam or service space in the cargo area or between the engine room and a hold space may be fitted with penetrations provided that they conform to the provisions of 9.3.2.1.7.5.

The bulkhead between the cargo tank and the cargo pump-room below deck may be fitted with penetrations provided that they conform to the provisions of 9.3.2.1.7.6. If the vessel is fitted with a cargo pump-room below deck, the bulkheads between the cargo tanks may be fitted with passages provided that the loading pipes are fitted with shut-off devices at the outlet from the cargo tank and in the cargo pump-room direct at the bulkhead. The shut-off devices shall be capable of being activated from the deck.

9.3.2.11.5   Double-hull spaces and double bottoms in the cargo area shall be arranged for being filled with ballast water only. Double bottoms may, however, be used as oil fuel tanks, provided they comply with the provisions of 9.3.2.32.

9.3.2.11.6   (a)   A cofferdam, the centre part of a cofferdam or another space below deck in the cargo area may be arranged as a service space, provided the bulkheads bounding the service space extend vertically to the bottom. This service space shall only be accessible from the deck.

(b)   The service space shall be watertight with the exception of its access hatches and ventilation inlets.

(c) No pipes for loading and unloading shall be fitted within the service space referred to under (a) above.

Pipes for loading and unloading may be fitted in the cargo pump-rooms below deck only when they conform to the provisions of 9.3.2.17.6.

9.3.2.11.7 For double-hull construction with the cargo tanks integrated in the vessel's structure, the distance between the side wall of the vessel and the longitudinal bulkhead of the cargo tanks shall be not less than 1.00 m. A distance of 0.80 m may however be permitted, provided that, compared with the scantling requirements specified in the rules for construction of a recognised classification society, the following reinforcements have been made:

(a) 25% increase in the thickness of the deck stringer plate;

(b) 15% increase in the side plating thickness;

(c) Arrangement of a longitudinal framing system at the vessel's side, where depth of the longitudinals shall be not less than 0.15 m and the longitudinals shall have a face plate with the cross-sectional area of at least 7.0 cm^2.

(d) The stringer or longitudinal framing systems shall be supported by web frames, and like bottom girders fitted with lightening holes, at a maximum spacing of 1.80 m. These distances may be increased if the longitudinals are strengthened accordingly.

When a vessel is built according to the transverse framing system, a longitudinal stringer system shall be arranged instead of (c) above. The distance between the longitudinal stringers shall not exceed 0.80 m and their depth shall be not less than 0.15 m, provided they are completely welded to the frames. The cross-sectional area of the facebar or faceplate shall be not less than 7.0 cm^2 as in (c) above. Where cut-outs are arranged in the stringer at the connection with the frames, the web depth of the stringer shall be increased with the depth of cut-outs.

The mean depth of the double bottoms shall be not less than 0.70 m. It shall, however, never be less than 0.60 m.

The depth below the suction wells may be reduced to 0.50 m.

9.3.2.11.8 When a vessel is built with cargo tanks located in a hold space or refrigerated cargo tanks, the distance between the double walls of the hold space shall be not less than 0.80 m and the depth of the double bottom shall be not less than 0.60 m.

9.3.2.11.9 Where service spaces are located in the cargo area under deck, they shall be arranged so as to be easily accessible and to permit persons wearing protective clothing and breathing apparatus to safely operate the service equipment contained therein. They shall be designed so as to allow injured or unconscious personnel to be removed from such spaces without difficulties, if necessary by means of fixed equipment.

9.3.2.11.10 Cofferdams, double-hull spaces, double bottoms, cargo tanks, hold spaces and other accessible spaces within the cargo area shall be arranged so that they may be completely inspected and cleaned in an appropriate manner. The dimensions of openings except for those of double-hull spaces and double bottoms which do not have a wall adjoining the cargo tanks shall be sufficient to allow a person wearing breathing apparatus to enter or leave the space without difficulties. These openings shall have a minimum cross-sectional area of 0.36 m^2 and a minimum side length of 0.50 m. They shall be designed so as to allow injured or unconscious personnel to be removed from the bottom of such a space without difficulties, if necessary by means of fixed equipment. In these spaces the distance between the reinforcements shall not be less than 0.50 m. In double bottoms this distance may be reduced to 0.45 m.

Cargo tanks may have circular openings with a diameter of not less than 0.68 m.

9.3.2.12   *Ventilation*

9.3.2.12.1   Each hold space shall have two openings the dimensions and location of which shall be such as to permit effective ventilation of any part of the hold space. If there are no such openings, it shall be possible to fill the hold spaces with inert gas or dry air.

9.3.2.12.2   Double-hull spaces and double bottoms within the cargo area which are not arranged for being filled with ballast water, hold spaces and cofferdams shall be provided with ventilation systems.

9.3.2.12.3   Any service spaces located in the cargo area below deck shall be provided with a system of forced ventilation with sufficient power for ensuring at least 20 changes of air per hour based on the volume of the space. The ventilator fan shall be designed so that no sparks may be emitted on contact of the impeller blades with the housing and no static electricity may be generated.

The ventilation exhaust ducts shall extend down to 50 mm above the bottom of the service space. The air shall be supplied through a duct at the top of the service space. The air inlets shall be located not less than 2.00 m above the deck, at a distance of not less than 2.00 m from tank openings and 6.00 m from the outlets of safety valves.

The extension pipes, which may be necessary, may be of the hinged type.

9.3.2.12.4   Ventilation of accommodation and service spaces shall be possible.

9.3.2.12.5   Ventilators used for gas-freeing of tanks shall be designed so that no sparks may be emitted on contact of the impeller blades with the housing and no static electricity may be generated.

9.3.2.12.6   Notice boards shall be fitted at the ventilation inlets indicating the conditions when they shall be closed. Any ventilation inlets of accommodation and service spaces leading outside shall be fitted with fire flaps. Such ventilation inlets shall be located not less than 2.00 m from the cargo area.

Ventilation inlets of service spaces in the cargo area below deck may be located within such area.

9.3.2.12.7   The flame-arresters prescribed in 9.3.2.20.4, 9.3.2.21.11, 9.3.2.22.4, 9.3.2.22.5 and 9.3.2.26.3 shall be of a type approved for this purpose by the competent authority.

9.3.2.13   *Stability (general)*

9.3.2.13.1   Proof of sufficient stability shall be furnished including for stability in damaged condition.

9.3.2.13.2   The basic values for the stability calculation - the vessel's lightweight and location of the centre of gravity - shall be determined either by means of an inclining experiment or by detailed mass and moment calculation. In the latter case the lightweight of the vessel shall be checked by means of a lightweight test with a tolerance limit of ± 5% between the mass determined by calculation and the displacement determined by the draught readings.

9.3.2.13.3   Proof of sufficient intact stability shall be furnished for all stages of loading and unloading and for the final loading condition.

Floatability after damage shall be proved for the most unfavourable loading condition. For this purpose, calculated proof of sufficient stability shall be established for critical intermediate stages of flooding and for the final stage of flooding. Negative values of stability in intermediate stages of flooding may be accepted only if the continued range of curve of righting lever in damaged condition indicates adequate positive values of stability.

9.3.2.14   *Stability (intact)*

9.3.2.14.1   The requirements for intact stability resulting from the damage stability calculation shall be fully complied with.

9.3.2.14.2   For vessels with cargo tanks of more than 0.70 B in width, additional proof shall be furnished that, at an angle of 5° or, when this angle is less, at a heeling angle at which an opening becomes immersed, the righting arm is 0.10 m. The stability-reducing free surface effect in the case of cargo tanks filled to less than 95% of their capacity shall be taken into account.

9.3.2.14.3   The most stringent requirement of 9.3.2.14.1 and 9.3.2.14.2 is applicable to the vessel.

9.3.2.15   *Stability (damaged condition)*

9.3.2.15.1   The following assumptions shall be taken into consideration for the damaged condition:

(a)   The extent of side damage is as follows:

longitudinal extent:	at least 0.10 L, but not less than 5.00 m;
transverse extent:	0.79 m;
vertical extent:	from the base line upwards without limit.

(b)   The extent of bottom damage is as follows:

longitudinal extent:	at least 0.10 L, but not less than 5.00 m;
transverse extent:	3.00 m;
vertical extent:	from the base 0.59 m upwards, the sump excepted.

(c)   Any bulkheads within the damaged area shall be assumed damaged, which means that the location of bulkheads shall be chosen so as to ensure that the vessel remains afloat after the flooding of two or more adjacent compartments in the longitudinal direction.

The following provisions are applicable:

–   For bottom damage, adjacent athwartship compartments shall also be assumed as flooded;

–   The lower edge of any non-watertight openings (e.g. doors, windows, access hatchways) shall, at the final stage of flooding, be not less than 0.10 m above the damage waterline;

–   In general, permeability shall be assumed to be 95%. Where an average permeability of less than 95% is calculated for any compartment, this calculated value obtained may be used. However, the following minimum values shall be used:

–   engine rooms: 85%;

– accommodation:	95%;
– double bottoms, oil fuel tanks, ballast tanks, etc., depending on whether, according to their function, they have to be assumed as full or empty for the vessel floating at the maximum permissible draught:	0% or 95%.

For the main engine room only the one-compartment standard need be taken into account, i.e. the end bulkheads of the engine room shall be assumed as not damaged.

9.3.2.15.2   At the stage of equilibrium (final stage of flooding), the angle of heel shall not exceed 12°. Non-watertight openings shall not be flooded before reaching the stage of equilibrium. If such openings are immersed before that stage, the corresponding spaces shall be considered as flooded for the purpose of the stability calculation.

The positive range of the righting lever curve beyond the stage of equilibrium shall have a righting lever of ≥0.05 m in association with an area under the curve of ≥0.0065 m.rad. The minimum values of stability shall be satisfied up to immersion of the first non-watertight opening and in any event up to an angle of heel ≤27°. If non-watertight openings are immersed before that stage, the corresponding spaces shall be considered as flooded for the purposes of stability calculation.

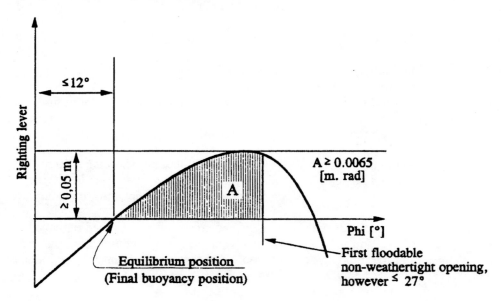

9.3.2.15.3   If openings through which undamaged compartments may additionally become flooded are capable of being closed watertight, the closing appliances shall be marked accordingly.

9.3.2.15.4   Where cross- or down-flooding openings are provided for reduction of unsymmetrical flooding, the time for equalisation shall not exceed 15 minutes, if during the intermediate stages of flooding sufficient stability has been proved.

9.3.2.16   *Engine rooms*

9.3.2.16.1   Internal combustion engines for the vessel's propulsion as well as internal combustion engines for auxiliary machinery shall be located outside the cargo area. Entrances and other openings of engine rooms shall be at a distance of not less than 2.00 m from the cargo area.

| 9.3.2.16.2 | The engine rooms shall be accessible from the deck; the entrances shall not face the cargo area. Where the doors are not located in a recess whose depth is at least equal to the door width, the hinges shall face the cargo area. |

9.3.2.17 *Accommodation and service spaces*

| 9.3.2.17.1 | Accommodation spaces and the wheelhouse shall be located outside the cargo area forward of the fore vertical plane or abaft the aft vertical plane bounding the part of cargo area below deck. Windows of the wheelhouse which are located not less than 1.00 m above the bottom of the wheelhouse may tilt forward. |

| 9.3.2.17.2 | Entrances to spaces and openings of superstructures shall not face the cargo area. Doors opening outward and not located in a recess the depth of which is at least equal to the width of the doors shall have their hinges face the cargo area. |

| 9.3.2.17.3 | Entrances from the deck and openings of spaces facing the weather shall be capable of being closed. The following instruction shall be displayed at the entrance of such spaces: |

**DO NOT OPEN DURING LOADING, UNLOADING OR GAS-FREEING
WITHOUT PERMISSION FROM THE MASTER.
CLOSE IMMEDIATELY.**

| 9.3.2.17.4 | Entrances and windows of superstructures and accommodation spaces which can be opened as well as other openings of these spaces shall be located not less than 2.00 m from the cargo area. No wheelhouse doors and windows shall be located within 2.00 m from the cargo area, except where there is no direct connection between the wheelhouse and the accommodation. |

| 9.3.2.17.5 | (a) | Driving shafts of the bilge or ballast pumps in the cargo area may penetrate through the bulkhead between the service space and the engine room, provided the arrangement of the service space is in compliance with 9.3.2.11.6. |

(b) The penetration of the shaft through the bulkhead shall be gastight and shall have been approved by a recognised classification society.

(c) The necessary operating instructions shall be displayed.

(d) Penetrations through the bulkhead between the engine room and the service space in the cargo area and the bulkhead between the engine room and the hold spaces may be provided for electrical cables, hydraulic and piping for measuring, control and alarm systems, provided that the penetration have been approved by a recognised classification society. The penetrations shall be gastight. Penetrations through a bulkhead with an "A-60" fire protection insulation according to SOLAS 74, Chapter II-2, Regulation 3, shall have an equivalent fire protection.

(e) Pipes may penetrate the bulkhead between the engine room and the service space in the cargo area provided that these are pipes between the mechanical equipment in the engine room and the service space which do not have any openings within the service space and which are provided with shut-off devices at the bulkhead in the engine room.

(f) Pipes from the engine room may pass through the service space in the cargo area or a cofferdam or a hold space to the outside provided that within the service space or cofferdam or hold space they are of the thick-walled type and have no flanges or openings.

(g)   Where a driving shaft of auxiliary machinery penetrates through a wall located above the deck the penetration shall be gastight.

9.3.2.17.6   A service space located within the cargo area below deck shall not be used as a cargo pump-room for the loading and unloading system, except where:

–   the pump room is separated from the engine room or from service spaces outside the cargo area by a cofferdam or a bulkhead with an "A-60" fire protection insulation according to SOLAS 74, Chapter II-2, Regulation 3, or by a service space or a hold space;

–   the "A-60" bulkhead required above does not include penetrations referred to in 9.3.2.17.5 (a);

–   ventilation exhaust outlets are located not less than 6.00 m from entrances and openings of the accommodation and service spaces outside the cargo area;

–   the access hatches and ventilation inlets can be closed from the outside;

–   all pipes for loading and unloading as well as those of stripping systems are provided with shut-off devices at the pump suction side in the cargo pump-room immediately at the bulkhead. The necessary operation of the control devices in the pump-room, starting of pumps and control of the liquid flow rate shall be effected from the deck;

–   the bilge of the cargo pump-room is equipped with a gauging device for measuring the filling level which activates a visual and audible alarm in the wheelhouse when liquid is accumulating in the cargo pump-room bilge;

–   the cargo pump-room is provided with a permanent gas-detection system which automatically indicates the presence of explosive gases or lack of oxygen by means of direct-measuring sensors and which actuates a visual and audible alarm when the gas concentration has reached 20% of the lower explosive limit. The sensors of this system shall be placed at suitable positions at the bottom and directly below the deck.

Measurement shall be continuous.

The audible and visual alarms are installed in the wheelhouse and in the cargo pump-room and, when the alarm is actuated, the loading and unloading system is shut down. Failure of the gas detection system shall be immediately signalled in the wheelhouse and on deck by means of audible and visual alarms;

–   the ventilation system prescribed in 9.3.9.12.3 has a capacity of not less than 30 changes of air per hour based on the total volume of the service space.

9.3.2.17.7   The following instruction shall be displayed at the entrance of the cargo pump-room:

**BEFORE ENTERING THE CARGO PUMP-ROOM CHECK WHETHER
IT IS FREE FROM GASES AND CONTAINS SUFFICIENT OXYGEN.
DO NOT OPEN DOORS AND ENTRANCE OPENINGS WITHOUT
THE PERMISSION OF THE MASTER.
LEAVE IMMEDIATELY IN THE EVENT OF ALARM.**

9.3.2.18-   (*Reserved*)
9.3.2.19

9.3.2.20   *Arrangement of cofferdams*

9.3.2.20.1   Cofferdams or cofferdam compartments located next to a service space which has been arranged in accordance with 9.3.2.11.6 shall be accessible through an access hatch.

The access hatches and ventilation inlets shall be located not less than 0.50 m above the deck.

9.3.2.20.2   Cofferdams shall be capable of being filled with water and emptied by means of a pump. Filling shall be effected within 30 minutes. These requirements are not applicable when the bulkhead between the engine room and the cofferdam comprises fire-protection insulation "A-60" in accordance with SOLAS 74, Chapter II-2, Regulation 3, or has been fitted out as a service space. The cofferdams shall not be fitted with inlet valves.

9.3.2.20.3   No fixed pipe shall permit connection between a cofferdam and other piping of the vessel outside the cargo area.

9.3.2.20.4   The ventilation openings of cofferdams shall be fitted with a flame-arrester withstanding a deflagration.

9.3.2.21   *Safety and control installations*

9.3.2.21.1   Cargo tanks shall be provided with the following equipment:

(a)   a mark inside the tank indicating the liquid level of 95%;

(b)   a level gauge;

(c)   a level alarm device which is activated at the latest when a degree of filling of 90% is reached;

(d)   a high level sensor for actuating the facility against overflowing at the latest when a degree of filling of 97.5% is reached;

(e)   an instrument for measuring the pressure of the vapour phase inside the cargo tank;

(f)   an instrument for measuring the temperature of the cargo, if in column (9) of Table C of Chapter 3.2 a heating installation is required, or if a maximum temperature is indicated in column (20) of that list;

(g)   a nozzle with a closure connected to a sampling device, closed or partially closed, and/or a sampling opening as required in column (13) of Table C of Chapter 3.2.

9.3.2.21.2   When the degree of filling in per cent is determined, an error of not more than 0.5% is permitted. It shall be calculated on the basis of the total cargo tank capacity including the expansion trunk.

9.3.2.21.3   The level gauge shall allow readings from the control position of the shut-off devices of the particular cargo tank.

9.3.2.21.4   The level alarm device shall give a visual and audible warning on board when actuated. The level alarm device shall be independent of the level gauge.

9.3.2.21.5   The high level sensor referred to in 9.3.2.21.1 (d) above shall give a visual and audible alarm on board and at the same time actuate an electrical contact which in the form of a binary signal interrupts the electric current loop provided and fed by the shore facility, thus initiating measures at the shore facility against overflowing during loading operations.

The signal shall be transmitted to the shore facility via a watertight two-pin plug of a connector device in accordance with IEC Publication No. 309 (1992) for direct current of 40 to 50 volts, identification colour white, position of the nose 10 h.

The plug shall be permanently fitted to the vessel close to the shore connections of the loading and unloading pipes.

The high level sensor shall also be capable of switching off the vessel's own discharging pump. The high level sensor shall be independent of the level alarm device, but it may be connected to the level gauge.

9.3.2.21.6   The visual and audible signals given by the level alarm device shall be clearly distinguishable from those of the high level sensor.

The visual alarm shall be visible at each control position on deck of the cargo tank stop valves. It shall be possible to easily check the functioning of the sensors and electric circuits or these shall be "intrinsically safe apparatus".

9.3.2.21.7   When the pressure or temperature exceeds a set value, instruments for measuring the vacuum or overpressure of the gaseous phase in the cargo tank or the temperature of the cargo, shall activate a visual and audible alarm in the wheelhouse. When the wheelhouse is unoccupied the alarm shall also be perceptible in a location occupied by a crew member.

When the pressure exceeds the set value during loading, the instrument for measuring the pressure shall, by means of the plug referred to in 9.3.2.21.5 above, initiate immediately an electrical contact which shall put into effect measures to interrupt the loading operation. If the vessel's own discharge pump is used, it shall be switched off automatically.

The instrument for measuring the overpressure or vacuum shall activate the alarm at latest when an overpressure equal to 1.15 times the opening pressure of the pressure relief device, or a vacuum pressure of 1.1 times the opening pressure of the vacuum valve is reached. The maximum allowable temperature is indicated in column (20) of Table C of Chapter 3.2. The sensors for the alarms mentioned in this paragraph may be connected to the alarm device of the sensor.

When it is prescribed in column (20) of Table C of Chapter 3.2, the instrument for measuring the overpressure of the gaseous phase shall activate a visible and audible alarm in the wheelhouse when the overpressure exceeds 40 kPa during the voyage. When the wheelhouse is unoccupied, the alarm shall also be perceptible in a location occupied by a crew member.

When a manometer is used to measure the overpressure or the vacuum pressure, its indicator scale shall not be less than 0.14 m in diameter. The maximum permissible overpressure or vacuum values shall be indicated by a red mark.

The manometers shall be capable of being read at any time from the location where it is possible to interrupt loading or unloading or in the immediate vicinity of the water-spray system control.

9.3.2.21.8   Where the control elements of the shut-off devices of the cargo tanks are located in a control room, reading of the level gauges shall be possible in the control room and the visual and audible warning given by the level alarm device, the high level sensor referred to in 9.3.2.21.1 (d) and the instruments for measuring the pressure of the vapour phase and temperature of the cargo shall be noticeable in the control room and on deck.

Satisfactory monitoring of the cargo area shall be ensured from the control room.

9.3.2.21.9   The closed-type sampling device penetrating through the boundary of the cargo tank but constituting a part of a closed system shall be designed so that during sampling no gas or liquid may escape from the cargo tank. The device shall be of a type approved by the competent authority for this purpose.

9.3.2.21.10   The partly closed sampling device penetrating through the boundary of the cargo tank shall be such that during sampling only a small quantity of gaseous or liquid cargo can escape into the open air. As long as the device is not used it shall be closed completely. The device shall be of a type approved by the competent authority for this purpose.

9.3.2.21.11   The sampling openings shall have a diameter of not more than 0.30 m. They shall be fitted with a flame arrester plate stack, capable of withstanding steady burning and shall be so designed that the opening period will be as short as possible and that the flame arrester plate stack cannot remain open without external intervention. The manometers shall be capable of being read in the immediate vicinity of the water-spray system control.

9.3.2.21.12   The vessel shall be so equipped that loading or unloading operations can be interrupted by means of switches, i.e. the quick-action stop valve located on the flexible vessel-to-shore connecting line must be capable of being closed. The switch shall be placed at two points on the vessel (fore and aft).

This provision applies only when prescribed in column (20) of Table C of Chapter 3.2.

The interruption system shall be designed according to the quiescent current principle.

9.3.2.22   *Cargo tank openings*

9.3.2.22.1   (a)   Cargo tank openings shall be located on deck in the cargo area.

(b)   Cargo tank openings with a cross-section of more than 0.10 m² and openings of safety devices for preventing overpressures shall be located not less than 0.50 m above deck.

9.3.2.22.2   Cargo tank openings shall be fitted with gastight closures capable of withstanding the test pressure in accordance with 9.3.2.23.1.

9.3.2.22.3   Closures which are normally used during loading or unloading operations shall not cause sparking when operated.

9.3.2.22.4   (a)   Each cargo tank or group of cargo tanks connected to a common vapour pipe shall be fitted with:

–   safety devices for preventing unacceptable overpressures or vacuums. When anti-explosion protection is required in column (17) of Table C of Chapter 3.2, the vacuum valve shall be fitted with a flame arrester capable of withstanding a deflagration and the pressure-relief valve with a high-velocity vent valve capable of withstanding steady burning.

The gases shall be discharged upwards. The opening pressure of the high-velocity vent valve and the opening pressure of the vacuum valve shall be indelibly indicated on the valves;

–   a connection for the safe return ashore of gases expelled during loading;

–   a device for the safe depressurisation of the tanks consisting of at least a fire-resistant flame-arrester and a stop valve which clearly indicates whether it is open or shut.

(b)   The outlets of high-velocity vent valves shall be located not less than 2.00 m above the deck and at a distance of not less than 6.00 m from the accommodation and from the service spaces outside the cargo area. This height may be reduced when within a radius of 1.00 m round the outlet of the high-velocity vent valve, there is no equipment, no work is being carried out and signs indicate the area. The setting of the high-velocity vent valves shall be such that during the transport operation they do not blow off until the maximum permissible working pressure of the cargo tanks is reached.

9.3.2.22.5   (a)   Insofar as anti-explosion protection is prescribed in column (17) of Table C of Chapter 3.2, a vapour pipe connecting two or more cargo tanks shall be fitted, at the connection to each cargo tank, with a flame arrester with a fixed or spring-loaded plate stack, capable of withstanding a detonation. This equipment may consist of:

(i)   a flame arrester fitted with a fixed plate stack, where each cargo tank is fitted with a vacuum valve capable of withstanding a deflagration and a high-velocity vent valve capable of withstanding steady burning;

(ii)   a flame arrester fitted with a spring-loaded plate stack, where each cargo tank is fitted with a vacuum valve capable of withstanding a deflagration;

(iii)   a flame arrester with a fixed plate stack;

(iv)   a flame arrester with a fixed plate stack, where the pressure-measuring device is fitted with an alarm system in accordance with 9.3.2.21.7;

(v)   a flame arrester with a spring-loaded plate stack, where the pressure-measuring device is fitted with an alarm system in accordance with 9.3.2.21.7.

When a fire-fighting installation is permanently mounted on deck in the cargo area and can be brought into service from the deck and from the wheelhouse, flame arresters need not be required for individual cargo tanks.

Only substances which do not mix and which do not react dangerously with each other may be carried simultaneously in cargo tanks connected to a common vapour pipe;

or

(b)   Insofar as anti-explosion protection is prescribed in column (17) of Table C of Chapter 3.2, a vapour pipe connecting two or more cargo tanks shall be fitted, at the connection to each cargo tank, with a pressure/vacuum relief valve incorporating a flame arrester capable of withstanding a detonation/deflagration.

Only substances which do not mix and which do not react dangerously with each other may be carried simultaneously in cargo tanks connected to a common vapour pipe;

or

(c)   Insofar as anti-explosion protection is prescribed in column (17) of Table C of Chapter 3.2, an independent vapour pipe for each cargo tank, fitted with a pressure/vacuum valve incorporating a flame arrester capable of withstanding a deflagration and a high velocity vent valve incorporating a flame arrester capable of withstanding steady burning. Several different substances may be carried simultaneously;

or

(d) Insofar as anti-explosion protection is prescribed in column (17) of Table C of Chapter 3.2, a vapour pipe connecting two or more cargo tanks shall be fitted, at the connection to each cargo tank, with a shut-off device capable of withstanding a detonation, where each cargo tank is fitted with a vacuum valve capable of withstanding a deflagration and a high-velocity vent valve capable of withstanding steady burning.

Only substances which do not mix and which do not react dangerously with each other may be carried simultaneously in cargo tanks connected to a common vapour pipe.

9.3.2.23   *Pressure tests*

9.3.2.23.1 The cargo tanks, residual cargo tanks, cofferdams, pipes for loading and unloading shall be subjected to initial tests before being put into service and thereafter at prescribed intervals.

Where a heating system is provided inside the cargo tanks, the heating coils shall be subjected to initial tests before being put into service and thereafter at prescribed intervals.

9.3.2.23.2 The test pressure for the cargo tanks and residual cargo tanks shall be not less than 1.3 times the construction pressure. The test pressure for the cofferdams and open cargo tanks shall be not less than 10 kPa (0.10 bar) gauge pressure.

9.3.2.23.3 The test pressure for pipes for loading and unloading shall be not less than 1,000 kPa (10 bar) gauge pressure.

9.3.2.23.4 The maximum intervals for the periodic tests shall be 11 years.

9.3.2.23.5 The procedure for pressure tests shall comply with the provisions established by the competent authority or a recognised classification society.

9.3.2.24   (*Reserved*)

9.3.2.25   *Pumps and piping*

9.3.2.25.1 Pumps, compressors and accessory loading and unloading piping shall be placed in the cargo area. Cargo pumps shall be capable of being shut down from the cargo area and, in addition, from a position outside the cargo area. Cargo pumps situated on deck shall be located not less than 6.00 m from entrances to, or openings of, the accommodation and service spaces outside the cargo area.

9.3.2.25.2 (a) Pipes for loading and unloading shall be independent of any other piping of the vessel. No cargo piping shall be located below deck, except those inside the cargo tanks and inside the cargo pump-room.

(b) The pipes for loading and unloading shall be arranged so that, after loading or unloading operations, the liquid remaining in these pipes may be safely removed and may flow either into the vessel's tanks or the tanks ashore.

(c) Pipes for loading and unloading shall be clearly distinguishable from other piping, e.g. by means of colour marking.

(d) The pipes for loading and unloading located on deck, with the exception of the shore connections, shall be located not less than a quarter of the vessel's breadth from the outer shell.

(e) The shore connections shall be located not less than 6.00 m from the entrances to, or openings of, the accommodation and service spaces outside the cargo area.

(f) Each shore connection of the vapour pipe and shore connections of the pipes for loading and unloading, through which the loading or unloading operation is carried out, shall be fitted with a shut-off device. However, each shore connection shall be fitted with a blind flange when it is not in operation.

Each shore connection of the pipes for loading and unloading through which the loading or unloading operation is carried out shall be fitted with the device intended for the discharge of residual cargo described in 8.6.4.1.

(g) The vessel shall be equipped with an additional stripping system.

(h) The flanges and stuffing boxes shall be provided with a spray protection device.

9.3.2.25.3 The distance referred to in 9.3.2.25.1 and 9.3.2.25.2 (e) may be reduced to 3.00 m if a transverse bulkhead complying with 9.3.2.10.2 is situated at the end of the cargo area. The openings shall be provided with doors.

The following notice shall be displayed on the doors:

**DO NOT OPEN DURING LOADING AND UNLOADING
WITHOUT THE PERMISSION OF THE MASTER.
CLOSE IMMEDIATELY.**

9.3.2.25.4 (a) Every component of the pipes for loading and unloading shall be electrically connected to the hull.

(b) The pipes for loading shall extend down to the bottom of the cargo tanks.

9.3.2.25.5 The stop valves or other shut-off devices of the pipes for loading and unloading shall indicate whether they are open or shut.

9.3.2.25.6 The pipes for loading and unloading shall have, at the test pressure, the required elasticity, leakproofness and resistance to pressure.

9.3.2.25.7 The pipes for loading and unloading shall be fitted with pressure gauges at the pump outlet.

Where these pressure gauges are manometers, the indicator scale shall have a diameter of not less than 0.14 m.

Reading of the pressure gauges shall be possible from the control position of the loading pump at any time. The maximum permissible overpressure or vacuum shall be indicated by a red mark.

9.3.2.25.8 (a) When pipes for loading and unloading are used for supplying the cargo tanks with washing or ballast water, the suctions of these pipes shall be located within the cargo area but outside the cargo tanks.

Pumps for tank washing systems with associated connections may be located outside the cargo area, provided the discharge side of the system is arranged in such a way that the suction is not possible through that part.

A spring-loaded non-return valve shall be provided to prevent any gases from being expelled from the cargo area through the tank washing system.

(b)   A non-return valve shall be fitted at the junction between the water suction pipe and the cargo loading pipe.

9.3.2.25.9   The permissible loading and unloading flows shall be calculated.

Calculations concern the permissible maximum loading and unloading flow for each cargo tank or each group of cargo tanks, taking into account the design of the ventilation system. These calculations shall take into consideration the fact that in the event of an unforeseen cut-off of the gas return piping or the compensation piping of the shore facility, the safety devices of the cargo tanks will prevent pressure in the cargo tanks from exceeding the following values:

over-pressure: 115% of the opening pressure of the high-velocity vent valve;

vacuum pressure: 110% of the opening pressure of the vacuum valve but not more than 3.85 kPa.

The main factors to be considered are the following:

1.   Dimensions of the ventilation system of the cargo tanks;

2.   Gas formation during loading: multiply the largest loading flow by a factor of not less than 1.25;

3.   Density of the vapour mixture of the cargo based on 50% volume vapour of 50% volume air;

4.   Loss of pressure through ventilation pipes, valves and fittings. Account will be taken of a 30% clogging of the mesh of the flame-arrester;

5.   Chocking pressure of the safety valves.

The permissible maximum loading and unloading pressure for each cargo tank or for each group of cargo tanks shall be given in an on-board instruction.

9.3.2.25.10   The stripping system shall be subjected to initial tests before being put into service or thereafter if any alteration has been made to it, using water as test medium. The test and the determination of the residual quantities shall be carried out in accordance with the requirements of 8.6.4.2.

In this test, the following residual quantities shall not be exceeded:

(a)   5 l for each cargo tank;

(b)   15 l for each pipe system.

The residual quantities obtained in the test shall be entered in the certificate for the test of the stripping system referred to in 8.6.4.3.

9.3.2.25.11   If the vessel is carrying several dangerous substances liable to react dangerously with each other, a separate pump with its own piping for loading and unloading shall be installed for each substance. The piping shall not pass through a cargo tank containing dangerous substances with which the substance in question is liable to react.

9.3.2.26   *Residual cargo tanks and slop tanks*

9.3.2.26.1   The vessel shall be provided with at least one residual cargo tank and with slop tanks for slops which are not suitable for pumping. These tanks shall be located only in the cargo area. Intermediate bulk containers or tank-containers or portable tanks in accordance with 7.2.4.1 may be used instead of a fixed residual cargo tank. During filling of these intermediate bulk containers or tank-containers or portable tanks, means for collecting any leakage shall be placed under the filling connections.

9.3.2.26.2   Slop tanks shall be fire resistant and shall be capable of being closed with lids (e.g. drums with lever closing ring lids). The tanks shall be marked and easy to handle.

9.3.2.26.3   The maximum capacity of a residual cargo tank is 30 m^3.

9.3.2.26.4   The residual cargo tank shall be equipped with:

–   pressure-relief and a-vacuum relief valves.

    The high velocity vent valve shall be so regulated as not to open during carriage. This condition is met when the opening pressure of the valve meets the conditions set out in column (109) of Table C of Chapter 3.2;

    When anti-explosion protection is required in column (17) of Table C of Chapter 3.2, the vacuum-relief valve shall be capable of withstanding deflagrations and the high-velocity vent valve shall withstand steady burning;

–   a level indicator;

–   connections with shut-off devices, for pipes and hoses.

Intermediate bulk containers (IBCs), tank containers and portable tanks intended to collect cargo remains, cargo residues or slops shall be equipped with:

-    a connection enabling gases released during filling to be evacuated safely;

-    a possibility of indicating the degree of filling;

-    connections with shut-off devices, for pipes and hoses.

Residual cargo tanks, intermediate bulk containers (IBCs), tank containers and portable tanks shall be connected to the vapour pipe of cargo tanks only for the time necessary to fill them in accordance with 7.2.4.15.2.

Residual cargo tanks, intermediate bulk containers (IBCs), tank-containers and portable tanks placed on the deck shall be located at a minimum distance from the hull equal to one quarter of the vessel's breadth.

9.3.2.27   (*Reserved*)

9.3.2.28 *Water-spray system*

When water-spraying is required in column (9) of Table C of Chapter 3.2, a water-spray system shall be installed in the cargo area on deck to enable gas emissions from loading to be precipitated and to cool the tops of cargo tanks by spraying water over the whole surface so as to avoid safely the activation of the high-velocity vent valve at 50 kPa.

The gas precipitation system shall be fitted with a connection device for supply from a shore installation.

The spray nozzles shall be so installed that the entire cargo deck area is covered and the gases released are precipitated safely.

The system shall be capable of being put into operation from the wheelhouse and from the deck. Its capacity shall be such that when all the spray nozzles are in operation, the outflow is not less than 50 litres per square metre of deck area and per hour.

9.3.2.29- *(Reserved)*
9.3.2.30

9.3.2.31 *Engines*

9.3.2.31.1 Only internal combustion engines running on fuel with a flashpoint of more than 55° C are allowed.

9.3.2.31.2. Ventilation inlets of the engine room, and when the engines do not take in air directly from the engine room, air intakes of the engines shall be located not less than 2.00 m from the cargo area.

9.3.2.31.3 Sparking shall not be possible within the cargo area.

9.3.2.31.4 The surface temperature of the outer parts of engines used during loading or unloading operations, as well as that of their air inlets and exhaust ducts shall not exceed the allowable temperature according to the temperature class. This provision does not apply to engines installed in service spaces provided the provisions of 9.3.2.52.3 (b) are fully complied with.

9.3.2.31.5 The ventilation in the closed engine room shall be designed so that, at an ambient temperature of 20 °C, the average temperature in the engine room does not exceed 40° C.

9.3.2.32 *Oil fuel tanks*

9.3.2.32.1 Where the vessel is provided with hold spaces, the double bottoms within these spaces may be arranged as a liquid oil fuel tanks, provided their depth is not less than 0.60 m.

Liquid oil fuel pipes and openings of such tanks are not permitted in the hold space.

9.3.2.32.2 The open ends of the air pipes of all liquid oil fuel tanks shall extend to not less than 0.50 m above the open deck. Their open ends and the open ends of overflow pipes leading to the deck shall be fitted with a protective device consisting of a gauze diaphragm or a perforated plate.

9.3.2.33 *(Reserved)*

9.3.2.34   *Exhaust pipes*

9.3.2.34.1   Exhausts shall be evacuated from the vessel into the open air either upwards through an exhaust pipe or through the shell plating. The exhaust outlet shall be located not less than 2.00 m from the cargo area. The exhaust pipes of engines shall be arranged so that the exhausts are led away from the vessel. The exhaust pipes shall not be located within the cargo area.

9.3.2.34.2   Exhaust pipes shall be provided with a device preventing the escape of sparks, e.g. spark arresters.

9.3.2.35   *Bilge pumping and ballasting arrangements*

9.3.2.35.1   Bilge and ballast pumps for spaces within the cargo area shall be installed within such area.

This provision does not apply to:

– double-hull spaces and double bottoms which do not have a common boundary wall with the cargo tanks;

– cofferdams and hold spaces where ballasting is carried out using the piping of the fire-fighting system in the cargo area and bilge-pumping is performed using educators.

9.3.2.35.2   Where the double bottom is used as a liquid oil fuel tank, it shall not be connected to the bilge piping system.

9.3.2.35.3   Where the ballast pump is installed in the cargo area, the standpipe and its outboard connection for suction of ballast water shall be located within the cargo area but outside the cargo tanks.

9.3.2.35.4   A cargo pump-room below deck shall be capable of being drained in an emergency by an installation located in the cargo area and independent from any other installation. This installation shall be provided outside the cargo pump-room.

9.3.2.36-
9.3.2.39   *(Reserved)*

9.3.2.40   *Fire-extinguishing arrangements*

9.3.2.40.1   A fire-extinguishing system shall be installed on the vessel. This system shall comply with the following requirements:

– It shall be supplied by two independent fire or ballast pumps, one of which shall be ready for use at any time. These pumps shall not be installed in the same space;

– It shall be provided with a water main fitted with at least three hydrants in the cargo area above deck. Three suitable and sufficiently long hoses with spray nozzles having a diameter of not less than 12 mm shall be provided. It shall be possible to reach any point of the deck in the cargo area simultaneously with at least two jets of water which do not emanate from the same hydrant.

A spring-loaded non-return valve shall be fitted to ensure that no gases can escape through the fire-extinguishing system into the accommodation or service spaces outside the cargo area;

      –   The capacity of the system shall be at least sufficient for a jet of water to have a minimum reach of not less than the vessel's breadth from any location on board with two spray nozzles being used at the same time.

9.3.2.40.2   In addition, the engine rooms, the pump-room and all spaces containing essential equipment (switchboards, compressors, etc.) for the refrigeration equipment, if any, shall be provided with a permanently fixed fire-extinguishing system meeting the following requirements:

9.3.2.40.2.1   *Extinguishing agents*

For the protection of spaces in engine rooms, boiler rooms and pump rooms, only permanently fixed fire-extinguishing systems using the following extinguishing agents are permitted:

(a) CO_2 (carbon dioxide);

(b)   HFC 227 ea (heptafluoropropane);

(c)   IG-541 (52% nitrogen, 40% argon, 8% carbon dioxide).

Other extinguishing agents are permitted only on the basis of recommendations by the Administrative Committee.

9.3.2.40.2.2   *Ventilation, air extraction*

(a)   The combustion air required by the combustion engines which ensure propulsion should not come from spaces protected by permanently fixed fire-extinguishing systems. This requirement is not mandatory if the vessel has two independent main engine rooms with a gastight separation or if, in addition to the main engine room, there is a separate engine room installed with a bow thruster that can independently ensure propulsion in the event of a fire in the main engine room.

(b)   All forced ventilation systems in the space to be protected shall be shut down automatically as soon as the fire-extinguishing system is activated.

(c)   All openings in the space to be protected which permit air to enter or gas to escape shall be fitted with devices enabling them to be closed rapidly. It shall be clear whether they are open or closed.

(d)   Air escaping from the pressure-relief valves of the pressurised air tanks installed in the engine rooms shall be evacuated to the open air.

(e)   Overpressure or negative pressure caused by the diffusion of the extinguishing agent shall not destroy the constituent elements of the space to be protected. It shall be possible to ensure the safe equalisation of pressure.

(f)   Protected spaces shall be provided with a means of extracting the extinguishing agent. If extraction devices are installed, it shall not be possible to start them up during extinguishing.

9.3.2.40.2.3   *Fire alarm system*

The space to be protected shall be monitored by an appropriate fire alarm system. The alarm signal shall be audible in the wheelhouse, the accommodation and the space to be protected.

9.3.2.40.2.4   *Piping system*

(a)   The extinguishing agent shall be routed to and distributed in the space to be protected by means of a permanent piping system. Piping installed in the space to be protected and the reinforcements it incorporates shall be made of steel. This shall not apply to the connecting nozzles of tanks and compensators provided that the materials used have equivalent fire-retardant properties. Piping shall be protected against corrosion both internally and externally.

(b)   The discharge nozzles shall be so arranged as to ensure the regular diffusion of the extinguishing agent.

9.3.2.40.2.5   *Triggering device*

(a)   Automatically activated fire-extinguishing systems are not permitted.

(b)   It shall be possible to activate the fire-extinguishing system from a suitable point located outside the space to be protected.

(c)   Triggering devices shall be so installed that they can be activated in the event of a fire and so that the risk of their breakdown in the event of a fire or an explosion in the space to be protected is reduced as far as possible.

Systems which are not mechanically activated shall be supplied from two energy sources independent of each other. These energy sources shall be located outside the space to be protected. The control lines located in the space to be protected shall be so designed as to remain capable of operating in the event of a fire for a minimum of 30 minutes. The electrical installations are deemed to meet this requirement if they conform to the IEC 60331-21:1999 standard.

When the triggering devices are so placed as not to be visible, the component concealing them shall carry the "Fire-fighting system" symbol, each side being not less than 10 cm in length, with the following text in red letters on a white ground:

Fire-extinguishing system

(d)   If the fire-extinguishing system is intended to protect several spaces, it shall comprise a separate and clearly-marked triggering device for each space.

(e)   The instructions shall be posted alongside all triggering devices and shall be clearly visible and indelible. The instructions shall be in a language the master can read and understand and if this language is not English, French or German, they shall be in English, French or German. They shall include information concerning:

(i)   the activation of the fire-extinguishing system;

(ii)   the need to ensure that all persons have left the space to be protected;

(iii)   the correct behaviour of the crew in the event of activation;

(iv)   the correct behaviour of the crew in the event of the failure of the fire-extinguishing system to function properly.

(f)   The instructions shall mention that prior to the activation of the fire-extinguishing system, combustion engines installed in the space and aspirating air from the space to be protected, shall be shut down.

9.3.2.40.2.6   *Alarm device*

(a)   Permanently fixed fire-extinguishing systems shall be fitted with an audible and visual alarm device.

(b)   The alarm device shall be set off automatically as soon as the fire-extinguishing system is first activated. The alarm device shall function for an appropriate period of time before the extinguishing agent is released; it shall not be possible to turn it off.

(c)   Alarm signals shall be clearly visible in the spaces to be protected and their access points and be clearly audible under operating conditions corresponding to the highest possible sound level. It shall be possible to distinguish them clearly from all other sound and visual signals in the space to be protected.

(d)   Sound alarms shall also be clearly audible in adjoining spaces, with the communicating doors shut, and under operating conditions corresponding to the highest possible sound level.

(e)   If the alarm device is not intrinsically protected against short circuits, broken wires and drops in voltage, it shall be possible to monitor its operation.

(f)   A sign with the following text in red letters on a white ground shall be clearly posted at the entrance to any space the extinguishing agent may reach:

WARNING, FIRE-EXTINGUISHING SYSTEM!
LEAVE THIS SPACE IMMEDIATELY WHEN THE … (DESCRIPTION) ALARM
IS ACTIVATED!

9.3.2.40.2.7   *Pressurised tanks, fittings and piping*

(a)   Pressurised tanks, fittings and piping shall conform to the requirements of the competent authority.

(b)   Pressurised tanks shall be installed in accordance with the manufacturer's instructions.

(c)   Pressurised tanks, fittings and piping shall not be installed in the accommodation.

(d)   The temperature of cabinets and storage spaces for pressurised tanks shall not exceed 50 °C.

(e)   Cabinets or storage spaces on deck shall be securely stowed and shall have vents so placed that in the event of a pressurised tank not being gastight, the escaping gas cannot penetrate into the vessel. Direct connections with other spaces are not permitted.

9.3.1.40.2.8   *Quantity of extinguishing agent*

If the quantity of extinguishing agent is intended for more than one space, the quantity of extinguishing agent available does not need to be greater than the quantity required for the largest of the spaces thus protected.

9.3.1.40.2.9   *Installation, maintenance, monitoring and documents*

(a)   The mounting or modification of the system shall only be performed by a company specialised in fire-extinguishing systems. The instructions (product data sheet, safety data sheet) provided by the manufacturer of the extinguishing agent or the system shall be followed.

(b) The system shall be inspected by an expert:

    (i) before being brought into service;

    (ii) each time it is put back into service after activation;

    (iii) after every modification or repair;

    (iv) regularly, not less than every two years.

(c) During the inspection, the expert is required to check that the system conforms to the requirements of 9.3.2.40.2.

(d) The inspection shall include, as a minimum:

    (i) an external inspection of the entire system;

    (ii) an inspection to ensure that the piping is leakproof;

    (iii) an inspection to ensure that the control and activation systems are in good working order;

    (iv) an inspection of the pressure and contents of tanks;

    (v) an inspection to ensure that the means of closing the space to be protected are leakproof;

    (vi) an inspection of the fire alarm system;

    (vii) an inspection of the alarm device.

(e) The person performing the inspection shall establish, sign and date a certificate of inspection.

(f) The number of permanently fixed fire-extinguishing systems shall be mentioned in the inspection certificate.

9.3.2.40.2.10 *Fire-extinguishing system operating with CO_2*

In addition to the requirements contained in 9.3.2.40.2.1 to 9.3.2.40.2.9, fire-extinguishing systems using CO_2 as an extinguishing agent shall conform to the following provisions:

(a) Tanks of CO_2 shall be placed in a gastight space or cabinet separated from other spaces. The doors of such storage spaces and cabinets shall open outwards; they shall be capable of being locked and shall carry on the outside the symbol "Warning: danger", not less than 5 cm high and "CO_2" in the same colours and the same size;

(b) Storage cabinets or spaces for CO_2 tanks located below deck shall only be accessible from the outside. These spaces shall have an artificial ventilation system with extractor hoods and shall be completely independent of the other ventilation systems on board;

(c) The level of filling of CO_2 tanks shall not exceed 0.75 kg/l. The volume of depressurised CO_2 shall be taken to be 0.56 m³/kg;

(d) The concentration of CO_2 in the space to be protected shall be not less than 40% of the gross volume of the space. This quantity shall be released within 120 seconds. It shall be possible to monitor whether diffusion is proceeding correctly;

(e) The opening of the tank valves and the control of the diffusing valve shall correspond to two different operations;

(f) The appropriate period of time mentioned in 9.3.2.40.2.6 (b) shall be not less than 20 seconds. A reliable installation shall ensure the timing of the diffusion of CO_2.

9.3.2.40.2.11 *Fire-extinguishing system operating with HFC-227 ea (heptafluoropropane)*

In addition to the requirements of 9.3.2.40.2.1 to 9.3.2.40.2.9, fire-extinguishing systems using HFC-227 ea as an extinguishing agent shall conform to the following provisions:

(a) Where there are several spaces with different gross volumes, each space shall be equipped with its own fire-extinguishing system;

(b) Every tank containing HFC-227 ea placed in the space to be protected shall be fitted with a device to prevent overpressure. This device shall ensure that the contents of the tank are safely diffused in the space to be protected if the tank is subjected to fire, when the fire-extinguishing system has not been brought into service;

(c) Every tank shall be fitted with a device permitting control of the gas pressure;

(d) The level of filling of tanks shall not exceed 1.15 kg/l. The specific volume of depressurised HFC-227 ea shall be taken to be 0.1374 m³/kg;

(e) The concentration of HFC-227 ea in the space to be protected shall be not less than 8% of the gross volume of the space. This quantity shall be released within 10 seconds;

(f) Tanks of HFC-227 ea shall be fitted with a pressure monitoring device which triggers an audible and visual alarm in the wheelhouse in the event of an unscheduled loss of propellant gas. Where there is no wheelhouse, the alarm shall be triggered outside the space to be protected;

(g) After discharge, the concentration in the space to be protected shall not exceed 10.5% (volume);

(h) The fire-extinguishing system shall not comprise aluminium parts.

9.3.2.40.2.12 *Fire-extinguishing system operating with IG-541*

In addition to the requirements of 9.3.2.40.2.1 to 9.3.2.40.2.9, fire-extinguishing systems using IG-541 as an extinguishing agent shall conform to the following provisions:

(a) Where there are several spaces with different gross volumes, every space shall be equipped with its own fire-extinguishing system;

(b) Every tank containing IG-541 placed in the space to be protected shall be fitted with a device to prevent overpressure. This device shall ensure that the contents of the tank are safely diffused in the space to be protected if the tank is subjected to fire, when the fire-extinguishing system has not been brought into service;

(c)   Each tank shall be fitted with a device for checking the contents;

(d)   The filling pressure of the tanks shall not exceed 200 bar at a temperature of +15 °C;

(e)   The concentration of IG-541 in the space to be protected shall be not less than 44% and not more than 50% of the gross volume of the space. This quantity shall be released within 120 seconds.

9.3.2.40.2.13   *Fire-extinguishing system for physical protection*

In order to ensure physical protection in the engine rooms, boiler rooms and pump rooms, fire-extinguishing systems are accepted solely on the basis of recommendations by the Administrative Committee.

9.3.2.40.3   The two hand fire-extinguishers referred to in 8.1.4 shall be located in the cargo area.

9.3.2.40.4   The fire-extinguishing agent and the quantity contained in the permanently fixed fire-extinguishing system shall be suitable and sufficient for fighting fires.

9.3.2.41   *Fire and naked light*

9.3.2.41.1   The outlets of funnels shall be located not less than 2.00 m from the cargo area. Arrangements shall be provided to prevent the escape of sparks and the entry of water.

9.3.2.41.2   Heating, cooking and refrigerating appliances shall not be fuelled with liquid fuels, liquid gas or solid fuels.

The installation in the engine room or in another separate space of heating appliances fuelled with liquid fuel having a flash-point above 55 °C is, however, permitted.

Cooking and refrigerating appliances are permitted only in the accommodation.

9.3.2.41.3   Only electrical lighting appliances are permitted.

9.3.2.42   *Cargo heating system*

9.3.2.42.1   Boilers which are used for heating the cargo shall be fuelled with a liquid fuel having a flashpoint of more than 55 °C. They shall be placed either in the engine room or in another separate space below deck and outside the cargo area, which is accessible from the deck or from the engine room.

9.3.2.42.2   The cargo heating system shall be designed so that the cargo cannot penetrate into the boiler in the case of a leak in the heating coils. A cargo heating system with artificial draught shall be ignited electrically.

9.3.2.42.3   The ventilation system of the engine room shall be designed taking into account the air required for the boiler.

9.3.2.42.4   Where the cargo heating system is used during loading, unloading or gas-freeing, the service space which contains this system shall fully comply with the requirements of 9.3.2.52.3 (b). This requirement does not apply to the inlets of the ventilation system. These inlets shall be located at a minimum distance of 2.00 m from the cargo area and 6.00 m from the openings of cargo tanks or residual cargo tanks, loading pumps situated on deck, openings of high velocity vent valves, pressure relief devices and shore connections of loading and unloading pipes and must be located not less than 2.00 m above the deck.

The requirements of 9.3.2.52.3 (b) are not applicable to the unloading of substances having a flash point of 61 °C or more when the temperature of the product is at least 15 K lower at the flash point.

| 9.3.2.43-
9.3.2.49 | (*Reserved*) |

9.3.2.50   *Documents concerning electrical installations*

9.3.2.50.1   In addition to the documents required in accordance with the Regulations referred to in 1.1.4.6, the following documents shall be on board:

(a)   a drawing indicating the boundaries of the cargo area and the location of the electrical equipment installed in this area;

(b)   a list of the electrical equipment referred to in (a) above including the following particulars:

machine or appliance, location, type of protection, type of protection against explosion, testing body and approval number;

(c)   a list of or general plan indicating the electrical equipment outside the cargo area which may be operated during loading, unloading or gas-freeing. All other electrical equipment shall be marked in red. See 9.3.2.52.3 and 9.3.2.52.4.

9.3.2.50.2   The documents listed above shall bear the stamp of the competent authority issuing the certificate of approval.

9.3.2.51   *Electrical installations*

9.3.2.51.1   Only distribution systems without return connection to the hull are permitted:

This provision does not apply to:

–   local installations outside the cargo area (e.g. connections of starters of diesel engines);

–   the device for checking the insulation level referred to in 9.3.2.51.2 below.

9.3.2.51.2   Every insulated distribution network shall be fitted with an automatic device with a visual and audible alarm for checking the insulation level.

9.3.2.51.3   For the selection of electrical equipment to be used in zones presenting an explosion risk, the explosion groups and temperature classes assigned to the substances carried in accordance with columns (15) and (16) of Table C of Chapter 3.2 shall be taken into consideration.

9.3.2.52   *Type and location of electrical equipment*

9.3.2.52.1   (a)   Only the following equipment may be installed in cargo tanks, residual cargo tanks and pipes for loading and unloading (comparable to zone 0):

–   measuring, regulation and alarm devices of the EEx (ia) type of protection.

(b) Only the following equipment may be installed in the cofferdams, double-hull spaces, double bottoms and hold spaces (comparable to zone 1):

    – measuring, regulation and alarm devices of the certified safe type;

    – lighting appliances of the "flame-proof enclosure" or "pressurised enclosure" type of protection;

    – hermetically sealed echo sounding devices the cables of which are led through thick-walled steel tubes with gastight connections up to the main deck;

    – cables for the active cathodic protection of the shell plating in protective steel tubes such as those provided for echo sounding devices.

(c) Only the following equipment may be installed in the service spaces in the cargo area below deck (comparable to zone 1):

    – measuring, regulation and alarm devices of the certified safe type;

    – lighting appliances of the "flame-proof enclosure" or "apparatus protected by pressurization" type of protection;

    – motors driving essential equipment such as ballast pumps; they shall be of the certified safe type.

(d) The control and protective equipment of the electrical equipment referred to in paragraphs (a), (b) and (c) above shall be located outside the cargo area if they are not intrinsically safe.

(e) The electrical equipment in the cargo area on deck (comparable to zone 1) shall be of the certified safe type.

9.3.2.52.2 *Accumulators shall be located outside the cargo area.*

9.3.2.52.3 (a) Electrical equipment used during loading, unloading and gas-freeing during berthing and which are located outside the cargo area shall (comparable to zone 2) be at least of the "limited explosion risk" type.

(b) This provision does not apply to:

    (i) lighting installations in the accommodation, except for switches near entrances to accommodation;

    (ii) radiotelephone installations in the accommodation or the wheelhouse;

    (iii) electrical installations in the accommodation, the wheelhouse or the service spaces outside the cargo areas if:

        1. These spaces are fitted with a ventilation system ensuring an overpressure of 0.1 kPa (0.001 bar) and none of the windows is capable of being opened; the air intakes of the ventilation system shall be located as far away as possible, however, not less than 6.00 m from the cargo area and not less than 2.00 m above the deck;

        2. The spaces are fitted with a gas detection system with sensors:

–   at the suction inlets of the ventilation system;

–   directly at the top edge of the sill of the entrance doors of the accommodation and service spaces;

3.   The gas concentration measurement is continuous;

4.   When the gas concentration reaches 20% of the lower explosive limit, the ventilators are switched off. In such a case and when the overpressure is not maintained or in the event of failure of the gas detection system, the electrical installations which do not comply with (a) above, shall be switched off. These operations shall be performed immediately and automatically and activate the emergency lighting in the accommodation, the wheelhouse and the service spaces, which shall comply at least with the "limited explosion risk" type. The switching-off shall be indicated in the accommodation and wheelhouse by visual and audible signals;

5.   The ventilation system, the gas detection system and the alarm of the switch-off device fully comply with the requirements of (a) above;

6.   The automatic switching-off device is set so that no automatic switch off may occur while the vessel is under way.

9.3.2.52.4   The electrical equipment which does not meet the requirements set out in 9.3.2.52.3 above together with its switches shall be marked in red. The disconnection of such equipment shall be operated from a centralised location on board.

9.3.2.52.5   An electric generator which is permanently driven by an engine and which does not meet the requirements of 9.3.2.52.3 above, shall be fitted with a switch capable of shutting down the excitation of the generator. A notice board with the operating instructions shall be displayed near the switch.

9.3.2.52.6   Sockets for the connection of signal lights and gangway lighting shall be permanently fitted to the vessel close to the signal mast or the gangway. Connecting and disconnecting shall not be possible except when the sockets are not live.

9.3.2.52.7   The failure of the power supply for the safety and control equipment shall be immediately indicated by visual and audible signals at the locations where the alarms are usually actuated.

9.3.2.53   *Earthing*

9.3.2.53.1   The metal parts of electrical appliances in the cargo area which are not live as well as protective metal tubes or metal sheaths of cables in normal service shall be earthed, unless they are so arranged that they are automatically earthed by bonding to the metal structure of the vessel.

9.3.2.53.2   The provisions of 9.3.2.53.1 above apply also to equipment having service voltages of less than 50 V.

9.3.2.53.3   Independent cargo tanks, metal intermediate bulk containers and tank-containers shall be earthed.

9.3.2.53.4   Metal intermediate bulk containers (IBCs) and tank-containers, used as residual cargo tanks or slop tanks, shall be capable of being earthed.

| 9.3.2.54- 9.3.2.55 | (*Reserved*) |

9.3.2.56 *Electrical cables*

9.3.2.56.1 All cables in the cargo area shall have a metallic sheath.

9.3.2.56.2 Cables and sockets in the cargo area shall be protected against mechanical damage.

9.3.2.56.3 Movable cables are prohibited in the cargo area, except for intrinsically safe electric circuits or for the supply of signal lights and gangway lighting.

9.3.2.56.4 Cables of intrinsically safe circuits shall only be used for such circuits and shall be separated from other cables not intended for being used in such circuits (e.g. they shall not be installed together in the same string of cables and they shall not be fixed by the same cable clamps).

9.3.2.56.5 For movable cables intended for signal lights and gangway lighting, only sheathed cables of type H 07 RN-F in accordance with 245 IEC 66 or cables of at least equivalent design having conductors with a cross-section of not less than 1.5 mm² shall be used.

These cables shall be as short as possible and installed so that damage is not likely to occur.

| 9.3.2.57- 9.3.2.59 | (*Reserved*) |

9.3.2.60 *Special equipment*

A shower and an eye and face bath shall be provided on the vessel at a location which is directly accessible from the cargo area.

| 9.3.2.61- 9.3.2.70 | (*Reserved*) |

9.3.2.71 *Admittance on board*

The notice boards displaying the prohibition of admittance in accordance with 8.3.3 shall be clearly legible from either side of the vessel.

| 9.3.2.72- 9.3.2.73 | (*Reserved*) |

9.3.2.74 *Prohibition of smoking, fire or naked light*

9.3.2.74.1 The notice boards displaying the prohibition of smoking in accordance with 8.3.4 shall be clearly legible from either side of the vessel.

9.3.2.74.2 Notice boards indicating the circumstances under which the prohibition is applicable shall be fitted near the entrances to the spaces where smoking or the use of fire or naked light is not always prohibited.

9.3.2.74.3 Ashtrays shall be provided close to each exit of the accommodation and the wheelhouse.

| 9.3.2.75- 9.3.2.91 | (*Reserved*) |

9.3.2.92   *Emergency exit*

Spaces the entrances or exits of which are likely to become partly or completely immersed in the damaged condition shall have an emergency exit which is situated not less than 0.10 m above the damage waterline. This requirement does not apply to forepeak and afterpeak.

9.3.2.93-   *(Reserved)*
9.3.2.99

9.3.3   **Rules for construction of type N tank vessels**

The rules for construction of 9.3.3.0 to 9.3.3.99 apply to type N tank vessels.

9.3.3.0   *Materials of construction*

9.3.3.0.1   (a)   The vessel's hull and the cargo tanks shall be constructed of shipbuilding steel or other at least equivalent metal.

The independent cargo tanks may also be constructed of other materials, provided these have at least equivalent mechanical properties and resistance against the effects of temperature and fire.

(b)   Every part of the vessel including any installation and equipment which may come into contact with the cargo shall consist of materials which can neither be dangerously affected by the cargo nor cause decomposition of the cargo or react with it so as to form harmful or hazardous products.

(c)   Inside vapour pipes and gas discharge pipes shall be protected against erosion.

9.3.3.0.2   Except where explicitly permitted in 9.3.3.03 below or in the certificate of approval, the use of wood, aluminium alloys or plastic materials within the cargo area is prohibited.

9.3.3.0.3   (a)   The use of wood, aluminium alloys or plastic materials within the cargo area is only permitted for:

- gangways and external ladders;

- movable items of equipment (aluminium gauging rods are, however, permitted provided that they are fitted with brass feet or protected in another way to avoid sparking);

- chocking of cargo tanks which are independent of the vessel's hull and chocking of installations and equipment;

- masts and similar round timber;

- engine parts;

- parts of the electrical installation;

- loading and unloading appliances;

- lids of boxes which are placed on the deck.

(b)   The use of wood or plastic materials within the cargo area is only permitted for:

–   supports and stops of any kind.

(c)   The use of plastic materials or rubber within the cargo area is only permitted for:

–   coating of cargo tanks and of hoses for loading and unloading;

–   all kinds of gaskets (e.g. for dome or hatch covers);

–   electric cables;

–   hoses for loading and unloading;

–   insulation of cargo tanks and of hoses for loading and unloading.

(d)   All permanently fitted materials in the accommodation or wheelhouse, with the exception of furniture, shall not readily ignite. They shall not evolve fumes or toxic gases in dangerous quantities, if involved in a fire.

9.3.3.0.4   The paint used in the cargo area shall not be liable to produce sparks in case of impact.

9.3.3.0.5   The use of plastic material for vessel's boats is permitted only if the material does not readily ignite.

9.3.3.1-
9.3.3.7   *(Reserved)*

9.3.3.8   *Classification*

9.3.3.8.1   The tank vessel shall be built under survey of a recognised classification society in accordance with the rules established by that classification society for its highest class, and the tank vessel shall be classed accordingly.

The vessel's class shall be continued.

The classification society shall issue a certificate certifying that the vessel is in conformity with the rules of this section.

The design pressure and the test pressure of cargo tanks shall be entered in the certificate.

If a vessel has cargo tanks with different valve opening pressures, the design and test pressures of each tank shall be entered in the certificate.

The classification society shall draw up a certificate mentioning all the dangerous goods accepted for carriage by the vessel (see also 1.16.1.2.5).

9.3.3.8.2   The cargo pump-rooms shall be inspected by a recognised classification society whenever the certificate of approval has to be renewed as well as during the third year of validity of the certificate of approval. The inspection shall comprise at least:

–   an inspection of the whole system for its condition, for corrosion, leakage or conversion works which have not been approved;

–   a checking of the condition of the gas detection system in the cargo pump-rooms.

Inspection certificates signed by the recognised classification society with respect to the inspection of the cargo pump-rooms shall be kept on board. The inspection certificates shall at least include particulars of the above inspection and the results obtained as well as the date of the inspection.

9.3.3.8.3   The condition of the gas detection system referred to in 9.3.3.52.3 (b) shall be checked by a recognised classification society whenever the certificate of approval has to be renewed and during the third year of validity of the certificate of approval. A certificate signed by the recognised classification society shall be kept on board.

9.3.3.8.4   9.3.3.8.2 and 9.3.3.8.3, checking of the condition of the gas detection system, do not apply to open type N.

9.3.3.9   *(Reserved)*

9.3.3.10   ***Protection against the penetration of gases***

9.3.3.10.1   The vessel shall be designed so as to prevent gases from penetrating into the accommodation and the service spaces.

9.3.3.10.2   The lower edges of door-openings in the sidewalls of superstructures and the coaming of access hatches to under-deck spaces shall have a height of not less than 0.50 m above the deck.

This requirement need not be complied with if the wall of the superstructures facing the cargo area extends from one side of the ship to the other and has doors the sills of which have a height of not less than 0.50 m above the deck. The height of this wall shall be not less than 2.00 m. In this case, the lower edges of door-openings in the sidewalls of superstructures and the coamings of access hatches behind this wall shall have a height of not less than 0.10 m above the deck. The sills of engine room doors and the coamings of its access hatches shall, however, always have a height of not less than 0.50 m.

9.3.3.10.3   The bulwarks, foot-rails etc. shall be provided with sufficiently large openings which are located directly above the deck.

9.3.3.10.4   9.3.3.10.1 to 9.3.3.10.3 above do not apply to open type N.

9.3.3.11   ***Hold spaces and cargo tanks***

9.3.3.11.1   (a)   The maximum permissible capacity of a cargo tank shall be determined in accordance with the following table:

$L \times B \times H$ (m^3)	Maximum permissible capacity of a cargo tank (m^3)
up to 600	$L \times B \times H \times 0.3$
600 to 3 750	$180 + (L \times B \times H - 600) \times 0.0635$
> 3 750	380

In the table above $L \times B \times H$ is the product of the main dimensions of the tank vessel in metres (according to the measurement certificate), where:

L = overall length of the hull;
B = extreme breadth of the hull;
H = shortest vertical distance between the top of the keel and the lowest point of the deck at the side of the vessel (moulded depth) within the cargo area.

For trunk vessels, H shall be replaced by H', where H' shall be obtained from the following formula:

$$H' = H + \left(ht \times \frac{bt}{B} \times \frac{lt}{L} \right)$$

where:

ht = trunk height (distance between trunk deck and main deck measured on trunk side at L/2);
bt = trunk breadth;
lt = trunk length.

(b) The relative density of the substances to be carried shall be taken into consideration in the design of the cargo tanks. The maximum relative density shall be indicated in the certificate of approval.

(c) When the vessel is provided with pressure cargo tanks, these tanks shall be designed for a working pressure of 400 kPa (4 bar).

(d) For vessels with a length of not more than 50.00 m, the length of a cargo tank shall not exceed 10.00 m; and

For vessels with a length of more than 50.00 m, the length of a cargo tank shall not exceed 0.20 L.

This provision does not apply to vessels with independent built-in cylindrical tanks having a length to diameter ratio ≤7.

9.3.3.11.2 (a) The cargo tanks independent of the vessel's hull shall be fixed so that they cannot float.

(b) The capacity of a suction well shall be limited to not more than 0.10 m³.

9.3.3.11.3 (a) The cargo tanks shall be separated by cofferdams of at least 0.60 m in width from the accommodation, engine room and service spaces outside the cargo area below deck or, if there are no such accommodation, engine room and service spaces, from the vessel's ends. Where the cargo tanks are installed in a hold space, a space of not less than 0.50 m shall be provided between such tanks and the end bulkheads of the hold space. In this case an insulated end bulkhead meeting the definition for Class "A-60" according to SOLAS 74, Chapter II-2, Regulation 3, shall be deemed equivalent to a cofferdam. For pressure cargo tanks, the 0.50 m distance may be reduced to 0.20 m.

(b) Hold spaces, cofferdams and cargo tanks shall be capable of being inspected.

(c) All spaces in the cargo area shall be capable of being ventilated. Means for checking their gas-free condition shall be provided.

9.3.3.11.4 The bulkheads bounding the cargo tanks, cofferdams and hold spaces shall be watertight. The cargo tanks, cofferdams and the end bulkheads of the hold spaces, as well as the bulkheads bounding the cargo area shall have no openings or penetrations below deck. Penetrations through bulkheads between two hold spaces are, however, permitted.

The bulkhead between the engine room and the cofferdam or service space in the cargo area or between the engine room and a hold space may be fitted with penetrations provided that they conform to the provisions of 9.3.3.17.5.

The bulkhead between the cargo tank and the cargo pump-room below deck may be fitted with penetrations provided that they conform to the provisions of 9.3.3.17.6. If the vessel is fitted with a cargo pump-room below deck, the bulkheads between the cargo tanks may be fitted with passages provided that the discharge pipes are fitted with shut-off devices at the outlet from the cargo tank and in the cargo pump-room direct at the bulkhead. All penetrations in cargo tanks shall be fitted with stop valves. The shut-off devices shall be capable of being activated from the deck.

9.3.3.11.5   Double-hull spaces and double bottoms in the cargo area shall be arranged for being filled with ballast water only. Double bottoms may, however, be used as oil fuel tanks, provided they comply with the provisions of 9.3.3.32.

9.3.3.11.6   (a)   A cofferdam, the centre part of a cofferdam or another space below deck in the cargo area may be arranged as a service space, provided the bulkheads bounding the service space extend vertically to the bottom. This service space shall only be accessible from the deck.

    (b)   The service space shall be watertight with the exception of its access hatches and ventilation inlets.

    (c)   No pipes for loading and unloading shall be fitted within the service space referred to under 9.3.3.11.4 above.

        Pipes for loading and unloading may be fitted in the cargo pump-rooms below deck only when they conform to the provisions of 9.3.3.17.6.

9.3.3.11.7   Where a vessel is constructed with hold spaces containing cargo tanks which are independent of the structure of the vessel, the space between the wall of the hold space and the wall of the cargo tanks shall be not less than 0.60 m. The space between the bottom of the hold space and the bottom of the cargo tanks shall be not less than 0.50 m. The space between the suction well and the bottom structures shall be not less than 0.10 m.

The space may be reduced to 0.40 m under the pump sumps.

If the above-mentioned spaces are not feasible, it shall be possible to remove the cargo tanks easily.

9.3.3.11.8   Where service spaces are located in the cargo area under deck, they shall be arranged so as to be easily accessible and to permit persons wearing protective clothing and breathing apparatus to safely operate the service equipment contained therein. They shall be designed so as to allow injured or unconscious personnel to be removed from such spaces without difficulties, if necessary by means of fixed equipment.

9.3.3.11.9   Cofferdams, double-hull spaces, double bottoms, cargo tanks, hold spaces and other accessible spaces within the cargo area shall be arranged so that they may be completely inspected and cleaned. The dimensions of openings except for those of double-hull spaces and double bottoms which do not have a wall adjoining the cargo tanks shall be sufficient to allow a person wearing breathing apparatus to enter or leave the space without difficulties. These openings shall have a minimum cross-section of 0.36 m^2 and a minimum side length of 0.50 m. They shall be designed so as to allow injured or unconscious personnel to be removed from the bottom of such a space without difficulties, if necessary by means of fixed equipment. In these spaces the distance between the reinforcements shall not be less than 0.50 m. In double bottoms this distance may be reduced to 0.45 m.

Cargo tanks may have circular openings with a diameter of not less than 0.68 m.

9.3.3.11.10   9.3.3.11.6 (c) above does not apply to open type N.

9.3.3.12   *Ventilation*

9.3.3.12.1   Each hold space shall have two openings the dimensions and location of which shall be such as to permit effective ventilation of any part of the hold space. If there are no such openings, it shall be possible to fill the hold spaces with inert gas or dry air.

9.3.3.12.2   Double-hull spaces and double bottoms within the cargo area which are not arranged for being filled with ballast water, hold spaces and cofferdams shall be provided with ventilation systems.

9.3.3.12.3   Any service spaces located in the cargo area below deck shall be provided with a system of forced ventilation with sufficient power for ensuring at least 20 changes of air per hour based on the volume of the space. The ventilator fan shall be designed so that no sparks may be emitted on contact of the impeller blades with the housing and no static electricity may be generated.

The ventilation exhaust ducts shall be located up to 50 mm above the bottom of the service space. The fresh air inlets shall be located in the upper part; they shall be not less than 2.00 m above the deck, not less than 2.00 m from the openings of the cargo tanks and not less than 6.00 m from the outlets of safety valves.

The extension pipes which may be necessary may be of the hinged type.

On board open type N vessels other suitable installations without ventilator fans shall be sufficient.

9.3.3.12.4   Ventilation of accommodation and service spaces shall be possible.

9.3.3.12.5   Ventilators used for gas-freeing of tanks shall be designed so that no sparks may be emitted on contact of the impeller blades with the housing and no static electricity may be generated.

9.3.3.12.6   Notice boards shall be fitted at the ventilation inlets indicating the conditions when they shall be closed. Any ventilation inlets of accommodation and service spaces leading outside shall be fitted with fire flaps. Such ventilation inlets shall be located not less than 2.00 m from the cargo area.

Ventilation inlets of service spaces in the cargo area below deck may be located within such area.

9.3.3.12.7   Flame-arresters prescribed in 9.3.3.20.4, 9.3.3.21.11, 9.3.3.22.4, 9.3.3.22.5 and 9.3.3.26.3 shall be of a type approved for this purpose by the competent authority.

9.3.3.12.8   9.3.3.12.5, 9.3.3.12.6 and 9.3.3.12.7 above do not apply to open type N.

9.3.3.13   *Stability (general)*

9.3.3.13.1   Proof of sufficient stability shall be furnished. This proof is not required for vessels with cargo tanks the width of which is not more than 0.70 B.

9.3.3.13.2   The basic values for the stability calculation - the vessel's lightweight and location of the centre of gravity - shall be determined either by means of an inclining experiment or by detailed mass and moment calculation. In the latter case the lightweight of the vessel shall be checked by means of a lightweight test with a tolerance limit of ± 5% between the mass determined by calculation and the displacement determined by the draught readings.

9.3.3.13.3   Proof of sufficient intact stability shall be furnished for all stages of loading and unloading and for the final loading condition.

9.3.3.14   *Stability (intact)*

For vessels with cargo tanks the width of which is more than $0.70 \cdot B$, proof shall be furnished that, at an angle of 5° or, when this angle is less, at a heeling angle at which an opening becomes immersed, the righting arm is 0.10 m. The stability-reducing free surface effect in the case of cargo tanks filled to less than 95% of their capacity shall be taken into account.

9.3.3.15   (*Reserved*)

9.3.3.16   *Engine rooms*

9.3.3.16.1   Internal combustion engines for the vessel's propulsion as well as internal combustion engines for auxiliary machinery shall be located outside the cargo area. Entrances and other openings of engine rooms shall be at a distance of not less than 2.00 m from the cargo area.

9.3.3.16.2   The engine rooms shall be accessible from the deck; the entrances shall not face the cargo area. Where the doors are not located in a recess whose depth is at least equal to the door width, the hinges shall face the cargo area.

9.3.3.16.3   The last sentence of 9.3.3.16.2 does not apply to oil separator or supply vessels.

9.3.3.17   *Accommodation and service spaces*

9.3.3.17.1   Accommodation spaces and the wheelhouse shall be located outside the cargo area forward of the fore vertical plane or abaft the aft vertical plane bounding the part of cargo area below deck. Windows of the wheelhouse which are located not less than 1.00 m above the bottom of the wheelhouse may tilt forward.

9.3.3.17.2   Entrances to spaces and openings of superstructures shall not face the cargo area. Doors opening outward and not located in a recess whose depth is at least equal to the width of the doors shall have their hinges face the cargo area.

9.3.3.17.3   Entrances from the deck and openings of spaces facing the weather shall be capable of being closed. The following instruction shall be displayed at the entrance of such spaces:

DO NOT OPEN DURING LOADING, UNLOADING OR GAS-FREEING
WITHOUT PERMISSION FROM THE MASTER.
CLOSE IMMEDIATELY.

9.3.3.17.4   Entrances and windows of superstructures and accommodation spaces which can be opened as well as other openings of these spaces shall be located not less than 2.00 m from the cargo area. No wheelhouse doors and windows shall be located within 2.00 m from the cargo area, except where there is no direct connection between the wheelhouse and the accommodation.

9.3.3.17.5   (a)   Driving shafts of the bilge or ballast pumps may penetrate through the bulkhead between the service space and the engine room, provided the arrangement of the service space is in compliance with 9.3.3.11.6.

(b)   The penetration of the shaft through the bulkhead shall be gastight and shall have been approved by a recognised classification society.

(c)   The necessary operating instructions shall be displayed.

(d)   Penetrations through the bulkhead between the engine room and the service space in the cargo area and the bulkhead between the engine room and the hold spaces may be provided for electrical cables, hydraulic lines and piping for measuring, control and alarm systems, provided that the penetrations have been approved by a recognised classification society. The penetrations shall be gastight. Penetrations through a bulkhead with an "A-60" fire protection insulation according to SOLAS 74, Chapter II-2, Regulation 3, shall have an equivalent fire protection.

(e)   Pipes may penetrate the bulkhead between the engine room and the service space in the cargo area provided that these are pipes between the mechanical equipment in the engine room and the service space which do not have any openings within the service space and which are provided with shut-off devices at the bulkhead in the engine room.

(f)   Pipes from the engine room may penetrate through the service space in the cargo area or a cofferdam or a hold space to the outside provided that within the service space or cofferdam or hold space they are of the thick-walled type and have no flanges or openings.

(g)   Where a driving shaft of auxiliary machinery penetrates through a wall located above the deck the penetration shall be gastight.

9.3.3.17.6   A service space located within the cargo area below deck shall not be used as a cargo pump-room for the loading and unloading system, except where:

–   the cargo pump-room is separated from the engine room or from service spaces outside the cargo area by a cofferdam or a bulkhead with an "A-60" fire protection insulation according to SOLAS 74, Chapter II-2, Regulation 3, or by a service space or a hold space;

–   the "A-60" bulkhead required above does not include penetrations referred to in 9.3.3.17.5 (a);

–   ventilation exhaust outlets are located not less than 6.00 m from entrances and openings of the accommodation and service spaces outside the cargo area;

–   the access hatches and ventilation inlets can be closed from the outside;

–   all pipes for loading and unloading as well as those of stripping systems are provided with shut-off devices at the pump suction side in the cargo pump-room immediately at the bulkhead. The necessary operation of the control devices in the pump-room, starting of pumps and control of the liquid flow rate shall be effected from the deck;

–   the bilge of the cargo pump-room is equipped with a gauging device for measuring the filling level which activates a visual and audible alarm in the wheelhouse when liquid is accumulating in the cargo pump-room bilge;

–   the cargo pump-room is provided with a permanent gas detection system which automatically indicates the presence of explosive gases or lack of oxygen by means of direct-measuring sensors and which actuates a visual and audible alarm when the gas concentration has reached 20% of the lower explosive limit. The sensors of this system shall be placed at suitable positions at the bottom and directly below the deck.

Measurement shall be continuous.

The audible and visual alarms are installed in the wheelhouse and in the cargo pump-room and, when the alarm is actuated, the loading and unloading system is shut down. Failure of the gas detection system shall be immediately signalled in the wheelhouse and on deck by means of audible and visual alarms;

–   the ventilation system prescribed in 9.3.3.12.3 has a capacity of not less than 30 changes of air per hour based on the total volume of the service space.

9.3.3.17.7   The following instruction shall be displayed at the entrance of the cargo pump-room:

BEFORE ENTERING THE CARGO PUMP-ROOM CHECK WHETHER IT IS FREE FROM GASES AND CONTAINS SUFFICIENT OXYGEN. DO NOT OPEN DOORS AND ENTRANCE OPENINGS WITHOUT THE PERMISSION OF THE MASTER. LEAVE IMMEDIATELY IN THE EVENT OF ALARM.

9.3.3.17.8   9.3.3.17.5 (g), 9.3.3.17.6 and 9.3.3.17.7 do not apply to open type N.

9.3.3.17.2, last sentence, 9.3.3.17.3, last sentence and 9.3.3.17.4 do not apply to oil separator and supply vessels.

9.3.3.18-   (*Reserved*)
9.3.3.19

9.3.3.20   *Arrangement of cofferdams*

9.3.3.20.1   Cofferdams or cofferdam compartments located next to a service space which has been arranged in accordance with 9.3.3.11.6 shall be accessible through an access hatch.

The access hatch and ventilation inlets shall be located not less than 0.50 m above the deck.

9.3.3.20.2   Cofferdams shall be capable of being filled with water and emptied by means of a pump. Filling shall be effected within 30 minutes. These requirements are not applicable when the bulkhead between the engine room and the cofferdam has an "A-16" fire protection insulation according to SOLAS 74, Chapter II-2, Regulation 3.

The cofferdams shall not be fitted with inlet valves.

9.3.3.20.3   No fixed pipe shall permit connection between a cofferdam and other piping of the vessel outside the cargo area.

9.3.3.20.4   The ventilation openings of cofferdams shall be fitted with a flame-arrester.

9.3.3.20.5   9.3.3.20.4 above does not apply to open type N.

9.3.3.20.2 above does not apply to oil separator and supply vessels.

9.3.3.21   *Safety and control installations*

9.3.3.21.1   Cargo tanks shall be provided with the following equipment:

(a)   a mark inside the tank indicating the liquid level of 97%;

(b)   a level gauge;

(c)   a level alarm device which is activated at the latest when a degree of filling of 90% is reached;

(d)   a high level sensor for actuating the facility against overflowing when a degree of filling of 97.5% is reached;

(e)   an instrument for measuring the pressure of the vapour phase inside the cargo tank;

(f)   an instrument for measuring the temperature of the cargo if in column (9) of Table C of Chapter 3.2 a heating installation is required or if in column (20) a possibility of heating the cargo is required or if a maximum temperature is indicated;

(g)   a nozzle with a closure connected to a sampling device of the closed or partially closed type and/or a sampling opening as required in column (13) of Table C of Chapter 3.2;

(h)   an ullage opening.

9.3.3.21.2   When the degree of filling in per cent is determined, an error of not more than 0.5% is permitted. It shall be calculated on the basis of the total cargo tank capacity including the expansion trunk.

9.3.3.21.3   The level gauge shall allow readings from the control position of the shut-off devices of the particular cargo tank.

9.3.3.21.4   The level alarm device shall give a visual and audible warning on board when actuated. The level alarm device shall be independent of the level gauge.

9.3.3.21.5   (a)   The high level sensor referred to in 9.3.3.21.1 (d) above shall give a visual and audible alarm on board and at the same time actuate an electrical contact which in the form of a binary signal interrupts the electric current loop provided and fed by the shore facility, thus initiating measures at the shore facility against overflowing during loading operations. The signal shall be transmitted to the shore facility via a watertight two-pin plug of a connector device in accordance with IEC Publication No. 309 (1992) for direct current of 40 to 50 volts, identification colour white, position of the nose 10 h.

The plug shall be permanently fitted to the vessel close to the shore connections of the loading and unloading pipes.

The high level sensor shall also be capable of switching off the vessel's own discharging pump.

The high level sensor shall be independent of the level alarm device, but it may be connected to the level gauge.

(b)   On board oil separator vessels the sensor referred to in 9.3.3.21.1 (d) shall activate a visual and audible alarm and switch off the pump used to evacuate bilge water.

(c)   Supply vessels and other vessels which may be delivering products required for operation shall be equipped with a connecting nozzle conforming to European standard EN 12 827 and a rapid closing device enabling refuelling to be interrupted. A control facility shall actuate this device by a binary signal from the section of the facility for the prevention of overflowing located on the supply vessel. It shall be possible to actuate the rapid closing device independently of the binary signal.

The control facility shall convert the binary signal into a signal actuating the rapid closing device.

The electrical circuits actuating the rapid closing device shall be secured according to the quiescent current principle or other appropriate error detection measures. The state of operation of electrical circuits which cannot be controlled using the quiescent current principle shall be capable of being easily checked.

It shall be possible to transmit the binary signal to the control facility using a fail-safe electrical circuit fitted with a connector device in accordance with IEC publication 309, for direct current of 40 to 50 volts, identification colour white, position of the nose 10 h.

The rapid closing device shall actuate a visual and an audible alarm on board.

9.3.3.21.6   The visual and audible signals given by the level alarm device shall be clearly distinguishable from those of the high level sensor.

The visual alarm shall be visible at each control position on deck of the cargo tank stop valves. It shall be possible to easily check the functioning of the sensors and electric circuits or these shall be intrinsically safe apparatus.

9.3.3.21.7   When the pressure or temperature exceeds a set value, instruments for measuring the vacuum or overpressure of the gaseous phase in the cargo tank or the temperature of the cargo, shall activate a visual and audible alarm in the wheelhouse. When the wheelhouse is unoccupied, the alarm shall also be perceptible in a location occupied by a crew member.

When the pressure exceeds the set value during loading, the instrument for measuring the pressure shall, by means of the plug referred to in 9.3.3.21.5, initiate simultaneously an electrical contact which shall put into effect measures to interrupt the loading operation. If the vessel's own discharge pump is used, it shall be switched off automatically.

The instrument for measuring the overpressure or vacuum shall activate the alarm at latest when an overpressure equal to 1.15 times the opening pressure of the pressure relief device, or a vacuum pressure of 1.1 times the opening pressure of the vacuum valve is reached. The maximum allowable temperature is indicated in column (20) of Table C of Chapter 3.2. The sensors for the alarms mentioned in this paragraph may be connected to the alarm device of the sensor.

When it is prescribed in column (20) of Table C of Chapter 3.2 the instrument for measuring the overpressure of the gaseous phase shall activate a visible and audible alarm in the wheelhouse when the overpressure exceeds 40 kPa during the voyage. When the wheelhouse is unoccupied, the alarm shall also be perceptible in a location occupied by a crew member.

When a manometer is used to measure the overpressure or the vacuum pressure, its indicator scale shall not be less than 0.14 m in diameter. The maximum permissible overpressure or vacuum values shall be indicated by a red mark.

The manometers shall be capable of being read at any time from the location where it is possible to interrupt loading or unloading or in the immediate vicinity of the water-spray system control.

9.3.3.21.8 Where the control elements of the shut-off devices of the cargo tanks are located in a control room, reading of the level gauges shall be possible in the control room and the visual and audible warning given by the level alarm device, the high level sensor referred to in 9.3.3.21 (d) and the instruments for measuring the pressure of the vapour phase and temperature of the cargo shall be noticeable in the control room and on deck.

Satisfactory monitoring of the cargo area shall be ensured from the control room.

9.3.3.21.9 The closed-type sampling device penetrating through the boundary of the cargo tank but constituting a part of a closed system shall be designed so that during sampling no gas or liquid may escape from the cargo tank. The device shall be of a type approved by the competent authority for this purpose.

9.3.3.21.10 The partly closed sampling device penetrating through the boundary of the cargo tank shall be such that during sampling only a small quantity of gaseous or liquid cargo can escape into open air. As long as the device is not used it shall be closed completely. The device shall be of a type approved by the competent authority for this purpose.

9.3.3.21.11 The sampling openings shall have a diameter of not more than 0.30 m. They shall be fitted with a flame-arrester plate stack capable of withstanding steady burning and shall be so designed that the period during which they remain open is as short as possible and the flame-arrester plate stack does not remain open without external intervention.

Flame-arrester plate stacks are not required on board open type N tank vessels.

9.3.3.21.12 The ullage openings shall be such that the filling level may be measured by means of a gauging rod. The ullage openings shall be fitted with a self-closing lid.

9.3.3.21.13 9.3.3.21.1 (h) does not apply to closed type N.

9.3.3.21.1 (e), 9.3.3.21.7 as regards measuring the pressure, 9.3.3.21.9 and 9.3.3.21.10 do not apply to open type N with flame-arrester and to open type N.

9.3.3.21.1 (h) and 9.3.3.21.12 do not apply to open type N.

9.3.3.21.1 (b), (c) and (g), 9.3.3.21.3, 9.3.3.21.4 and 9.3.3.21.11 do not apply to oil separator and supply vessels.

9.3.3.21.1 (f) and 9.3.3.21.7 do not apply to supply vessels.

9.3.3.21.5 (a) does not apply to oil separator vessels.

9.3.3.22 *Cargo tank openings*

9.3.3.22.1 (a) Cargo tank openings shall be located on deck in the cargo area.

(b) Cargo tank openings with a cross-section of more than 0.10 m² and openings of safety devices for preventing overpressures shall be located not less than 0.50 m above deck.

9.3.3.22.2 Cargo tank openings shall be fitted with gastight closures capable of withstanding the test pressure in accordance with 9.3.3.23.1.

9.3.3.22.3   Closures which are normally used during loading or unloading operations shall not cause sparking when operated.

9.3.3.22.4   (a)   Each cargo tank or group of cargo tanks connected to a common vapour pipe shall be fitted with safety devices for preventing unacceptable overpressures or vacuums.

These safety devices shall be as follows:

for the open N type:

–   safety devices designed to prevent any accumulation of water and its penetration into the cargo tanks;

for the open N type with flame-arresters:

–   safety equipment fitted with flame-arresters capable of withstanding steady burning and designed to prevent any accumulation of water and its penetration into the cargo tank;

for the closed N type:

–   safety devices for preventing unacceptable overpressure or vacuum. Where anti-explosion protection is required in column (17) of Table C of Chapter 3.2, the vacuum valve shall be fitted with a flame arrester capable of withstanding a deflagration and the pressure relief valve with a high-velocity vent valve acting as a flame arrester capable of withstanding steady burning. Gases shall be discharged upwards. The opening pressure of the high-velocity vent valve and the opening pressure of the vacuum valve shall be permanently marked on the valves.

–   a connection for the safe return ashore of gases expelled during loading;

–   a device for the safe depressurisation of the cargo tanks consisting of at least a flame-arresters and a stop valve the position of which shall clearly indicate whether it is open or shut.

(b)   The outlets of high-velocity vent valves shall be located not less than 2.00 m above the deck and at a distance of not less than 6.00 m from the accommodation and from the service spaces outside the cargo area. This height may be reduced when within a radius of 1.00 m round the outlet of the high-velocity vent valve, there is no equipment, no work is being carried out and signs indicate the area. The setting of the high-velocity vent valves shall be such that during the transport operation they do not blow off until the maximum permissible working pressure of the cargo tanks is reached.

9.3.3.22.5   (a)   Insofar as anti-explosion protection is prescribed in column (17) of Table C of Chapter 3.2, a vapour pipe connecting two or more cargo tanks shall be fitted, at the connection to each cargo tank, with a flame arrester with a fixed or spring-loaded plate stack, capable of withstanding detonation. This equipment may consist of:

(i)   a flame arrester fitted with a fixed plate stack, where each cargo tank is fitted with a vacuum valve capable of withstanding a deflagration and a high-velocity vent valve capable of withstanding steady burning;

(ii)   a flame arrester fitted with a spring-loaded plate stack, where each cargo tank is fitted with a vacuum valve capable of withstanding a deflagration;

(iii) a flame arrester with a fixed plate stack;

(iv) a flame arrester with a fixed plate stack, where the pressure measurement device is fitted with an alarm system in accordance with 9.3.3.21.7;

(v) a flame arrester with a spring-loaded plate stack, where the pressure measurement device is fitted with an alarm system in accordance with 9.3.3.21.7.

Only substances which do not mix and which do not react dangerously with each other may be carried simultaneously in cargo tanks connected to a common vapour pipe;

or

(b) Insofar as anti-explosion protection is prescribed in column (17) of Table C of Chapter 3.2, a vapour pipe connecting two or more cargo tanks shall be fitted, at the connection to each cargo tank, with a pressure/vacuum valve incorporating a flame arrester capable of withstanding a detonation/deflagration.

Only substances which do not mix and which do not react dangerously with each other may be carried simultaneously in cargo tanks connected to a common vapour pipe;

or

(c) Insofar as anti-explosion protection is prescribed in column (17) of Table C of Chapter 3.2, an independent vapour pipe for each cargo tank, fitted with a pressure/vacuum valve incorporating a flame arrester capable of withstanding a deflagration and a high-velocity vent value incorporating a flame arrester capable of withstanding steady burning. Several difference substances may be carried simultaneously;

or

(d) Insofar as anti-explosion protection is prescribed in column (17) of Table C of Chapter 3.2, a vapour pipe connecting two or more cargo tanks shall be fitted, at the connection to each cargo tank, with a shut-off device capable of withstanding a detonation, where each cargo tank is fitted with a vacuum valve capable of withstanding a deflagration and a high-velocity vent valve capable of withstanding steady burning.

Only substances which do not mix and which do not react dangerously with each other may be carried simultaneously in cargo tanks connected to a common vapour pipe.

9.3.3.22.6   9.3.3.22.2, 9.3.3.22.4 (b) and 9.3.3.22.5 do not apply to open type N with flame-arrester and to open type N.

9.3.3.22.3 does not apply to open type N.

9.3.3.23   *Pressure tests*

9.3.3.23.1   The cargo tanks, residual cargo tanks, cofferdams, pipes for loading and unloading, with the exception of discharge hoses shall be subjected to initial tests before being put into service and thereafter at prescribed intervals.

Where a heating system is provided inside the cargo tanks, the heating coils shall be subjected to initial tests before being put into service and thereafter at prescribed intervals.

9.3.3.23.2 The test pressure for the cargo tanks and residual cargo tanks shall be not less than 1.3 times the construction pressure. The test pressure for the cofferdams and open cargo tanks shall be not less than 10 kPa (0.10 bar) gauge pressure.

9.3.3.23.3 The test pressure for pipes for loading and unloading shall be not less than 1,000 kPa (10 bar) gauge pressure.

9.3.3.23.4 The maximum intervals for the periodic tests shall be 11 years.

9.3.3.23.5 The procedure for pressure tests shall comply with the provisions established by the competent authority or a recognised classification society.

9.3.3.24 (*Reserved*)

9.3.3.25 *Pumps and piping*

9.3.3.25.1 (a) Pumps and accessory loading and unloading piping shall be located in the cargo area.

(b) Cargo pumps shall be capable of being shut down from the cargo area and from a position outside the cargo area.

(c) Cargo pumps situated on deck shall be located not less than 6.00 m from entrances to, or openings of, the accommodation and service spaces outside the cargo area.

9.3.3.25.2 (a) Pipes for loading and unloading shall be independent of any other piping of the vessel. No cargo piping shall be located below deck, except those inside the cargo tanks and inside the cargo pump-room.

(b) The pipes for loading and unloading shall be arranged so that, after loading or unloading operations, the liquid remaining in these pipes may be safely removed and may flow either into the vessel's cargo tanks or the tanks ashore.

(c) Pipes for loading and unloading shall be clearly distinguishable from other piping, e.g. by means of colour marking.

(d) (*Reserved*)

(e) The shore connections shall be located not less than 6.00 m from the entrances to, or openings of, the accommodation and service spaces outside the cargo area.

(f) Each shore connection of the vapour pipe and shore connections of the pipes for loading and unloading, through which the loading or unloading operation is carried out, shall be fitted with a shut-off device. However, each shore connection shall be fitted with a blind flange when it is not in operation.

Each shore connection of the pipes for loading and unloading through which the loading or unloading operation is carried out shall be fitted with the device intended for the discharge of residual cargo described in the model in 8.6.4.1.

(g) The vessel shall be equipped with a stripping system.

9.3.3.25.3   The distance referred to in 9.3.3.25.1 (c) and (e) and 9.3.3.25.2 (e) may be reduced to 3.00 m if a transverse bulkhead complying with 9.3.3.10.2 is situated at the end of the cargo area. The openings shall be provided with doors.

The following notice shall be displayed on the doors:

DO NOT OPEN DURING LOADING AND UNLOADING WITHOUT
THE PERMISSION OF THE MASTER.
CLOSE IMMEDIATELY.

9.3.3.25.4   (a)   Every component of the pipes for loading and unloading shall be electrically connected to the hull.

(b)   The pipes for loading shall extend down to the bottom of the cargo tanks.

9.3.3.25.5   The stop valves or other shut-off devices of the pipes for loading and unloading shall indicate whether they are open or shut.

9.3.3.25.6   The pipes for loading and unloading shall have, at the test pressure, the required elasticity, leakproofness and resistance to pressure.

9.3.3.25.7   The pipes for loading and unloading shall be fitted with pressure gauges at the pump outlet.

Where these pressure gauges are manometers, the indicator scale shall have a diameter of not less than 0.14 m.

Reading of the pressure gauges shall be possible from the control position of the loading pump at any time. The maximum permissible overpressure or vacuum shall be indicated by a red mark.

9.3.3.25.8   (a)   When pipes for loading and unloading are used for supplying the cargo tanks with washing or ballast water, the suctions of these pipes shall be located within the cargo area but outside the cargo tanks.

Pumps for tank washing systems with associated connections may be located outside the cargo area, provided the discharge side of the system is arranged in such a way that suction is not possible through that part.

A spring-loaded non-return valve shall be provided to prevent any gases from being expelled from the cargo area through the tank washing system.

(b)   A non-return valve shall be fitted at the junction between the water suction pipe and the cargo loading pipe.

9.3.3.25.9   The permissible loading and unloading flows shall be calculated. For open type N with flame-arrester and open type N the loading and unloading flows depend on the total cross-section of the exhaust ducts.

Calculations concerning the permissible maximum loading and unloading flows for each cargo tank or each group of cargo tanks, taking into account the design of the ventilation system. These calculations shall take into consideration the fact that in the event of an unforeseen cut-off of the gas return piping or the compensation piping of the shore facility, the safety devices of the cargo tanks will prevent pressure in the cargo tanks from exceeding the following values:

over pressure: 115% of the opening pressure of the high velocity vent valve vacuum pressure: 110% of the opening pressure of the vacuum valve but not more than 3.85 kPa

The main factors to be considered are the following:

1. Dimensions of the ventilation system of the cargo tanks;

2. Gas formation during loading: multiply the largest loading flow by a factor of not less than 1.25;

3. Density of the vapour mixture of the cargo based on 50% volume vapour of 50% volume air;

4. Loss of pressure through ventilation pipes, valves and fittings. Account will be taken of a 30% clogging of the mesh of the flame-arrester;

5. Chocking pressure of the safety valves.

The permissible maximum loading and unloading pressure for each cargo tank or for each group of cargo tanks shall be given in an on-board instruction.

9.3.3.25.10 The stripping system shall be subjected to initial tests before being put into service or thereafter if any alteration has been made to it, using water as test medium. The test and the determination of the residual quantities shall be carried out in accordance with the requirements of 8.6.4.2.

In this test, the following residual quantities shall not be exceeded:

(a) 5 l for each cargo tank;

(b) 15 l for each pipe system.

The residual quantities obtained in the test shall be entered in the certificate in 8.6.4.3.

9.3.3.25.11 If the vessels is carrying several dangerous substances liable to react dangerously with each other, a separate pump with its own piping for loading and unloading shall be installed for each substance. The piping shall not pass through a cargo tank containing dangerous substances with which the substance in question is liable to react.

9.3.3.25.12 9.3.3.25.1 (a) and (c), 9.3.3.25.2 (e), 9.3.3.25.3 and 9.3.3.25.4 (a) do not apply to type N open unless the substance carried has corrosive properties (see column (5) of Table C of Chapter 3.2, hazard 8).

9.3.3.25.4 (b) does not apply to open type N.

9.3.3.25.2 (f), last sentence, 9.3.3.25.2 (g), 9.3.3.25.8 (a), last sentence and 9.3.3.25.10 do not apply to oil separator and supply vessels.

9.3.3.25.9 does not apply to oil separator vessels.

9.3.3.25.2 (h) does not apply to supply vessels.

9.3.3.26 *Residual cargo tanks and slop tanks*

9.3.3.26.1 The vessel shall be provided with at least one residual cargo tank and with at least one tank for slops. These tanks shall be located only in the cargo area. Intermediate bulk containers or tank-containers or portable tanks in accordance with 7.2.4.1 may be used instead of a fixed residual cargo tank. During filling of intermediate bulk containers or tank-containers or portable tanks, means for collecting any leakage shall be placed under the filling connections.

9.3.3.26.2 Slop tanks shall be fire resistant and shall be capable of being closed with lids (e.g. drums with lever closing ring lids). The tanks shall be marked and easy to handle.

9.3.3.26.3 The maximum permissible capacity of a residual cargo tank is 30 m³.

9.3.3.26.4 The residual cargo tanks shall be equipped with:

- in the case of an open system:

  - a device for ensuring pressure equilibrium;

  - an ullage opening;

  - connections, with stop valves, for pipes and hoses;

- in the case of a protected system:

  - a device for ensuring pressure equilibrium, fitted with a flame-arrester capable of withstanding steady burning;

  - an ullage opening;

  - connections, with stop valves, for pipes and hoses;

- in the case of a closed system:

  - a vacuum valve and a high-velocity vent valve.

    The high-velocity vent valve shall be so regulated that it does not open during carriage. This condition is met when the opening pressure of the valve meets the conditions required in column (10) of Table C of Chapter 3.2 for the substance to be carried. When anti-explosion protection is required in column (17) of Table C of Chapter 3.2, the vacuum valve shall be capable of withstanding deflagrations and the high-velocity vent valve steady burning;

  - a device for measuring the degree of filling;

  - connections, with stop valves, for pipes and hoses.

Intermediate bulk containers (IBCs), tank containers and portable tanks intended to collect cargo remains, cargo residues or slops shall be equipped with:

- a connection enabling gases released during filling to be evacuated safely;

- a possibility of indicating the degree of filling;

- connections with shut-off devices, for pipes and hoses.

Residual cargo tanks, intermediate bulk containers (IBCs), tank containers and portable tanks shall be connected to the vapour pipe of cargo tanks only for the time necessary to fill them in accordance with 7.2.4.15.2.

Residual cargo tanks, intermediate bulk containers (IBCs), tank containers and portable tanks placed on the deck shall be located at a minimum distance from the hull equal to one quarter of the vessel's breadth.

9.3.3.26.5   9.3.3.26.1 and 9.3.3.26.3 above do not apply to oil separator vessels.

9.3.3.27   (*Reserved*)

9.3.3.28   *Water-spray system*

When water-spraying is required in column (9) of Table C of Chapter 3.2, a water-spray system shall be installed in the cargo area on deck for the purpose of cooling the tops of cargo tanks by spraying water over the whole surface so as to avoid safely the activation of the high-velocity vent valve at 10 kPa or as regulated.

The spray nozzles shall be so installed that the entire cargo deck area is covered and the gases released are precipitated safely.
The system shall be capable of being put into operation from the wheelhouse and from the deck. Its capacity shall be such that when all the spray nozzles are in operation, the outflow is not less than 50 litres per square metre of deck area and per hour.

9.3.3.29-
9.3.3.30   (*Reserved*)

9.3.3.31   *Engines*

9.3.3.31.1   Only internal combustion engines running on fuel with a flashpoint of more than 55 °C are allowed.

9.3.3.31.2   Ventilation inlets of the engine room and, when the engines do not take in air directly from the engine room, air intakes of the engines shall be located not less than 2.00 m from the cargo area.

9.3.3.31.3   Sparking shall not be possible within the cargo area.

9.3.3.31.4   The surface temperature of the outer parts of engines used during loading or unloading operations, as well as that of their air inlets and exhaust ducts shall not exceed the allowable temperature according to the temperature class. This provision does not apply to engines installed in service spaces provided the provisions of 9.3.3.52.3 (b) are fully complied with.

9.3.3.31.5   The ventilation in the closed engine room shall be designed so that, at an ambient temperature of 20 °C, the average temperature in the engine room does not exceed 40 °C.

9.3.3.31.6   9.3.3.31.2 above does not apply to oil separator or supply vessels.

9.3.3.32   *Oil fuel tanks*

9.3.3.32.1   Where the vessel is provided with hold spaces, the double bottoms within these spaces may be arranged as liquid oil fuel tanks, provided their depth is not less than 0.60 m.

Liquid oil fuel pipes and openings of such tanks are not permitted in the hold space.

| 9.3.3.32.2 | The open ends of the air pipes of each liquid oil fuel tank shall extend to 0.5 m above the open deck. These open ends and the open ends of overflow pipes leading to the deck shall be provided with a protective device consisting of a gauze diaphragm or a perforated plate. |

9.3.3.33   (*Reserved*)

9.3.3.34   *Exhaust pipes*

9.3.3.34.1   Exhaust shall be evacuated from the vessel into the open air either upwards through an exhaust pipe or through the shell plating. The exhaust outlet shall be located not less than 2.00 m from the cargo area. The exhaust pipes of engines shall be arranged so that the exhausts are led away from the vessel. The exhaust pipes shall not be located within the cargo area.

9.3.3.34.2   Exhaust pipes shall be provided with a device preventing the escape of sparks, e.g. spark arresters.

9.3.3.34.3   The distance prescribed in 9.3.3.34.1 above does not apply to oil separator or supply vessels.

9.3.3.35   *Bilge pumping and ballasting arrangements*

9.3.3.35.1   Bilge and ballast pumps for spaces within the cargo area shall be installed within such area.

This provision does not apply to:

– double-hull spaces and double bottoms which do not have a common boundary wall with the cargo tanks;

– cofferdams and hold spaces where ballasting is carried out using the piping of the fire-fighting system in the cargo area and bilge-pumping is performed using eductors.

9.3.3.35.2   Where the double bottom is used as a liquid oil fuel tank, it shall not be connected to the bilge piping system.

9.3.3.35.3   Where the ballast pump is installed in the cargo area, the standpipe and its outboard connection for suction of ballast water shall be located within the cargo area but outside the cargo tanks.

9.3.3.35.4   A cargo pump-room below deck shall be capable of being drained in an emergency by an installation located in the cargo area and independent from any other installation. The installation shall be provided outside the cargo pump-room.

9.3.3.36-   (*Reserved*)
9.3.3.39

9.3.3.40   *Fire-extinguishing arrangements*

9.3.3.40.1   A fire-extinguishing system shall be installed on the vessel. This system shall comply with the following requirements:

– It shall be supplied by two independent fire or ballast pumps, one of which shall be ready for use at any time. These pumps shall not be installed in the same space;

– It shall be provided with a water main fitted with at least three hydrants in the cargo area above deck. Three suitable and sufficiently long hoses with spray nozzles having a diameter of not less than 12 mm shall be provided. It shall be possible to reach any point of the deck in the cargo area simultaneously with at least two jets of water which do not emanate from the same hydrant;

A spring-loaded non-return valve shall be fitted to ensure that no gases can escape through the fire-extinguishing system into the accommodation or service spaces outside the cargo area;

— The capacity of the system shall be at least sufficient for a jet of water to have a minimum reach of not less than the vessel's breadth from any location on board with two spray nozzles being used at the same time.

9.3.3.40.2 In addition the engine room, the pump-room and all spaces containing essential equipment (switchboards, compressors, etc.) for the refrigeration equipment, if any, shall be provided with a fixed fire-extinguishing system meeting the following requirements:

9.3.3.40.2.1 *Extinguishing agents*

For the protection of spaces in engine rooms, boiler rooms and pump rooms, only permanently fixed fire-extinguishing systems using the following extinguishing agents are permitted:

(a) CO_2 (carbon dioxide);

(b) HFC 227 ea (heptafluoropropane);

(c) IG-541 (52% nitrogen, 40% argon, 8% carbon dioxide).

Other extinguishing agents are permitted only on the basis of recommendations by the Administrative Committee.

9.3.3.40.2.2 *Ventilation, air extraction*

(a) The combustion air required by the combustion engines which ensure propulsion should not come from spaces protected by permanently fixed fire-extinguishing systems. This requirement is not mandatory if the vessel has two independent main engine rooms with a gastight separation or if, in addition to the main engine room, there is a separate engine room installed with a bow thruster that can independently ensure propulsion in the event of a fire in the main engine room.

(b) All forced ventilation systems in the space to be protected shall be shut down automatically as soon as the fire-extinguishing system is activated.

(c) All openings in the space to be protected which permit air to enter or gas to escape shall be fitted with devices enabling them to be closed rapidly. It shall be clear whether they are open or closed.

(d) Air escaping from the pressure-relief valves of the pressurised air tanks installed in the engine rooms shall be evacuated to the open air.

(e) Overpressure or negative pressure caused by the diffusion of the extinguishing agent shall not destroy the constituent elements of the space to be protected. It shall be possible to ensure the safe equalisation of pressure.

(f)   Protected spaces shall be provided with a means of extracting the extinguishing agent. If extraction devices are installed, it shall not be possible to start them up during extinguishing.

9.3.3.40.2.3   *Fire alarm system*

The space to be protected shall be monitored by an appropriate fire alarm system. The alarm signal shall be audible in the wheelhouse, the accommodation and the space to be protected.

9.3.3.40.2.4   *Piping system*

(a)   The extinguishing agent shall be routed to and distributed in the space to be protected by means of a permanent piping system. Piping installed in the space to be protected and the reinforcements it incorporates shall be made of steel. This shall not apply to the connecting nozzles of tanks and compensators provided that the materials used have equivalent fire-retardant properties. Piping shall be protected against corrosion both internally and externally.

(b)   The discharge nozzles shall be so arranged as to ensure the regular diffusion of the extinguishing agent.

9.3.3.40.2.5   *Triggering device*

(a)   Automatically activated fire-extinguishing systems are not permitted.

(b)   It shall be possible to activate the fire-extinguishing system from a suitable point located outside the space to be protected.

(c)   Triggering devices shall be so installed that they can be activated in the event of a fire and so that the risk of their breakdown in the event of a fire or an explosion in the space to be protected is reduced as far as possible.

Systems which are not mechanically activated shall be supplied from two energy sources independent of each other. These energy sources shall be located outside the space to be protected. The control lines located in the space to be protected shall be so designed as to remain capable of operating in the event of a fire for a minimum of 30 minutes. The electrical installations are deemed to meet this requirement if they conform to the IEC 60331-21:1999 standard.

When the triggering devices are so placed as not to be visible, the component concealing them shall carry the "Fire-fighting system" symbol, each side being not less than 10 cm in length, with the following text in red letters on a white ground:

Fire-extinguishing system

(d)   If the fire-extinguishing system is intended to protect several spaces, it shall comprise a separate and clearly-marked triggering device for each space.

(e)   The instructions shall be posted alongside all triggering devices and shall be clearly visible and indelible. The instructions shall be in a language the master can read and understand and if this language is not English, French or German, they shall be in English, French or German. They shall include information concerning:

(i)   the activation of the fire-extinguishing system;

(ii)   the need to ensure that all persons have left the space to be protected;

        (iii)   the correct behaviour of the crew in the event of activation;

        (iv)   the correct behaviour of the crew in the event of the failure of the fire-extinguishing system to function properly.

(f)   The instructions shall mention that prior to the activation of the fire-extinguishing system, combustion engines installed in the space and aspirating air from the space to be protected, shall be shut down.

9.3.3.40.2.6   *Alarm device*

(a)   Permanently fixed fire-extinguishing systems shall be fitted with an audible and visual alarm device.

(b)   The alarm device shall be set off automatically as soon as the fire-extinguishing system is first activated. The alarm device shall function for an appropriate period of time before the extinguishing agent is released; it shall not be possible to turn it off;

(c)   Alarm signals shall be clearly visible in the spaces to be protected and their access points and be clearly audible under operating conditions corresponding to the highest possible sound level. It shall be possible to distinguish them clearly from all other sound and visual signals in the space to be protected.

(d)   Sound alarms shall also be clearly audible in adjoining spaces, with the communicating doors shut, and under operating conditions corresponding to the highest possible sound level.

(e)   If the alarm device is not intrinsically protected against short circuits, broken wires and drops in voltage, it shall be possible to monitor its operation.

(f)   A sign with the following text in red letters on a white ground shall be clearly posted at the entrance to any space the extinguishing agent may reach:

WARNING, FIRE-EXTINGUISHING SYSTEM!
LEAVE THIS SPACE IMMEDIATELY WHEN THE ... (DESCRIPTION) ALARM
IS ACTIVATED!

9.3.3.40.2.7   *Pressurised tanks, fittings and piping*

(a)   Pressurised tanks, fittings and piping shall conform to the requirements of the competent authority.

(b)   Pressurised tanks shall be installed in accordance with the manufacturer's instructions.

(c)   Pressurised tanks, fittings and piping shall not be installed in the accommodation.

(d)   The temperature of cabinets and storage spaces for pressurised tanks shall not exceed 50 °C.

(e)   Cabinets or storage spaces on deck shall be securely stowed and shall have vents so placed that in the event of a pressurised tank not being gastight, the escaping gas cannot penetrate into the vessel. Direct connections with other spaces are not permitted.

9.3.3.40.2.8   *Quantity of extinguishing agent*

If the quantity of extinguishing agent is intended for more than one space, the quantity of extinguishing agent available does not need to be greater than the quantity required for the largest of the spaces thus protected.

9.3.3.40.2.9   *Installation, maintenance, monitoring and documents*

(a)   The mounting or modification of the system shall only be performed by a company specialised in fire-extinguishing systems. The instructions (product data sheet, safety data sheet) provided by the manufacturer of the extinguishing agent or the system shall be followed.

(b)   The system shall be inspected by an expert:

(i)   before being brought into service;

(ii)   each time it is put back into service after activation;

(iii)   after every modification or repair;

(iv)   regularly, not less than every two years.

(c)   During the inspection, the expert is required to check that the system conforms to the requirements of 9.3.3.40.2.

(d)   The inspection shall include, as a minimum:

(i)   an external inspection of the entire system;

(ii)   an inspection to ensure that the piping is leakproof;

(iii)   an inspection to ensure that the control and activation systems are in good working order;

(iv)   an inspection of the pressure and contents of tanks;

(v)   an inspection to ensure that the means of closing the space to be protected are leakproof;

(vi)   an inspection of the fire alarm system;

(vii)   an inspection of the alarm device.

(e)   The person performing the inspection shall establish, sign and date a certificate of inspection.

(f)   The number of permanently fixed fire-extinguishing systems shall be mentioned in the inspection certificate.

9.3.3.40.2.10   *Fire-extinguishing system operating with CO_2*

In addition to the requirements contained in 9.3.3.40.2.1 to 9.3.3.40.2.9, fire-extinguishing systems using CO_2 as an extinguishing agent shall conform to the following provisions:

(a)   Tanks of CO_2 shall be placed in a gastight space or cabinet separated from other spaces. The doors of such storage spaces and cabinets shall open outwards; they shall be capable of being locked and shall carry on the outside the symbol "Warning: danger", not less than 5 cm high and "CO_2" in the same colours and the same size;

(b)   Storage cabinets or spaces for CO_2 tanks located below deck shall only be accessible from the outside. These spaces shall have an artificial ventilation system with extractor hoods and shall be completely independent of the other ventilation systems on board;

(c)   The level of filling of CO_2 tanks shall not exceed 0.75 kg/l. The volume of depressurised CO_2 shall be taken to be 0.56 m^3/kg;

(d)   The concentration of CO_2 in the space to be protected shall be not less than 40% of the gross volume of the space. This quantity shall be released within 120 seconds. It shall be possible to monitor whether diffusion is proceeding correctly;

(e)   The opening of the tank valves and the control of the diffusing valve shall correspond to two different operations;

(f)   The appropriate period of time mentioned in 9.3.3.40.2.6 (b) shall be not less than 20 seconds. A reliable installation shall ensure the timing of the diffusion of CO_2.

9.3.3.40.2.11   *Fire-extinguishing system operating with HFC-227 ea (heptafluoropropane)*

In addition to the requirements of 9.3.0.40.2.1 to 9.3.0.40.2.9, fire-extinguishing systems using HFC-227 ea as an extinguishing agent shall conform to the following provisions:

(a)   Where there are several spaces with different gross volumes, each space shall be equipped with its own fire-extinguishing system;

(b)   Every tank containing HFC-227 ea placed in the space to be protected shall be fitted with a device to prevent overpressure. This device shall ensure that the contents of the tank are safely diffused in the space to be protected if the tank is subjected to fire, when the fire-extinguishing system has not been brought into service;

(c)   Every tank shall be fitted with a device permitting control of the gas pressure;

(d)   The level of filling of tanks shall not exceed 1.15 kg/l. The specific volume of depressurised HFC-227 ea shall be taken to be 0.1374 m^3/kg;

(e)   The concentration of HFC-227 ea in the space to be protected shall be not less than 8% of the gross volume of the space. This quantity shall be released within 10 seconds;

(f)   Tanks of HFC-227 ea shall be fitted with a pressure monitoring device which triggers an audible and visual alarm in the wheelhouse in the event of an unscheduled loss of propellant gas. Where there is no wheelhouse, the alarm shall be triggered outside the space to be protected;

(g)   After discharge, the concentration in the space to be protected shall not exceed 10.5% (volume);

(h)   The fire-extinguishing system shall not comprise aluminium parts.

9.3.3.40.2.12 *Fire-extinguishing system operating with IG-541*

In addition to the requirements of 9.3.3.40.2.1 to 9.3.3.40.2.9, fire-extinguishing systems using IG-541 as an extinguishing agent shall conform to the following provisions:

(a)　Where there are several spaces with different gross volumes, every space shall be equipped with its own fire-extinguishing system;

(b)　Every tank containing IG-541 placed in the space to be protected shall be fitted with a device to prevent overpressure. This device shall ensure that the contents of the tank are safely diffused in the space to be protected if the tank is subjected to fire, when the fire-extinguishing system has not been brought into service;

(c)　Each tank shall be fitted with a device for checking the contents;

(d)　The filling pressure of the tanks shall not exceed 200 bar at a temperature of +15 °C;

(e)　The concentration of IG-541 in the space to be protected shall be not less than 44% and not more than 50% of the gross volume of the space. This quantity shall be released within 120 seconds.

9.3.3.40.2.13 *Fire-extinguishing system for physical protection*

In order to ensure physical protection in the engine rooms, boiler rooms and pump rooms, fire-extinguishing systems are accepted solely on the basis of recommendations by the Administrative Committee.

9.3.3.40.3　The two hand fire-extinguishers referred to in 8.1.4 shall be located in the cargo area.

9.3.3.40.4　The fire-extinguishing agent and the quantity contained in the permanently fixed fire-extinguishing system shall be suitable and sufficient for fighting fires.

9.3.3.40.5　9.3.3.40 and 9.3.3.40.2 above do not apply to oil separator or supply vessels.

9.3.3.41　*Fire and naked light*

9.3.3.41.1　The outlets of funnels shall be located not less than 2.00 m from the cargo area. Arrangements shall be provided to prevent the escape of sparks and the entry of water.

9.3.3.41.2　Heating, cooking and refrigerating appliances shall not be fuelled with liquid fuels, liquid gas or solid fuels.

The installation in the engine room or in another separate space of heating appliances fuelled with liquid fuel having a flashpoint above 55 °C is, however, permitted.

Cooking and refrigerating appliances are permitted only in the accommodation.

9.3.3.41.3　Only electrical lighting appliances are permitted.

9.3.3.42　*Cargo heating system*

9.3.3.42.1　Boilers which are used for heating the cargo shall be fuelled with a liquid fuel having a flashpoint of more than 55 °C. They shall be placed either in the engine room or in another separate space below deck and outside the cargo area, which is accessible from the deck or from the engine room.

9.3.3.42.2　　The cargo heating system shall be designed so that the cargo cannot penetrate into the boiler in the case of a leak in the heating coils. A cargo heating system with artificial draught shall be ignited electrically.

9.3.3.42.3　　The ventilation system of the engine room shall be designed taking into account the air required for the boiler.

9.3.3.42.4　　Where the cargo heating system is used during loading, unloading or gas-freeing, the service space which contains this system shall fully comply with the requirements of 9.3.3.52.3 (b). This requirement does not apply to the inlets of the ventilation system. These inlets shall be located at a minimum distance of 2.00 m from the cargo area and 6.00 m from the openings of cargo tanks or residual cargo tanks, loading pumps situated on deck, openings of high-velocity vent valves, pressure relief devices and shore connections of loading and unloading pipes and must be located not less than 2.00 m above the deck.

The requirements of 9.3.3.52.3 (b) are not applicable to the unloading of substances having a flashpoint of 61 °C or more when the temperature of the product is at least 15 K lower at the flashpoint.

9.3.3.43-
9.3.3.49　　　*(Reserved)*

9.3.3.50　　*Documents concerning electrical installations*

9.3.3.50.1　　In addition to the documents required in accordance with the Regulations referred to in 1.1.4.6, the following documents shall be on board:

(a)　a drawing indicating the boundaries of the cargo area and the location of the electrical equipment installed in this area;

(b)　a list of the electrical equipment referred to in (a) above including the following particulars:

machine or appliance, location, type of protection, type of protection against explosion, testing body and approval number;

(c)　a list of or general plan indicating the electrical equipment outside the cargo area which may be operated during loading, unloading or gas-freeing. All other electrical equipment shall be marked in red. See 9.3.3.52.3 and 9.3.3.52.4.

9.3.3.50.2　　The documents listed above shall bear the stamp of the competent authority issuing the certificate of approval.

9.3.3.51　　*Electrical installations*

9.3.3.51.1　　Only distribution systems without return connection to the hull are permitted.

This provision does not apply to:

−　certain limited sections of the installations situated outside the cargo area (e.g. connections of starters of diesel engines);

−　the device for checking the insulation level referred to in 9.3.3.51.2 below.

9.3.3.51.2　　Every insulated distribution network shall be fitted with an automatic device with a visual and audible alarm for checking the insulation level.

9.3.3.51.3   For the selection of electrical equipment to be used in zones presenting an explosion risk, the explosion groups and temperature classes assigned to the substances carried in columns (15) and (16) of Table C of Chapter 3.2 shall be taken into consideration.

9.3.3.52   *Type and location of electrical equipment*

9.3.3.52.1   (a)   Only the following equipment may be installed in cargo tanks, residual cargo tanks, and pipes for loading and unloading (comparable to zone 0):

–   measuring, regulation and alarm devices of the EEx (ia) type of protection.

(b)   Only the following equipment may be installed in the cofferdams, double-hull spaces, double bottoms and hold spaces (comparable to zone 1):

–   measuring, regulation and alarm devices of the certified safe type;

–   lighting appliances of the "flame-proof enclosure" or "apparatus protected by pressurization" type of protection;

–   hermetically sealed echo sounding devices the cables of which are led through thick-walled steel tubes with gastight connections up to the main deck;

–   cables for the active cathodic protection of the shell plating in protective steel tubes such as those provided for echo sounding devices.

(c)   Only the following equipment may be installed in the service spaces in the cargo area below deck (comparable to zone 1):

–   measuring, regulation and alarm devices of the certified safe type;

–   lighting appliances of the "flame-proof enclosure" or "apparatus protected by pressurization" type of protection;

–   motors driving essential equipment such as ballast pumps; they shall be of the certified safe type.

(d)   The control and protective equipment of the electrical equipment referred to in paragraphs (a), (b) and (c) above shall be located outside the cargo area if they are not intrinsically safe.

(e)   The electrical equipment in the cargo area on deck (comparable to zone 1) shall be of the certified safe type.

9.3.3.52.2   Accumulators shall be located outside the cargo area.

9.3.3.52.3   (a)   Electrical equipment used during loading, unloading and gas-freeing during berthing and which are located outside the cargo area shall (comparable to zone 2) be at least of the "limited explosion risk" type.

(b)   This provision does not apply to:

(i)   lighting installations in the accommodation, except for switches near entrances to accommodation;

(ii)   radiotelephone installations in the accommodation or the wheelhouse;

(iii) electrical installations in the accommodation, the wheelhouse or the service spaces outside the cargo areas if:

1. These spaces are fitted with a ventilation system ensuring an overpressure of 0.1 kPa (0.001 bar) and none of the windows is capable of being opened; the air intakes of the ventilation system shall be located as far away as possible, however, not less than 6.00 m from the cargo area and not less than 2.00 m above the deck;

2. The spaces are fitted with a gas detection system with sensors:

    – at the suction inlets of the ventilation system;

    – directly at the top edge of the sill of the entrance doors of the accommodation and service spaces;

3. The gas concentration measurement is continuous;

4. When the gas concentration reaches 20% of the lower explosive limit, the ventilators are switched off. In such a case and when the overpressure is not maintained or in the event of failure of the gas detection system, the electrical installations which do not comply with (a) above, shall be switched off. These operations shall be performed immediately and automatically and activate the emergency lighting in the accommodation, the wheelhouse and the service spaces, which shall comply at least with the "limited explosion risk" type. The switching-off shall be indicated in the accommodation and wheelhouse by visual and audible signals;

5. The ventilation system, the gas detection system and the alarm of the switch-off device fully comply with the requirements of (a) above;

6. The automatic switch-off device is set so that no automatic switching-off may occur while the vessel is under way.

9.3.3.52.4 The electrical equipment which does not meet the requirements set out in 9.3.3.52.3 above together with its switches shall be marked in red. The disconnection of such equipment shall be operated from a centralised location on board.

9.3.3.52.5 An electric generator which is permanently driven by an engine and which does not meet the requirements of 9.3.3.52.3 above, shall be fitted with a switch capable of shutting down the excitation of the generator. A notice board with the operating instructions shall be displayed near the switch.

9.3.3.52.6 Sockets for the connection of signal lights and gangway lighting shall be permanently fitted to the vessel close to the signal mast or the gangway. Connecting and disconnecting shall not be possible except when the sockets are not live.

9.3.3.52.7 The failure of the power supply for the safety and control equipment shall be immediately indicated by visual and audible signals at the locations where the alarms are usually actuated.

9.3.3.53 *Earthing*

9.3.3.53.1 The metal parts of electrical appliances in the cargo area which are not live as well as protective metal tubes or metal sheaths of cables in normal service shall be earthed, unless they are so arranged that they are automatically earthed by bonding to the metal structure of the vessel.

9.3.3.53.2   The provisions of 9.3.3.53.1 above apply also to equipment having service voltages of less than 50 V.

9.3.3.53.3   Independent cargo tanks, metal intermediate bulk containers and tank-containers shall be earthed.

9.3.3.53.4   Metal intermediate bulk containers (IBCs) and tank-containers, used as residual cargo tanks or slop tanks, shall be capable of being earthed.

9.3.3.54-
9.3.3.55   (*Reserved*)

9.3.3.56   *Electrical cables*

9.3.3.56.1   All cables in the cargo area shall have a metallic sheath.

9.3.3.56.2   Cables and sockets in the cargo area shall be protected against mechanical damage.

9.3.3.56.3   Movable cables are prohibited in the cargo area, except for intrinsically safe electric circuits or for the supply of signal lights, gangway lighting and submerged pumps on board oil separator vessels.

9.3.3.56.4   Cables of intrinsically safe circuits shall only be used for such circuits and shall be separated from other cables not intended for being used in such circuits (e.g. they shall not be installed together in the same string of cables and they shall not be fixed by the same cable clamps).

9.3.3.56.5   For movable cables intended for signal lights, gangway lighting, and submerged pumps on board oil separator vessels, only sheathed cables of type H 07 RN-F in accordance with 245 IEC 66 or cables of at least equivalent design having conductors with a cross-section of not less than 1.5 mm^2 shall be used.

These cables shall be as short as possible and installed so that damage is not likely to occur.

9.3.3.57-
9.3.3.59   (*Reserved*)

9.3.3.60   *Special equipment*

A shower and an eye and face bath shall be provided on the vessel at a location which is directly accessible from the cargo area.

This requirement does not apply to oil separator and supply vessels.

9.3.3.61-
9.3.3.70   (*Reserved*)

9.3.3.71   *Admittance on board*

The notice boards displaying the prohibition of admittance in accordance with 8.3.3 shall be clearly legible from either side of the vessel.

9.3.3.72-
9.3.3.73   (*Reserved*)

9.3.3.74 *Prohibition of smoking, fire or naked light*

9.3.3.74.1 The notice boards displaying the prohibition of smoking in accordance with 8.3.4 shall be clearly legible from either side of the vessel.

9.3.3.74.2 Notice boards indicating the circumstances under which the prohibition is applicable shall be fitted near the entrances to the spaces where smoking or the use of fire or naked light is not always prohibited.

9.3.3.74.3 Ashtrays shall be provided close to each exit in the accommodation and the wheelhouse.

9.3.3.75-
9.3.3.99 *(Reserved)*

Printed at United Nations, Geneva
GE.04-23243–September 2004–495
Reprinted at United Nations, Geneva
GE.04-81657–October 2004–1,770

Complete set of two volumes: ISBN 92-1-139102-4
Volumes I and II not to be sold separately

United Nations publication
Sales No. E.04.VIII.2

ISBN 92-1-139100-8 (Vol. I)

ECE/TRANS/182/VOL.I